Money, Oil, and Empire in the Middle East

An important new political and economic history of the unraveling of the British empire and its connection to the decline of sterling as a leading international currency. Analyzing events such as the 1951 Iranian oil nationalization crisis and the 1956 Suez crisis, Steven G. Galpern provides a new perspective on British imperialism in the Middle East by reframing British policy in the context of the government's postwar efforts to maintain the international prestige of the pound. He reveals the link that British officials made between the Middle Eastern oil trade and the strength of sterling, and how this influenced government policy and strained relationships with the Middle East, the United States, and multinational oil firms. In so doing, this book draws revealing parallels between the British experience and that of the United States today, and will be essential reading for scholars of the British empire, Middle East studies, and economic history.

STEVEN G. GALPERN received his PhD in history from the University of Texas at Austin after which he worked for five years as a historian at the US Department of State, where he currently works as a Middle East Analyst.

Frontispiece The last of the Anglo-Iranian Oil Company's British staff leaving Abadan, October 1951.

Money, Oil, and Empire in the Middle East

Sterling and Postwar Imperialism, 1944–1971

Steven G. Galpern

CAMBRIDGE
UNIVERSITY PRESS

CAMBRIDGE UNIVERSITY PRESS
Cambridge, New York, Melbourne, Madrid, Cape Town, Singapore,
São Paulo, Delhi

Cambridge University Press
The Edinburgh Building, Cambridge CB2 8RU, UK

Published in the United States of America by Cambridge University Press,
New York

www.cambridge.org
Information on this title: www.cambridge.org/9780521767903

First published 2009

Printed in the United Kingdom at the University Press, Cambridge

A catalogue record for this publication is available from the British Library

Library of Congress Cataloguing in Publication data
Galpern, Steven G., 1969–
Money, oil, and empire in the Middle East : sterling and postwar imperialism,
1944–1971 / Steven G. Galpern.
   p.   cm.
Includes bibliographical references and index.
ISBN 978-0-521-76790-3 (hardback)
1. Petroleum industry and trade – Great Britain – History – 20th century.
2. Petroleum industry and trade – Middle East – History – 20th century.
3. Pound, British – History – 20th century.   4. Imperialism – History – 20th
century. I. Title.
HD9571.5.G35   2009
332.4′4109045 – dc22   2009029438

ISBN 978-0-521-76790-3 Hardback

For Patti

Contents

Illustrations

Tables

Acknowledgements

This book is the result of generous support from many people over the years, both for me personally and for this project. First, I would like to thank my mother, my father, my grandmother, Gertrude, and my late grandfather, Jay, for their unwavering faith in me, a source of great strength when my academic pursuits did not necessarily lead me on a logical path from point A to point B. Deep gratitude goes to Steve Sommers, Ingrid Dorer-Fitzpatrick, and Mark Germano, the dynamic and wonderful teachers who sparked and nurtured my early interest in the field of history. I would also like to thank Carl Petry for serving as an inspirational gateway to the Middle East and Rashid Khalidi for helping me to develop and refine my knowledge of the region in the modern era.

Research for this book could not have been completed without the help of numerous people and institutions. Generous grants from the Graduate School, the History Department, and the British Studies Program at the University of Texas at Austin funded travel to the necessary archives. The staff at the British National Archives in Kew, where I did the bulk of my research, was particularly helpful and made my many visits there a genuine pleasure. I would like to thank Henry Gillett and Sarah Millard at the Bank of England Archive in the City of London and Michael Gasson and Vicki Stretch at the BP Archive at the University of Warwick for all of their efforts to bring the relevant records to my attention. Bethan Thomas at the BP Archive deserves special recognition for finding and reproducing photos for me, and I must also thank the staff at the National Archives and Records Administration in Washington, DC.

This book went through many drafts on which I obtained invaluable input, a process during which I was fortunate to receive lots of encouragement. Of course, any mistakes are my own, and for them I take full responsibility. Many thanks are due to Jimmy McWilliams and Mark Lawrence for providing comments on individual chapters as I wrote them. Mark, Tony Hopkins, and Michael Stoff should be recognized for their wonderful suggestions that helped turn my dissertation into this book. I am grateful to Brad Coleman for his advice on improving the

Introduction and to Ahmed al-Rahim, Al Wood, and John Wiecking for their recommendations on the Afterword. Frank Gavin's belief in this project and Hafez Farmayan's insistence that I say something new about Iran and the oil nationalization episode provided added motivation, while thanks are due to Conny Mayer and Nabeel Khoury for enabling me to take critical time off work – very soon after starting a new job – so that I could make final revisions to the manuscript. For shepherding the book through the publication process, Michael Watson, Helen Waterhouse, Christopher Hills, and Rosina Di Marzo at Cambridge University Press deserve my utmost appreciation. I would also like to thank my copy-editor, Carol Fellingham Webb, for her exceptional work, as well as the readers at Cambridge for their help in fine-tuning the manuscript.

In the end, however, no single individual contributed more to this book than Roger Louis. From the moment that I conceived the project as a third-year graduate student until the manuscript reached its final stages, he has been a critical sounding board and a tireless advocate. He read more than a few drafts along the way and pushed me to get the manuscript published when my faith was in short supply. Most of all, no one has taught me more about what it means to be a scholar, a teacher, and a mentor. To him I owe a debt of gratitude that can never be repaid.

This book is dedicated to Patti Simon, who not only read and offered comments on different sections as they evolved but also became twice the parent to our toddler (Sol, please forgive me for my moments of impatience) as I finished it. Indeed, she kept our family whole during my bouts of distraction and sometimes-unhealthy focus on revisions. She was and is my rock, and for that I am eternally grateful.

Abbreviations

AIOC	Anglo-Iranian Oil Company
Aminoil	American Independent Oil Company
APOC	Anglo-Persian Oil Company
Aramco	Arabian-American Oil Company
BE	Bank of England
BIS	Bank for International Settlements
BP	British Petroleum
CAB	Cabinet Office
Casoc	California-Arabian Standard Oil Company
ECA	Economic Cooperation Authority
ENI	Ente Nazionale Idrocarburi
EPU	European Payments Union
ERP	European Recovery Program
EXIM	Export-Import Bank of the United States
FCO	Foreign and Commonwealth Office
FO	Foreign Office
FRUS	*Foreign Relations of the United States*
HMG	His/Her Majesty's Government
IBRD	International Bank of Reconstruction and Development (now the World Bank)
IMF	International Monetary Fund
IOP	Iranian Oil Participants
IPC	Iraq Petroleum Company
ISA	Independent Sterling Area
KCC	Kuwait Capital Corporation
KFAED	Kuwait Fund for Arab Economic Development
KFTCIC	Kuwait Foreign Trading, Contracting and Investment Company
KIB	Kuwait Investment Board
KIC	Kuwait Investment Company
KIO	Kuwait Investment Office
KOC	Kuwait Oil Company

MEEC	Middle East Emergency Committee
NA	National Archives of the United Kingdom
NARA	United States National Archives and Records Administration
NIOC	National Iranian Oil Company
OSA	Overseas Sterling Area (same as Rest of the Sterling Area)
POWE	Ministry of Fuel and Power
PREM	Prime Minister's Office
RSA	Rest of the Sterling Area (same as Overseas Sterling Area)
SCUA	Suez Canal Users Association
Socal	Standard Oil of California (now Chevron)
Socony	Standard Oil of New York (now Exxon-Mobil)
T	Treasury Office
VLCC	very large crude carrier

Introduction

On October 4, 1951, the last of the Anglo-Iranian Oil Company's senior staff evacuated Iran's Abadan Island. There, the firm had built, owned, and operated the world's largest oil refinery, which Iran had nationalized several months earlier along with the rest of the country's petroleum industry.[1] A majority of Anglo-Iranian's British personnel left Abadan the previous day on the HMS *Mauritius*. Before boarding the small crafts that would shuttle them to the *Mauritius*, AIOC employees gathered with their bags and other belongings in the hot sun outside the Gymkhana social club, a potent symbol of the kind of informal colonial outpost that Abadan had become.[2] Indeed, while British imperialism in the Middle East was mostly informal, the British cultural and economic presence at Abadan demonstrated how, on the ground, the operation of informal influence could approximate formal control. Britain ceded that control when the *Mauritius* left that October, revealing the empire's vulnerability both within the Middle East and beyond. Possibly in an attempt to deny this fact – or at least to compensate for it – the ship's band gave a rousing, stiff-upper-lip performance of "Colonel Bogey" (the oft-whistled British military song made famous by David Lean's *The Bridge on the River Kwai*), as it traveled the short distance upriver to Basra, Iraq, which remained an important sphere of British influence.[3] The next day, after dominating the Iranian oil industry for half a century, the Anglo-Iranian Oil Company – in which the British government itself had a majority stake – was gone from Iran.

The AIOC's eviction from Iran represented more than a decline in British imperial status, however; it also meant real economic loss for the

---

[1] The views expressed herein are my own and do not necessarily reflect those of the US Department of State. This book is based entirely upon declassified, publicly available documents.

[2] See illustration 85 in J. H. Bamberg, *The History of the British Petroleum Company, Volume 2: The Anglo-Iranian Years, 1928–1954* (Cambridge University Press, 1994), 456.

[3] As described in Daniel Yergin, *The Prize: The Epic Quest for Oil, Money and Power* (New York: Simon and Schuster, 1991), 463.

United Kingdom. After all, the Abadan refinery was the nation's largest single overseas asset. But of greater significance was the fact that Britain imported much of its oil from Iran, where crude and its derivatives were produced more cheaply than in other countries. Given that the AIOC had exclusive rights to develop and market Iranian petroleum, Britain was able to pay for the oil in its own currency, the pound sterling. This and the company's huge profits greatly benefited the credit side of the country's balance sheet for international trade and payments, and, with a treasury as depleted by war as Britain's, being able to acquire oil with sterling proved vital to the strength of the currency and the larger economy. As one might expect, British officials worked feverishly to find a way to return the AIOC to Iran.

Examining the British experience in Iran uncovers a larger trend in British policy-making after World War II that involved the government's efforts to control the flow of Middle Eastern oil and the money associated with it. Britain's desire to preserve the international prestige of sterling motivated these efforts and, in the process, strained relations with countries and companies involved in the production, sale, and transport of Middle Eastern oil. The rising tide of nationalism in the postwar Middle East and the emergence of the United States as a competing power in the region circumscribed the way British officials were able to defend sterling through their Middle Eastern oil policy and thereby demonstrated the currency's vulnerability, sometimes in stark terms. Indeed, it had become clear to policy-makers that Britain's dependence on foreign oil exposed it to the constant risk of financial crisis – even more so as the nation's precarious balance-of-payments position persisted in the 1950s and 1960s. Thus, British officials viewed the Middle Eastern oil trade as critical not only to preserving sterling's international stature but also to protecting the currency from ruin, reinforcing the already powerful imperative to safeguard the nation's strategic and economic interests in the Middle East after World War II.

British external sterling policy after 1945

In the aftermath of World War II, British officials still considered their country a first-class power, despite the overwhelming physical and economic devastation that the conflict wreaked upon it. After all, London continued to serve as the seat of an empire that stretched into all corners of the globe, and its currency still facilitated half of all international trade. As long as Britain could rely upon financial support from the United States, the world's dominant power after the war, policy-makers across the political spectrum saw no reason why it could not participate in international affairs as it had done previously. Although Britain reduced its commitments in some parts of the empire soon after the hostilities ended, most notably in India and Palestine in 1947, it reinvigorated its commitments in others, including Africa, Southeast Asia, and the Middle East. Indeed, a combination of perceived economic advantage and a potent sense of pride and prestige would sustain Britain's imperial will well into the 1960s, encompassing the political, military, and economic spheres.[4] The last of these three categories frames the issues under consideration in this book, specifically British postwar external sterling policy.

After spending most of the nineteenth century as the world's preeminent trading and reserve currency, the pound entered a period of decline triggered by World War I. Because of its global reach, the First World War disrupted and permanently realigned international trade patterns and, in the process, diminished both sterling and the City of London (the capital's financial district, usually referred to as "the City"), the world's leading financial center. By the 1930s, worldwide economic depression had forced Britain and sterling into retreat into a neo-mercantilist, imperial trading system that during World War II evolved into the currency bloc known as the sterling area. Nothing did more damage to the status of both sterling and the City of London than the Second World War. Six years of conflict precipitated a financial hemorrhage so great that the British government could not sustain the pound as an international currency without putting intense pressure on the domestic economy and keeping the sterling area and its rigid exchange controls intact.

Nonetheless, until its devaluation in 1967, both Labour and Conservative governments struggled to strengthen sterling in an effort to preserve

---

[4] A number of historians have demonstrated the persistence of Britain's imperial will in the postwar era. See John Gallagher, *The Decline, Revival and Fall of the British Empire: The Ford Lectures and Other Essays* (Cambridge University Press, 1982); John Darwin, *Britain and Decolonization: The Retreat from Empire in the Post-War World* (New York: St. Martin's Press, 1988); Wm. Roger Louis and Ronald Robinson, "The Imperialism of Decolonization" in Wm. Roger Louis (ed.), *Ends of British Imperialism: The Scramble for Empire, Suez and Decolonization* (London: I. B. Tauris, 2006), 451–502; and most recently Ronald Hyam, *Britain's Declining Empire: The Road to Decolonisation, 1918–1968* (Cambridge University Press, 2006). For a discussion of this subject in the context of the Middle East, see Wm. Roger Louis, *The British Empire in the Middle East, 1945–1951: Arab Nationalism, the United States, and Postwar Imperialism* (Oxford: Clarendon Press, 1984). In her classic work, *Britain's Moment in the Middle East, 1914–1971*, new and revised edition (London: Chatto and Windus, 1981), Elizabeth Monroe contends that Britain suffered a "decline of confidence about empire" during World War II but that protecting the flow of oil and stopping communism reinvigorated Britain's imperial mission in the Middle East to some degree.

the currency's international standing.[5] Clement Attlee's Labour government of 1946–1951 believed that a strong pound was the lifeblood of the sterling area, economically binding together the British empire and Commonwealth, the very existence of which demonstrated Britain's continuing importance in the world. Although Labour officials figured that sterling's strength also promoted London's position as one of the world's foremost financial centers, they considered this benefit ancillary to the currency's vital role within the empire.[6] In contrast, the Conservative governments that ruled Britain from 1951 to 1964 under Winston Churchill, Anthony Eden, and Harold Macmillan, respectively, were convinced that Britain's influence in world affairs depended on London's status as a financial center – which they thought depended on sterling convertibility – and, therefore, sought to bolster the pound before removing it from its safe haven of exchange controls.[7] They also believed that the future of sterling and the British economy lay outside the empire, a destiny that depended on the currency's strength and convertibility.[8] The Labour government that took power under Harold Wilson in 1964 fought to defend the pound's value for yet another reason: Wilson believed that the currency represented one of the two major pillars – along with the dollar – of the postwar international financial system. That sterling was considered the first line of defense for the dollar, the monetary foundation on

[5] Susan Strange believes that British officials suffered from "Top Currency syndrome," which she explains was a collective unwillingness of these officials to accept the declining position of sterling after World War II. Consequently, they followed an economic program ill-suited to the pound's fallen stature, having mistakenly assumed that the advantages of maintaining sterling as an international reserve currency outweighed the costs of such an effort. See *Sterling and British Policy* (London: Oxford University Press, 1971), 43–73. Catherine Schenk describes this view, widely held at the time that she published her book, as a "popular myth" in *Britain and the Sterling Area: From Devaluation to Convertibility in the 1950s* (London: Routledge, 1994), 1. That Whitehall promoted the strength of sterling after World War II, regardless of the party in power, has been well documented. See, for example, Andrew Shonfield, *British Economic Policy since the War* (London: Penguin Books, 1958); Frank Longstreth, "The City, Industry and the State" in Colin Crouch (ed.), *State and Economy in Contemporary Capitalism* (London: Croom Helm, 1979); David Sanders, *Losing an Empire, Finding a Role: An Introduction to British Foreign Policy since 1945* (New York: St. Martin's Press, 1989), ch. 7; P. J. Cain and A. G. Hopkins, *British Imperialism, 1688–2000*, second edition (London: Longman, 2002), Part 8; and Philip Williamson, "The City of London and Government in Modern Britain: Debates and Politics" in Ranald Michie and Philip Williamson (eds.), *The British Government and the City of London in the Twentieth Century* (Cambridge University Press, 2004), 5–30.
[6] Jim Tomlinson, "Labour Party and the City, 1945–1970" in Michie and Williamson, *The British Government and the City of London in the Twentieth Century*, 183.
[7] Scott Newton, "Keynesianism, Sterling Convertibility, and British Reconstruction, 1940–1952" in Michie and Williamson, *The British Government and the City of London in the Twentieth Century*, 269–275.
[8] Gerold Krozewski, *Money and the End of Empire: British International Economic Policy and the Colonies, 1947–1958* (Houndmills: Palgrave, 2001).

which the Bretton Woods system rested, contributed to Wilson's view that the system would not survive if Britain devalued the pound.[9]

Within the British government, officials at the Treasury and the Bank of England[10] represented a sustained, one-note chorus of voices on the question of postwar international sterling policy that found a receptive audience in the Conservative Party. Advocating for sterling convertibility immediately after the war – and doing so until Churchill's government lifted exchange restrictions in 1954–1955 – they, like the Conservatives, believed that the City profited greatly from the pound's widespread use.[11] As the City went, they thought, so did Britain. Only in 1967 did these officials undertake a rigorous examination of whether or not the City's success depended on sterling's international role, eventually reaching the conclusion that it did not.[12]

[9] Tomlinson, "Labour Party and the City, 1945–1970," 187; Diane Kunz, "'Somewhat Mixed Up Together': Anglo-American Defence and Financial Policy during the 1960s" in Robert D. King and Robin Kilson (eds.), *The Statecraft of British Imperialism: Essays in Honour of Wm. Roger Louis* (London: Frank Cass, 1999), 213–232. The pound's devaluation in 1967 indeed paved the way for the dollar's separation from gold in 1973 and the consequent unraveling of the entire Bretton Woods system. Saki Dockrill writes: "Wilson was determined to avoid devaluation not least because Attlee's Labour Government had been compelled, with serious consequences for Britain's international prestige, to devalue the pound in 1949, and he saw the maintenance of the existing policy of the parity of the pound as a crucial factor in keeping up his reputation as a Labour Prime Minister," *Britain's Retreat from East of Suez: The Choice between Europe and the World?* (New York: Palgrave Macmillan, 2002), 216.

[10] The Bank of England was not a public institution until 1946 when the Labour government nationalized it. Only then did it undertake functions characteristic of a central bank whose policies conformed to the government's economic agenda. Originally established to raise money and to lend it to the government, the Bank of England was, before 1946, merely one of many joint-stock banks – but one that maintained a close relationship with Whitehall. Its chief responsibility across the nineteenth century was to secure sterling's convertibility into gold. See Alec Cairncross, "The Bank of England and the British Economy" in Richard Roberts and David Kynaston (eds.), *The Bank of England: Money, Power and Influence, 1694–1994* (Oxford: Clarendon Press, 1995), 56–82.

[11] A report by a working party of the Treasury and the Bank of England read: "The fact that sterling is an international currency gives to the United Kingdom important advantages. The banking, insurance, and similar transactions carried out in London, largely because of the international character of sterling, bring in substantial current earnings," "Problems of the Sterling Area," June 25, 1956, National Archives of the United Kingdom (hereafter cited as "NA"), T 236/5362.

[12] "Costs and Benefits of the International Role of Sterling and its Reduction," Group on the International Monetary System, IM (69) 31, September 9, 1969, NA, T 312/2305. In my research in the Treasury files, I found only two statements by officials expressing serious doubt about the strong-pound policy. The first was by Under-Secretary R. W .B. Clarke in November 1951: "Over the next ten years, sterling is unlikely to be strong. There is no real solution to the UK balance of payments in sight . . . If a genuine doubt exists about the ability of the country to concentrate whole-heartedly upon paying its way during the next ten years (to the exclusion of defence and consumption), it may not be very sensible to seek to foster the use of sterling as an international currency . . . The

Treasury and Bank officials also noted other benefits to sterling's international presence. British merchants could use their own currency "over a large part of the world" and be saved the "expense and inconvenience" of operating in foreign currency, they explained in a 1956 working party report. They also pointed out that Britain could keep smaller working balances of other currencies if it tended to buy and sell goods in such currencies. Ultimately, though, they felt that the British government had no choice other than to maintain the pound's international role. Even if it wanted to reduce the pound to a purely domestic vehicle of exchange, Britain did not have the financial resources necessary to buy back the sterling held in the reserves of countries all over the world.[13]

To strengthen and stabilize sterling, postwar British governments had to rebuild the gold and international monetary reserves depleted by the conflict. In a gold standard or gold-exchange standard international monetary regime – both of which will be discussed in chapter 1 – the reserves of a country's central bank help to determine its currency's value.[14] A country adds to its reserves by absorbing more gold and foreign exchange from the rest of the world than it releases, which is known as running a balance-of-payments, or current account, surplus.[15] Consistent surpluses will result in upward pressure on a currency's value, while consistent deficits will do the opposite. A country will generally run a current account surplus if it exports more goods than it imports, that is, if it develops a surplus on its visible trade – physical products – with the rest of the world. A country's invisible trade, which includes the interest and dividends earned on foreign investments, as well as the earnings from services such as banking, shipping, and insurance, also constitutes part of the current account. Because the City developed such superior financial services across the nineteenth century, Britain's invisible income became an increasingly important element in the nation's balance of payments.

reasoning behind this policy during the last few years has never been very clear," "Future of the Sterling Area," Memorandum by Clarke, November 20, 1951, NA, T 236/4611. The second reconsideration, by D. M. B. Butt, came in October 1957: "The more I think of it the more I am convinced that we are mistaken or at best shortsighted in both our lines of defence of sterling's status as an 'international currency,'" Butt to Rickett, October 31, 1957, NA, T 236/6051.

[13] "Problems of the Sterling Area," June 25, 1956, NA, T 236/5362.
[14] In the case of sterling, Treasury official J. A. Ford wrote, "The United Kingdom's reserves are generally watched as the sole index of sterling's strength." See "Iraq: Diversification of Currency Cover," September 10, 1957, NA, T 236/4796.
[15] The balance of payments is the total account of a country's trade and capital transactions with the rest of the world. The current account measures the difference between the sale of goods and services to foreign residents and the purchase of goods and services from them, while the capital account refers to the difference between the sales of assets to foreign residents and the purchase of assets from them.

And as the decline of Britain's industrial sector relative to its competitors led to progressively smaller visible earnings – a trend accelerated by the destruction World War II wreaked on the British mainland – the country's invisible earnings became even more valuable.

The invisible side of a country's current account also includes the profits generated by its multinational corporations, and no two firms contributed more to Britain's balance of payments in the postwar era than the Anglo-Iranian Oil Company (AIOC)[16] and Royal Dutch-Shell,[17] the two major multinational oil firms residing in the United Kingdom. They both produced enormous invisible income flows for Britain, particularly the AIOC, whose production facilities were located almost entirely in the Middle East, where oil was the cheapest in the world to produce. Not only did the profits of the companies help increase Britain's invisible earnings, but by virtue of the fact that they were treated as British residents, their operations also protected and bolstered the visible side of the nation's current account, simultaneously saving and earning foreign exchange for Britain's reserves. For a country so dependent on imported oil, it is impossible to exaggerate the advantages that Anglo-Iranian and Shell afforded Britain – and never more so than after the war when domestic petroleum consumption almost doubled and British imports of crude grew more than six-fold between 1946 and 1955.[18] As countless files at the Bank of England and the records of the Foreign Office, the Treasury Office, the Ministry of Fuel and Power, the Cabinet Office, and the Prime Minister's Office illustrate, British officials fixated on the connection between the state of the nation's balance of

[16] In 1954, the Anglo-Iranian Oil Company was renamed British Petroleum (BP). Since almost all subsequent discussion regarding the firm concerns the Anglo-Iranian years, the name British Petroleum is not used here.

[17] The ownership and management structure of Shell was complex. When Royal Dutch, a Dutch firm, and Shell Transport, a British firm, merged their interests on January 1, 1907, the two corporations kept their separate identities. They earned their income from the various operating companies that they co-owned, but they did not become operating companies themselves. The Anglo-Saxon Petroleum Company, based in London, owned and ran the transportation and storage facilities, while the Bataafsche Petroleum Maatschappij, based in The Hague, owned and ran the production facilities and the refineries. Oil historian Anthony Sampson described "the Group" as having "a hundred different faces," and in the 1970s three of those faces, at least in terms of shareholding, were British (39 percent), American (19 percent), and Dutch (18 percent). Dutch interests had 60 percent management control in the postwar era. See Stephen Howarth, *A Century in Oil: The "Shell" Transport and Trading Company, 1897–1997* (London: Weidenfeld and Nicholson, 1997), 75–77, and Anthony Sampson, *The Seven Sisters: The Great Oil Companies and the World They Shaped* (New York: The Viking Press, 1975), 11–12.

[18] M. F. G. Scott, *A Study of United Kingdom Imports* (Cambridge University Press, 1963), 33–40.

payments, the strength of sterling, and the operations of the AIOC and Shell.

Given how much the British government's sterling policy seemed to undermine the nation's manufacturing sector – by making exports more expensive and imports cheaper – and benefit the nation's service sector – by attracting foreign investment – it is worth asking whether there was an official bias in favor of finance. After all, the City did not generate enough national income to justify such favoritism in material terms.[19] P. J. Cain and A. G. Hopkins address the issue of financial influence on British imperial and foreign policy by describing a common worldview among policy-makers within Whitehall and City elites based on their similar socioeconomic backgrounds and experiences, something they call "gentlemanly capitalism."[20] From the Cain and Hopkins perspective, gentlemanly capitalists in government were, in effect, socialized to pursue an imperial or foreign policy agenda that would inherently benefit financial interests. Thus, it was not simply the physical proximity of the City to the machinery of government that enabled this sector to have more political influence than northern-based manufacturing interests, but the sociocultural proximity as well.[21]

Without dismissing the merits of the Cain and Hopkins argument, a more compelling explanation for official bias in favor of finance in British policy is that the Treasury Office had enormous influence over policy-making after World War II. According to one historian, the department had attained a "zenith of responsibility and power" not seen since the late seventeenth century as a result of the nationalization of British industries, as well as the dire financial straits in which Britain found itself after

---

[19] Shonfield, *British Economic Policy since the War*, 153–159. Shonfield makes this point in the context of blaming the sterling area for draining investment away from the domestic British economy. He also believes that the sterling area persisted after World War II merely to bolster the international status of the pound. Catherine Schenk challenges this view in *Britain and the Sterling Area*.

[20] Cain and Hopkins, *British Imperialism*, 43–53, 619–622. J. A. Hobson was the first to address the issue of the influence of financial elites on British foreign policy in his landmark *Imperialism: A Study* (Ann Arbor: University of Michigan Press, 1965), first published in 1902. In it, he argues that the British financial class had "the largest definite stake" in nineteenth-century British imperial expansion, so it must have provided the primary impulse for it.

[21] It is important to note, however, that several large companies, especially in newer industries, moved their head offices to London in the 1920s, including the Anglo-Iranian Oil Company, Courtaulds, GEC, GKN, ICI, Shell, Unilever, and Vickers. As a result, "top industrialists" were "much closer to the country's social and political heart, including a residence in London or the Home Counties and membership of a London club." See Youssef Cassis, "Financial Elites Revisited" in Michie and Williamson, *The British Government and the City of London in the Twentieth Century*, 89.

the war.[22] Because Treasury officials regularly sought advice from their colleagues at the Bank of England, who in turn had a great deal of contact with their like-minded associates in the City, conditions were ripe for the City to influence policy on behalf of its interests.[23] But, as recent studies have demonstrated, scholars should avoid broad generalizations about the historic relationship between the British government and the City: it was complex and changed over time based on the party in power and the domestic and international economic context.[24] While a financial bias undoubtedly existed at the Treasury and the Bank, such favoritism did not guarantee that City interests got everything they wanted from the British government, nor was it a prerequisite for Whitehall's support for a strong and stable pound. Ultimately, the desire to maintain Britain's place in world affairs provided enough incentive for both Labour and Conservative governments to pursue policies that promoted sterling's international role.[25]

That said, the philosophy that seemed to underpin foreign economic policy in the British government in the 1950s and 1960s could not help but reflect the shift in the center of gravity in the British economy from manufacturing to finance that began to occur earlier in the century.[26] In

[22] Henry Roseveare, *The Treasury: The Evolution of a British Institution* (New York: Columbia University Press, 1969), 282.

[23] The Treasury and the Bank of England worked very closely together in the post-World War II era. According to Roger Makins, the Joint Permanent Secretary of the Treasury, "in practice the relationship between the Treasury and the Bank is necessarily very closely knit . . . This relationship and the mutual responsibilities to which it gives rise call for close and continual contact and co-operation between the Treasury and the Bank, and this, in my brief experience, has been the rule at all levels in both organisations," from "Radcliffe Committee: Opening Statement by Sir Roger Makins," September 1957, NA, T 236/6050. G. C. Peden writes: "There are good grounds for believing that the City would have influence on the Treasury. The Chancellor's responsibilities included public loans, the national debt, banking and currency, foreign exchanges and international financial relations. Chancellors rarely brought economic or financial expertise to their office and normally depended upon their officials for advice," and "expert advice regarding most matters that would affect the City would be sought from the Bank of England." He also notes that "Treasury officials maintained informal links with the City on a personal basis." But he is careful to point out: "The fact that the City was well placed to influence policy does not, however, establish that its influence was always predominant." See "The Treasury and the City" in Michie and Williamson, *The British Government and the City of London in the Twentieth Century*, 119–120.

[24] See in particular Ranald Michie, "The City of London and the British Government: The Changing Relationship," Peden, "The Treasury and the City," E. H. H. Green, "The Conservatives and the City," Tomlinson, "Labour Party and the City, 1945–1970," and Catherine R. Schenk, "The New City and the State in the 1960s" in Michie and Williamson, *The British Government and the City of London in the Twentieth Century*.

[25] Williamson, "The City of London and Government in Modern Britain," 22.

[26] Eric Hobsbawm, *Industry and Empire: An Economic History of Britain since 1750* (London: Weidenfeld and Nicolson, 1968).

this way, postwar British political economy followed a pattern of development experienced by other leading economic powers. The internationalization of the economies of Spain in the sixteenth century, Holland in the seventeenth century, and the United States in the twentieth century, through the export of goods and capital, led to the development of advanced commercial and banking sectors. As these countries became more willing to pay emerging economic powers to manufacture what they wanted and needed than they were to make such things themselves – because the emerging powers could do so better, more cheaply, or both – their economies became dominated by financial services. And because they had more developed capital markets and financial services than those of their manufacturing competitors, they tended to place increasing value on the financial sector of their economies, an area where they had the greatest comparative advantage.[27]

In the years after World War II, Britain ceded its advantage in financial services to the United States, which raises the issue of British economic decline, the timing and nature of which has been a subject of vigorous debate among scholars, politicians, and others over the past century.[28] First and foremost, any discussion of economic decline must be based on precisely defined terms. To what sector of the economy are we referring? Are we referring to relative decline, meaning a country's performance measured against the performance of others, or absolute decline, meaning a country's performance measured against its own past performance? This book deals specifically with the decline of sterling as a leading international currency and deals with it in both relative and absolute terms. There is no question that the dollar superseded the pound as the world's preferred trading and reserve currency after World War II, a point best exemplified by the decision to underpin the Bretton Woods international monetary system with it. There is also no question that fewer and fewer countries wanted to use sterling as either a trading or reserve currency after World War II: Britain was forced to maintain capital controls in the sterling area until 1958 to prevent member countries from abandoning the pound; and after 1958, those countries began diversifying their reserves out of sterling and into gold and dollars.

[27] For a provocative discussion of these issues, see David Landes, *The Wealth and Poverty of Nations: Why Some are so Rich and Some so Poor* (New York: W. W. Norton, 1998), 171–174, 444–446.
[28] The best survey of this debate is in Barry Supple, "Fear of Failing: Economic History and the Decline of Britain" in Peter Clarke and Clive Trebilcock (eds.), *Understanding Decline: Perceptions and Realities of British Economic Performance* (Cambridge University Press, 1997).

Informal empire in the Middle East

"In decline" is hardly how one would describe Britain's position in the Middle East after World War II. A century and a half of experience in the region enabled Britain to develop an extensive network of political, military, and economic influence there, mostly by establishing and nurturing relationships with local elites. Its initial contact derived from the government's desire to protect the land and sea routes to India, while an emerging trade with East Asia – and the need to defend that trade against piracy – deepened the country's involvement further.[29] In support of these endeavors, Britain established treaty relationships with the Persian Gulf sheikhdoms on the northeastern flank of the Arabian Peninsula, colonized southern Arabia, and developed diplomatic ties with Iran. Near the end of the century, Britain occupied Egypt in an effort to secure trade and strategic links to Asia via the Suez Canal. The discovery of oil in Iran and Iraq in the first part of the twentieth century, combined with petroleum's critical role in fueling the British navy during World War I, ensured that Britain would further tighten its grip around the Middle East. And when the British government assumed mandate authority over large parts of the disintegrating Ottoman empire, including Palestine, Iraq, and Transjordan (modern-day Jordan) after World War I – as sanctioned by the newly established League of Nations – Britain's influence in the region reached a high water mark that would last until Britain left Palestine in 1948.

While Britain had granted independence to most Middle Eastern territories under its formal control by the late 1940s – with the exception of Aden and the Persian Gulf sheikhdoms – it sought to preserve informal influence over the entire region.[30] The decline of India's strategic and economic importance to the empire, which became fully evident in the wake of World War II, led the postwar Labour government to place greater emphasis on the Middle East as a source of imperial strength.[31] Labour Foreign Secretary Ernest Bevin went so far as to characterize the Middle East as of "cardinal importance . . . second only to the United

---

[29] Edward Ingram, *Britain's Persian Connection, 1798–1828: Prelude to the Great Game in Asia* (Oxford: Clarendon Press, 1992), 23. Monroe, *Britain's Moment in the Middle East*, 13–14.

[30] For discussions of British informal empire in the Middle East, see Louis, *The British Empire in the Middle East*; Glen Balfour-Paul, "Britain's Informal Empire in the Middle East" in Judith Brown and Wm. Roger Louis (eds.), *The Oxford History of the British Empire, Volume IV: The Twentieth Century* (Oxford University Press, 1999), 490–514; and Daniel Silverfarb, *Britain's Informal Empire in the Middle East: A Case Study of Iraq, 1929–1941* (New York: Oxford University Press, 1986).

[31] Louis, *The British Empire in the Middle East*.

Kingdom itself," and certainly never more so than when Britain quit India in 1947.[32] The region's strategic value lay in the numerous British bases there – especially the enormous military complex along the Suez Canal – which were well placed for the dual purpose of defending the African colonies and striking the Soviet Union. Moreover, the Middle East was a critical center of communications between Europe and Asia.[33] As for Britain's economic interests, they were diverse, many, and large, including banking, insurance, aviation, shipping, construction, mining, and, of course, oil, the most significant of all.

No asset was worth more than the Anglo-Iranian Oil Company's stake in Iran – and in ways that cannot be measured by oil imports and sterling revenues alone. Since the AIOC was the sole concession holder, the firm was a gateway to British informal control in the country, exercising overwhelming authority over daily life in the south through its provision of employment, housing, and municipal services. Anglo-Iranian's command over oil production and Iran's use of sterling meant that Britain had some sway in the Iranian economy as well. This is not to say that the British government conspired to use the AIOC or other companies as hidden instruments of imperial or foreign policy or as substitutes for colonial administration.[34] Generally speaking, in capitalist democracies, governments and multinational enterprises have their own respective interests and only when those interests coincide do the two act in concert – and sometimes not even then. Nonetheless, it is fair to argue that the British government viewed firms like the AIOC as useful tools, in a range of options, through which to exert influence as those companies operated in parts of the world critical to British interests.

As noted in the case of Iran, Britain demonstrated a certain measure of control in the Middle East through its role as the central banker to the many countries that traded and held reserves in sterling (see Table 1.1 on p. 30 for a complete list of the countries in the sterling account system in 1952). Britain imposed its authority through the crude

---

[32] Quoted in Nicholas Owen, "Britain and Decolonization: The Labour Governments and the Middle East" in Michael J. Cohen and Martin Kolinsky (eds.), *Demise of the British Empire in the Middle East: Britain's Responses to Nationalist Movements, 1943–1955* (London: Frank Cass, 1998), 5.

[33] Ibid., 10–16; Michael J. Cohen, "The Strategic Role of the Middle East after the War" in Cohen and Kolinsky, *Demise of the British Empire in the Middle East*, 26–28.

[34] J. A. Hobson makes this argument regarding British imperialism in *Imperialism: A Study*. Others in this camp are Paul Baran, *The Political Economy of Growth* (New York: Monthly Review Press, 1957); André Gunder Frank, *Capitalism and Underdevelopment in South America* (New York: Monthly Review Press, 1967); and Immanuel Wallerstein, *The Capitalist World Economy* (Cambridge University Press, 1979). A chief critic of this view is D. C. M. Platt in *Finance, Trade, and Politics in British Foreign Policy, 1815–1914* (Oxford: Clarendon Press, 1968).

mechanics of exchange control as well as the blocking of accounts in London. It also demonstrated influence through more subtle methods, such as the extension of credit and the steering of investment to the City and the empire. But the effectiveness of Britain's control depended on its economic strength. Consequently, as sterling exhibited increasing weakness over the course of the postwar era, the tail could also wag the dog. Indeed, sterling holders transferred money out of London to punish Britain for political reasons, making themselves heard by exacerbating balance-of-payments problems at key moments. Furthermore, when sterling became convertible in 1958, holders of the currency exploited their access to capital markets beyond London and also diversified their reserves into gold and currencies that they considered more stable, usually the dollar.[35] Without diminishing the palpability of British control over states on the imperial periphery through their use of sterling, such examples of pushback demonstrate the complexity of power dynamics in informal imperial relationships. The balance of power in these relationships is context-dependent and, thus, they defy monolithic characterization.[36]

Oil and economics in postwar Anglo-American relations

Because of the Middle East's vast petroleum resources, the region became an important sphere of Anglo-American competition and cooperation in the postwar era. The competition was triggered by the realization among US officials that the United States would become a major petroleum importer after World War II. Consequently, the US government tried to assert greater control over the production and distribution of Middle Eastern oil, over which British influence had been paramount for nearly half a century. One need not guess how the British felt about this encroachment in their sphere of influence: "Oil is the single greatest post-war asset remaining to us. We should refuse to divide our last asset with the Americans," remarked a British official.[37] Nonetheless, Britain and the United States worked throughout the postwar period to collaborate in the region both strategically and economically on behalf of their mutual interests, most notably the larger effort to defend the area against real and perceived communist threats.[38]

---

[35] Krozewski, *Money and the End of Empire*, ch. 9.
[36] See, for example, Frank, *Capitalism and Underdevelopment*.
[37] Quoted in Yergin, *The Prize*, 401.
[38] Louis and Robinson, "The Imperialism of Decolonization."

With cooperation, however, came conflicts over the best way to achieve ostensibly shared goals. That the United States found itself with unprecedented power after the war and Britain was fighting tooth and nail to stave off decline embittered their disagreements. Concerned about increasing financial and strategic vulnerability, Whitehall pursued economic and Middle East policies designed to protect and advance British interests. Whereas British officials believed such policies promoted the welfare of the West – because they thought that the spread of liberal capitalism depended on Britain's ability to remain an important player in world affairs – US officials believed that they did the opposite by subverting American interests.[39] Relations stabilized after Britain's disastrous invasion of Egypt in 1956, which, while relegating London to the role of junior partner to Washington in the region, left intact Britain's critical responsibility for protecting Western oil interests in the Persian Gulf. By the mid-1960s, however, tensions rose once again when Britain's continuing postwar economic troubles forced it to make decisions that did not square with US definitions of Western economic and strategic priorities.

The paramountcy of oil

Why focus on oil rather than any other commodity? Given that Britain reinvigorated its imperial mission during and after World War II primarily

[39] The literature on Anglo-American relations after 1945 is extensive, and Anglo-American conflicts over economic issues and over questions of Middle East policy are well documented. For general surveys of Anglo-American relations that consider or include the post-World War II period, see Wm. Roger Louis and Hedley Bull (eds.), The "Special Relationship": Anglo-American Relations since 1945 (Oxford: Clarendon Press, 1986); Robert M. Hathaway, Great Britain and the United States: Special Relations since World War II (Boston: Twayne, 1990); C. J. Bartlett, "The Special Relationship": A Political History of Anglo-American Relations since 1945 (London: Longman, 1992); D. Cameron Watt, Succeeding John Bull: America in Britain's Place, 1900–1975 (Cambridge University Press, 1984); Ritchie Ovendale, Anglo-American Relations in the Twentieth Century (New York: St. Martin's Press, 1998); and Jonathan Hollowell (ed.), Twentieth-Century Anglo-American Relations (Houndmills: Palgrave, 2001). For Anglo-American relations in the context of economic issues, see Richard N. Gardner, Sterling–Dollar Diplomacy: The Origins of the Prospects of Our International Economic Order, new expanded edition (New York: McGraw-Hill, 1969), which is the classic work; L. S. Pressnell, External Economic Policy since the War, Volume I: The Post-War Financial Settlement (London: Her Majesty's Stationery Office, 1986); and Alan P. Dobson, The Politics of the Anglo-American Economic Special Relationship, 1940–1987 (New York: St. Martin's Press, 1988). For general Anglo-American relations in the Middle East after World War II, see Louis, The British Empire in the Middle East; Ritchie Ovendale, Britain, the United States, and the Transfer of Power in the Middle East, 1945–1962 (London: Leicester University Press, 1996); and Tore T. Petersen, The Middle East between the Great Powers: Anglo-American Conflict and Cooperation, 1952–1957 (Houndmills: Macmillan, 2000).

to secure control over as many essential raw materials as possible – in part because of the huge dollar income that they generated – it would indeed be worthwhile to consider other primary exports.[40] But it is clear that no commodity created as much anxiety or hope regarding Britain's balance of payments as oil because no commodity figured as prominently in Britain's current account. In a 1955 paper prepared for the Working Party on the Treatment of Oil in the Balance of Payments, the Treasury and the Ministry of Fuel and Power wrote:

The international ramifications of the oil industry (including its tanker operations) are so large and so complex as almost to constitute oil a currency in itself. Its size and complexity, and the fact that the fullest statistics are those relating to currency movements, and that any other basis of treatment would mean very substantial corrections in a Balance of Payments account, are, in our view, sufficient reasons for treating oil differently from other trade.[41]

Leslie Rowan, a career Treasury official who led the Overseas Finance Division from 1951 to 1958, put a finer point on the matter when he asserted, "Oil is the largest single item among the dollar payments in the Sterling Area and a substantial reduction in the dollar drain which this represents must be a dominant element in our economic policy."[42]

It should be noted, though, that because of the huge volume of trade in goods, services, and capital that flows back and forth across the borders of an advanced, industrialized country, calculating the balance of payments is an inexact science.[43] The process becomes even more inexact when trying to determine precisely how the operations of the international petroleum industry figured into Britain's balance of payments in the postwar era – as the documentary evidence

[40] Cabinet Office Deputy Secretary W. S. Murrie wrote to Prime Minister Clement Attlee, "It is necessary to take into account the raw material resources of the Empire and to develop and utilise them in order to contribute to the balance of payments, all being coordinated with a development of our own industries, and to grant priorities in the light of this," September 13, 1947, NA, PREM 8/493; Allister Hinds, *Britain's Sterling Colonial Policy and Decolonization, 1939–1958* (Westport: Greenwood Press, 2001), ch. 4; Gallagher, *The Decline, Revival and Fall of the British Empire*; John Darwin covers the literature on this subject in *The End of the British Empire: The Historical Debate* (Oxford: Basil Blackwell, 1992), ch. 3, "Economics and the End of Empire."
[41] "Paper for the Working Party on the Treatment of Oil in the Balance of Payments," Note by the Treasury and Ministry of Fuel and Power, TO (55) 2, January 28, 1955, NA, T 277/506.
[42] "Sterling Oil–Dollar Oil Problem: Oil in Relation to the UK and Sterling Area Balance of Payments," Memorandum by the United Kingdom (prepared by Leslie Rowan), February 1950, BP Archive (hereafter cited as "BP") 96429.
[43] In fact, balance-of-payments statistics are often revised, which will account for any discrepancies between the figures in the tables in Appendix 1 and figures cited by British officials in the course of this book.

reveals.[44] One member of the Treasury wrote, "There are so many peculiar elements in the oil calculations in the balance of payments that this will be a formidable thing to get straight."[45] Of course, such problems did not stop British officials from attempting to make these calculations anyway, and they are included in the Appendices. What matters most is that British officials firmly believed that oil was a major factor in Britain's trade account and that this belief greatly influenced British policy because of the potential repercussions for sterling.

The Anglo-Iranian Oil Company

The Anglo-Iranian Oil Company is the focus of attention here – and not Royal Dutch-Shell – because Anglo-Iranian procured its petroleum from the Middle East, whereas Shell acquired most of its crude from Indonesia and Venezuela. The AIOC controlled 100 percent of the production in Iran, 50 percent of the production in Kuwait, and 23.75 percent of the production in Iraq.[46] Another reason for the concentration on Anglo-Iranian is because of its special relationship with Whitehall, based on the British government's majority shareholding position in the company, which lasted from 1914 until 1979.[47] The combination of the British government's stake in the AIOC and the firm's all-British nationality convinced many British officials that they could rely on company executives to consider the British national interest in the conduct of their business. At the very least, they thought, the British directors at Shell were much less likely to put British interests ahead of the company's commercial welfare than Anglo-Iranian directors, especially concerning the British balance of payments and sterling.[48]

---

[44] See, for example, the documents of the Working Party of the Treatment of Oil in the Balance of Payments in NA, T 277/506; "Ideal Requirements for Balance of Payments Statistics," Note by the Treasury RES (57) 2, May 22, 1957, NA, T 230/426; "The Oil Balance of Payments," Memorandum by the Ministry of Fuel and Power, GEN. 295/101, Oct 13, 1950, Bank of England Archive (hereafter cited as "BE")/EC5/258; and "Oil Balance of Payments Statistics," Central Statistical Office, December 5, 1960, BE/EID3/340.

[45] Clarke to Figgures, September 14, 1956, NA, T 236/4842.

[46] The extent of Shell's Middle East interests was a 23.75 percent share of the Iraq Petroleum Company.

[47] The British government had a 51 percent stake in the company, which, in 1945, produced 16,839,000 tons of oil. Royal Dutch-Shell produced 29,794,000 tons that year. Production data from *Oil and Petroleum Yearbook, 1945* (London: Walter E. Skinner, 1945), xi–xii. When relevant, Shell will be addressed.

[48] That said, in the context of financial issues, a study of Whitehall's relationships with Shell, the Dutch government, and the United States, where the company had extensive market outlets, would certainly be valuable because of the substantial number of dollars that Shell's operations added to Britain's reserves.

One might expect that the mutual desire of the British government and the AIOC to obtain Middle Eastern oil as cheaply as possible would lead to stable relations between Whitehall and company executives. More often than not it did. But official perceptions of the British national interest and company perceptions of Anglo-Iranian's commercial interest did not always dovetail. In fact, they clashed on two major occasions in the postwar era regarding sterling and oil. Thus, analyzing the consequences of the British government's sterling-driven Middle East petroleum policy provides an opportunity to reflect on the nebulous nature of the boundary between the public and private sectors in a case in which the lines were especially blurred.[49]

Tensions and conflict arose between the British government and the AIOC for the same reasons that they did between the British government and other multinational petroleum firms and between Britain and other countries involved in Middle Eastern oil: Whitehall's desire to protect and promote sterling. Throughout the postwar era, both Labour and Conservative governments sought to control all of the ways that the Middle Eastern oil trade could help or harm the country's balance of payments. Officials wanted to control: (1) what kind of oil Britain imported, ensuring the flow of Middle Eastern oil into the United Kingdom; (2) the production of Middle Eastern oil and the share of the profits that British companies received after selling it; (3) the transportation of Middle Eastern oil through the Suez Canal; and (4) where the sterling revenues of the countries that produced Middle Eastern oil were invested. At least until 1956, the British government pursued this agenda with such boldness that it left a trail of frayed relations in its wake.

The structure of the book

Chapter 1 explores the disputes between Britain and the United States over Britain's defense of its right to discriminate against oil imports from

[49] For a discussion of the literature dealing with the difficulties of defining the boundaries between the state and society, see Timothy Mitchell, "The Limits of the State: Beyond Statist Approaches and their Critics," *American Political Science Review*, 85, 1 (1991), 77–96. Also see Stephen Krasner, *Defending the National Interest: Raw Materials Investments and US Foreign Policy* (Princeton University Press, 1978) for an analysis of the relationship between the state and private enterprise regarding commodities such as oil in the American context. Of the best historical works that deal with the world's major multinational oil firms, only Bamberg, *The History of the British Petroleum Company, Volume II*, considers the impact of sterling on Britain's relations with the AIOC (see 321–324). In *The Seven Sisters*, Anthony Sampson mentions the sterling-oil connection, writing that the British Treasury regarded oil companies as "geese laying golden eggs, in the form of huge contributions to the balance of payments," 137. Yergin refers to the link between sterling and oil in *The Prize* during a section on the Suez crisis (485). Benjamin Shwadran addresses the issue in a footnote in *The Middle East, Oil and the Great Powers*, third edition (Jerusalem: Israel Universities Press, 1973), 541, fn 16.

US multinational petroleum firms in the wake of World War II. The first section describes the creation and evolution of the sterling area – the exchange control structure that supported the British empire's closed trading system – as well as the establishment of the Bretton Woods international monetary regime. The next section reviews the clashes that occurred between British and American officials as they strove to negotiate an agreement that would regulate the international production and distribution of oil in the postwar era. These clashes revealed, for the first time, Whitehall's intention to prevent British dependence on foreign oil from undermining the nation's balance of payments. They also mark the earliest occasion on which the British government's postwar sterling-oil agenda strained relations with another party with interests in Middle Eastern petroleum. The third section discusses the severe economic problems that Britain experienced in 1947 and the strategic consequences that those problems either triggered or accentuated, all of which had an impact on Britain's role in the Middle East. The section ends with a description of the currency crisis that struck Britain in 1949 and subsequently led to the large-scale oil-discrimination policy that Britain unveiled that year, which is the subject of the final section of this first chapter. Known as the oil-substitution program, it demonstrated the seriousness of the British government's previously expressed threats to use Middle Eastern oil to protect sterling and also added the Anglo-Iranian Oil Company to a growing list of parties that Whitehall would frustrate with its sterling-driven petroleum and foreign policies. Chapter 1 stands apart from the chapters that follow it in that it does not concern a particular Middle Eastern country and that it deals mainly with the politics that were beginning to dominate the region by way of foreshadowing.

The bitter disagreement between Iran and the Anglo-Iranian Oil Company over a new petroleum contract, culminating in the nationalization of the Iranian petroleum industry in 1951, is the subject of chapter 2.[50] British officials, especially at the Treasury and the Bank

---

[50] There is a wealth of material on this topic from a wide range of perspectives. See the chapters in James A. Bill and Wm. Roger Louis (eds.), *Musaddiq, Iranian Nationalism, and Oil* (Austin: The University of Texas Press, 1988); Mary Ann Heiss, *Empire and Nationhood: The United States, Great Britain, and Iranian Oil, 1950–1954* (New York: Columbia University Press, 1997); Mostafa Elm, *Oil, Power, and Principle: Iran's Oil Nationalization and its Aftermath* (Syracuse University Press, 1992); L. P. Elwell-Sutton, *Persian Oil: A Study in Power Politics* (Westport: Greenwood Press, 1975); Louis, *The British Empire in the Middle East*, ch. 5, Part 3; Bamberg, *The History of the British Petroleum Company, Volume II*, Part III; Steve Marsh, *Anglo-American Relations and Cold War Oil: Crisis in Iran* (New York: Palgrave Macmillan, 2003); and most recently Steve Marsh, "Anglo-American Crude Diplomacy: Multinational Oil and the Iranian Oil Crisis, 1951–1953," *Contemporary British History*, 21, 1 (March 2007), 25–53.

of England, believed that the future of the pound as an international currency depended on British control over the production of Iranian oil and Britain's ability to enforce international contracts. Thus, they proved particularly stubborn about accepting any changes in the status quo or how much they would have to give up in a negotiated settlement.[51] As in chapter 1, the issue of Anglo-American conflict over the convergence of Britain's economic and Middle Eastern oil policies occurred once again. This time, US officials criticized their British counterparts for neglecting Western interests in the Middle East, particularly given the threat of Soviet influence in the region, and used the rhetoric of anti-colonialism to express their dissatisfaction with British policy. A new theme emerges as well, one that lasts through the rest of the book: that is, how the rise of nationalism in the postwar Middle East helped to frustrate Whitehall's efforts to stabilize and strengthen sterling.

Chapter 3 examines Britain's response to the nationalization of the Suez Canal, the country's main artery to Middle Eastern oil, in 1956. It details the economic consequences for Britain of the canal's nationalization and considers the resulting Anglo-French-Israeli invasion of Egypt in the context of the government's efforts to revamp sterling.[52] Top US officials, especially President Dwight D. Eisenhower, were furious over the British government's participation in the tripartite invasion, once again using the language of anti-colonialism to criticize British officials. As led by Eisenhower, the US government economically punished Britain in a way that signified a kind of climax to the tensions that had developed around Whitehall's attitude of defending the pound at all costs. For sterling, the consequences were catastrophic. The aim here – as well as in chapter 2 – is not to privilege sterling considerations over all others in explaining British policy, but rather to demonstrate their importance

[51] Scholars have previously noted the link that the British government made between Iranian oil and the British balance of payments. See, for example, Elm, *Oil, Power, and Principle*, 99, 105, 128, 323; Heiss, *Empire and Nationhood*, 15, 24, 45; and Louis, *The British Empire in the Middle East*, 670, 688, 740. Louis laments that, given the scope of his work, it was "not possible to discuss the broader economic dimension of the [Iranian oil crisis]," 670.

[52] Two historians, Diane Kunz in *The Economic Diplomacy of the Suez Crisis* (Chapel Hill: University of North Carolina Press, 1991) and Lewis Johnman in "Defending the Pound: The Economics of the Suez Crisis, 1956" in Anthony Gorst, Lewis Johnman, and W. Scott Lucas (eds.), *Post-war Britain, 1945–64: Themes and Perspectives* (London: Pinter, 1989), 166–188, have considered the sterling issues that preoccupied British officials during the crisis. Kunz is more concerned with the measures taken by the United States to change British policy than she is with the economic considerations that motivated British actions in the first place. Even though Johnman entitles his chapter "Defending the Pound," he does not contextualize it by examining the broader economic goals of the British government during this period.

in the policy-making process because of their critical role in shaping the environment in which decisions were made.[53]

Chapter 4 explores the concern among British officials over where Kuwait invested its oil-driven, surplus sterling revenue. Starting in the early 1950s, Whitehall sought to ensure, by informal means, that Kuwait's ruling family invested its revenue in London and kept it there. British officials feared that if the sheikhdom rapidly transferred a large portion of its holdings out of sterling, the consequences for the currency's international position would be devastating, especially as colonies with large sterling balances became independent and sought to use those balances for development. As already seen in chapters 2 and 3, the British government's attempts to exert influence over the affairs of a Middle Eastern country clashed with an emerging nationalist sentiment that expressed itself in demands for local autonomy. In this case, the issue was Kuwait's desire for increased control over the investment of its oil income. Unlike in chapters 2 and 3, however, in which British officials acted with audacity and obstinacy when confronting a crisis that threatened sterling, Whitehall displayed impressive flexibility regarding Kuwait. Mutual dependence in the Anglo-Kuwaiti relationship, based on Britain's economic weakness and Kuwait's strategic vulnerability, as well as Britain's greatly diminished stature in the Middle East, ensured that British officials would deal with Kuwaiti nationalism in a way that prevented tension from exploding into crisis. At relevant moments, chapter 4 also addresses the evolution of the Anglo-American relationship as it pertained to the Middle East during the late 1950s and 1960s, focusing primarily on Britain's role in policing the Persian Gulf as part of the Anglo-American security structure in the region.

An important point must be made about the decision not to focus on certain Middle Eastern oil-producing states, both in chapter 4 and in the book as a whole. Iraq, a member of the sterling area until 1958 and a source of petroleum that both the Anglo-Iranian Oil Company and Royal Dutch-Shell bought with sterling, is hardly discussed except for several pages in chapter 4 concerning the Iraqi Revolution of 1958. The reason is that nothing happened in Iraq that British officials believed

---

[53] Readers interested in more indepth or multi-faceted coverage of both the Suez and Iranian oil crises are encouraged to explore the enormous body of literature available on both subjects. For the Suez crisis, a good place to begin is Wm. Roger Louis and Roger Owen (eds.), *Suez 1956: The Crisis and its Consequences* (Oxford: Clarendon Press, 1989) and Keith Kyle, *Suez* (London: Weidenfeld and Nicolson, 1991). For a collection of primary source documents related to the Suez crisis, see Anthony Gorst and Lewis Johnman (eds.), *The Suez Crisis* (London: Routledge, 1997).

would put sterling in jeopardy. Even the revolution, loaded with anti-British overtones, did not prompt the sort of aggressive reaction at Whitehall that occurred over the respective nationalizations of the Iranian oil industry and the Suez Canal. By the end of the decade, Britain's approach to nationalist movements in the Middle East, especially as they related to oil's impact on sterling, had become much more realistic and accommodating. Naturally, Britain was concerned about the effect on the pound of Iraq's departure from the sterling area – an issue raised in chapter 4 – but not so much so that Whitehall felt compelled to do anything drastic, a response that Britain's devastating experience at Suez had checked anyway. As for the investment of Iraq's sterling revenues, the Iraqi government spent so much of its oil-generated income on development that it never accumulated balances near the scale of Kuwait's. The same was true of the British-controlled, oil-producing sheikhdoms in the Persian Gulf, such as Dubai and Abu Dhabi. Their much smaller oil industries did not produce large enough sterling receipts to worry British officials. Therefore, chapter 4 deals with Kuwait to the exclusion of the other sheikhdoms, despite the fact that they formed a kind of administrative unit under the authority of the British Resident at Bahrain.[54]

The story ends with Britain's devaluation of sterling in November 1967 and its subsequent decision to withdraw British forces from the Persian Gulf in 1971, a tandem of watershed moments in postwar British history. The devaluation represented the abandonment of Whitehall's strong pound policy and marked the demise of the sterling area – although convertibility had already signaled the death knell of the currency group at the end of the 1950s.[55] By devaluing sterling, the Labour government demonstrated that it had finally acknowledged that fundamental adjustments were required to alleviate Britain's deeply entrenched balance-of-payments problems. Reducing overseas expenditure by eliminating the costs associated with British military commitments east of Suez was next. The decision to withdraw British forces from east of Suez, announced in January 1968, included the British presence in the Gulf, the elimination of which lowered the curtain on the British empire in the Middle East.

[54] In his "Report on Situation in Kuwait," Sir Thomas Rapp, the Head of the British Middle East Office in Cairo, wrote to the Foreign Office, "In general, the problems of Kuwait have little in common with the rest of the Gulf, and this is particularly true of the present difficulties, the causes of which are exclusively economic and financial . . . Moreover, the magnitude of Kuwait's problems and their vital importance to us, give Kuwait a claim to special and separate consideration," No. 20, June 17, 1953, NA, POWE 33/2081.
[55] Krozewski, *Money and the End of Empire*, chs. 8 and 9.

It provoked shock, dismay, and disappointment from US officials and Gulf sheikhs alike, sentiments that reflected concern over the strategic vacuum that Britain would leave behind. Because Britain's decision to devalue sterling and its myriad consequences concern some of the central questions raised by this book, the episode sets the stage for a concluding discussion.

1 Anglo-American conflict over oil and the sterling area

> With our dollar reserves in such a precarious state oil could make or break our plans for recovery.
>
> Victor Butler, Chairman, Committee of Officials on European Economic Co-operation and Britain's Under-Secretary of the Ministry of Fuel and Power[1]

> . . . our interest in helping their balance of payments problem cannot go so far as to wreck American oil operations in the Middle East.
>
> Robert Eakens, Chief of the Petroleum Division, US State Department[2]

To defend the British economy from the worst effects of the world-wide depression of the 1930s and the mobilization for the world war that followed, Britain rigidly regulated trade between the empire and the rest of the world. This neo-mercantilist system was supported by a regime of exchange controls that applied to colonies – both formal and semi-formal – and independent nations that primarily used sterling to conduct their business, a group that officially became known as the sterling area during World War II. After the war, officials in the administration of US President Harry Truman expected that Britain would dismantle the sterling area in support of the Anglo-American goal of liberating international trade under the Bretton Woods international monetary system, which the two countries had jointly developed based on the lessons that they drew from the economic experience of the interwar years.

But the Attlee government believed that to save and earn the dollars necessary to rebuild Britain, it would have to preserve the sterling area and capitalize on the assets that remained within it. One of those assets was the favorable position of Royal Dutch-Shell and the Anglo-Iranian Oil Company in the international oil industry, which enabled the sterling area to protect its collective gold and dollar reserves by selling petroleum to it for pounds. Moreover, the companies also infused Britain's reserves with dollars by selling crude and petroleum products to dollar markets in

---

[1] BP 66887.

[2] *Foreign Relations of the United States* (hereafter cited as "*FRUS*"), *1949, Vol. VI*, 145.

the Western Hemisphere and to the major US multinationals for dollars to sell to their own markets.[3]

British officials sought to exploit this advantage by discriminating against so-called "dollar" oil in favor of "sterling" oil after the war, a policy that understandably upset both US multinational oil companies and US officials.[4] Britain had begun restricting imports of dollar oil as early as 1940, but the issue never became controversial until the British government raised the prospect of doing so in the postwar era, when it seemed to US officials that such a policy could no longer be justified. Conflict over this question, which would wax and wane for the rest of the decade, can be traced back to Anglo-American petroleum talks of 1944–1945. The talks were designed to produce an agreement that would rationalize the development of Middle Eastern oil, but disputes over the discrimination issue almost scuttled the whole process.[5]

American frustration with British behavior during these discussions, however, did not compare with the anger that US policy-makers expressed when Whitehall announced that it would implement a large-scale, petroleum-discrimination program in January 1950. Britain's balance-of-payments struggles and the emergence of a large surplus of sterling oil from Iran during the latter half of the 1940s provided the catalyst for the program's implementation, which contemporaries called "substitution," shorthand for the substitution of sterling oil for imports of dollar oil from US multinationals. After months of negotiations with the firms disadvantaged by the policy, the British government eventually allowed them to sell oil in the sterling area in a way that protected the sterling area's dollar position. Nonetheless, London had served notice to Washington that it would use any means at its disposal to defend the pound.

---

[3] See "Oil in Relation to Foreign Exchange Balances," August 1945, NA, T 236/219 and "Working Party on the Dollar Element in Oil," OWP (49) 4, April 28, 1949, BP 66889.

[4] Sterling and dollar oil were defined, respectively, as oil sold by British-registered companies for sterling and oil sold by US-registered companies for dollars. The British government first made this distinction early in World War II, when a Treasury official wrote: "It is of primary importance if we are to conserve the dollars required for the necessary purchases for the arming of the fighting services and the feeding etc. of the civil population that purchases from the United States should, as far as possible, be diverted towards countries where payments need not be made in dollars," BE/EC4/111. In fact, during the first part of the war, the British government decreed that companies owned or operated within the sterling area that sold oil outside the sterling area could only accept payment in US dollars, regardless of where the oil was sold. See Bolton to Rowe-Dutton, October 16, 1945, NA, T 236/2144.

[5] The best work on these talks is Michael B. Stoff, *Oil, War, and American Security: The Search for a National Policy on Foreign Oil, 1941–1947* (New Haven: Yale University Press, 1980), chs. 5–7.

Along with creating turmoil in the Anglo-American relationship, disputes over the sterling–dollar oil issue also revealed tensions between multinational oil companies and their governments in both the United States and Britain. As Britain began to indicate that it would discriminate against dollar oil, the American majors lobbied the US Department of State to defend their interests. Department officials asked the British government to reach agreements with the US firms that would enable those companies to sell oil in the sterling area while still protecting Britain's balance of payments, but they refused to become entangled in negotiations between the two sides. As a result, petroleum executives often complained that the Department of State was not putting enough pressure on Britain to settle the matter quickly, thereby placing their firms' market share at risk.

Directors at Anglo-Iranian were equally upset with the British government for instituting the discrimination policy in the first place. At first glance, this reaction is unexpected given that the program appeared to benefit the company.[6] In fact, AIOC executives feared that their "friends" at the US firms would think that Anglo-Iranian encouraged the policy to steal American markets, a misconception that would disrupt the company's critical business relationships across the Atlantic. Officials at the AIOC also believed that the government had overstepped its bounds, violating a longtime understanding that, despite the latter's controlling interest in the firm, it would not interfere in the company's day-to-day commercial operations. Clearly, the short-term effects of the dollar shortage concerned the British government more than the impact of discrimination on Anglo-Iranian's transatlantic relations.

Referring to the Anglo-American clash over a postwar loan for Britain, noted diplomatic historian Bradford Perkins wrote, "what Americans liked to describe as economic imperialism and the British simply to call the sterling system, produced one sharp controversy but otherwise less tension than might have been anticipated [in the postwar period]."[7] The conflict over sterling and dollar oil constitutes a second sharp controversy. At first glance, the disagreements concerning the sterling–dollar oil question may seem like petty squabbling over a mundane and highly technical economic matter. It is important to recognize, however, that these arguments shed light on a major debate over an issue that would plague Anglo-American relations in the wake of World War II: that is, Britain's use of

---

[6] J. H. Bamberg addresses the Anglo-Iranian perspective on the discrimination issue in *The History of the British Petroleum Company, Volume II*, 309–315, 321–324.

[7] See Bradford Perkins, "Unequal Partners: The Truman Administration and Great Britain" in Louis and Bull, *The "Special Relationship"*, 51.

the discriminatory sterling area to defend its economic interests versus the United States' quest to implement its vision of a worldwide, multilateral trade regime in the face of communist expansion.[8] In other words, the British government resented what it viewed as American insensitivity to its postwar economic plight while the United States grew increasingly frustrated with what it perceived to be Britain's pursuit of narrow, short-term, economic goals at the expense of both countries' long-term interest in establishing international free trade and defeating communism.

This chapter seeks to achieve two objectives. First, it attempts to lift the Anglo-American disputes over sterling and dollar oil out of obscurity by placing them in the context of the larger economic and political arguments that occurred between Britain and the United States during the postwar era. In doing so, it makes a crucial connection between the Anglo-American disagreement over the shape of an international petroleum accord in 1944 and the row over the implementation of Britain's substitution program little more than five years later.[9] Second, the British government's defiant protection of its right to discriminate against dollar oil in 1944 marks the beginning of a long-term policy in which the British government would use its influence in Middle Eastern oil-producing countries to preserve sterling's international viability. Therefore, this chapter sets the Anglo-American disputes over sterling and dollar oil against the larger background of Whitehall's sustained effort to prevent Britain's dependence on foreign oil from undermining its postwar international economic goals.

---

[8] There were those on the British Right who had no interest in free trade and "wanted to make Imperial Preference and the sterling area the basis for a post-war order." See Richard N. Gardner, "Sterling–Dollar Diplomacy in Current Perspective" in Louis and Bull, *The "Special Relationship"*, 187.

[9] Very few scholars have considered the sterling–dollar oil question. Horst Menderhausen, "Dollar Shortage and Oil Surplus in 1949–1950," *Essays in International Finance*, No. 11, November 1950, is a more or less technical and descriptive work about Britain's substitution policy, the value of which – as historical scholarship – is reduced by the fact that it was written so soon after the policy was implemented. Catherine Schenk, "Exchange Controls and Multinational Enterprise: The Sterling–Dollar Oil Controversy in the 1950s," *Business History*, 38, 4 (1996), 21–41, focuses on the period after Whitehall repealed substitution and is more concerned with the effectiveness of exchange control and the impact of exchange control on multinational oil companies. Bamberg, *The History of the British Petroleum Company, Volume II* examines the substitution episode only over the course of a few pages and, even then, only in the context of the AIOC's relationship with the British government. David S. Painter, *Oil and the American Century: The Political Economy of US Foreign Oil Policy, 1941–1954* (Baltimore: The Johns Hopkins University Press, 1986), 160–165, explores the sterling–dollar oil controversy tangentially. Finally, because Stoff, *Oil, War, and American Security* provides such indepth treatment of the Anglo-American oil talks after World War II, it deals with some of the sterling–dollar issues. But Stoff's interests lie elsewhere, and the book concludes before substitution was enacted.

1.1   The rise of the sterling area and the creation of the Bretton Woods international monetary system, 1932–1944

In the worldwide economic crisis of the early 1930s, Britain, the leading proponent of free trade for the better part of a century, sought to return sterling and the British economy to stability by creating a closed trading system within the boundaries of the empire.[10] The process began in the first part of 1932, when Britain imposed a tariff on manufactured imports and continued over the summer at the Imperial Economic Conference in Ottawa, Canada. From London's perspective, the goal of the conference was to establish empire free trade – the abolition of trade barriers within the imperial system – allowing those territories that were not exempt from the new tariff, mainly the Dominions (Australia, New Zealand, South Africa, and Canada), to negotiate for privileged access to the British market in exchange for a reduction in their own tariffs on British manufactures.[11] Rather than achieving a multilateral agreement based on a broad, coherent plan, though, the rough-and-tumble bargaining sessions merely produced a series of bilateral accords. The accords gave the Dominions the protected markets in Britain that they coveted without requiring them to forfeit the right to raise tariffs to defend their own industries. Likewise, Britain secured the protection of its farmers and set aside parts of its own market for certain trading partners outside the empire, such as Argentina and Denmark. While the Dominions got the better of Britain on manufactured goods, neither side emerged from Ottawa completely satisfied. Those who had hoped that the bilateral agreements would increase economic activity and trade within the empire, moreover, would be left disappointed at the end of the 1930s. Perhaps most discouraging to British policy-makers was the failure of the Imperial Economic Conference to establish empire free trade.[12]

Regardless, the conference cannot be viewed as a total failure, especially in terms of sterling's rehabilitation. The Ottawa accords, along with London's policy of allowing the pound to float, led to more tightly

---

[10] Some British officials had wanted to establish such a system for years, starting with Colonial Secretary Joseph Chamberlain in 1897. The pressure to do so increased when Chamberlain launched the tariff reform movement in 1903.

[11] Dominions were former colonies that had achieved self-governing status and freely associated with Britain. A good survey of the evolution of Britain's relationship with Australia, New Zealand, South Africa, and Canada is J. D. B. Miller, *Britain and the Old Dominions* (Baltimore: The Johns Hopkins University Press, 1966). India and Southern Rhodesia also participated in the conference, while Britain represented the crown colonies.

[12] Ian M. Drummond, *Imperial Economic Policy, 1917–1939: Studies in Expansion and Protection* (London: George Allen and Unwin, 1974), chs. 5 and 6; Cain and Hopkins, *British Imperialism*, 464–478.

integrated financial networks within the empire. Furthermore, the system of "imperial preference" through which Britain, the Dominions, and the colonies afforded each other favored trading status, provided sterling with a large and insulated area in which to operate and prosper. What emerged was a trading and financial halfway house in which sterling found stability and in which the City of London could continue to operate on a large, albeit reduced, scale.[13]

Rising up alongside the trade area created by the Ottawa agreements was a kind of currency club organized around the pound. Referred to as the sterling bloc, the group had no formal association or rules to follow, but it nonetheless possessed certain recognizable characteristics: "member" countries pegged their exchange rates to sterling, traded predominantly in sterling, held sterling as the major part of their international reserves, and looked primarily to London for their capital.[14] Countries that were considered part of the sterling bloc included Britain, the Dominions (except for Canada, which linked itself to the US dollar), India, the dependent empire, Egypt, Iraq, and Britain's Middle Eastern protectorates.[15] The Scandinavian countries also fell into the currency group because of their "particularly close" financial and commercial ties to Britain. Japan, Greece, Iran, and the Baltic states, which pegged their exchange rates to the pound, did not make widespread enough use of sterling, either in their international trade and payments or in their reserves, to be affiliated with it.[16]

The sterling bloc developed a more formal structure during World War II to conserve foreign exchange on behalf of the British war effort. After the outbreak of hostilities in September 1939, foreign countries that belonged to the sterling bloc abandoned the group as they liquidated their sterling assets, leaving behind mostly members of the British empire. It

---

[13] Cain and Hopkins, *British Imperialism*, 464–465; Ian M. Drummond, *The Floating Pound and the Sterling Area, 1931–1939* (Cambridge University Press, 1981), 253–254; Drummond, *Imperial Economic Policy*, 279–289.

[14] Eventually, sterling area members would have privileged access to the London capital market. The classic work on the sterling area is A. R. Conan, *The Sterling Area* (London: Macmillan, 1952). For a survey of the sterling area during the 1930s, see Drummond, *The Floating Pound and the Sterling Area*. For an examination of the currency group in the immediate postwar period, see Philip W. Bell, *The Sterling Area in the Postwar World: Internal Mechanism and Cohesion, 1946–1952* (Oxford: Clarendon Press, 1956). In *Britain and the Sterling Area*, Catherine Schenk picks up where Bell leaves off and provides a revisionist interpretation.

[15] Drummond, *The Floating Pound and the Sterling Area*, 3.

[16] "A History of the Sterling Area," prepared by the Treasury and sent to the Bank of England in March 1957, undated, BE/OV 44/10 and "Outline History of the Sterling Area," Treasury/Bank Working Party on the Sterling Area, SAWP (56) 26, May 29, 1956, BE/OV 44/32.

was during this period that the sterling bloc became more closely associated with the empire as well as when it assumed the name by which it has since become known: the sterling area. In response to the unrelenting flight from the pound that occurred at the outset of World War II, Britain erected a "ring fence" of exchange control around the sterling area. The control, designed in part to promote the accumulation of dollars and other foreign currencies, limited trade and payments with countries outside the currency group. Each member of the sterling area coordinated its exchange control policies with London but took responsibility for its own enforcement program. Therefore, territories in the Overseas Sterling Area (OSA) participated in the exchange control regime voluntarily and did so because, as large users and holders of sterling, they shared an interest in protecting the currency.[17] Exchange control also served the purpose of mobilizing capital in support of the war by encouraging the unfettered flow of money between London, the empire, and other sterling area members without allowing currency to leak into the wider world. Ultimately, the liberal transfer of capital within the sterling area was as important to the successful outcome of the war as the movement of troops and the production of materials. In a global conflict, advantage accrued to the combatants that could shift money the most efficiently.[18]

Much like the impetus for the rise of the sterling bloc in the 1930s, and the rationale behind its formalization during World War II, the sterling area carried on after the war to protect the pound during yet another episode of disequilibrium in the international economy: the postwar dollar shortage. The problem developed because the United States and Canada were the only major industrialized nations to emerge from the conflict with their economic bases intact. Countries around the globe turned to North America for imports to help them rebuild their tattered economies. But because of their diminished capacity to export, Britain and others could not earn the dollars necessary to pay for the imported goods and services. Thus, to conserve dollars and other kinds of foreign exchange, the British government consolidated the discriminatory controls on trade and payments instituted at the beginning of World War II by passing an Exchange Control Act in 1947.[19] Because the complex web of

[17] The Overseas Sterling Area, sometimes called the Rest of the Sterling Area (RSA), refers to all members except Britain.

[18] "A History of the Sterling Area," BE/OV 44/10 and "Outline History of the Sterling Area," SAWP (56) 26, May 29, 1956, BE/OV 44/32.

[19] The act made the sterling area official by listing, for the first and only time, the countries that were considered members of the currency group, calling them the "Scheduled Territories." See "Sterling and the Sterling Area," sent by J. E. Lucas to E. H. Boothroyd on January 11, 1962, NA, T 317/844.

Table 1.1 *The sterling account system, April 1952*

Sterling area	American account area	Transferable account area	Bilateral account area
Australia	Bolivia	Austria	Argentina
British Colonies	Central America	Chile	Belgium
Burma	Colombia	Czechoslovakia	Brazil
Ceylon	Cuba	Denmark	China
Great Britain	Dominica	Egypt	Formosa
Iceland	Ecuador	Ethiopia	France
India	Philippines	Finland	East Germany
Iraq	United States	Greece	Hungary
Jordan	Venezuela	Italy	Iran
Libya		Netherlands	Israel
New Zealand		Norway	Japan
Pakistan		Poland	Lebanon
Persian Gulf Territories		Spain	Paraguay
South Africa		Sweden	Peru
		Thailand	Portugal
		USSR	Romania
		West Germany	Switzerland
			Syria
			Tangier
			Turkey
			Uruguay
			Yugoslavia

Source: Schenk, *Britain and the Sterling Area*, 9.

controls associated with the act treated non-residents (non-members) of the sterling area differently from one another – based on the kind of currency they used and the nature of their trade patterns with the sterling area – the group's financial inner-workings can be somewhat difficult to penetrate. As shown in Table 1.1, four general account areas arose for exchange control purposes, reflecting the various levels of restriction that Britain imposed on transfers between certain countries and between those countries and the sterling area.[20]

[20] For the most part, sterling transfers were permitted within each account area without permission. As a result of their perpetual balance-of-payments surpluses with the sterling area, bilateral account countries were the most strictly monitored, with transfers between them requiring sanction from the Bank of England. Automatic transfers between the bilateral account countries and the sterling area were conducted through bilateral agreements, hence the name of the group. The transferable account countries could exchange sterling freely with each other and the sterling area but not with the bilateral or dollar account countries. Finally, the American account area included dollar area countries that were allowed to exchange sterling earnings for dollars – and dollars

Another motivation for perpetuating and tightening the wartime exchange controls in the postwar period was the enormous debt that Britain had built up during the war. To help finance the Allied victory, Britain borrowed billions of pounds from members of the sterling area by crediting sterling to their accounts in London, with Egypt and India accumulating the largest so-called "sterling balances." Since the total balances by the end of the war were estimated to be £14 billion, almost six times the worth of Britain's gold and dollar reserves in 1945, Whitehall had to prevent holders from running them down, meaning that it had to restrict their transferability to other currency areas to avoid a financial meltdown.[21] Thus, Britain arranged the blocking of their sterling balances with India, Egypt, and others in return for guaranteed repayment over a period of years.[22]

In addition to tightening the sterling area's exchange control regime, Britain sought to overcome its dollar shortage by creating a central pool in which sterling area members agreed to deposit their gold and dollar earnings. The overriding objective of the gold and dollar pool was to enable the sterling area as a whole to balance its payments with the rest of the world, especially the dollar area. In other words, it did not matter if Britain ran balance-of-payments deficits with the United States as long as significant dollar earners in the sterling area, with whom Britain ran balance-of-payments surpluses, kept exporting the dollar-generating raw materials that helped maintain symmetry between the sterling and dollar worlds. Exchange control and the gold and dollar pool were the two most important instruments employed by Whitehall to incubate sterling until policy-makers felt the currency was strong enough to achieve convertibility – at least those policy-makers who did not believe that the sterling area system was an end unto itself. In this way, the discriminatory sterling area was nothing less than the vehicle through which the pound and Britain would regain past glory.[23]

---

for sterling. They could also make payments in sterling to transferable account and sterling area countries. See Schenk, *Britain and the Sterling Area*, 8–10.

[21] Sir Alexander Cairncross, "A British Perspective on Bretton Woods" in Orin Kirshner (ed.), *The Bretton Woods–GATT System: Retrospect and Prospect after Fifty Years* (New York: M. E. Sharpe, 1996), 71.

[22] In other, less common instances, as in the cases of Australia and New Zealand, sterling area members agreed to write down the value of their holdings. See "A History of the Sterling Area," BE/OV 44/10. The balances would be the subject of discussion, concern, and debate for many years, both within Whitehall and between Britain and the US government, which viewed them as an impediment to the free flow of trade and capital in the postwar world. Whether or not they were a burden on the British economy and contributed to sterling's weakness during the 1950s is a matter of debate. See Schenk, *Britain and the Sterling Area*, ch. 2.

[23] Cain and Hopkins, *British Imperialism*, 631–632.

While the sterling area achieved its main purpose of protecting the pound during both World War II and the postwar era, its success came at the political cost of hampering relations with the United States. US policy-makers had chafed at the notion of "imperial preference" since its inception, and the discriminatory sterling area proved to be no less of an irritant. When British and US representatives met during the war to conceive a blueprint for the postwar system of international trade and payments, the Americans, especially Secretary of State Cordell Hull, let it be known that the walls of the sterling area would have to come down.[24] Early in the war, John Maynard Keynes, the renowned economist and leading British delegate to many of the Anglo-American talks, rejected this notion. He told US officials that the prognosis for Britain's financial health in the postwar era looked so grave that to survive it would have to continue its discriminatory trade practices.[25] His position exasperated members of the US Department of State. Having digested the lessons of the 1930s, and foreseeing a world in which no country could compete with the United States in trade, they and other US policy-makers insisted on the establishment of a multilateral economic order at the war's end. The British, however, would continue to defend their right to discriminate until the British economy got back on its feet, if not longer.[26]

The two major wartime statements regarding Anglo-American economic objectives for the postwar world reflected both the British and US imperatives. The first, the Atlantic Charter, was made public on August 14, 1941, and included a definition of multilateralism in its last two paragraphs.[27] Had Under-Secretary of State Sumner Welles had his way, the United States would have inserted the phrase "without discrimination" into the fourth paragraph concerning "equal access to raw materials." But British Prime Minister Winston Churchill insisted that

[24] The classic and best work on the Anglo-American discussions remains Gardner, *Sterling–Dollar Diplomacy*. Also see L. S. Pressnell, *External Economic Policy since the War*.

[25] Wanting to avoid alienating the United States, the constructive relations with which he viewed as critical to Britain's future, Keynes would soften his tone by 1944. He agreed that the sterling area should be phased out and multilateralism achieved as soon as possible, but without further gutting a British Treasury that had been eviscerated by the war. For Keynes the issue became *when and how* Britain made the move to multilateralism, not *if* it did so. See Robert Skidelsky, *John Maynard Keynes, Volume III: Fighting for Britain, 1937–1946* (London: Macmillan, 2000), ch. 9.

[26] Gardner, *Sterling–Dollar Diplomacy*, 41–43.

[27] The fourth and fifth paragraphs read: "(a) 'Fourth, they will endeavour, with due respect for their existing obligations, to further the enjoyment by all States, great or small, victor or vanquished, of access, on equal terms to the trade and to the raw materials of the world which are needed for their prosperity.' (b) 'Fifth, they desire to bring about the fullest collaboration between all nations in the economic field, with the object of securing for all improved labour standards, economic advancement and social security.'" See Pressnell, *External Economic Policy since the War*, Appendix 9(a) and (b), 380.

"without discrimination" would have abrogated the Ottawa agreements and, thus, would never have been accepted by either the British government or the Dominions. Churchill also reserved Britain's right to maintain imperial preference, raising the point that Britain had sustained free trade for eighty years "in the face of ever-mounting American tariffs." "All we got in reciprocation was successive doses of American protection," he scoffed. The prime minister's gift for persuasion and the US desire to produce a joint statement as quickly as possible ensured that "without discrimination" would not be included in the Charter.[28] The second statement was Article VII of the Mutual Aid Agreement – otherwise known as the Lend-Lease program – the vehicle through which the United States provided aid to countries whose defense was deemed vital to the United States during the war. Unlike the Atlantic Charter, it was the product of months of negotiations, and it also went much farther than the Charter on the matter of discrimination, tying Lend-Lease aid to "the elimination of all forms of discriminatory treatment in international commerce." Like the Charter, though, it recognized British concerns about the dire state of its economy by leaving room for future conversations that would determine "the best means of attaining" free trade "in the light of governing economic conditions."[29]

The two plans that the United States and Britain submitted for a new international monetary system reflected not only the ideals of the Atlantic Charter and Article VII but also the competing goals and interests of the two countries. Not surprisingly, the American plan, drafted by US Treasury economist Harry Dexter White, envisioned a global economy devoid of trade and finance controls. It also conceived of a monetary regime with fixed exchange rates, like the old gold standard, in which countries could only adjust parities as sanctioned by an international authority. Keynes's plan, on the other hand, allowed for greater flexibility in adjusting currency rates. It also granted countries the freedom to implement exchange and trade controls to harmonize their balance-of-payments and full employment objectives. Keynes expected that the United States, moreover, as the world's largest creditor, would finance trade deficits up to $23 billion.[30]

The agreement that established the Bretton Woods international monetary regime in 1944, which was named for the town in New Hampshire where the conference that produced the accord took place, represented a concerted, albeit not entirely successful, effort by Britain and the United

[28] Gardner, *Sterling–Dollar Diplomacy*, 42–47.   [29] Ibid., 54–59.
[30] Barry Eichengreen, *Globalizing Capital: A History of the International Monetary System* (Princeton University Press, 1996), 96.

States to correct the mistakes of the interwar period.[31] In response to
the balance-of-payments fiascos of the 1920s and the liquidity crisis of
the 1930s, the Articles of Agreement created the International Monetary Fund (IMF) to regulate the world's exchange rates and to disburse
loans to countries with severe trade account problems. Member nations
funded the IMF at varying levels, with the United States contributing
$2.75 billion, far short of the $23 billion suggested by Keynes. Countries
could draw upon "quotas" of up to $8.8 billion – again, a far cry from
the $26 billion recommended by Keynes and more like White's sugges-
tion of $5 billion. The system operated under a gold-exchange standard,
in which the gold-backed dollar served as the world's main reserve currency to which all other currencies were pegged.[32] Unlike the former
gold standard regime, nations could adjust their exchange rates as much
as 10 percent or more, upon approval by the IMF, to correct a fundamental balance-of-payments disequilibrium (a concession to Keynes).
What exactly constituted a "fundamental disequilibrium," the Articles
of Agreement did not specify.[33] This "compromise" agreement between
the US and British plans clearly revealed the much stronger bargaining
position of the United States.

On the issue of discrimination, however, Britain achieved two victories that proved important in the conduct of British international economic policy after the war. First, Britain was able to have a scarce-
currency clause inserted into the Bretton Woods Articles of Agreement.
This allowed a country to implement extraordinary exchange restrictions against nations that ran consistent enough balance-of-payments
surpluses to make scarce the IMF's holdings of their currencies (because
of borrowing by deficit members). Second, the Articles of Agreement
also permitted countries to preserve controls over the flow of international capital. While the IMF was supposed to assess these controls
and then recommend policies for their elimination after a period of
five years, the postwar economic environment was distorted enough for
Britain and the Western European countries to maintain controls until
1958 and later.[34] Despite these allowances, British trade and currency
restrictions would continue to bother US officials well into the postwar
period.

[31] Forty-four Allied and Associated Nations attended the conference. For a multifaceted
examination of the history and legacy of Bretton Woods, see Orin Kirshner (ed.), *The
Bretton Woods–GATT System: Retrospect and Prospect after Fifty Years* (New York: M. E.
Sharpe, 1996). Also see Armand Van Dormael, *Bretton Woods: Birth of a Monetary
System* (New York: Holmes and Meier, 1978).
[32] Dollars could be exchanged for gold at $35 an ounce.
[33] Eichengreen, *Globalizing Capital*, 97.   [34] Ibid, 97–98, 113–114.

1.2   Anglo-American petroleum talks, 1944–1945

The push for a comprehensive oil agreement came primarily from the United States, particularly because economic growth projections and dwindling underground reserves led American planners to conclude that the nation would become a net importer of oil soon after the war.[35] They also knew that the world would need considerable amounts of petroleum to fuel reconstruction – and that much of the supply for this massive project would come from the Middle East. In terms of production, the region was fast becoming the international oil industry's center of gravity, with Saudi Arabia having the greatest proven reserves in the world. In fact, US officials were so concerned about protecting the country's interest in Arabian oil that, in 1943, Harold Ickes, US Secretary of the Interior and Petroleum Administrator for War, established the government-owned Petroleum Reserves Corporation in part to buy the California-Arabian Standard Oil Company (Casoc) from its American partners, which had signed a concession agreement with the desert kingdom in 1933.[36] At the time, the firm's directors had simply asked the US government to provide financial assistance to Saudi Arabia to help stabilize the country and to protect its concession from the British, who had longstanding ties with its ruler, Ibn Saud.[37] Shocked at Washington's bold foray into the private sector and unwilling to part with an extremely profitable investment, Casoc officials rejected the offer.[38] The US government nonetheless found a way to help insure the

---

[35] The British Ambassador in Washington received a memorandum from the Department of State at the end of May 1943 that read: "It is suggested to His Majesty's government in the United Kingdom that discussions be undertaken for the purpose of arriving at an understanding as regards concessions to or related rights of development of sub-soil resources . . . ," "Oil Policy: Introductory Note," undated (but to be discussed by the War Cabinet's Ministerial Oil Committee on April 4, 1944), from the Papers, Agendas, and Minutes of the Meetings of the Ministerial Oil Committee, NA, POWE 33/1491.

[36] Standard Oil of California (Socal), which then became Chevron) signed the initial concession and incorporated the California-Arabian Standard Oil Company (Casoc). It eventually brought in the Texas Company (which became Texaco) in 1936 to provide market outlets. In 1944, they renamed the firm the Arabian-American Oil Company (Aramco), and in 1948, Standard Oil of New Jersey (which became Exxon) and Standard Oil of New York (Socony, which became Mobil) purchased 30 and 10 percent shares in the company respectively. Exxon and Mobil merged in 1998 to become the Exxon-Mobil Corporation, in part reversing the 1911 US Supreme Court decision that broke up the Standard Oil Company.

[37] About a year later the Acting Secretary of State wrote to Winant, the ambassador in the United Kingdom, that he was "disturbed about the rumor" that the British wanted to "horn in on Saudi Arabian oil reserves," February 22, 1944, *FRUS, 1944, Vol. III*, 101.

[38] Herbert Feis, the economic advisor to the State Department, wrote that the Casoc directors had "gone fishing for a cod, and caught a whale." Quoted in Sampson, *The Seven Sisters*, 95.

American investment in Saudi Arabia. After a historic meeting with Ibn Saud on a battleship in Egypt's Suez Canal zone, US President Franklin Roosevelt arranged for the country to receive Lend-Lease aid by executive order. For American policy-makers, maintaining the Saudi regime was a matter of national security, and, thus, the US government sought other ways to protect American interests there and elsewhere in the Middle East. One was by obtaining a petroleum agreement from Great Britain, the most influential power in the region and one with significant Middle Eastern oil investments.[39]

What the United States government hoped to achieve with a petroleum accord was the full development of oil production in the Middle East in a way that was efficient, stable, and non-discriminatory. Although the issue of discrimination had been a significant bone of contention between the United States and Britain since the early 1930s, regarding Middle Eastern oil, disputes over restrictive trade practices stretched back even further – to when the British government tried to prevent US companies from exploring for oil in British-controlled, League of Nations mandates after World War I.[40] Consequently, the Inter-Divisional Petroleum Committee of the Department of State, a working group of economic and political officers formed in December 1943, prepared a memorandum on the "Foreign Petroleum Policy of the United States." It emphasized the US government's desire to reach an agreement with Britain that would "include reciprocal assurances that petroleum development, processing, and marketing" would not be impeded "either by restrictions imposed unilaterally by either government or by inter-company arrangements." The memorandum's authors also explained that, based on the equal access clause of the Atlantic Charter, this agreement, like any, "should guarantee equality of treatment to all purchasers in respect of prices, quantities, and terms and conditions of sale."[41] For US policy-makers, if an accord with Britain did not promote and protect free trade

---

[39] As noted in the Introduction, the Anglo-Iranian Oil Company controlled 100 percent of the production in Iran, together with half of that in Kuwait and almost a quarter in Iraq.

[40] When Britain tried to keep Socony out of its League of Nations mandate in Palestine after World War I, the company asked the Department of State to pressure Britain into allowing US firms to explore for oil in the mandate areas. This paved the way for the Red Line Agreement (1928), which opened the door to American participation in Middle Eastern oil. See Cole to Polk, March 15, 1919, *FRUS, 1919, Vol. II*, 251, and Yergin, *The Prize*, 194–206. Even as late as World War II, Britain only allowed companies registered in the United Kingdom, with British directors and staff, to explore for oil in its Persian Gulf protectorates. See Stoff, *Oil, War, and American Security*, 130–131.

[41] *FRUS, 1944, Vol. V*, 31–32.

in oil, particularly in the Middle East, then there would be no point in ratifying it.

For their part, British officials viewed an oil agreement with the United States as advantageous to British interests as well. They argued that "orderly and efficient development can do nothing but good, but can only be ensured by common consent," and that no alternatives existed to "rivalry or co-operation, competition or a common policy." The government also believed that there was strength in numbers: together, Britain and the United States would be better able to prevent Middle Eastern oil from falling into the hands of parties hostile to their welfare. According to British policy-makers, finding common ground with the United States on Middle Eastern oil was also important because of the larger implications surrounding an agreement. They felt that people in both countries, and elsewhere, were "firmly convinced that future peace and prosperity of the world" would "depend on close understanding and unity of policy between the English-speaking nations."[42] Regardless of that statement's blatant Anglo-centrism, it must be regarded as a significant factor motivating Britain's self-interested desire to enter into oil discussions with the US government.[43] British officials also viewed an accord with the United States as an opportunity to expand Britain's influence in US-dominated, Latin American oil, if, as expected, US representatives demanded greater participation for American firms in the Middle East.[44] Finally, Basil Jackson, the outspoken AIOC representative in the United States, believed that Anglo-American cooperation in Iran might bring security to the firm's concession there if the Soviet Union decided to make any aggressive moves toward the country.[45]

Even though British officials believed that the implementation of some kind of joint oil agreement with the United States was a good idea, they did not enter into discussions with their American counterparts without anxiety. Writing to Franklin Roosevelt about the upcoming discussions on petroleum in February 1944, Winston Churchill warned, "there is apprehension in some quarters here that the United States has a desire to deprive us of our oil assets in the Middle East." He added that when an Anglo-American conference on Middle Eastern oil was finally

---

[42] "Oil Policy: Introductory Note," undated (but to be discussed by the War Cabinet's Ministerial Oil Committee on April 4, 1944), from the Papers, Agendas, and Minutes of the Meetings of the Ministerial Oil Committee, NA, POWE 33/1491.

[43] During preliminary technical discussions with the US group, the British delegation "emphasised the importance of avoiding a failure in the first big experiment in multilateral commodity organisation," "Minutes of a Meeting of the War Cabinet's Ministerial Oil Committee," MOC (44) 8, May 15, 1944, NA, FO 371/42696.

[44] Stoff, Oil, War, and American Security, 146–147.

[45] No. 172 from Jackson to Fraser, January 25, 1945, BP 70986.

announced, the subject would attract negative attention in the British Parliament, especially because the secretary of state was tapped to head the US delegation: "It will be felt that we are being hustled and may be subjected to pressure," Churchill explained.[46] Britain's Ministerial Oil Committee echoed the prime minister's sentiments, contending, "it is not improbable that some sections of American opinion may seek an opportunity to improve their position at our expense."[47] But British officials believed that if they made clear their determination to maintain the country's oil interests in the Middle East, there would still be "plenty of room for a constructive agreement which would be of benefit to both parties while harming neither."[48] Nevertheless, Churchill warned Roosevelt that "a wrangle about oil would be a poor prelude for the tremendous joint enterprise and sacrifice to which we have bound ourselves."[49]

One of the main reasons British officials worried about US encroachment on British-controlled oil concessions was the detrimental effect that it would have on the country's balance of payments.[50] By purchasing oil with sterling from companies registered in Britain, the nation saved dollars on a commodity that represented the greatest drain on the country's dollar supply. Consequently, after the war, policy-makers intended to exploit British-controlled oil resources as much as possible by encouraging the "maximum" expansion of production and refining capacity by British companies.[51] But this expansion would not achieve the dollar-saving that they desired if the companies did not have somewhere to sell the extra crude and products. Thus, the British government sought to limit the "unreasonable development by other interests" that would infringe on the ability of British companies to find the markets necessary to absorb the increased production.[52] Not surprisingly, then, British officials wanted a petroleum agreement with the United States that would

---

[46] No. 583 from Churchill to Roosevelt, February 20, 1944, NA, POWE 33/1495. The United States made the announcement on March 7, 1944.

[47] "Oil Policy: Introductory Note," undated (but to be discussed by the War Cabinet's Ministerial Oil Committee on April 4, 1944), from the Papers, Agendas, and Minutes of the Meetings of the Ministerial Oil Committee, NA, POWE 33/1491.

[48] Ibid.

[49] No. 583 from Churchill to Roosevelt, February 20, 1944, NA, POWE 33/1495.

[50] The Ministerial Oil Committee wrote in the "Introductory Note" that "any contraction of British-owned oil resources in the Middle East by surrender to American interests would have a most damaging effect on our future balance of payments," NA, POWE 33/1491. See also "Anglo-American Oil Policy: Memorandum Prepared by the Petroleum Division for the Chairman of the Oil Control Board," January 27, 1944, NA, FO 371/42686.

[51] Ibid.

[52] "Minutes of a Meeting of the War Cabinet's Ministerial Oil Committee Concerning a Draft by Sir William Brown," MOC (44) 3, April 3, 1944, NA, POWE 33/1491.

regulate the development of Middle Eastern oil, while simultaneously allowing Britain to increase its production and refining capacity. They also hoped to be able to reduce the sale of dollar oil to sterling markets if Britain was running dangerously high balance-of-payments deficits.

Official discussions to lay the groundwork for an oil agreement began in mid-April 1944, when British and US delegates met for two weeks in Washington, DC, for preliminary technical conversations. These exploratory discussions were characterized by accommodation rather than conflict thanks in part to the "conciliatory tone" set at the beginning by Charles Rayner, the petroleum advisor to the Department of State. The defensive-minded British delegates, who entered the talks suspicious of American intentions, relaxed as a result, and the discussions that followed produced a "Memorandum of Understanding" between the two sides. The delegates wanted the Memorandum to be general in scope "to ensure the broadest possible support," so that it could eventually serve the multilateral purposes for which it was intended.[53]

Indeed, the Memorandum's preamble and subsequent clauses reflected the free trade goals that the US government had sought for the postwar world since 1941. The preamble included the notion that "ample supplies" of petroleum were "essential for both the security and economic well being of nations"; that the development of these supplies should take into account the interests of countries involved in both the production and consumption of oil; that the level of supplies drawn from around the world should pay "due consideration" to, among other things, "relevant economic factors"; and that "such supplies should be available in accordance with the principles of the Atlantic Charter."[54] Article I of the document reflected the spirit of the Atlantic Charter and was clearly meant to correct the historic and continuing practices of the British government regarding oil. The first clause of Article I advocated that oil should be made available to "the nationals of all peace-loving countries in adequate volume, at fair prices and on an equitable and nondiscriminatory basis." Continuing this theme, the sixth clause rejected "restrictions imposed by either Government or its nationals" that would hamper the distribution of petroleum in ways "inconsistent with the purposes" of the Memorandum. As it had in the past, this last point would create friction between Britain and the United States on petroleum.

---

[53] For a copy of the "Memorandum" see *FRUS, 1944, Vol. III*, 112–115; Stoff, *Oil, War, and American Security*, 155–157.
[54] *FRUS, 1944, Vol. III*, 112–115.

Although the exploratory discussions that led to the Memorandum were amicable, British delegates did express some reservations about the document during the talks, even as they agreed to it, because of balance-of-payments concerns. They worried mostly that the Memorandum did not take into account the fact that the United States was naturally endowed with a great deal more oil than Britain. After all, British officials said, their country was dependent on foreign sources of supply for almost all of its petroleum while the United States was not. Consequently, they wanted the Memorandum to include a statement that would allow their government special privileges regarding the importation of oil based on economic need, an issue tied directly to their concern for the security of sterling. In response to the US claim that such a statement would defeat the entire purpose of the agreement, the British delegation explained that the British government would probably not agree to "any abrogation of its right to use what measures it felt appropriate to protect the security and well being of the British empire."[55] The US delegates assured them that the words "relevant economic factors" in the preamble would secure their right to enact such measures, covering such issues as "the protection of national currencies."[56] They also explained that they had already assumed that Britain would use resources under its control "primarily" on behalf of its national interest.[57] Regardless, one member of the British delegation was disappointed that the US representatives "could not meet, on the face of the document and in definite terms, the position that the United Kingdom was dependent upon imports for petroleum supplies."[58] In the end, the British were left dissatisfied about the lack of precise language that would give them a loophole out of the agreement in times of economic difficulty.

During the interim period between the end of the exploratory discussions in early May and the beginning of the Oil Conference in late July, British officials focused on how they could reconcile the Memorandum with Britain's need to protect sterling. The Treasury, which sought to defend the pound throughout the postwar era at all costs, expressed "satisfaction" with the outcome of the negotiations with the United States. But the department remained concerned about the foreign exchange

---

[55] Stoff, *Oil, War, and American Security*, 158–159; "Report to the War Cabinet's Ministerial Oil Committee of the UK Delegation to Washington on their Negotiations," MOC (44) 8, May 15, 1944, NA, FO 371/42696.
[56] Ibid.
[57] "Draft Report of the War Cabinet's Ministerial Oil Committee," MOC (44) 11, May 23, 1944, NA, FO 371/42696.
[58] "Minutes of Joint Session No. VIII of the Anglo-American Exploratory Discussions on Petroleum," April 26, 1944, NA, FO 371/42696.

question – about whether Britain could buy as much oil from non-dollar sources as it wanted to safeguard the country's balance of payments.[59] In June, British officials began talking about the "one-sided nature of the arrangements" contained in the Memorandum, believing it "essential that the balance be redressed," if the British government was to support it. While understanding that it would be difficult for Britain to exclude US oil companies from sterling area markets, British officials thought that they might have to do just that, exclaiming, "Our post-war exchange position may be involved, and we must be free without any suggestion of bad faith to look at our oil commitments from that point of view." The matter was of the "gravest consequence," Chancellor of the Exchequer J. A. Anderson said.[60] Thus, British delegates were prepared to enter the Oil Conference with the United States, due to take place in the dog days of a typically humid Washington summer, arguing this point, much to the dismay of their American counterparts.[61]

Anticipating a single-minded British opposition, US representatives were determined to reject further British efforts to "urge" upon them a "preferential treatment proviso" that would subvert their free trade agenda. One Department of State official warned petroleum advisor Charles Rayner: "It is a dangerous hallucination to suppose that the British can be talked out of their bluntly and strongly stated ambitions in this matter." That Whitehall had "overweighted" its delegation with "no less than four" cabinet ministers raised the eyebrows of US officials, signaling to them that the British intended to bring their "heavy artillery" to "make some bread in the memorandum of the agreement."[62] Mixed metaphors aside, the comment referred to Article I (3), which concerned

[59] "Minutes of a Meeting of the Ministerial Oil Committee," MOC (44) 6, May 16, 1944, NA, FO 371/42696.

[60] "Oil Discussions with the United States Government: Report of the Special Oil Committee," War Cabinet, June 14, 1944, WP (44) 313, NA, FO 371/42697; "Note by the Chairman of the War Cabinet's Special Oil Committee," J. A. Anderson, Chancellor of the Exchequer, June 11, 1944, NA, POWE 33/1493.

[61] J. A. Anderson wrote, "Our negotiators should make it clear on the resumption of discussions that our right, in relation to oil, to resort to any fiscal methods compatible with any international agreements for the time being in force remain intact; and that the Memorandum of Understanding does not, apart from any wider international arrangement, curtail in any way our freedom of action for securing this end," in ibid. Stoff, *Oil, War, and American Security*, 172.

[62] Unsigned to Rayner, July 11, 1944, US National Archives and Records Administration (hereafter cited as "NARA"), Office of International Trade Policy, Petroleum Division, Subject File, 1943–1949, Box 8, "CCBR Working Papers/Anglo-American Agreements President's Com" folder; "Minute of a Conversation between a Member of Ronald I. Campbell's Staff at the British Embassy," Washington, DC and James C. Sappington of the State Department, August 17, 1944, NA, FO 371/42701; Stoff, *Oil, War, and American Security*, 172–173.

the conditions under which the development of oil resources would be conducted, focusing on such issues as "availability of supply" and "collective security arrangements."[63] In its report to the War Cabinet, the British Special Oil Committee wrote that the Article should include the phrase, "with due regard to the right of each country to draw from the production under its control to the extent that may be considered necessary."[64] Its inclusion would allow Britain, in the event of a balance-of-payments crisis, to conserve dollars by supplying the sterling area with oil exclusively from sterling sources, like the Anglo-Iranian Oil Company, without violating the petroleum agreement.

On the second day of the conference, Ralph Assheton, Financial Secretary to the Treasury and the chairman of the British delegation at the joint sub-committee meetings, raised the issue of amending Article I (3) to safeguard sterling. In a long statement, he described, in great detail, Britain's economic plight, focusing in particular on the country's indebtedness, the damage the war had done to its export trade, and its need to find a way to pay for imports. He went so far as to characterize what happened to Britain's economy during the war as a "revolution as complete and swift as any in history." Therefore, Assheton explained, Britain had to safeguard its freedom to intervene in the international oil industry in ways that would bolster the country's foreign exchange position. He could not be specific about the degree to which the British government might have to disrupt normal trade flows in petroleum, but he could say for certain that the government was not planning "drastic alterations." He also wanted to clarify that Britain's motives were based purely on financial need and not something more sinister. Assheton continued by stating that all that Britain really wanted was to "make her position comparable to that of the United States," a country which, at the time, could satisfy its petroleum needs from domestic sources. The way to do so, he asserted, was to allow Britain to supply itself and its colonies with oil from production under British control "to the extent necessary for purposes of economic security."[65]

"Dumbfounded" by Assheton's remarks, US delegates argued that his recommendation would undermine both British and American

[63] Article I (3) read: "That the development of these resources shall be conducted with a view to the availability of adequate supplies of petroleum to both countries as well as to all other peace-loving countries, subject to the provisions of such collective security arrangements as may be established," *FRUS, 1944, Vol. III*, 113.

[64] "Oil Discussions with the United States Government: Report of the Special Oil Committee," WP (44) 313, June 14, 1944, NA, FO 371/42697.

[65] "Minutes of the Joint Sub-Committee, Session I, Anglo-American Conversations on Petroleum," July 26, 1944, NA, FO 371/42700.

interests.[66] Charles Rayner insisted that the British request was "inconsistent with the ideals of free and flexible international trade" that the agreement sought to promote. He also thought that giving "undue emphasis" to the foreign exchange question was unnecessary "in view of the language of the Preamble," repeating comments made a few months earlier. Deputy Petroleum Administrator Ralph K. Davies, "very much surprised and troubled" by Assheton's statement, thought from previous discussions that Britain had only wanted a "first call" on British-controlled oil in times of economic difficulty. But it was clear, Davies said, that the British delegation was "asking the United States government publicly to endorse the right of the United Kingdom Government to exclude United States oil from the UK market." Furthermore, he insisted, British discrimination against dollar oil would backfire and harm British interests rather than advance them. Disruptions in the flow of the international oil trade would, Davies said, "precipitate disorderly and perhaps chaotic markets, with a resultant loss to the United Kingdom itself greater than any temporary gain."[67] Over the next several days, British and American delegates rehashed these arguments, raised new ones, and pushed the limits of each other's patience as they went around and around discussing the vulnerability of sterling on the one hand and free trade on the other.

Eventually, a dispute arose about whether discrimination against dollar oil was an effective way of dealing with a potential foreign exchange crisis. The US delegation came armed with statistics to demonstrate that restricting imports of dollar oil would backfire. In his presentation, Charles Rayner explained that if Britain kept dollar oil out of the sterling area, 35 million barrels of dollar oil a year would seek markets elsewhere, thereby reducing Britain's share of those markets by the same amount. The implication was that even though Britain's balance of payments would benefit from a British monopoly on oil sales within the sterling area, Britain would offset these gains by forfeiting valuable business in non-sterling, non-dollar markets. British delegate Frank Lee replied that, while he was not in a position to deal "off-hand" with Rayner's figures, the British government had done its own statistical analysis, which showed that the country's balance of payments might lose $100 million a year on oil – "not an insignificant amount," he said. Therefore, if Rayner proved correct that discriminating against dollar oil would not produce

[66] "Minutes of a Conversation between a Member of Ronald I. Campbell's Staff at the British Embassy, Washington, DC and James C. Sappington of the State Department," August 17, 1944, NA, FO 371/42701.
[67] Ibid.

the desired result, then, obviously, the British government would have to weigh other options. However, Lee explained, the point that he and his colleagues were trying to impress upon the Americans was that the problem was serious enough for the government to consider *whatever* measures seemed necessary to resolve it, including discrimination.[68]

Exacerbating the inflexibility of both delegations was the fear that an oil agreement that appeared to sell out either British or US interests would never be accepted back home. Ralph Assheton insisted that if he and his colleagues could not expand Article I (3) to allow Britain some leeway on oil importation in times of severe economic difficulty, Parliament would characterize the agreement as an "uneven deal," since it would permit the United States to control its domestic market without providing Britain with the same luxury.[69] In a similar vein, Harry Hawkins, Director of the Office of Economic Affairs at the Department of State, commented that if the US delegation accepted the British revision, the government would have to explain to the American people why it had "authorized" the British to exclude dollar oil from sterling markets. Because "such disclosure would spell the political ruin of the Agreement in the United States," Hawkins continued, the revision "should be regarded as simply impossible" for that reason alone.[70] Moreover, American officials asked how the US government would explain the change to American oil companies. Ralph Davies asserted that the firms would never go along with it, and that the US government had no authority to force them to adhere to the agreement, which, consequently, would become nothing more than a "dishonest" and "empty" gesture. "You cannot ask American companies to give up a trade advantage or to give up a substantial segment of their volume of business without offering them anything in return," Davies declared.[71] As the positions of both sides hardened, it seemed that the Oil Conference would come to a close having achieved nothing other than animosity between Britain and the United States.

What did the British *really* want? According to delegate Frank Lee, his government simply sought to "go on record as having warned" the United States that "circumstances in the post-war period might be such as to make it necessary to take abnormal steps," not wanting to be party to an agreement that would prevent it from taking those

---

[68] "Minutes of the Joint Sub-Committee, Session II, Anglo-American Conversations on Petroleum," July 27, 1944, NA, FO 371/42700.
[69] "Minutes of the Joint Sub-Committee, Session I, Anglo-American Conversations on Petroleum," July 26, 1944, NA, FO 371/42700.
[70] Ibid.
[71] "Minutes of the Joint Sub-Committee, Session III, Anglo-American Conversations on Petroleum," July 28, 1944, NA, FO 371/42700.

steps.[72] They also hoped for some understanding from US representatives on why Britain would have to take such unusual measures during a difficult "transitional period," and, as a result, give Britain their blessing as they had on other agreements.[73] Just as important, the British delegation wanted US officials *and* the UK audience watching at home to know that it refused to be pushed around – that it had fought hard for British interests. Lord Beaverbrook, who was chosen by Winston Churchill to lead the British team, in part because he was known as a skilled negotiator and especially because he was devoted to "protecting British interests and private enterprise," said that there was merit in "standing up to the Americans and avoiding becoming a subservient nation."[74] It seems that the British delegation believed that, if it could walk away from the Oil Conference having achieved these goals, then it could be satisfied in its success without actually having amended Article I (3). Nonetheless, a change to the Article would certainly have represented a much greater accomplishment.

In the end, the two sides reached a compromise that would give Britain what it desired without including a clause in the agreement that would, in effect, undermine the entire document, which is what the United States hoped to prevent. Lord Beaverbrook, having concluded that the American delegation would not budge on the issue of amending Article I (3), said that the British were willing to take their revision off the table if the future Petroleum Commission was given specific direction based on: (1) "a statement of the British position as it had been explained" during the discussions; (2) "a statement that the US Delegation had taken note of the UK position"; and (3) "a statement that if the UK felt itself compelled to pursue the course of action which had been discussed, and if agreement could not be reached in the Petroleum Commission, then the US Government should have the right to terminate the Agreement without notice."[75] Harold Ickes did not want such language included in the document itself because he thought that "it would add nothing" to the

[72] "Minutes of the Joint Sub-Committee, Session IV, Anglo-American Conversations on Petroleum, July 31, 1944," NA, FO 371/42700.

[73] Examples of this are the draft Commercial Agreement, the draft Commodity Agreement, and the Bretton Woods Agreement. See "Minutes of the Plenary Session No. III of Anglo-American Conversations on Petroleum," August 1, 1944, NA, FO 371/42701.

[74] Stoff, *Oil, War, and American Security*, 170; Campbell to Sargent, August 22, 1944, NA, FO 371/42702. It is important to note that Beaverbrook's comment reflects an attitude consistent with future British approaches to the United States regarding sterling and oil.

[75] Ronald Campbell, the chargé d'affaires at the British Embassy in Washington, wrote to the Foreign Office that "it is the unanimous view of the British delegates that the Americans cannot be persuaded to yield by argument; they have fixed views and apparently they are acting in unison. They have given us a rough ride and the road gets worse." No. 4136, August 2, 1944, NA, FO 371/42699.

agreement, arguing that regardless of any "specific language" the British government "had the right to adopt any policy it chose with respect to its own market." Without insisting that the language be written into the accord, British delegate Richard Law disagreed that it "would add nothing" to the agreement, repeating what other British representatives had said before: that the British government simply "wished to have it on record that circumstances outside their control might make it impossible for them to fulfill the terms of the Agreement during the transitional period."[76]

The joint delegations unanimously approved a statement that satisfied the conditions that Lord Beaverbrook outlined.[77] They would be included in the minutes of the plenary session, which would be made available to the US Congress and the British Parliament, thus ending the increasingly bitter dispute that had begun the moment Ralph Assheton fired his opening salvo on July 26.[78] After further talks in September of the following year, convened to discuss an American redraft of the Petroleum Agreement, it was finally signed on September 24, 1945.

The accord was never ratified, however, in part because of the US domestic oil industry's hostility to it. In fact, the independent oil companies, which exerted enormous influence on Congress – especially the Texas representatives – forced American officials to amend the agreement.[79] According to Ralph K. Davies, the independents remembered all too well past attempts by the US government (most recently during the New Deal) "to enact legislation for Federal control of their operations." This, he said, had filled their representatives with "suspicion" that the federal government "would take advantage of any opportunity, direct or indirect, to gain authority over their activities."[80] The

[76] "Minutes of the Plenary Session No. III of Anglo-American Conversations on Petroleum," August 1, 1944, NA, FO 371/42701.

[77] J. A. Anderson said that Beaverbrook's solution corresponded "very closely to that which the War Cabinet had decided on 3rd August to suggest to the delegation" and that the "generally adequate" terms of the statement "appeared to safeguard" the British exchange position. From an undated draft telegram from the War Cabinet Ministers to the British Embassy in Washington, DC, NA, FO 371/42699.

[78] No. 4179 from R. I. Campbell to the Foreign Office, August 4, 1944, NA, FO 371/42699; "Minutes of the Joint Sub-Committee, Session V, Anglo-American Conversations on Petroleum, August 1, 1944," NA, FO 371/42701.

[79] Texas was home to the most influential group of American independent oil producers. One of their senators, Tom Connally, was chairman of the Senate's Foreign Relations Committee.

[80] "Minutes of the Anglo-American Conversations on Petroleum, Joint Official Sub-Committee Meeting No. 2," September 20, 1945, NARA, RG 59, Records of the Petroleum Division, Box 20, Records of Committees, 1942–1947. Among the changes that the US government made to satisfy the domestic oil industry was the addition of Article VII, which actually proved advantageous to Britain. It assured that nothing in

independents claimed that the agreement not only violated anti-trust laws through its cartel-like arrangements, but also allowed Britain to force open the US market to duty free oil, much to their disadvantage.[81] When the Senate Foreign Relations Committee finally voted on the Petroleum Agreement in the summer of 1947, Texas Senator Tom Connally was the lone dissenter, promising a "bitter fight" if it ever came to the Senate floor. On the cusp of a difficult re-election campaign, Harry Truman did not welcome a tough battle over an agreement that he did not think was worth the energy and political capital needed to enact it.[82]

Ultimately, the ability of private companies to accomplish the goals that the US government initially sought to achieve through the Petroleum Agreement undermined support for it. Because of their valuable market outlets, American multinationals Socony-Vacuum and Standard Oil of New Jersey were asked by Standard Oil of California and Texaco to participate in the Aramco concession in Saudi Arabia, involving no fewer than four major American firms in the Middle East's most prolific petroleum source. Also, left to their own devices, British and US companies were able to establish the rational development and stable price structure within the Middle Eastern oil industry that the US government had desired.[83] On the other side of the Atlantic, British officials seemed content to let sleeping dogs lie, since they had become much more anxious about how the oil accord could hurt Britain than they were enthusiastic about its benefits. In the end, the document simply faded away.

Even though the effort to produce a comprehensive petroleum agreement resulted in failure, it is important to consider the arguments that dominated the Anglo-American oil talks. Exploring the Anglo-American conversations on petroleum from 1944 to 1945 helps to provide the

the agreement "shall be construed as impairing . . . the right to enact any law or regulation, relating to the importation of petroleum into the country of either Government." Wilfred Eady of the British Treasury thought that this was "better than the words in the old Agreement – 'relevant economic factors,'" in ibid. and NA, T 236/1311. Also see the "Minutes of Joint Official Sub-Committee Meeting No. 1," September 19, 1945, NA, FO 371/50388.

[81] H. Wilkinson to Congressman Richard Law, included in a cable sent to the Foreign Office on December 9, 1944, NA, POWE 33/1499; No. 1127 from the Earl of Halifax at the British Embassy in Washington to the Ministry of Fuel and Power, November 9, 1945, NA, FO 371/50390.

[82] Stoff, *Oil, War, American Security*, 194.

[83] Ibid., 195–208. Also see the "Record of Discussion of the 'Informal Anglo/US Oil Talks,'" November 2, 1946, for a comment on how the multinational oil companies sought a new international price structure no longer based primarily on the Gulf of Mexico since the United States "would no longer be the principal source of oil supplies for international trade in the not too distant future," NA, FO 371/53056.

necessary context from which Britain's future decision to discriminate against dollar oil emerged. By examining the ways in which British officials fought to preserve their right to discriminate against non-sterling oil in 1944 and 1945 – and whenever they said non-sterling, they really meant dollar – one better understands how seriously they took the link between the strength of the pound and British production and consumption of petroleum. Even though the British delegates to the petroleum talks always spoke of discrimination against dollar oil in hypothetical terms, the evidence demonstrates that the British government was intent on implementing substitution at some point in the postwar period. This explains why the British delegates were so adamant about not signing an accord that limited their ability to import oil in ways that protected sterling. The Anglo-American dispute over this issue in 1944 was merely a dress rehearsal for the much larger conflict that would occur when Britain finally did execute its large-scale discrimination policy, a decision influenced by the severe balance-of-payments setbacks that the country suffered in the latter half of the 1940s.

1.3   Balance-of-payments crises and strategic turning points, 1947–1949

The difficult winter of 1946–1947 could not have come at a worse time. With Britain struggling to pay for the cost of reconstruction, the bitter cold caused a fuel shortage that reduced British exports by £100 million for 1947.[84] Fortunately, Britain had just secured a major loan from the United States in July to help bail the country out of its postwar financial troubles.[85] The protracted and rancorous discussions that produced the loan, officially called the Anglo-American Financial Agreement, made the oil talks seem almost pleasant by comparison. Nonetheless, the negotiations resulted in an aid package that included a $3.75 billion loan plus $650 million to settle outstanding Lend-Lease debts, all of which was to be paid back over a fifty-year period at an annual rate of 2 percent starting in 1951. British officials had initially hoped for an outright grant of $4–6 billion, and some resented what they considered US parsimony given the invaluable sacrifices that they felt Britain had made on behalf of the Allies during the war. Others believed the loan to have been generous.[86] But

---

[84] Cairncross, *The British Economy since 1945*, 54–55.
[85] Britain and the United States agreed to the loan in December 1945, but Congress did not ratify it until July of the following year.
[86] Cairncross maintains that the loan was not only "generous by commercial standards" but also "allowed the United Kingdom to borrow on a scale that was several times larger than what might have been raised on commercial terms," *The British Economy since*

just about every British official bristled at what American policy-makers were asking them to relinquish in return for the loan, namely the end of discrimination within the sterling area and a commitment to making sterling convertible by the end of 1946. In other words, the United States was asking the British government to give up two of the most important tools by which it planned to nurse the country's economy back to good health. Faced with the inconceivable possibility of walking away with nothing, British officials acceded to the American terms.[87]

Much to the astonishment of both Britain and the United States, most of the US loan was wiped out in the balance-of-payments crisis of 1947. Striking in midsummer, the problem had started with the previous winter's fuel shortage, which had dramatically reduced export-led income. Furthermore, Britain was spending more on imports because of the continued failure of worldwide primary production to recover from the war: insufficient production increased international demand, which drove up the price of food and raw materials, 42 percent of which came from dollar sources in the Western Hemisphere.[88] Making matters worse, the slow return of international primary production meant smaller contributions from the British colonies to the sterling area dollar pool, thereby limiting Britain's ability to exploit the dollar pool to pay for imports from the United States.[89] Finally, the British government's commitment to stabilizing Europe and Asia after the war exacerbated the country's economic problems by forcing Britain to maintain a level of military, administrative, and relief spending that it had not anticipated nor could it afford.[90] The result was that while the sterling area's dollar deficit amounted to $510 million for all of 1946, it totaled $1,620 million for the first half of 1947 – a breathtaking increase to say the least, and this was *before* the

---

1945, 53. The US government had already disturbed British officials by "abruptly" and "unexpectedly" ending Lend-Lease aid when Japan surrendered in 1945. See J. C. R. Dow, *The Management of the British Economy, 1945–60* (Cambridge University Press, 1964), 17.

[87] The best accounts of these negotiations can be found in Gardner, *Sterling–Dollar Diplomacy*, 199–223, and Pressnell, *External Economic Policy since the War*, 262–330.

[88] "United Kingdom Financial Position and the World Dollar Shortage," a "Memorandum from the British Embassy in Washington to the State Department," delivered by the British Ambassador, Lord Inverchapel to the Secretary of State, George Marshall, on June 18, 1947, *FRUS, 1947, Vol. III*, 17–24; Gardner, *Sterling–Dollar Diplomacy*, 308.

[89] "United Kingdom Financial Position and the World Dollar Shortage," *FRUS, 1947, Vol. III*, 17–24; Scott Newton, "Britain, the Sterling Area and European Integration, 1945–50," *The Journal of Imperial and Commonwealth History*, 13, 3 (1985), 163–182; Gardner, *Sterling–Dollar Diplomacy*, 308.

[90] Gardner, *Sterling–Dollar Diplomacy*, 309.

British government made the pound convertible, an act that plunged the country deeper into financial crisis.[91]

US pressure, a desire among British officials to honor their commitments to the United States, and old-fashioned pride in Britain's historic "financial eminence," all contributed to sterling convertibility on July 15, 1947, exactly one year after the Anglo-American Financial Agreement was ratified – a symbolic gesture to be sure.[92] In response, worldwide holders of sterling who purchased goods from the Western Hemisphere, and whose own currencies were not convertible, began changing large amounts of sterling into dollars. Some transfers were to be expected, but no one on either side of the Atlantic envisioned the hemorrhaging that would ensue. By August 1, Britain's dollar drain totaled $650 million a month, and had the British government not suspended convertibility on August 20, the American loan would have been exhausted by September. Despite British warnings, US officials failed to understand that Britain's economic problems comprised one part, albeit a significant one, of a much larger international crisis stemming from the worldwide scarcity of dollars.[93] The British government knew that by making sterling convertible, especially while other currencies remained non-convertible, Britain would be shouldering the burden of the world's dollar shortage. But a mixture of self-deception and pride led the British government to proceed with convertibility anyway.[94]

Because the Anglo-American Financial Agreement did not address the greater issue of the worldwide dollar shortage, it could never have provided an adequate shield for Britain to defend against the attacks to which convertibility rendered sterling vulnerable. Furthermore, by making the British loan contingent upon an end to discrimination and sterling convertibility, US officials coerced Britain into removing its most effective armor against those attacks.[95] Reflecting the continued resentment in some British circles over the way the US government had handled the

[91] These figures are from the Annex of a Memorandum from Hugh Dalton, Chancellor of the Exchequer, for the Cabinet Committee on Balance of Payments and Convertibility, CP (47) 227, August 5, 1947, NA, PREM 8/489.
[92] Newton, "Britain, the Sterling Area and European Integration, 1945–50," 166; Gardner, *Sterling–Dollar Diplomacy*, 318.
[93] "United Kingdom Financial Position and the World Dollar Shortage," *FRUS, 1947, Vol. III*, 17–24.
[94] Richard Gardner argues that the blame for convertibility's part in Britain's balance-of-payments troubles in 1947 cannot be laid solely at the feet of the United States, but that Britain should have taken some responsibility as well. See *Sterling–Dollar Diplomacy*, 312–325. As early as 1945, Keynes insisted it was in Britain's interests for the country to begin an interim program for getting rid of exchange restrictions "immediately," Memorandum of Conversation, August 3, 1945, *FRUS, 1945, Vol. VI*, 79–87.
[95] Newton, "Britain, the Sterling Area and European Integration, 1945–50," 166.

Financial Agreement, Sir John Balfour, an official at the British Embassy in Washington, remarked that the loan was "over-sold to Congress and the United States public as a cure all and the medicine men must now be prepared to give convincing explanations as to why their medicine failed to work."[96] In mid-1947, British and American officials learned the hard way that the UK economy was only at the beginning of a long and difficult road to recovery. Moreover, they both learned that more drastic measures would have to be taken to return both Britain and the world to economic equilibrium. On the US side, this included the European Recovery Program (ERP) – better known as the Marshall Plan – which, by providing direct aid to help Western Europe rebuild itself, was designed, in part, to help correct the trade imbalances that led to dollar scarcity.[97] On the British side, this meant the resumption of rigid sterling area controls like rationing, licensing, exchange control, and, eventually, large-scale discrimination against dollar oil.[98]

Even before the financial crisis of 1947, economic conditions in Britain were severe enough to affect the government's strategic policy in the Middle East, specifically Britain's defense of the eastern Mediterranean. When the Soviet Union, having already delayed in pulling its troops out of northern Iran in the first half of 1946, unsettled the Turkish government by proposing joint control of the Dardanelles in August of that year, British officials coordinated with their US counterparts to provide military aid to Turkey. Given Britain's worsening economic problems, however, the question remained whether it would be able to continue furnishing such aid to either Turkey or its neighbors. The answer came at the beginning of 1947, when a civil war in Greece – which started during World War II but escalated in the autumn of 1946 – proved to be a source of increasing instability in the eastern Mediterranean and raised concerns about Soviet pressure there. The civil war set communist insurgents against a royalist government backed by the United States and Britain, the latter of which announced in February 1947 that it could no longer afford to keep its troops in Greece or finance the government's

[96] No. 195 from the British Embassy in Washington, DC to the Foreign Office on August 1, 1947, NA, T 236/2426.
[97] That Secretary of State George Marshall made the speech that laid the groundwork for the ERP in June of that year suggests that some US officials had already recognized a need to think more creatively about rescuing Europe from its economic plight. In addition, Marshall believed that the United States "must accede [sic]" to British "demands for permission to discriminate." Quoted in Dobson, The Politics of the Anglo-American Economic Special Relationship, 110.
[98] Newton, "Britain, the Sterling Area and European Integration, 1945–50," 171–172; Alec Cairncross and Barry Eichengreen, Sterling in Decline: The Devaluations of 1931, 1949 and 1967 (Oxford: Basil Blackwell, 1983), 114.

civil and military needs.[99] Fearing the consequences for Western interests of a British decision that US Secretary of State George Marshall described as "tantamount to British abdication from the Middle East," US President Harry Truman and his advisors conceived a plan for Soviet containment that would fill the British void.[100] Truman unveiled the new approach in a speech before a joint session of Congress on March 12, 1947, declaring it the "policy of the United States to support free peoples" who were "resisting attempted subjugation by armed minorities or by outside pressures," later called the Truman Doctrine.[101] Congress subsequently approved $400 million in economic and military aid for Greece and Turkey to help fight communism on behalf of that goal, marking the beginning of an era of deeper US involvement in the Middle East.

Britain's transfer of responsibility for the eastern Mediterranean to the United States spurred efforts to define a joint security strategy for the region. In discussions at the US Department of Defense in September and October of 1947, known as "The Pentagon Talks,"[102] British and US planners characterized the eastern Mediterranean and the Middle East as "vital" to the security of both Britain and the United States, requiring Anglo-American support for the region's defense against Soviet influence.[103] Critical to these efforts, according to US officials, was maintaining "the British position in the Middle East area to the greatest possible extent."[104] While emphasizing Britain's continued "primary responsibility for military security" in the region, US policy-makers did not intend for the United States to "become a sort of Middle Eastern junior partner" of the British or to be "placed in the position of more or less following the British lead."[105] Given the British view of the United States as a novice in the region – at least compared with Britain's much longer experience there – this is precisely how many at Whitehall perceived the American role.[106] Nonetheless, British officials agreed with their US

---

[99] Douglas Little, *American Orientalism: The United States and the Middle East since 1945* (Chapel Hill: University of North Carolina Press, 2002), 121–123.

[100] Quoted in ibid., 123.   [101] Quoted in ibid.

[102] "'The Pentagon Talks of 1947' between the United States and the United Kingdom Concerning the Middle East and the Eastern Mediterranean," *FRUS, 1947, Vol. V*, 488–626.

[103] Undated Memorandum Prepared in the Department of State, "The American Paper," *FRUS, 1947, vol. V*, 575–576; Undated Memorandum on Policy in the Middle East and Eastern Mediterranean by the British Group, *FRUS, 1947, Vol. V*, 580–582.

[104] Undated Memorandum Prepared in the Department of State, "The British and American Positions," *FRUS, 1947, Vol. V*, 511–521.

[105] Undated Memorandum Prepared in the Department of State, "The American Paper."

[106] This is a subject of discussion in the context of the Iranian oil crisis in chapter 2.

counterparts that the two governments should develop "parallel" policies to solve common problems.[107] Indeed, US officials expected that Britain well understood that it could not fulfill its political and economic obligations in the Middle East without US help.[108]

The British government's decision to withdraw from the eastern Mediterranean was the first of three major turning points in British foreign and imperial policy in 1947, all of which are important to the larger narrative of this book. The next was the decision to quit India in August. Britain's departure from the subcontinent was the culmination of transformations in the imperial relationship that started during World War I. On the Indian side, the war precipitated domestic changes in the economic, social, and political spheres that developed during the interwar period and paved the way for local demands for independence. Under pressure to maintain India's loyalty in the face of the advancing Japanese army in Asia in 1942, Britain promised to meet those demands after the war.[109] Simultaneous with the rise of Indian nationalism was a decline in British imperial interest in the subcontinent. Economically, a combination of changes in the world, British, and Indian economies transformed the Anglo-Indian relationship and diminished India's value to Britain.[110] Strategically, the escalating cost of maintaining the Indian army precluded India's worth as a defense asset, even considering the country's location at a critical juncture between the eastern and western parts of the empire.[111] Thus, when the Indian National Congress pushed for independence after World War II, rather than stand in the way, Britain looked to depart peacefully and with honor – although there was hardly official agreement on the decision to leave in the first place.[112] The price of keeping India had simply become too high in British calculations, especially given Britain's ailing postwar economy as reflected by the nation's balance-of-payments struggles in 1947.

---

[107] Undated Memorandum on Policy in the Middle East and Eastern Mediterranean by the British Group, *FRUS, 1947, Vol. V*, 580–582.

[108] Undated Memorandum Prepared in the Department of State, "The British and American Positions."

[109] Judith Brown, "India" in Brown and Louis, *The Oxford History of the British Empire, Volume IV*, 436.

[110] B. R. Tomlinson, *The Political Economy of the Raj: The Economics of Decolonization in India, 1914–1947* (London: Macmillan, 1979).

[111] Brown, "India," 439.

[112] Ibid., 436. Ernest Bevin is a notable example of official British opposition to quitting India, which he based on the possible negative consequences for the rest of the empire, including the Middle East. See Wm. Roger Louis, "The Dissolution of the British Empire" in Brown and Louis, *The Oxford History of the British Empire, Volume IV*, 333–334.

With India gone, Britain reoriented the empire around the Middle East. It was Labour Foreign Secretary Ernest Bevin's vision that the region should replace India as the engine that turned the gears of the British empire. He believed that the Middle East would prove itself to be as economically and strategically valuable to the postwar imperial system as India was in the heyday of the Raj. Unlike colonial relations during the Victorian era, however, cooperation and mutual benefit would define the relationship between Britain and the Arab people, who certainly viewed such rhetoric as akin to a wolf dressing in sheep's clothing. Regardless, Bevin insisted that, as partners, Britain and the Arab states would economically develop the Middle East and defend the empire – particularly the African colonies vital for postwar reconstruction – against Soviet aggression. Britain's strength would flow from this partnership, which Bevin considered critical to the nation's ability to remain a world power. Winning the support of Prime Minister Clement Attlee, the foreign secretary's framework became the cornerstone of the postwar Labour government's imperial policy.[113]

Understanding the Middle East's critical role in Labour's vision of the postwar empire sheds light on British policy toward Palestine at the end of the mandate period, which culminated in Britain's withdrawal in May 1948. The decision to leave Palestine, reached in September 1947, represented the third major turning point in British foreign and imperial policy that year. Momentum toward resolution of the Palestine question – that is, what shape a future state inhabited by Jews and Arabs would take – gained speed after World War II because of international concern over the Jewish refugee problem created by the Holocaust. Britain faced a dilemma in working towards a solution, however, in that its postwar ambitions in the Middle East depended on support from two groups whose respective ideas about how the Palestine question should be resolved conflicted with one another. On the one hand, the Truman Administration, as represented by the president himself, supported partition of the mandate into Jewish and Arab states for moral as well as domestic political reasons – a plan advocated by the Zionist community in Palestine and abroad. Such an outcome was anathema to the Arab world, which supported the mandate's future as a binational state, as did British officials, not least because they feared that fervent Arab opposition to partition would undermine Britain's position in the Middle East. Given the wave of nationalism that swept the region in the 1950s as a result of the humiliation associated with the Arab defeat in the first war with Israel, they were not wrong. Ultimately, the British chiefs of

---

[113] Louis, *British Empire in the Middle East*, 15–21.

staff concluded that, regardless of which plan triumphed, Britain could not impose a solution in Palestine by force. Thus, when the United Nations Special Committee on Palestine (UNSCOP) voted in favor of partition in September 1947 – a decision ratified two months later by the UN General Assembly under US pressure – Britain announced that it would leave when the mandate expired on May 14–15, 1948. The sterling crisis that September provided further impetus for Britain to go.[114]

Arab-Jewish fighting in Palestine from the end of 1947 until mid-1948 – and the Arab-Israeli war that followed Israel's declaration of independence on May 14 – delivered a major blow to Britain's balance of payments. The conflict effectively shut down a major British oil refinery in the Israeli port city of Haifa, a valuable sterling area asset that produced four million tons of sterling oil a year and which allowed Britain to save $50 million on its balance of payments.[115] Activity at the refinery was disrupted in two ways: first, violence in and around the facility, which began soon after the UN Partition Plan for Palestine was announced in November 1947, prevented Jewish and Arab employees from working; second, Arab states hostile to Israel stopped the flow of oil to the refinery, including two million tons of crude oil a year by pipeline from Iraq, and another two million by sea – one million from the Persian Gulf through Egypt's Suez Canal and one million by ship from an outlet in Lebanon.[116] When Israel declared statehood, Egypt began to prevent any British tankers bound for Haifa from passing through the Suez Canal, and Iraq shut down the Iraq Petroleum Company's pipeline to Israel. Despite British efforts to compel Egypt and Iraq to cooperate, neither country would permit the flow of oil to resume unless the other did so

---

[114] Wm. Roger Louis, "The End of the Palestine Mandate" in Louis, *Ends of British Imperialism*, 419–447; Louis, "The Dissolution of the British Empire," 336.

[115] Consolidated Refineries Limited, a company owned equally by the Anglo-Iranian Oil Company and Royal Dutch-Shell, operated the refinery. For the most complete examination of the politics surrounding the operation of the Haifa refinery, see Uri Bialer, *Oil and the Arab-Israeli Conflict, 1948–1963* (New York: St. Martin's Press, 1999). Chapman Andrews at the British Embassy in Alexandria wrote to the Foreign Office that "in the Haifa refinery Great Britain has an interest of vital importance to herself, her allies and all her friends in the free world. This interest is in part financial in so far as it affects the dollar sterling position, and part economic as it affects the recovery of Britain . . ." No. 152, September 3, 1949, NA, FO 371/75405. For these figures, see an undated memorandum by the Ministry of Fuel and Power entitled "Palestine – British Oil Companies," NA, POWE 33/17, and "Statement by the United States and United Kingdom Groups" regarding "Discussions on the Haifa Refinery," November 17, 1949, *FRUS, 1949, Vol. VI*, 80–82.

[116] See BP 71849 for a number of documents that detail the ways in which Arab-Israeli fighting curtailed operations; "Palestine – British Oil Companies," NA, POWE 33/17.

1.1 The Haifa oil refinery.

first.[117] As one Baghdad newspaper put it, "No Iraqi leader can bear the historic responsibility of allowing the pumping of oil to Haifa or face the indignation of the people if he decides to do so."[118] Failing to persuade Egypt or Iraq to change its policy, Britain tried other avenues to bring oil to Haifa, including temporarily arranging for Royal Dutch-Shell to ship crude from Venezuela.[119] But this proved economically inefficient and eventually Consolidated Refineries Ltd. and Israel had to find other sources of crude, including Kuwait, the Soviet Union, and Iran.[120]

The Haifa episode is important not only because of the economic threat it posed to Britain during a period of balance-of-payments weakness, but also because of the attitudes of the various actors involved and how their attitudes foreshadowed future behavior. US officials did not want to expend any political capital in helping Britain to reopen the refinery, but instead were satisfied to remain on the sidelines and provide

[117] See NA, FO 371/75403–9 for the details of Britain's efforts to persuade Egypt and Iraq to allow oil to reach the Haifa refinery.
[118] Trevelyan to Burrows, July 22, 1949, NA, FO 371/75404.
[119] See BP 69761 for discussions of the Venezuelan option.
[120] Bialer, *Oil and the Arab-Israeli Conflict*, chs. 8–10.

moral support as long as British action did not harm US welfare. The Department of State's Chief of the Petroleum Division, Robert Eakens, recognized the "primary interest" of the refinery question for Britain on balance-of-payments grounds, but he considered it only of "secondary interest" to the United States. In fact, Eakens believed that the refinery's reopening would actually harm both US oil companies and Saudi Arabia by displacing Saudi oil in worldwide markets.[121] Future disputes between Britain and the United States over joint policy in the Middle East, based on conflicting interpretations of the importance of Britain's balance-of-payments troubles – and how much these troubles should impinge on ostensibly common policy in the region – are not hard to imagine after this episode. The attitudes of Egypt and Iraq are important to acknowledge as well. Their refusal to bow to British pressure on Haifa set the stage for future clashes, first between Britain and Iran, and then between Britain and Egypt, over the production and transport of oil. Only these battles would have far worse consequences for Britain's balance-of-payments position.

The effect of the closing of the Haifa refinery on Britain's balance of payments was marginal, though, when compared with the financial crisis of 1949. Despite the efforts of the United States to revitalize Europe through an injection of dollars under the Marshall Plan – as well as the recovery of worldwide primary production – international dollar scarcity persisted as a result of a recession in the United States. In Britain's case, because US consumption diminished, commodity producers within the empire did not earn enough dollars to compensate for the sterling area's purchases in the Western Hemisphere. Also, the return of Western Europe to respectable levels of production also meant little if the region could not sell to the American market.[122] Thus, unlike in 1947, the problem was on the demand side rather than the supply side. Commonwealth countries added to Britain's difficulties by circumventing sterling area controls to buy dollar goods that were cheaper than equivalent sterling products and by purchasing finished goods, such as machine tools, that the sterling area could not provide. These consumption patterns sent a message around the world that the pound was overvalued. Anticipating a devaluation, merchants speculated against sterling by delaying payments in their normal trading operations.[123] Such speculative movements can

---

[121] Eakens to Barrow, August 19, 1949, *FRUS, 1949, Vol. VI*, 144–145.
[122] Newton, "Britain, the Sterling Area and European Integration, 1945–50," 173–174.
[123] Note by the Permanent Secretary, HM Treasury, E. E. Bridges, July 26, 1949, BE/G1/109; Samuel I. Katz, "Sterling's Recurring Postwar Payments Crises," *The Journal of Political Economy*, 68, 3 (1955), 222–223; Newton, "Britain, the Sterling Area and European Integration, 1945–50," 173–174.

quickly spell disaster for a currency by compounding preexisting weaknesses – and this is exactly what happened in the summer of 1949. Consequently, in September, the British government took the dramatic step of devaluing the pound from $4.03 to $2.80, a measure designed to reverse the rapid outflow of reserves by igniting the country's export sector.[124]

In mid-1949, the state of Britain's balance of payments did not seem any more secure than at the end of the war. Chancellor of the Exchequer Sir Stafford Cripps wrote: "The experience of this year has shown how vulnerable our position is to the merest ripple in world economy especially in the dollar area."[125] Britain had received billions of dollars in aid from the United States through the Anglo-American Financial Agreement and the Marshall Plan; the British government locked down the sterling area as tightly as was reasonably possible to accumulate dollars, or, at the very least, to limit dollar depletion; and the Labour Party's chancellors of the exchequer faithfully followed disinflationary economic policies. But balance-of-payments problems continued to plague Britain nonetheless. In preparing for the Commonwealth Finance Ministers' Conference on July 13, two months before devaluation, a Cabinet working party prepared an economic policy paper that considered, among other things, ways for the sterling area to earn and save dollars by changing the pattern of its commodity trade. From butter in Australia and New Zealand to sugar in the West Indies, the paper investigated how the sterling area could divert primary products from its usual buyers to the United States. The commodity that received the most attention was oil. In fact, the authors suggested that the conference treat oil as a separate issue, unsurprising given that British officials estimated that oil would cost Britain around $600 million in 1949–1950 because of the complex of ways that both British and US operations leaked dollars from the sterling area.[126] The moment was ripe for the British government to do what it warned American officials it might do back in 1944: discriminate against dollar oil. After all, Victor Butler, an under-secretary at the Ministry of Fuel and Power, once wrote: "Oil seems to me to be the biggest potential dollar earner or saver that we have."[127]

124 According to Scott Newton, "By 16 June Britain's dollar drain was running at an annual rate of $600 million and the reserves faced exhaustion by the end of the year," ibid., 174. For the most complete discussion of this entire episode see Cairncross and Eichengreen, *Sterling in Decline*, 111–155.
125 Cripps to Snyder, December 23, 1949, NA, T 172/2121.
126 "Draft Economic Policy Committee Paper" for the Cabinet Commonwealth Finance Ministers' Conference Working Party, GEN 297/5 (Revise), July 7, 1949, BE/G1/108.
127 Memorandum by the Minister of Fuel and Power on "Oil" for the Cabinet Production Committee, PC (47) 24, December 10, 1947, NA, T 236/2133. The supplies of the

1.4   Substitution of sterling oil for dollar oil, 1949–1950

The first serious statement on a program to substitute sterling for dollar oil appeared in August 1949, during the heart of the balance-of-payments crisis of that year.[128] While this was no coincidence, Britain's economic problems represented only one of three factors that, occurring simultaneously, led to the program's implementation. The second was a fall in the price of oil, which reduced the level of foreign exchange that the British government had expected to earn on the sale of petroleum within competitive dollar markets. And the third was the emergence of a surplus of roughly four million tons of sterling oil in 1949–1950 – most of which was fuel oil used for heating and power – that needed to find markets. The surplus was the direct result of the oil expansion program initiated by the British government after World War II "to develop an export for which there is an assured and expanding market in the interest of [Britain's] overall balance of payments."[129] Unfortunately, this "assured" market was not expanding fast enough to keep pace with British and worldwide production, which had dramatically recovered from the scarcity of the immediate post-war period. To compensate for the lower levels of dollars coming into the sterling area on oil sales as a result of the lower price of petroleum and the US recession, Britain sought to save dollars by using the new surplus of sterling oil to displace a large part of the 13 million tons of crude and products that the major US firms sold in the sterling area for about $350 million.[130]

British officials raised concerns about Britain's "very large" dollar deficit on oil at financial and trade discussions with the United States and Canada in Washington during the second week of September 1949. The talks were designed to explore "various measures which the three governments might take to prevent a serious breakdown in the dollar–sterling relationships," and, thus, the parties considered, among other things, the sterling–dollar oil question. After the balance-of-payments crisis of 1947, Britain had resorted to tighter sterling area controls to defend its balance-of-payments position. The major US multinational

---

British companies to the sterling area were estimated to be worth $230 million and sales to third countries were estimated to yield foreign currencies worth the equivalent of $270 million. For these figures, see the Memorandum by the United Kingdom on "Oil in Relation to the UK and Sterling Area Balance of Payments," February 1950, BP 96429.

[128] Memorandum on "Oil and Dollars" for the Cabinet Working Party on the Dollar Element in Oil, CP (49) 176, August 18, 1949, NA, POWE 33/1683.

[129] Ibid.

[130] "Oil in Relation to the UK and Sterling Area Balance of Payments," February 1950, BP 96429.

oil companies suffered as a result, and American officials, eager for these firms to resume normal trading with the sterling area, hoped that the United States, Britain, and the companies could conceive an arrangement that promoted the interests of everyone involved.[131] But, as Secretary of State Dean Acheson wrote to the US Embassy in London regarding the financial talks, both American and British officials agreed that the sterling–dollar oil question was so complex that it "could not be resolved in the short time available to them, and that further study would be required."[132] By the time the discussions in Washington had begun, however, the three American multinationals most affected by discrimination against dollar oil – Caltex, Standard Oil of New Jersey, and Socony-Vacuum (as well as their joint ventures, such as Aramco and Standard-Vacuum) – had already proposed plans that they believed would enable them to operate in the sterling area while doing as little damage as possible to Britain's balance of payments.[133] At the center of these proposals was the notion that, because British oil companies also cost the sterling area a significant number of dollars, if the US firms were able to reduce their dollar-expenditure to levels comparable to that of the British companies, then, in all fairness, they should no longer be victimized by discrimination.

That Anglo-Iranian and Royal Dutch-Shell also drained dollars from the sterling area – roughly $275 million of the $600–625 million that the currency group spent on oil – warrants explanation.[134] British companies spent dollars in every stage of the supply chain to bring oil to market. First, they bought American crude and products to sell to areas that they could not supply from their own sources. Second, to reduce expenditure on US petroleum products, they spent dollars on domestic

---

131 Certainly, other US industries were affected as well, but oil received the most attention because, as Paul Nitze pointed out several months before, oil represented "the largest foreign investments of the United States, the strategic interests represented chiefly by United States company control in the Middle East and Caribbean areas of nearly half the world's petroleum production outside the United States and control of more than 20 billion barrels of crude oil reserves." He added that American strategic interests in the Middle East also rested on "the influence of American oil companies and their contributions to the wealth and development of the areas in which they are engaged," Nitze to Acheson on "The Sterling Dollar Oil Problem," May 12, 1949, 1945–1949, RG 59, Decimal File, Box 5955, 841.6363/5–1349.

132 September 12, 1949, *FRUS, 1949, Vol. IV*, 833–839.

133 Painter, *Oil and the American Century*, 162.

134 After taking into account the $260 million in dollar receipts of the British companies, their net dollar expenditure was $275 million on the 80 million tons of oil that they expected to sell that year. See "Tripartite Talks, Sterling Oil–Dollar Oil Problem, Memorandum by the United Kingdom, Oil in Relation to the UK and Sterling Area Balance of Payments," January 1950, NARA, RG 59, Decimal File, 1950–1954, Box 4797, 841.2553/10–2750.

refinery expansion by using American engineering firms, personnel, and materials unavailable in Britain; in other words, British firms used short-term dollar investment on refineries to save dollars in the long run since importing finished products cost more than importing crude.[135] Finally, British companies spent dollars to hire American tankers to deliver crude and products that they bought from American firms.[136]

Because of the balance-of-payments consequences of this enormous dollar expenditure on oil, the British government did its best to restrict both the country's petroleum consumption and the dollar-spending of Anglo-Iranian and Royal Dutch-Shell. The oil-rationing program that the government established during World War II persisted until the latter half of the 1940s as a result of Britain's financial troubles. Whitehall also conceived a stringent authorization procedure with which all British industries had to comply if they wanted to spend dollars. While British oil companies were able to "enjoy a more favorable position" regarding authorization than other British firms because of their "dollar earning function," directors still had to make the case that whatever they wanted to buy with dollars could not be purchased in the sterling area, or from a "softer currency source." Furthermore, they had to demonstrate that "a certain amount of crude oil or refined products" would be "placed in jeopardy" if the dollar purchase was not authorized.[137]

The British government contemplated compelling the British companies to buy even less US oil but decided that such purchases were "already at a minimum." Any dollar oil that the British firms continued to buy resulted from contracts that they had signed during the period of oil scarcity or from their need to purchase products that they did not make – or did not make in sufficient quantities. The government also tried to reduce the dollar cost of oil production and refinery expansion by encouraging the use of domestic engineering firms, personnel, and material and discussed saving dollars by hiring more non-dollar tankers to transport oil.[138] In addition, British officials considered "ousting" US

---

[135] "Home Refining in the UK: Brief for Minister," undated, but likely written in June or July 1947, NA, POWE 33/2211; "Chapter VII or the First Report by OEEC on Co-ordination of Oil Refinery Expansion in the OEEC Countries," BP 70340.

[136] For a general discussion of these issues, as well as the statistics related to the multifarious aspects of the dollar drain on oil, see "Brief on Oil for Washington Talks" for the Cabinet Working Party on the Oil Expansion Programme, GEN. 295/16, August 16, 1949, NA, T 236/2886.

[137] "Oil Companies' Acquisition Procedure for UK and Foreign Equipment and Materials," September 20, 1948, NA, T 236/2139.

[138] "Brief on Oil for Washington Talks." See Colin E. Spearing's report to AIOC Deputy Chairman Basil Jackson for an expression of company resentment over the constraints that the government placed on the firm in this area, November 9, 1951, BP 66982.

oil from the sterling area through a price war, but believed such a strategy "most unlikely to succeed," in part because the reduction in prices would "have a markedly adverse effect" on Britain's "general balance of payments position."[139]

These measures, in combination with other forces at work in the oil industry, significantly reduced the dollar cost of British oil by 1949. According to a memorandum sent by the Ministry of Fuel and Power to US oil companies via the Department of State, the dollar component of British oil amounted to $0.92 a barrel, compared with $3.69 a barrel for the American firms operating in the sterling area. Not surprisingly, US petroleum executives challenged this data, calling it misleading. And because the Ministry of Fuel and Power never published the basis for its figures, they were impossible to verify.[140] The implication from the US side was that the British government had cooked the books to justify, after the fact, an import-restriction policy that appeared designed to increase the British share of the sterling area's petroleum trade. Regardless of whether the British government manipulated the data, it had always considered the dollar content of American oil large enough to contemplate major discrimination against it. Furthermore, the evidence does not demonstrate that an increase in the disparity between the dollar content of British and US oil was a decisive factor in launching the substitution program.[141]

The US multinationals worked to accommodate the British government in 1949, and Caltex's scheme for the "sterlingization" of its operations in the Empire-Commonwealth provides a notable example of this effort. In September, the company submitted to British officials an elaborate proposal, "The Caltex Plan," which was designed "to adjust the operations of the Caltex group to the developing pattern of international payments." It acknowledged "the great changes wrought by the war in the flow of world trade" and demonstrated the company's sincere desire to accommodate Britain's balance-of-payments concerns in order to maintain its business in the sterling area. The firm offered to accept sterling for its oil – as it and others had done before – and promised to reduce the dollar content of the crude and products that it sold in Britain and the Empire-Commonwealth from 84 percent to 20 percent by 1951 or

[139] Memorandum on "Oil and Dollars" for the Cabinet Working Party on the Dollar Element in Oil, CP (49) 176, August 18, 1949, NA, POWE 33/1683.

[140] Menderhausen, "Dollar Shortage and Oil Surplus," 9.

[141] While Menderhausen notes the increasing disparity between the dollar cost to Britain of British and US oil across 1949, the British government never – in private or public statements – lists it as a reason for implementing substitution. See "Dollar Shortage and Oil Surplus," 9–10.

1952.[142] Consequently, when the Ministry of Fuel and Power told Caltex's subsidiary in London, Regent Oil, at the end of November that the company would have to reduce its imports of dollar oil products from 100,000 to 45,000 tons in the first quarter of 1950, the announcement surprised and upset Caltex officials.[143] In a meeting at the Department of State, a Caltex representative remarked that he considered the British action "high-handed and arbitrary," especially since the government had not yet responded to the company's plan.[144] But Caltex was not the only US petroleum company affected: the Ministry of Fuel and Power notified Standard Oil of New Jersey and Socony-Vacuum that they would also have to make similarly drastic reductions in their import of oil products to the sterling area. Having told the three US multinationals with the largest sterling area operations of the British government's decision to displace their dollar oil imports, Britain announced its policy to discriminate against dollar oil at a level unseen in the postwar period.[145]

The unilateral nature of Britain's decision to replace dollar with sterling oil at the end of 1949 took the United States by surprise, but not because the issue of discrimination against dollar oil represented a major break from the past. American oilmen and government officials had become accustomed to dealing with British discrimination, and threats of further discrimination, for quite some time. In 1946, Don Bliss, the Commercial Attaché at the US Embassy in London, wrote to George Marshall that "it may be assumed" that British restrictions on the import of American oil products into the sterling area "will be continued for a considerable period, and a completely free market for petroleum cannot be anticipated until the British balance of payments permits or until agreements reached in the International Trade Organization come into effect."[146] Both government and company officials were stunned by the announcement of Britain's substitution policy because they had been working with

[142] The plan, dated September 9, 1949, is attached to Herrow to Perkins, September 14, 1949, NARA, RG 59, Decimal File, 1945–1949, Box 5955, 841.6363/9–1449.
[143] This represented 5,000 barrels a day or one-eighth of the company's gasoline production in the Persian Gulf.
[144] Memorandum of Conversation on "Petroleum – Cutback in Dollar Oil Sales to UK First Quarter 1950," December 2, 1949, NARA, RG 59, Decimal File, 1945–1949, Box 5955, 841.6363/12–249.
[145] The total amount of dollar oil to be substituted in 1950 was 3.8 million tons: 2,400,000 tons of fuel oil; 750,000 tons of motor spirit; 500,000 tons of gas/diesel oil; and 150,000 tons of kerosene. The figures are from "Tripartite Talks, Sterling Oil–Dollar Oil Problem, Memorandum by the United Kingdom, Oil in Relation to the UK and Sterling Area Balance of Payments," January 1950, NARA, RG 59, Decimal File, 1950–1954, Box 4797, 841.2553/10–2750.
[146] October 29, 1946, NARA, RG, 59, Decimal File, 1950–1954, Box 4797, 841.6363/10–2946.

the British government on ways for Britain to save dollars on petroleum without resorting to expansive discrimination against US firms. One Jersey Standard executive was not alone when he expressed his company's "surprise and shock" at the "speed and manner in which the British proposals had been introduced." He added that Britain's import-restriction policy "had been made in an unprecedented manner and in the midst of an attempt to reach a just and orderly solution."[147] Later in the month, Sir Oliver Franks, the British Ambassador to the United States, reported that some members of the company's board were "very angry."[148]

In response to the British measures, the American petroleum firms pressed the Department of State to become more involved in their negotiations with the British government, creating some friction between oil executives and US officials. One Caltex representative insisted that the Department take "as strong action as possible" to persuade Britain to abandon substitution, arguing that the company-to-government approach had failed.[149] A Socony-Vacuum executive echoed this sentiment, explaining at a Department of State meeting that the American firms "would be unable to get anywhere with the British unless and until the US government took a firm position with the British and insisted that a settlement of the matter be reached."[150] But while the Department urged Britain to strike a deal with the US oil companies that promoted both American and British interests, it refused, as a matter of policy, to become embroiled in the details of the negotiations. In a memorandum sent to the "American Oil Companies," the US government clarified that the oil firms "must exert their own efforts in maintaining their foreign markets," adding that they should "take prompt steps to work out arrangements."[151]

These comments did not prevent petroleum executives from continuing to press Department of State officials to become more involved. By March, with none of the big three US companies having reached an agreement with Whitehall, Jersey Standard's Eugene Holman wrote to Dean Acheson that "further discussions with the British will bear fruit only if the background of inter-governmental relationships and

---

[147] "Minutes of a Meeting Held at the Ministry of Fuel and Power," December 8, 1949, NA, POWE 33/1677.

[148] No. 5974 to the Foreign Office, December 29, 1949, NA, T 236/2877.

[149] Memorandum of Conversation on "Petroleum – Cutback in Dollar Oil Sales to UK First Quarter 1950," December 2, 1949, NARA, RG 59, Decimal File, 1945–1949, Box 5955, 841.6363/12–249.

[150] Memorandum of Conversation on "Sterling Dollar Oil," December 9, 1949, NARA, RG 59, Decimal File, 1945–1949, Box 5955, 841.6363/12–949.

[151] Memorandum for American Oil Companies, December 7, 1949, NARA, RG 59, Decimal File, 1945–1949, Box 5955, 841.6363/12–249.

attitudes on matters of principle is clear," adding that the Department of State should send Henry R. Labouisse, Jr., the Director of the Office of British Commonwealth and Northern European Affairs, to London to participate in scheduled talks with British officials.[152] Commenting on this overture, Labouisse affirmed that the Department had historically thought participation in such discussions to be undesirable, as it might find itself "supporting particular company plans," thereby setting a "precedent for other industries."[153]

By May, with no deal in sight, John J. Collins, an advisor at Jersey Standard Tanker Officers Association, wrote in frustration to Acheson:

We assume that one of the functions of the State Department is to protect legitimate interests of Americans wherever they properly may be engaging in commerce throughout the world; and since American jobs and therefore the American standard of living is being affected by the loss of markets to major American oil companies by this present British device, we are wondering what effective action the State Department has taken to protect American oil companies in their legitimate business enterprise.[154]

The oilmen were not wrong in believing that the Department of State was not acting entirely on behalf of their interests. According to the Anglo-Iranian Oil Company's representative in the United States, W. D. Heath Eves, Department officials gave him "the undercurrent impression" that they were so concerned with "steering all the Middle Eastern countries towards the West out of the sphere of Communistic influence" that they believed that US oil companies "should be content to give ground in their negotiations, even though the result might be considerable additional expense."[155] In the final analysis, the petroleum executives' unhappiness with the Department of State reveals a certain expectation that, because Department officials ostensibly recognized the link between the commercial interests of US oil firms and the strategic interests of the United States, the latter should have done everything it possibly could to help

---

[152] Holman to Acheson, March 19, 1950, NARA, RG 59, Department of State, Decimal File, 1950–1954, Box 4796, 841.2553/3–1550.

[153] Labouisse to the Under Secretary, March 24, 1950, NARA, RG 59, Department of State, Decimal File, 1950–1954, Box 4796, 841.2553/3–1550.

[154] Collins to Acheson, May 3, 1950, NARA, RG 59, Decimal File, 1950–1954, Box 4797, 841.2553/5–350. The approach that the major multinational oil firms took to the highest levels of the Department of State is consistent with previous approaches regarding the protection and promotion of their international operations; in particular, when Britain discriminated against US oil firms in British mandate areas after World War I and when the US government supported the UN Partition Plan for Palestine, which petroleum executives believed threatened their companies' concessions in Arab states.

[155] No. 91 from Heath Eves to Jackson, January 20, 1950, BP 78132.

the companies reach an agreement with Britain. Of course, the executives were nonplussed when they felt that the government did not act accordingly.[156]

Even though the Department of State was reluctant to become involved in discussions between the US firms and the British government, Britain's substitution policy greatly upset US officials, and, as a result, they put constant pressure on their British counterparts to find a way to save dollars on oil without prejudicing US interests. According to a January 7, 1950, Foreign Office memorandum, after first merely expressing "regret" at the British government's intentions and "surprise at the tonnages of oil involved," the response from Washington was "one of growing violence."[157] That same month, another Foreign Office official worried that the Department of State had "adopted a very much stronger line than was expected," something that had become all too clear to Victor Butler at the Ministry of Fuel and Power when he was "bitterly assailed about the substitution decision" at meetings in Washington.[158] In fact, some US officials wondered whether the British government was "influenced only by dollar saving or whether it might be seeking to build up the market position of the British Companies at the expense of US Companies under the cloak of dollar saving." They even raised the issue of the British government's shareholding position in the Anglo-Iranian Oil Company, implying that British officials "had a commercial axe to grind in increasing Anglo-Iranian's business."[159] Consequently, the Economic Cooperation Authority (ECA), the organization in Washington that administered Marshall aid, "lent their support" to the Department of State by threatening "financial sanctions" against Britain.[160] US officials also accused the British companies of "excessive" development in

---

[156] A report by the Committee of Petroleum Imports, adopted by the National Petroleum Council on January 26, 1950, read: "The British policies, if continued, could compel the petroleum industry of this nation to surrender the international oil trade to the British . . . with consequent serious injury to the domestic economy and national security. The Committee finds that participation by American nationals in the development of world oil resources is in the interest of the United States and of all nations." Representatives of Jersey Standard and the partners in Caltex served on this committee, BP 96429.

[157] January 7, 1950, NA, FO 371/82983.

[158] "Oil Negotiations in Washington," EPC (50) 15, January 16, 1950, NA, FO 371/82983; H. E. Snow's Record Note, dated January 12, 1950, of a joint meeting with Shell at the Petroleum Division on January 9, BP 96429.

[159] Ibid.

[160] The ECA provided "free" dollars for refinery development contingent upon its approval of expansion plans submitted by the British oil companies. ECA representatives argued that the emergence of such a large surplus of sterling oil demonstrated that British firms were overexpanding their refinery capacity and that the companies would be penalized if they used any ECA dollars for unapproved projects.

their crude production, and expressed the concern that "it was only a matter of time before HMG would be applying, to the detriment of the American industry, substitution to crude as well as products."[161]

American strategists seemed to resent most how, in their view, Britain's discriminatory oil policies undermined Western strategic interests in Saudi Arabia and the rest of the Middle East. Two members of the Department of State's Office of African and Near Eastern Affairs argued that substitution "and other United Kingdom currency and trade restrictions" on US oil companies "forced a serious cutback of Saudi Arabian oil production," while Britain was unfairly expanding production in Kuwait, Iraq, and Iran. They explained that Saudi Arabia was producing 200,000 barrels of crude per day less than had been anticipated in the previous year – and that it would have to cut an additional 100,000 barrels a day as a result of Aramco's shrinking markets. Consequently, the two officials wrote, "there has been set in motion reactions which not only place in jeopardy the stability of Saudi Arabia but will also, if unchecked, work to the detriment of general economic, political and strategic interests in the Near East area which are of mutual importance to both the United States and the United Kingdom.[162]

US policy-makers believed that the decline of their government's "prestige and influence" in Saudi Arabia, as a result of Aramco's inability to sell the kingdom's oil – with the massive layoffs of local personnel that would inevitably follow – would "strike a serious if not critical blow" to American prestige in the Middle East, especially if the oil operations of other countries grew at the expense of US firms.[163] Because of the vital strategic interests at stake, Henry Labouisse maintained that British officials should not have permitted "dollars and cents" alone to "govern their actions with respect to US companies."[164] In other words, Britain's limited and short-sighted approach to its dollar-drain problem would do untold damage to its most important ally, and, as a result, the British government would wind up cutting off its nose to spite its face. What use would Britain's dollar-saving, discriminatory petroleum policy be if it forced the United States out of the Middle East and enabled the Soviet Union to take over the oil wells that allowed Britain to save those dollars in the first place?

[161] "Oil Negotiations in Washington" and H. E. Snow's Record Note.
[162] March 15, 1950, *FRUS, 1950, Vol. V*, 34–35.
[163] "US Petroleum Policy and the UK," WGB D-20, prepared by Robert Eakens for the Working Group on Britain, August 23, 1949, NARA, Office of International Trade Policy, Petroleum Division, Subject File, 1943–1949, Box 2, "Near East Oil" folder.
[164] Labouisse to Hare, March 3, 1950, *FRUS, 1950, Vol. V*, 33–34.

US officials were not indifferent to Britain's economic plight, at the very least for strategic reasons, if not for sympathetic ones. They recognized Britain's critical role as an investor, banker, and trading partner for the rest of the sterling area and feared the "political and power consequences" of Britain's economic deterioration.[165] The country's sudden economic decline, they maintained, would cause the disintegration of the sterling area and deal a severe blow to Western strategic interests.[166] With the Cold War in full swing and showing no signs of abating, the US government prized the empire's "world-wide network of strategically located territories of great military value, which have served as defensive outposts, and as bridgeheads for operations."[167] The US government still supported the Wilsonian notion of "*eventual* self-determination of peoples" but wanted any British retrenchment to "take place in an orderly manner" to prevent the unwelcome event of former British territories falling into "unfriendly hands," namely communist ones.[168] Thus, because US policy-makers connected Britain's economic failure with the political unraveling of strategically vital parts of the globe, they appreciated the British government's efforts to take certain measures to protect its economic wellbeing, although Washington always qualified its statements of support in this regard.[169]

Acknowledging Britain's economic concerns, US officials simply wanted the government to be sensitive to American oil interests in the sterling area and minimize the damage that its dollar-saving measures would inflict upon them. Henry Labouisse telephoned Leslie Rowan at the British Treasury and explained that the United States "could understand the British desire" to implement a substitution policy, but that it "could not understand the necessity for such precipitate and unilateral action." He added that US officials had even "recognized that some substitution ultimately would be made," but that they "had expected that it would be done only after appropriate consultations with our companies and in such a manner as to cause the minimum amount of

---

[165] Douglas to Acheson, July 19, 1949, *FRUS, 1949, Vol. IV*, 803–805.   [166] Ibid.
[167] Department of State Policy Statement on "Great Britain," June 11, 1948, *FRUS, 1948, Vol. III*, 1091–1107.
[168] Ibid., my emphasis. Also see Louis and Robinson, "The Imperialism of Decolonization," for a discussion of the shift in American policy from an effort to urge Britain to relinquish its colonial possessions at the end of World War II to a more gradualist approach as the Cold War escalated.
[169] For example, in the aforementioned "Memorandum by the United States Government on the Sterling Oil–Dollar Oil Problem," US officials clarified that "the US Government may be willing to accept *on a temporary basis* some restrictions on the entry of oil into the sterling area, provided they can be justified on balance of payments grounds" (my emphasis).

dislocation."[170] From the US perspective, then, the British government's greatest offense was abandoning an attempt to resolve the sterling–dollar oil problem through negotiation in favor of a unilateral approach that showed a total disregard for American interests. This action compounded Britain's original sin of executing a policy based on its own narrow economic concerns that, for both strategic and free trade reasons, would benefit neither side in the long run, at least according to the US government view.

Why did the British government implement substitution rather than continue negotiating with the American companies when it knew that such a decision would most likely upset the United States? Why did British officials reject the "sterlingization" proposals of Caltex, Jersey Standard, and Socony-Vacuum when they seemed to offer a solution to Britain's dollar-saving worries? To answer both of these questions one has to consider the lengths to which the Treasury and the British government would go to protect the pound as well as the prevalence of the Treasury view in policy-making during this period.

First and foremost, Treasury officials would not accept the US companies' plans to sell oil to third parties for sterling because the result would be "the building up of large sterling balances," which was "as objectionable to the Treasury as dollar overdrafts."[171] Like the sterling balances held by India, Egypt, and other countries as a result of Britain's wartime borrowing, accumulations of sterling by the US petroleum firms represented a potential source of dollar outflow from the sterling area.[172] In other words, whatever pounds the companies did not spend in the Empire-Commonwealth, they would exchange for dollars when sterling eventually became convertible. The British government "could not assent to any arrangement which would result in the UK bearing the burden of other countries' dollar shortages," according to the deputy director of Anglo-Iranian's distribution department, H. E. Snow.[173] Such would have been the result of allowing US companies to sell oil to others for sterling, the consequences of which would have resembled the convertibility disaster of 1947, when third parties undermined the currency by

[170] Memorandum of Conversation, December 3, 1949, NARA, RG 59, Decimal File, 1945–1949, Box 5955, 841.6363/9–1449.
[171] Victor Butler's explanation as told to W. D. Heath Eves, No. 80 from Heath Eves to Jackson, December 29, 1949, BP 78132.
[172] "US Petroleum Policy and the UK," WGB D-20, prepared by Robert Eakens for the Working Group on Britain, August 23, 1949, NARA, Office of International Trade Policy, Petroleum Division, Subject File, 1943–1949, Box 2, "Near East Oil" folder.
[173] Snow to Fraser, May 18, 1949, BP 96429.

exchanging large amounts of sterling for dollars. In this case, the oil companies would have been doing the converting, but the effect would have been the same: the burden of worldwide dollar scarcity would have fallen upon Britain, at least from the Treasury's perspective.

While the restrictions on oil imports obviously gained enough support in the British Cabinet to be implemented, the Treasury was the policy's prime mover, sometimes putting it at odds with the Foreign Office, which was willing to sacrifice some dollars to maintain good relations with the United States. There is no better example of the clash between Treasury and Foreign Office interests than the disagreement that occurred over Victor Butler's "Incentive Scheme" to enable the US oil firms to avoid the substitution of sterling for dollar oil. Presented to the Department of State on January 30, 1950, the Butler Plan – as it was sometimes called – would have allowed US companies to import products into the sterling area if they: (1) registered subsidiaries in Britain that would be taxed by the British government; (2) spent their own dollars on the maintenance and expansion of their trade rather than obtaining those dollars from the British government in exchange for sterling; (3) accepted that any sterling earned for oil sold outside of the sterling area would be inconvertible (which irked the US government); and (4) spent the pounds that they accumulated within the sterling area, which would thereby limit the repatriation of capital; accordingly, the companies could increase their imports in direct one-to-one proportion with the value of their expenditures in the sterling area.[174] The proposal seemed to address the Treasury's concerns about the dollar drain on oil, but officials disliked the plan because it would have involved "an unacceptable risk of dollar loss" based on "the practical difficulties of administering the scheme." Sir Oscar Morland at the Foreign Office acknowledged this possibility, but he argued that it was "very questionable whether the extent of such possible loss is so great as to offset the political advantages" of adopting the Butler Plan.[175] The Treasury lost this particular battle, and the plan laid the groundwork for future agreements between Britain and the US companies. A second dispute between the Treasury and the Foreign Office over the petroleum import-restriction policy occurred at an Oil

---

[174] No. 389 from Miller to the Foreign Office, February 2, 1950, NA, FO 371/82984; "Appendix, US Companies' Trade in Third Countries and the Sterling Area, Outline of Incentive Scheme," "Tripartite Talks, Sterling Oil–Dollar Oil Problem, Memorandum by the United Kingdom, Oil in Relation to the UK and Sterling Area Balance of Payments," January 1950, NARA, RG 59, Decimal File, 1950–1954, Box 4797, 841.2553/10-2750.

[175] "Oil Negotiations in Washington," EPC (50) 15, January 16, 1950, NA, FO 371/82983.

Working Party discussion later in the year. The Foreign Office opposed a Treasury suggestion to increase the quantity of gas and diesel fuel to be substituted in 1951 because officials there believed that it would have been "unwise to risk controversy" over the government's oil policy while negotiating with the United States on defense assistance and oil stockpiling programs.[176] As they would in the future, the Treasury and the Foreign Office disagreed upon how much the protection of sterling should be allowed to shape Britain's foreign policy.

The Treasury appreciated the implications of its hard line on discrimination for Anglo-American relations, but department officials only seemed concerned with the program's effect on Britain's relationship with the United States when they feared that it would jeopardize US financial assistance, thereby harming sterling as much as helping it.[177] The key point to recognize is that during this period the Treasury believed that the health of the pound should be the primary determinant in developing British foreign policy. At a Department of State meeting in March 1950 on the future of cooperative action between the United States and Britain, Dean Rusk, the Deputy Under Secretary of State (and Secretary of State during the Kennedy and Johnson Administrations) declared that "the limits of foreign policy action by the British seem to be determined by what could pass through a fine treasury screen and that pennypinching [*sic*] seemed to be characteristic."[178]

The British government was not a monolith, and decisions were not reached without some departmental wrangling. But, in the case of defending the pound, policy disagreements seemed to concern style more than substance. Whether one believes that leading government officials shared a trans-departmental, "gentlemanly capitalist" worldview, that they suffered from "Top Currency syndrome," or that the Treasury achieved unprecedented influence in a period of postwar financial difficulty and nationalized domestic industries, there is no doubt that a consensus emerged that linked the prestige of Britain with a strong international pound. Even if sheer bureaucratic inertia continued the policies of a previous era, it is clear that the revitalization of sterling, as led by the

---

[176] Draft Minute, September 23, 1950, NA, POWE 33/1683.
[177] After meeting with British officials, Socony-Vacuum's director, Walter Faust, claimed that the Treasury was "prepared to have the British Government go as far as it [could]" without undermining this assistance; Memorandum of Conversation by Robert Eakens, December 13, 1949, NARA, RG 59, Decimal File, 1945–1949, Box 5955, 841.6363/12–1349.
[178] Memorandum of Conversation by the Officer in Charge of United Kingdom and Ireland Affairs, March 7, 1950, *FRUS, 1950, Vol. III*, 638–642.

Treasury, was a top priority at Whitehall in the postwar period.[179] The
implementation of the substitution program demonstrates the pervasive-
ness of the Treasury view, and the fact that it was allowed to hamper
Anglo-American relations as much as it did only serves to reinforce this
point.

Not only did the Treasury, Foreign Office, and the Ministry of Fuel
and Power all agree that replacing dollar with sterling oil was a good
way to protect Britain's balance of payments, but they also agreed that
the Anglo-Iranian Oil Company would have to play a significant role in
the program's implementation, much more so than Royal Dutch-Shell.
This was because of the all-British nature of the AIOC as well as the
government's 51 percent stake in the company: "While we can always rely
on the respect of AIOC for the national interests, it is at least doubtful
whether even the British directors of Shell would be prepared to put the
interests of the UK balance of payments above the commercial interests
of the Group," wrote Treasury official Martin Flett two years later.[180]
Beyond the issue of nationality, the two firms also had different petroleum
sources and market outlets, with the AIOC producing oil in the Middle
East and selling primarily to the sterling area, and Shell producing oil
in South America and Southeast Asia and selling more to the Western
Hemisphere. As a result, the two companies complemented each other
well in terms of earning and saving dollars for Britain. Despite Shell's
sizable dollar-expenditure on operations in South America, the firm's
large markets in the United States and in the Western Hemisphere in
general made it a valuable source of dollars and other hard currencies.[181]
On the other hand, Anglo-Iranian spent fewer dollars than Shell and
sold much of its oil in sterling markets, making the company a valuable
dollar-saver. Because of the AIOC's primary role as a dollar-saver – and
because the aforementioned four million tons of surplus oil that helped
trigger the substitution policy in the first place came from Anglo-Iranian's
Abadan refinery – the AIOC would carry the burden of executing the
program.

Executives at Anglo-Iranian initially took a "wait-and-see" attitude
toward Britain's discriminatory oil policies. Chairman Sir William Fraser
wrote to the firm's representative in New York and future chairman, Basil
Jackson, that "The full implications of the dollar/sterling issue are hard
to foresee, but there is nothing in that situation that need worry us fortunately and I think we would be well advised to sit back and let events take

[179] See Cain and Hopkins, *British Imperialism*; Strange, *Sterling and British Policy*; Roseveare, *The Treasury*, ch. 9; Shonfield, *British Economic Policy since the War*.
[180] Flett to Brittain and Rowan, January 31, 1952, NA, T 236/5874.   [181] Ibid.

their course – they can only inure to our advantage and any undue eagerness to take advantage of the position would be, I believe unbecoming,
as well as unwise."[182] Jackson agreed that Anglo-Iranian should refrain
from capitalizing on the misfortune of the US firms, writing to Fraser
that "so far as oil is concerned, it is important from the point of view of
good relations that we should show no undue eagerness in taking over
markets from our friends and competitors."[183]

Once the import-restriction program was announced, however, the
problem for Anglo-Iranian was that its US "friends and competitors"
thought that the company, in conjunction with Royal Dutch-Shell, had
orchestrated the policy. As early as July, when Victor Butler informed
Anglo-Iranian's H. E. Snow about the possibility of large-scale discrimination against dollar oil within the sterling area, Snow anticipated the
negative reaction in the United States and warned the government that
it was

essential that the situation should be adequately explained by HMG to the US
companies since otherwise there would be resentment and resistance and possibly
even the inference that this situation was being brought about as the result of the
pressure on HMG by the British companies seeking outlets for their increased
production – which would be very harmful to relations and would be likely to
cause a great deal of trouble in the markets.[184]

Snow's prescience was validated by W. D. Heath Eves, Basil Jackson's
replacement at AIOC's New York office, when he wrote that Pete Col-
lado of Jersey Standard was "very incensed about [substitution], and
that he and several others had no doubt that the British companies had
been largely responsible for the formulation of the plan."[185] Even Australian officials, who like other Commonwealth members had been asked
to assist in executing the oil discrimination program, were "under the
impression that the Substitution plan was a device conceived by the
British oil companies in order to sell their oil which the British government had subsequently been persuaded to accept."[186] According to
Heath Eves, while the US press mostly blamed the "British authorities" for substitution, many commentators believed that Anglo-Iranian
and Royal Dutch-Shell "could *show* more opposition to the plan."[187] He
even complained that he was getting a "little annoyed" with having to

[182] March 18, 1949, BP 60502.   [183] May 24, 1949, BP 96429.
[184] Snow to Fraser, July 5, 1949, BP 96429.
[185] Heath Eves to Jackson, January 12, 1950, BP 96429.
[186] Minutes of a Meeting of the Working Party on the Oil Expansion Programme,
       GEN.295/46th meeting, March 22, 1950, NA, T 236/2885.
[187] No. 108 from Heath Eves to Jackson, December 12, 1949, BP 96429.

"deny as strongly as possible" that the AIOC "had anything to do with the planning of the 'substitution' programme."[188]

Both AIOC and Royal Dutch-Shell directors began to worry about how the ill will would redound financially upon their companies. The Anglo-Dutch firm was particularly vulnerable to American reprisals given its dependence on the US market. Shell feared that because the US domestic oil lobby was putting its usual pressure on the federal government to place import restrictions on foreign oil, Britain's position in the sterling–dollar oil dispute might affect the firm's roughly $100 million worth of business there.[189] In a letter to Henry Wilson Smith at the Treasury, Shell Chairman Sir George Legh-Jones reminded him of the impact that such import restrictions would have on Britain's balance of payments and encouraged the British government, in the strongest possible terms, to resolve matters with the United States.[190]

Upon learning that Britain would continue its discrimination program in 1951, Anglo-Iranian's William Fraser expressed his displeasure in a letter to Donald Fergusson, the Minister of Fuel and Power, focusing primarily on how the policy was harming his company. He protested that the AIOC had alone "carried the load of providing the quantities required" for the program and wrote that "there is neither goodwill nor continuity in business" directed toward the company as a result of its oil being used for substitution. He then added that the "arbitrary absorption" of Anglo-Iranian's surplus products at Abadan was an "impediment to the progressive development" of the firm's business "on the only sound basis of freely acquired and continuing outlets." Continuing, Fraser declared, "From the commercial standpoint, it is very much in the Company's interest that we should be relieved of the potential obligation to provide oil for Substitution, and that it would be much better for us to be left to find our customers ourselves."[191] Fraser was clearly agitated by what he viewed as the British government's meddling in Anglo-Iranian's normal pattern of business.

Given that the government was a majority shareholder in the company, did it not have the right to use the firm to protect the national welfare as it saw fit? Not according to a thirty-six-year-old understanding between Anglo-Iranian and the British government. Even though the latter possessed controlling interest in the firm, it was not supposed to interfere in the company's day-to-day commercial operations. The

---

[188] No. 77 from Heath Eves to Jackson, December 22, 1949, BP 78132.
[189] "Possibility of US Restrictive Action on Oil Imports," Foreign Office Minute by T. F. Brenchley, May 8, 1950, NA, FO 371/82987.
[190] May 2, 1950, NA, FO 371/82987.
[191] Fraser to Fergusson, November 13, 1950, NA, POWE 33/1683.

nature of the government's relationship to Anglo-Iranian was defined when the former acquired its share of the company in 1914, signing an agreement that delineated the government's "minimum of interference with the conduct of [the company's] ordinary business."[192] The accord allowed for two Treasury representatives to sit on the board of directors and gave them veto power over "all acts of the Board and Committees of the Company and its subsidiaries." Also, if the government decided, it could appoint more representatives to the board in proportion to its share of the firm. Regardless, John Bradbury at the Treasury sent an official letter to Anglo-Iranian (then Anglo-Persian) that same year reaffirming its commitment to non-interference in the company's commercial affairs, maintaining that the right of veto would only be used in matters of "general policy." This included protecting the firm's contracts with the British navy; supervising matters that would affect foreign and military policy; and reviewing proposed sales, changes in the company's status, or new sources of exploitation. Bradbury added that "interference (if any) by the British Government in the ordinary administration of the Anglo-Persian Oil Company as a commercial concern would be strictly limited to the minimum necessary" to handle the aforementioned matters.[193] When the government explored with Anglo-Iranian the idea of shifting some of the company's exports toward dollar and other hard-currency markets, in addition to controlling the distribution of the company's surplus oil at Abadan, it had overstepped its bounds.[194] While the AIOC's directors were not indifferent to the national welfare, their first obligation was to the company's bottom line, and, consequently, they would not brook the government's disruption of its normal commercial operations.

In the end, pressure from the US government, a resurgent US economy, and the obvious benefits of reconciliation persuaded the British government to begin settling with the US oil companies in the spring of 1950. At least one American petroleum executive believed that the Department of State's efforts helped make the difference between success and failure.

---

[192] "*Agreement with the Anglo-Persian Oil Company, Limited*, as presented to Parliament by Command of His Majesty, 1914," BP 82347.

[193] "The Bradbury Letter 1914" in R. W. Ferrier, *The History of the British Petroleum Company, Volume I: The Developing Years, 1901–1932* (Cambridge University Press, 1982), Appendix 6.1, 645–646.

[194] Minutes of a meeting of the "Working Party on the Dollar Element in Oil: Sub-Committee on 1949/1950 Foreign Sales Programme," OWP/FS (49) 1, April 20, 1949, BP 66889. See Bamberg, *The History of the British Petroleum Company, Volume II*, 308–328, for a discussion of the relationship between Anglo-Iranian and the British government from 1946 to 1951.

Caltex official W. H. Pinckard thanked Dean Acheson in a note at the end of July 1950:

> I am writing this letter to express our great appreciation for the interest taken by the State Department in this matter and the help given to us in these negotiations by yourself and your associates, both in Washington and in the American Embassy in London. The very constructive and effective support given us by the Department were factors of the utmost importance in the successful outcome of these negotiations.[195]

Pinckard's comments reveal a much different attitude toward the Department than US oil executives had displayed previously, which suggests that either Department officials indeed played a critical role in advancing the negotiations – with or without sacrificing their aforementioned non-involvement policy – or a successful resolution to the sterling–dollar oil conflict simply put a bloom on Pinckard's rose. After all, the US economic recovery that year boosted oil sales for both British and American firms in North America and also increased the volume of business for sterling area countries there, which translated into a flow of dollars into the Empire-Commonwealth. Finally, Whitehall could hardly deny the benefits that Britain would reap by striking deals with the US majors. The new accords would limit the dollar drain on oil while also reducing friction in vital relationships with the United States and the Anglo-Iranian Oil Company. Another benefit was the expansion of British shipbuilding for American firms seeking to bring their rebranded, "sterling" oil to market.[196]

Because of the various sources from which the US companies acquired their petroleum, in addition to the range of destinations to which they sold their crude and products – factors that greatly affected the dollar content of their oil – the British government negotiated agreements with the firms on a case-by-case basis. All of the accords were based on Butler's Incentive Scheme to some degree, although Britain softened a bit on the issue of convertibility.[197] The details of the agreements are of limited importance here. It is critical to recognize, however, that a "general settlement on matters of principle" was never achieved when all of the deals were finally made.[198] The British government did not acknowledge any wrongdoing in using its control of oil to protect and revamp sterling

---

[195] July 25, 1950, NARA, RG 59, Decimal File, 1950–1954, 841.2553/7–2550.
[196] Menderhausen, "Dollar Shortage and Oil Surplus," 32.
[197] Menderhausen offers a good survey of the various settlements in "Dollar Shortage and Oil Surplus," 28–32. Details of the agreement with Standard-Vacuum can be found in NA, POWE 33/1674 and NA, T 236/2879; with Caltex in NA, FO 371/82988 and BE/EC5/253; and with Jersey Standard and Socony-Vacuum in BP 78133.
[198] Menderhausen, "Dollar Shortage and Oil Surplus," 28.

or to defend its economic interests in what it perceived as a time of grave economic weakness, which for British officials were one and the same mission. Clearly, the government was careful, as it was during the oil talks of 1944–1945, not to relinquish its right to exploit one of the few economic advantages that it possessed in the latter half of the 1940s and the early 1950s.

What, if anything, did substitution accomplish? In a statement to the House of Commons announcing the end of both oil rationing and the substitution program, Donald Fergusson estimated that substitution and the agreements that partially replaced it saved about $45 million on the oil supplied to the sterling area by the US companies in 1950. Later, he added that the Ministry of Fuel and Power's "provisional estimates" suggested that the sterling area's net dollar outflow was under $500 million – rather than the $625 million calculated the year before. Finally, he explained that the new petroleum accords, in addition to proposed action by the US companies themselves, would save the sterling area about $250 million by 1954.[199] As Horst Menderhausen argues, though, it is "next to impossible" to determine whether substitution saved more dollars than other courses that the British government might have pursued, such as reaching agreements with the US firms in 1949 or earlier. We can say for certain that the policy served at least one purpose: it let Washington know how seriously British officials took their sterling difficulties and that oil was indeed their weapon of choice in helping to solve this nagging problem.

The US government's displeasure with the petroleum substitution program transcended Britain's interference with the business interests of American nationals. US officials viewed the policy as a general violation of the free trade principles that Whitehall had agreed to support through various accords signed during and after World War II. Responding to a British memorandum entitled "The Sterling Oil–Dollar Oil Problem," Department of State officials wrote: "one of the basic objectives of the foreign economic policy of the United States Government is the early restoration of international trade on a multilateral basis free from the present artificial barriers and restrictions which tend to divert the world's resources from their most economic and efficient uses." Continuing, they explained that "it has been the understanding of the US Government that, as a contracting party to the General Agreement on Tariffs and Trade and as a signatory to the protocol of the Havana Charter for an International Trade Organization, the government of the United

---

[199] No. 533 from the Foreign Office to Washington, DC, February 10, 1951, NA, POWE 33/1683.

Kingdom seeks, as a matter of general economic and commercial policy, the attainment" of those multilateral objectives.[200] Particularly galling to the US government were the bilateral trade agreements that Britain had signed with Egypt and Argentina early in 1949, the latter of which gave Britain the exclusive right to supply the South American country with sterling oil in exchange for meat, displacing Standard Oil of New Jersey in the process.[201] Thus, from the US perspective, by discriminating against dollar oil, in addition to making restrictive oil arrangements with countries such as Argentina and Egypt, Britain was subverting the multilateral framework that it was ostensibly supposed to help the United States to establish in the postwar world.

Just as there were those in Washington who had long been vexed by Britain's discriminatory trade practices, there were those in London who questioned the US government's fervent advocacy of free trade. First, Britain's experience with massive unemployment and constant balance-of-payments pressure during the country's brief return to liberalism during the interwar period soured many leftists on the benefits of the free market and free trade.[202] Another camp, as represented by *The Economist*, believed that, because the US government tied loans to commercial concessions and passed restrictive shipping and immigration legislation, it failed to adhere to its own multilateral principles. Therefore, Britain should not have to do so either.[203] Others, such as Leopold Amery, a British official with almost fifty years of experience in empire affairs and

---

[200] "Memorandum by the United States Government on the Sterling Oil–Dollar Oil Problem," March 27, 1950, attached to Labouisse to Brown, Stinebower, and Eakens, NARA, RG 59, Decimal File, Box 4796, 1950–1954, 841.2553/3–2750. US officials briefly raised the issue of Section 9 of the Loan Agreement, which forbade both Britain and the United States from placing import restrictions on one another "in respect of any product." But they dropped it once Britain asserted that Section 9 "did not technically apply" in the case of substitution because the clause allowed for import restrictions based on the "special necessity" created by economic disruption from war. In fact, Dean Acheson wrote to the US Embassy in Britain that the US government "must regard such deviations from Section 9 of Financial Agreement as temporary measures to meet emergency situation." See No. 4995 from Sir O. Franks to the Foreign Office, October 20, 1949, NA, T 236/2876, Acheson to Embassy, June 30, 1949, *FRUS, 1949, Vol. IV*, 797–799, and Appendix 24 in Pressnell, *External Economic Policy since the War*, for a copy of the agreement.

[201] "The Sterling Dollar Oil Problem," an unsigned memorandum dated April 27, 1949, NARA, RG 59, Decimal File, 1945–1949, Box 5955, 841.6363/5–1349. The Minister of Fuel and Power, Donald Fergusson, believed that Britain, in bilateral bargaining with third countries, needed to preserve its right to force sterling oil upon them – to the exclusion of dollar oil – "in order to gain foreign exchange needed to purchase essential food stuffs," Foreign Office Minute by R. W. Jackling, February 1, 1950, NA, FO 371/82984.

[202] Gardner, *Sterling–Dollar Diplomacy*, 30–31.

[203] Cairncross, "A British Perspective on Bretton Woods," 77.

an ardent supporter of imperial preference, thought that free trade-driven American economic expansion "represented an attempt to reduce Britain to the status of a satellite state," as Wm. Roger Louis notes.[204] For Amery and others of his stripe, naked self-interest motivated US promotion of free trade, and they were not entirely wrong. When Britain was the world's dominant economic power in the nineteenth century, Whitehall proved equally as ardent an advocate for unrestricted access to markets and raw materials as the US government was after World War II, since it stood to receive the greatest benefit. Ultimately, the Anglo-American disputes over sterling and dollar oil, an extension of Anglo-American friction over the implementation of free trade in the postwar world, boiled down to two countries striving to protect their own interests.

As for the relationship between Whitehall and the Anglo-Iranian Oil Company, both sides were happy to see a major source of tension between them vanish. After learning about the agreements with the US oil firms, Sir William Fraser wrote to Donald Fergusson that he was "very glad to hear" that it was possible "to abandon the policy of Substitution."[205] Fergusson responded by expressing "relief to have substitution out of the way," offering the justification that "it was the only way in which [the government] could make immediate dollar savings in [its] period of dollar crisis." He then tried to alleviate any residual bad feelings on Fraser's part: "I fully appreciate that the implementation of substitution must have caused your company increasing trouble, and I can assure you that we are most grateful to you for your co-operation through this period."[206]

---

[204] Wm. Roger Louis, "American Anti-Colonialism and the Dissolution of the British Empire" in Louis and Bull, *The Special Relationship*, 262–263.

[205] Fraser to Fergusson, February 14, 1951, BP 58806.

[206] Fergusson to Fraser, February 19, 1951, BP 58806.

2 Sterling and Britain's confrontation with nationalism in Iran

Payments from the Anglo-Iranian Oil Company form a major item in [Britain's] revenue and balance of payments, and a short fall in them, resulting from an interruption in the smooth working of the AIOC's operations, would have disastrous effects on her economy.

Sir Reginald (James) Bowker, Assistant Under-Secretary of State, British Foreign Office[1]

... it was false to assume an identity of interests between the Western world and Persia over how much oil should be produced and to whom it should be sold on what terms. The Persians could get all the oil and foreign exchange they needed from much reduced operations, whereas our needs were both larger and different in nature. For all these reasons the United Kingdom had to keep control of the real resources involved.

Leslie Rowan, Second Secretary, British Treasury Office[2]

By the late 1940s, Britain and Iran had endured more than a century and a half of political and economic contact. Because Iran was located on the western border of India, the prize colony of the British empire, it became embroiled in a struggle between Britain and Russia for control over central Asia for much of the nineteenth century – popularly known as the Great Game. Owing to Russia's position along Iran's northern border, as well as repeated demonstrations of Czarist ambition southward, the Iranian government encouraged British investment in the region with the hope that a financial stake in Iran would give Britain a reason to defend the country against Russian encroachment. The Anglo-Iranian Oil Company's development of Iran's oil industry turned out to be the most lucrative and the most strategically important of any British venture there. As the sole concession holder, the AIOC exploited and marketed all of the country's oil, which helped Britain win two world wars and financed the company's share of Iraqi and Kuwaiti petroleum development.

---

[1] "Draft Brief for the British Delegation to the Washington Talks on Persia," Foreign Office Minute by Bowker, April 6, 1951, NA, FO 371/91470.

[2] British Record of the first meeting of the Anglo-American talks on Iran, April 9, 1951, NA, T 236/4425.

The British government's stake in the AIOC, as well as the company's total control of Iran's petroleum industry, made both the government and the firm targets for criticism by many Iranians after World War II. Angered by the fact that the British government was earning more in revenue on taxes and dividends from the AIOC than Iran was receiving in taxes and royalties from its own resources, the Iranian government demanded that the company's concession be renegotiated to give Iran a greater share of the profits. The new contract, signed in 1949, did not satisfy Iran's increasingly nationalistic parliament, the Majlis, and in May 1951, the country's newly appointed prime minister, Muhammad Mossadegh, led the government in nationalizing Iran's oil industry. For Britain, this turn of events was nothing less than catastrophic. In part because the loss of Iranian oil undermined Britain's capacity to defend and shore up sterling, the British government – first under Clement Attlee and then under Winston Churchill in October 1951 – worked hard to find a way to reestablish the AIOC's former position in Iran.

Neither Britain nor Iran would accept the other's control of Iranian petroleum. Because the commodity represented one of the largest items in the sterling area's balance of payments, British policy-makers in both the Labour and Conservative governments of this period were convinced that Iran's seizure of AIOC operations there would devastate the pound. These officials argued that it was critical for a British company to control Iranian oil, not only because Britain could buy it with sterling – as opposed to spending scarce dollars on oil from American firms – but also because an efficiently managed, British company would produce enough oil to protect Britain's balance of payments. A haphazardly run, Iranian-controlled oil industry would not. Furthermore, a British company might be willing to consider British foreign exchange concerns when setting production quotas, while the Iranian government would not. Of course, Iranians believed that they had every right to do what they wanted with their own oil and resented the treatment that they received from Whitehall and AIOC officials. Britain's refusal to entertain a fifty–fifty profit-sharing agreement with the Iranian government demonstrated to many Iranians that Britain was unwilling to view them as a partner in the exploitation of their petroleum. Iran was insulted by British offers for a new agreement that, while accepting nationalization "in principle," left management of the Iranian oil industry in British hands. For most Iranians, at least by the early 1950s, nationalization meant the ability to control their own resources without interference from foreigners, particularly British ones.

But Britain refused to accept the idea that nationalization meant the ability to tear up a binding agreement with impunity. Officials at Whitehall insisted that if Iran did not adequately compensate the AIOC, or received better terms on a new agreement than governments that respected their contracts, the effect on Britain's credit and standing throughout the world would be disastrous. Such an outcome would undermine Britain's invisible earnings and, thus, sterling's value as well. As a result, while the British government tried to encourage confidence in the pound through typical macroeconomic measures such as raising interest rates and controlling wages and spending, it also tried to do so with a foreign policy designed to project an image of Britain around the world as a country that would defend its economic interests. British officials dealt with their Iranian counterparts with this in mind, a stance that set them on a collision course with American Cold Warriors who believed that, if Iran fell to communism, the consequences would be devastating not only for Britain but for the entire Western world.

From the US perspective, it was more important to keep Iran and its oil from falling under Soviet influence than it was to support the Anglo-Iranian Oil Company, which leading US officials believed to be an anachronism. In fact, what mattered most to Washington was that Iran remain friendly to the West and that its oil be produced and sold by one or more American and Western European companies. Iran's geographic location along the southwestern border of the Soviet Union, in addition to its possession of a vital strategic commodity, made the country an important component in US Cold War planning. Along with Greece and Turkey, Iran formed part of the Northern Tier of nations under Western influence that would, in the hopes of US policy-makers, contain the Soviet Union from the south. And Washington grew more vigilant about the Soviet Union's expansionist aspirations after a succession of communist "victories" and threatening actions in Europe and Asia during the late 1940s. The US government, whether led by Democrat Harry Truman or Republican Dwight Eisenhower, would not abide communist incursions in the Middle East.

Given that the British government shared Washington's anti-communist agenda in the Middle East, US officials grew increasingly frustrated with what they perceived to be Whitehall's inability, or refusal, to soften Anglo-Iranian's hard line in its negotiations with Iran. In fact, British officials believed that the revised concession agreement that was signed by representatives of the company and Iran, but rejected by the Majlis, was fair. They considered the offer to be generous, given the standards in the Middle East at the time, and feared that surrendering any more profits would damage Britain's balance of payments. When it seemed, though, that the intransigence of Anglo-Iranian directors was beginning to harm the British national interest by jeopardizing the entire concession, Whitehall reexamined the government's relationship to the firm and became directly involved in the negotiations with Iran. Officials viewed the stakes for Britain as too high to let Anglo-Iranian representatives pursue a course that would never return their company, or any other British oil firm for that matter, to Iran.

As in the Anglo-American dispute over British discrimination against dollar oil, the British government's effort to defend its ability to use Middle Eastern petroleum to protect the pound precipitated a clash with the United States. Similar to what happened during the sterling–dollar oil controversy in the 1940s, Washington officials believed that Britain's narrow economic aims – in this case driving an outdated, unenlightened, colonial foreign policy – sabotaged Western influence in the Middle East. The continued failure of Britain and Iran to reach an oil agreement, which brought the latter's petroleum industry to a virtual standstill, created the kind of socioeconomic instability that US policy-makers insisted was ripening the country for communist insurgency. The view in London was that American officials were willing to sacrifice both the Anglo-Iranian Oil Company and sterling on the altar of their zealous anti-communist crusade, one that British policy-makers thought oversold the communist threat in Iran. As examined through the sterling lens, the oil crisis demonstrates how two allies, one in economic ascendance, one in economic decline, could come to blows over the execution of ostensibly shared foreign policy goals.

Using the British government's sterling policy to study Britain's relationship with Iran during the nationalization crisis also reveals the degree to which Iran, although not a formal possession painted red on the map, was perceived in London as a British colony of sorts. The British government exploited Iranian oil in the same way that it exploited the Indian economy: as a vehicle to benefit Britain's financial welfare, often at the expense of what Iranians and Indians wanted for themselves.[3] This chapter seeks to reexamine British imperial goals in Iran by exploring the oil nationalization question in the context of the British foreign economic agenda during this period. At the same time, it demonstrates the larger point that the link between Whitehall's sterling and Middle Eastern oil policies was not simply a phenomenon of the immediate postwar era.

2.1   The Anglo-Iranian Oil Company, Britain, and Iran, 1900–1946

The history of the Anglo-Iranian Oil Company begins at the end of 1900, when General Antoine Kitabgi, an influential confidant to the Persian

---

[3] For the Indian case, see Tomlinson, *The Political Economy of the Raj.*

prime minister, sought a British capitalist willing to invest in Persian oil.[4] Kitabgi's associate in Paris, Sir Henry Drummond Wolff, a former British minister in Persia, brought the confidant's interest to the attention of a wealthy but modest mining entrepreneur, William Knox D'Arcy. After months of being courted, and many more months of conducting negotiations in London, Paris, and Tehran, D'Arcy agreed to the terms of a concession with the Persian ruler, Muzaffar al-Din Shah. Signed in May 1901, the deal would pay the Persian government £20,000 in cash up front, £20,000 in shares, and 16 percent of the net profits from petroleum sales. Because the fledgling venture desperately needed financing after several years of unsuccessful exploration, it joined forces with the Burmah Oil Company, a well-established and capital-rich Scottish firm, to form the Concessions Syndicate Ltd. The British Admiralty, anxious for a reliable source of petroleum, had encouraged the union, and, in 1908, the Syndicate's team of geologists struck oil. D'Arcy's company and Burmah Oil officially merged to become the Anglo-Persian Oil Company (APOC) and gave birth to a new era in the international oil industry, one that would focus primarily on the Middle East.[5]

Early on, the unforeseen costs of developing the Persian concession left the APOC strapped for cash and paved the way for the British government's investment in the firm. The First Lord of the Admiralty and future Prime Minister, Winston Churchill, persuaded the government to acquire a majority stake in the APOC in 1914 to protect the British government from possible price exploitation by the major petroleum companies, especially since the Admiralty had recently converted its navy from coal-fired ships to lighter and faster oil-fueled vessels.[6] As discussed in chapter 1, Sir John Bradbury, the Joint Permanent Secretary of the Treasury, worked out the details of the government's relationship to the firm, establishing a somewhat loose arrangement, but leaving room for government intervention in the company's activities in certain cases, as when questions of foreign policy arose.

Whether the government's shareholding position in Anglo-Persian helped or hurt either Britain or the company in the long run is a matter of debate. The arrangement financially benefited the government, but its stake in the firm proved to be a diplomatic liability, one that would eventually have commercial ramifications. Middle Eastern oil-producing countries could not help but view Whitehall as a "self-interested

---

[4] Iran was referred to as Persia until 1936, when the country changed its English name to Iran. Thus, the Anglo-Persian Oil Company became the Anglo-Iranian Oil Company.

[5] Ferrier, *The History of the British Petroleum Company, Volume I*, 15–113.

[6] Ibid., 158–201; Monroe, *Britain's Moment in the Middle East*, 98–99.

shareholder" and the company as an agent of British imperialism.[7] In the nationalist hothouse of post-World War II Iran, there is no question that the relationship placed both the British government and the firm at a disadvantage.

Iran had first forced the APOC to change the terms of its original concession during the early 1930s. The country's ruler at the time, the autocratic Reza Shah, a former commander of Persia's fearsome Cossack Brigade, had ascended the throne by way of a military coup in 1921 and proceeded to undertake a series of economic and social reforms. These reforms, which included placing the nation's education and judicial systems under state control and forbidding Iranian women to wear veils, constituted the first steps in the ruler's plan to westernize Persian life. Other projects, such as building roads and railways, demanded high oil revenues that were greatly reduced by the oil glut and worldwide economic depression of the late 1920s. As a result, the Persian leader sought to renegotiate the original D'Arcy agreement. He believed all along, like the Iranian nationalists of the 1950s, that Anglo-Persian and the British government were cheating his country out of its rightful earnings. Thus, after four years of fruitless discussions, he cancelled the concession. Only upon the involvement of outside parties, including Iraqi Prime Minister Nuri al-Said, a leading figure in the Arab world, did the two sides reconvene to discuss a new agreement. It was signed in 1933 and gave Iran an initial £1 million payment, a royalty of 4 shillings per ton of oil based on volume sold, 20 percent of the dividends paid to the company's shareholders over £671,250, and other benefits.[8] The concession was supposed to last for sixty years, but, in the end, the company had bought itself only another fifteen years of contractual peace.

While the AIOC did not experience any disturbances in its concessionary relationship with Iran until the late 1940s, World War II disrupted the country by precipitating a joint British–Soviet occupation. Anxious about developing a supply route from the Persian Gulf and worried about Germany staging an invasion of the Soviet Union from Iran, the British and Soviet governments asked Reza Shah to expel all Germans from the country in 1941. When he balked, Britain occupied the south and the Soviet Union took over the north, overthrowing the Iranian ruler and installing his son Muhammad Reza Shah in the process. The two powers then signed an agreement with the new ruler that stipulated that they would not keep their troops in Iran for longer than six months after the war. They promised, moreover, to shield the country from the economic

---

[7] Monroe, *Britain's Moment in the Middle East*, 98–99.
[8] Bamberg, *The History of the British Petroleum Company, Volume II*, 30–50.

strains that their occupation and the conflict would inevitably produce.[9] The former condition proved much easier to uphold than the latter.

During this period, Britain sought to maintain as stable a monetary relationship with Iran as possible. In 1942, the two governments struck a currency deal that, owing to wartime pressures on Britain, Iran was able to tilt to its advantage. For its part, Britain sought to exchange an unlimited amount of sterling for rials, the Iranian currency, to pay for war-related production. In addition, it wanted to do so at a "more reasonable" rate than it had done previously. In return, Whitehall agreed to replace with gold – on a quarterly basis – 40 percent of Iran's sterling balances, which were growing rapidly as a result of the war. The British government also consented to exchange sterling for any dollars that Iran required to buy goods from the United States.[10] The agreement lapsed when Britain withdrew its forces in 1946, but Abul Hussein Ebtehaj, the brilliant and independent governor of Iran's central bank, the Bank Melli, ensured that an accord equally favorable to Iran, at least in terms of dollars, would replace it.[11] He used the Anglo-Iranian Oil Company as leverage, refusing to provide the firm with the rials that it needed to function until the Bank of England signed a "Memorandum of Understanding" with its Iranian counterpart, ensuring that the country would continue to receive enough dollars to import what it needed from the United States.[12] Ebtehaj's hard bargaining over Iran's currency relationship with Britain foreshadowed what was in store for Whitehall and the AIOC on the question of oil.

Economic change in conjunction with greater political freedom produced extraordinary social and political ferment in Iran during the war, catalyzing the nationalist movement that would eventually challenge the AIOC's position in the country. Wartime production expanded the working class and accelerated the process of urbanization, which in turn fed the growth of a variety of social groups. Trade unions reasserted themselves, and middle-class professionals became politically engaged. Meanwhile,

---

[9] Nikki R. Keddie, *Roots of Revolution: An Interpretive History of Modern Iran* (New Haven: Yale University Press, 1981).

[10] "Anglo-Persian Financial Agreement: Gold Clause," undated and unsigned, NA, T 236/223.

[11] Frances Bostock and Geoffrey Jones (eds.), *Planning and Power in Iran: Ebtehaj and Economic Development under the Shah* (London: Frank Cass, 1989) offers the most detailed portrait of the Bank Melli's governor and Iran's future chief economic planner.

[12] The Treasury wrote that the "very strong" bargaining position of the Iranian government, due to the fact that Iran was "the major source of sterling oil," justified making a currency arrangement with Iran that was more generous than that with any other country. See Note by the Treasury for the Cabinet Overseas Negotiations Committee, June 18, 1949, NA, T 236/3197 and "Report by the Working Party on Persia," Cabinet Overseas Negotiations Committee, ON (WP)(49)321, September 28, 1949, NA, T 236/3198.

competing groups and organizations communicated with larger audiences through protest and a flourishing free press. In the south, where the AIOC ran the country's oil industry, the British government was able to keep leftists and emerging nationalists at bay by backing the region's more conservative elements, such as landowners and tribal and religious leaders.[13] But Whitehall would not be able to hold the nationalists off for long.

In the parliamentary elections of 1943, Muhammad Mossadegh, the politically independent, European-educated aristocrat, who had served in a number of government posts in the 1920s, reentered politics. While not a member of the country's main nationalist organization, the Iran Party, he shared many of its views. One of the major issues on which he ran for office was an end to the government's longstanding policy of granting major concessions to foreign powers – namely Britain and Russia – with the goal of playing one off the other.[14] Having won a seat in the Majlis in 1943, Mossadegh would within several years join other like-minded deputies in not only denying the Soviet Union an oil concession but also challenging the existing concession of the Anglo-Iranian Oil Company.

2.2   From renegotiation to nationalization, 1947–1951

The British government's tax and dividend policies during and after World War II led to an increasing disparity between what Britain and Iran received on the sale of Iranian oil. Both the Conservative and the Labour governments increased taxes on corporate profits: the former to pay for the war and the latter to finance the welfare state afterwards. To help combat the inflationary pressures unleashed by postwar readjustment and Labour's full-employment agenda, the Chancellor of the Exchequer, Sir Stafford Cripps, encouraged British companies to limit the dividends they paid to their shareholders, hoping that such a gesture would persuade trade unions to curb their wage demands. Because of the structure of the Anglo-Iranian Oil Company's concession agreement with Iran, both the tax hike and the dividend limitation policy reduced Iran's potential oil revenue. At the same time, the higher tax rate increased the income received by the British government from the profits of the AIOC, such that in 1945, Britain received in taxation almost three times as much as Iran received in taxation and royalties on the sale of Iranian crude and products (see Table 2.1). Of course, Cripps's dividend limitation measure also reduced the British government's earnings

---

[13] Keddie, *Roots of Revolution*, 113–119.   [14] Elm, *Oil, Power, and Principle*, 135, 189.

Table 2.1 *Iran's oil production, AIOC net profits, British taxes, and payments to Iran, 1932–1950*

Year	Oil production (000s barrels)	AIOC net profits (£000s)	British taxes (£000s)	Payments to Iran (£000s)
1932	49,471	2,380	190	1,525
1933	54,392	2,654	460	1,812
1934	57,851	3,183	770	2,190
1935	57,283	3,519	400	2,221
1936	62,718	6,123	1,170	2,580
1937	77,804	7,455	2,610	3,525
1938	78,372	6,109	1,690	3,307
1939	78,151	2,986	3,320	4,271
1940	66,317	2,842	4,160	4,000
1941	50,777	3,222	3,280	4,000
1942	72,256	7,790	6,600	4,000
1943	74,612	5,639	12,070	4,000
1944	102,045	5,677	15,720	4,464
1945	130,526	5,792	15,630	5,624
1946	146,819	9,625	15,590	7,132
1947	154,998	18,565	16,820	7,104
1948	190,384	24,065	18,030	9,172
1949	204,712	18,390	16,930	13,489
1950	242,457	33,103	36,190	16,032

Sources: Elm, *Oil Power and Principle*, 38, Bamberg, *History of the British Petroleum Company, Volume 2*, 325, and DeGolyer and MacNaughton, *Twentieth Century Petroleum Statistics*, 9.

on Iranian oil because of its shareholding position within the firm. But this was no consolation to Iranians who were dismayed by the income disparity between Britain and Iran on the latter's resources.

On October 22, 1947, the Majlis passed a bill that paved the way for the Iranian government to open discussions with AIOC representatives regarding its grievances with the firm. Prompted by the Soviet Union's attempt to establish a joint Soviet–Iranian oil company, the new law prohibited the government from either granting petroleum concessions to foreigners or forming oil companies with them. The law also instructed the government "to undertake such negotiations and measures as may be necessary to secure the national rights, in all cases where the rights of the people have been violated in respect of the natural wealth of the country including its underground resources," focusing particularly on oil in southern Iran where the AIOC had its concession.[15] Because of

[15] Quoted in Elwell-Sutton, *Persian Oil*, 119.

the high price of oil in 1947 and 1948 – and because of increases in the British government's taxation of Anglo-Iranian – Britain was taking progressively larger shares of the profits on the sale of Iranian oil.[16] As the Majlis's criticism of the AIOC grew, Iran pressured the company to find a way to remedy what it viewed as the firm's violations of the country's rights concerning its own resources.[17]

The Iranian government presented the AIOC with a 50-page, 25-point memorandum detailing the injustices which required redress. In addition to its unhappiness with the consequences of Britain's taxation and dividend policies, the government complained about the small number of skilled Iranians employed by the company, especially in management positions. It also criticized the poor working conditions suffered by those who performed the firm's lowest-skilled labor. Furthermore, the memorandum assailed Anglo-Iranian's practice of selling discounted oil to the British Admiralty and US petroleum companies at the expense of the Iranian treasury. Another contentious issue was how unfavorably the Iranian government believed its agreement with the AIOC compared with those of other oil-producing states, such as Venezuela, which split the profits on the sale of its oil fifty–fifty with subsidiaries of Standard Oil of New Jersey and Royal Dutch-Shell. Iranians also did not appreciate the AIOC's habit of refining a large percentage of the country's crude overseas – instead of at the local Abadan refinery – without giving Iran a share of the profits from the overseas sales of the refined products. Finally, the memorandum pointed out that the "gold guarantee clause" of the 1933 agreement had to be adjusted to account for the declining value of sterling against gold, which had reduced Iran's royalty payments over the years.[18]

British officials, especially those at the Treasury, kept an eye on the AIOC's conversations with the Iranian government because of the connection between Iranian oil and sterling. In fact, Sir Wilfred Eady, the Treasury's joint second secretary, wanted the company to preserve the basic terms of the 1933 concession agreement. In August 1948, he told Neville Gass, Anglo-Iranian's managing director, that the Iranian government "should be satisfied with the progressively increasing amount of royalty" that would come from an expansion of the international oil trade and that Iran was not "entitled to any larger share of profits" than it had already been earning. He also maintained that the high price of

[16] Anglo-Iranian earned a net of £30 million in 1947 and was projected to earn twice that amount in 1948. See No. 334 from the Foreign Office to Tehran, April 27, 1949, NA, T 236/2817.

[17] Elm, *Oil, Power, and Principle*, 52.

[18] Ibid., 5; Bamberg, *The History of the British Petroleum Company, Volume II*, 387–389.

oil was "one of the great handicaps to world recovery."[19] Two months later, Eady explained to Abul Hussein Ebtehaj that, while the British government realized that its dividend limitation policy "had, in a sense, 'deprived' the Iranian Government of some share in the increased profits which the war had brought the company," he was "opposed to any fundamental change in the financial basis of the concession." Thus, any adjustment in the agreement designed to compensate for Iran's lost dividends would have to be temporary. The next day, Ebtehaj, a fervent defender of Iran's economic interests, responded that he was "very dissatisfied" with the 1933 concession agreement and believed that, because of the "enormous importance" of Iranian oil to Britain as a dollar earner, the AIOC should have been "very generous" in its treatment of his country's demands.[20] It was precisely because of the importance of Iranian oil to the British balance of payments that Mary Loughnane, a principal at the Treasury, "very much" hoped that, if the company did have to revise the 1933 concession agreement in Iran's favor, the directors would "give away as little as possible." She believed that "any increase in expenditure in Persia must worry" the British government because "every additional pound paid to Persian account is potentially an equivalent drain on [Britain's] dollar resources." Loughnane was particularly concerned by the fact that rising expenditure by British oil companies in the Middle East was "going to place an increasingly heavy burden on [the country's] balance of payments."[21]

While Treasury officials were the most outspoken about the damage that a change in the AIOC's concession could do to the British economy, members of the Foreign Office expressed similar concerns. E. A. Berthoud, the Foreign Office's assistant under-secretary at the Economic Relations Department, serves as a notable example. In August 1948, he agreed that the British government should not discourage the AIOC "from making a reasonable increase in royalty rates" but added that Whitehall had to consider the consequences of such an increase for Britain's economy. He explained that the higher Iran's royalty rate rose, the higher Britain would have to boost the level of its exports to pay for Iranian oil, suggesting that such an adjustment would be difficult to make: "The Persian oil fields," he wrote, "are our major overseas asset on which we depend to a considerable extent for achieving our own ultimate economic balance." Therefore, Berthoud believed that any generosity

[19] August 9, 1948, BP 8334.
[20] Eady to Sir H. Wilson Smith, October 26, 1948; Memorandum by Eady, October 27, 1948, NA, T 236/1337.
[21] Draft letter to Bevin, undated, but most likely written in March 1949, NA, T 236/2817.

on the part of the AIOC toward Iran should not lead to a permanent rise in the company's costs.[22] The following April, as the AIOC and the Iranian government continued their efforts to reach an accord, the assistant under-secretary told Jemal Emami, a member of the Majlis's Oil Committee and a delegate to the oil talks, that the British government "could not ignore the repercussions" for Britain's trade balances "resulting from increased payments" to Iran for its oil. Emami responded that the matter was "entirely separate" from Iran's negotiations with the AIOC, but that the Iranian government would be willing to review ways that it could help protect Britain's balance of payments. Commenting on his conversation with Emami in a note to Assistant Under-Secretary of State Michael Wright, Berthoud wrote that, because the company's negotiations would certainly lead to "large additional payments" to Iran, the British government would have to take another look at Anglo-Iranian financial agreements – in other words, make them more favorable to Britain.[23] A departmental brief for a meeting with AIOC representatives revealed further concern within the Foreign Office about the financial impact on Britain of a new oil accord with Iran: "We might, however make it clear that we hope the AIOC's Head Office will keep both us and the Treasury informed of the course of the negotiations and of any concession which they may have to make which will involve substantial changes in the sale of dollar oil and our balance of payments."[24] Later, when Iran nationalized its oil industry, other members of the Foreign Office expressed similar worries.

Generally speaking, however, under the leadership of Ernest Bevin, the Foreign Office encouraged the AIOC to reach a deal with Iran that offered more generous terms than provided under the existing concession agreement. In February 1949, the foreign secretary sent a note to Stafford Cripps, arguing that the Iranian government had "some legitimate grievance on the United Kingdom fiscal score" and that it was important, "both from the political point of view and for the future of the Company," that Iran "be satisfied that they are receiving an equitable return from the exploitation of their oil resources."[25] Little more than a month later, Sir William Strang, the permanent under-secretary of state, wrote to Cripps to reiterate Bevin's opinion on the matter. He explained that, while Bevin did not think that Iran "should necessarily be given all

---

[22] Berthoud to Sir Orme Sargent, August 27, 1948, NA, FO 371/68731.
[23] Berthoud to Wright, a "Record of Conversation with Mr. Emami, Persian Government Delegate to Anglo-Iranian Oil Company," April 8, 1949, NA, T 236/2817.
[24] January 25, 1949, NA, FO 371/75495.
[25] February 18, 1949, NA, T 236/2817.

they ask for," he did "feel strongly" that the country "should be given a more equitable arrangement than that now offered by the Company."[26]

Bevin's position, in part, reflected an effort to reconcile the contradictions between his personal commitment to the British welfare state and the less than palatable way that the AIOC treated Iran, especially its workers. The foreign secretary argued that "a British company ought to be a model employer and should go out of their way to improve upon [minimum conditions] and establish every possible relationship with the people in order to develop confidence between them and the company" – something he felt that the AIOC under the direction of William Fraser did not do.[27] That Bevin sent both correspondences regarding the AIOC's negotiations with Iran to the chancellor of the exchequer demonstrates that the Treasury may have been the most hesitant – save, perhaps, for the Ministry of Fuel and Power – about the AIOC ceding a larger share of its profits to Iran. Indeed, such an attitude squared with the Treasury view that British economic interests should dominate Britain's foreign oil policy, even if that meant ruffling a few feathers, whether in the Middle East or across the Atlantic.

After five months of negotiations, the AIOC and Iran signed a new agreement on July 17, 1949. Known as the Supplemental Agreement, the deal satisfied Ernest Bevin's goal of increased payments from the company to Iran. It raised the country's royalty rate from 4 to 6 shillings per ton and guaranteed the Iranian government a minimum annual payment of £4 million, something that E. A. Berthoud found "most undesirable" in terms of Britain's economic interests.[28] Based on these and other changes to the terms of the 1933 concession, Iran's earnings from the AIOC's operations jumped from what would have been £9,172,245 to £18,667,786 for 1948 and from £13,489,271 to £22,890,261 for 1949.[29] Accounting for variables in foreign exchange, the country stood to receive between 32 and 37.5 percent of the profits from the AIOC's worldwide operations, a figure that Mustafa Elm asserts is a far cry from the fifty–fifty split that Venezuela had achieved six years earlier.[30] In fact, Venezuela received 50 percent of the profits earned on the sale of its *own* oil only, not on the sale of petroleum that Standard Oil of New Jersey and Royal Dutch-Shell produced and refined around the world.

[26] March 29, 1949, NA, T 236/2817.
[27] Quoted in Louis, *The British Empire in the Middle East*, 56–57.
[28] "Record of a meeting in the Foreign Office on the 19th May with the Anglo-Iranian Oil Company," NA, T 236/2817. Berthoud believed that even £2.5–3 million was too high.
[29] Bamberg, *The History of the British Petroleum Company, Volume II*, 398.
[30] Elm, *Oil, Power, and Principle*, 55.

With the Supplemental Agreement, the Iranian government would, therefore, earn around 50 percent of the profits from the company's operations in Iran itself, which did make the contract comparable to that which Venezuela signed with its concessionaires, at least in terms of the way the revenues were divided. But, as Wm. Roger Louis has noted, there is a substantial psychological difference between a contract that uses complex calculations to produce royalties equivalent to 50 percent of a company's profits and one that emphasizes notions of profit-sharing between partners, even if the division of revenue is roughly the same.[31] That the AIOC historically kept its books in "deep secrecy" did not inspire confidence in Iran that the company was motivated by fairness or equity.[32] Consequently, while Bevin could be pleased that the AIOC demonstrated greater generosity toward Iran, the company's increase in payments did not persuade Iranians that they were "receiving an equitable return from the exploitation of their oil resources," as Bevin had wanted.[33]

Iranians who were aware of the terms that the AIOC had offered criticized both the company and the British government for not offering more. Even Iranian Finance Minister Abbas Golshayan, who signed the Supplemental Agreement, grumbled privately that the Shah and the prime minister had pressured him into accepting a contract less favorable than he could have won if they had left him alone. He secretly complained that "the British want the whole world for the furtherance of their own policy."[34] In his memoirs, Manucher Farmanfarmaian, the former director of the National Iranian Oil Company, assails the AIOC's William Fraser for having presented the Supplemental Agreement to Iranian officials "as a *fait accompli*" and issuing ultimatums during their negotiations.[35] An article in the semi-official government newspaper *Ittila'at*, written a few months before the Supplemental Agreement was signed, reflected what many Iranians felt in 1949. Its author, Mas'udi, pressed the AIOC to treat his country as the "American companies" had treated Venezuela, as a nation that was "in actual fact, a partner" with its concessionaires. He also celebrated "the feeling of assistance and cooperation" in Venezuela as a result of the sense of partnership that the oil firms fostered. Mas'udi then turned to the AIOC's long history in Iran, arguing that the AIOC should not have bargained with the government

[31] Louis, *The British Empire in the Middle East*, 646.
[32] Manucher Farmanfarmaian and Roxane Farmanfarmaian, *Memoirs of a Persian Prince* (New York: Random House, 1997), 210.
[33] Bevin to Cripps, February 18, 1949, NA, T 236/2817.
[34] Quoted in Elm, *Oil, Power, and Principle*, 55.
[35] Farmanfarmaian and Farmanfarmaian, *Memoirs of a Persian Prince*, 218.

as if it had been a "new customer." After all, he explained, the company had received a great many benefits during its fifty-year participation in Iranian oil.[36] Indeed, during that time, the AIOC was able to use the profits that it had collected on Iranian petroleum to help establish the Iraqi and Kuwaiti oil industries, where the AIOC operated in conjunction with other firms. The company repeatedly argued in its conversations with the Iranian government that, owing to the vastly different "economics and conditions" of the Venezuelan petroleum industry, it could not discuss the Iranian case in a similar fashion. Besides, AIOC directors declared, the terms that they were offering to Iran were as good as any in the Middle East.[37] Mas'udi addressed this issue, contending that arrangements between other Middle Eastern oil producers and their concessionaires were irrelevant as far as Iran was concerned because the oil industries in those countries were newer and, thus, demanded the kinds of higher costs that the AIOC no longer had to incur in his country. Therefore, the company could afford to be more generous with the Iranian government than other companies had been with their Middle Eastern partners. Like Mas'udi, well-informed Iranians had an answer for each argument that the AIOC used against signing a contract based on profit-sharing, but the firm's directors remained unpersuaded.

Despite the dissatisfaction that many Iranians expressed about the terms of the Supplemental Agreement, Whitehall considered it fair. Members of the Foreign Office believed that it would have been "unwise to press the company to go higher." The rationale was that, had the AIOC offered more, the firm would have found it difficult to compete in world markets, losing sterling sales as a result, with "serious repercussions" for Britain's balance of payments.[38] According to a telegram from the Foreign Office to the British Embassy in Tehran, "all concerned in London" were "in agreement" that the company's offer was "a fair one in comparison with oil concessions elsewhere."[39] At this point, it is clear that the company received the British government's complete support regarding the Supplemental Agreement. To a certain degree, this support was connected to the convergence of Britain's balance-of-payments interests and the interests of a commercial enterprise that wanted to maintain high profits.

The British government's defense of the AIOC's position also derived from a paternalistic attitude at Whitehall and the company that the British

[36] "Press Extracts No. 370," May 30, 1949, NA, T 236/2818.
[37] An account of the "Company's Activities in Persia during the Last Fifty Years," undated, from the files of Neville Gass, January 1951–December 1951, BP 9233.
[38] Foreign Office Minute, April 21, 1949, NA, FO 371/75496.
[39] No. 334 on April 27, 1949, NA, T 236/2817.

knew best how to safeguard Iranian welfare. On a number of occasions, Anglo-Iranian executives based their opposition to a fifty–fifty profit-sharing agreement on the fact that Iran's revenues would depend too much on the ever-changing price of oil.[40] They insisted that the Supplemental Agreement, with its flat rate system and guaranteed minimum payments, would "give [Iran] a stable income, fluctuating as little as possible."[41] Consistent revenues, the argument went, would ensure the country's political stability, something that would benefit both Iran and the AIOC.[42] A contract that helped stabilize the Iranian government was important to British policy-makers because, as some of them said, Iranians were a "volatile and unstable people" whose government was "inefficient" and lacked "leadership."[43] But Manucher Farmanfarmaian believes that stability would have best been achieved by negotiating a fifty–fifty agreement, which, by creating "harmony" and a "sense of equal partnership" between oil-producing states and their concession-aires, reconciled "the conflicting demands of economics and politics, of private enterprise and national pride."[44] A certain amount of prejudice prevented many figures at both the AIOC and Whitehall from viewing Iranians as equals or partners. After Iran nationalized its oil industry, preconceived notions of Iranian inefficiency would inform the conviction at Whitehall that some British company, be it the AIOC or any other, had to control Iranian oil to protect Britain's balance of payments. Most British officials believed that they knew what was best for Iran, and what was best for Iran from the Western perspective was, not coincidentally, what was best for Britain.

British prejudices aside, Iranian politics did, in fact, enter a period of great tumult and ferment after World War II. Factionalism within the Majlis hampered political stability, with six different prime ministers holding office between 1946 and 1951. Diverse coalitions, representing a vast array of interests within Iranian society, were constantly shifting and created a sort of parliamentary equilibrium that enabled the Shah to assert his authority. Once content to be a reigning, but not ruling, constitutional monarch in the early years after World War II, the Shah, bolstered by his expansion of the army, became involved in policy-making

---

[40] From an account of the "Company's Activities in Persia during the Last Fifty Years," BP 9223.

[41] Part of a response by W. D. Heath Eves to a question at the Near East Conference, Princeton University, June 2, 1951, regarding AIOC policy in Iran, BP 66237.

[42] Foreign Office Minute by D. P. Reilly, January 18, 1951, NA, FO 371/91244.

[43] Shepherd to Furlonge, June 5, 1951, FO371/91545; Le Rougetel to Attlee, August 1, 1949, NA, T 236/2818.

[44] Farmanfarmaian and Farmanfarmaian, *Memoirs of a Persian Prince*, 214.

by the late 1940s. In February 1949, he paid for his political activism with an attempt on his life by a would-be assassin affiliated with pro-labor groups and the rising religious opposition. The Shah's subsequent efforts to increase his power by suppressing challenges to his authority – in ways reminiscent of his autocratic father – made him a lightning rod for the grievances of a coalescing reformist movement that found expression in a political party called the National Front. Led by the "incorruptible populist" Muhammad Mossadegh, the National Front sought not only to achieve a legitimate form of constitutional government but also to wrest control of the nation's oil industry from Britain. These goals accommodated neither the Shah's authoritarian behavior nor his embrace of the Supplemental Agreement, both of which eroded his popular support.[45]

Given the anti-British sentiment that dominated the sixteenth session of the Majlis (February 1950–May 1951), the Supplemental Agreement stood almost no chance of being ratified. Most Iranians viewed the British as puppet masters who pulled the country's political and economic strings. Thus, to take a position that could in any way be interpreted as pro-British would be to commit political and, in some cases, literal suicide.[46] While Iranians often exaggerated the degree of control that the British government and the AIOC actually exerted over the nation, government officials and company representatives did have enormous influence over the political and economic life of Khuzistan, the southern province where the AIOC operated its concession.[47] Furthermore, Whitehall held some sway over the Shah, and Iran's wide use of sterling ensured a certain measure of financial control from London. For many Majlis deputies, then, the Supplemental Agreement represented the perpetuation of an intolerable status quo, and they never would have considered voting for it. Those deputies who did contemplate supporting the agreement would have been under an extraordinary amount of pressure not to do so. In this environment, the accord was virtually dead on arrival.

Regardless, in mid-1950, the Shah appointed General Razmara, a "no-nonsense" military strongman, to the job of prime minister to push the Supplemental Agreement through the Majlis – an effort that ended in failure and, eventually, the nationalization of Iran's oil industry.[48] When the agreement came up for debate, first in October and then in December

---

[45] Ervand Abrahamian, *Iran between Two Revolutions* (Princeton University Press, 1982), 240–261.
[46] Yergin, *The Prize*, 451.   [47] Abrahamian, *Iran between Two Revolutions*, 241.
[48] Ibid., 263.

of 1950, the sessions became little more than forums for National Front deputies and the clergy to attack the British and demand the nationalization of Iranian oil. On December 26, with opposition at a fever pitch and no majority to support the Supplementary Agreement, Razmara was forced to withdraw it before a vote could be called.[49] Two significant events sealed the accord's fate. First, four days after Razmara removed the oil bill from the floor of the Majlis, Saudi Arabia and Aramco announced that they had signed a historic deal to split the company's profits equally, rendering the AIOC's terms obsolete and sending a shockwave through the Middle East by establishing the fifty–fifty principle in the region; second, Razmara was assassinated on March 7, 1951, only days after he had publicly supported the Supplemental Agreement before the Majlis. His killer, who belonged to an Islamic group led by the nation's most vocal and best-known religious figure, Ayatollah Kashani, ensured that the "British stooge," Razmara, would no longer serve the "enemies of Islam," as Kashani referred to both the prime minister and the British.[50]

At this point, political events in Iran moved with almost unimaginable speed. On April 28, the National Front's Muhammad Mossadegh rode a tidal wave of popular support to the country's premiership, and on May 8, the Majlis Oil Committee unanimously approved a nine-point resolution that mandated the nationalization of Iranian oil. By July, Mossadegh had broken off negotiations with the AIOC, and the British government helplessly watched Iran confiscate Britain's greatest overseas asset. Pulling no punches, US Secretary of State Dean Acheson would later remark: "Never had so few lost so much so stupidly and so fast."[51]

Leading US officials accused the British government of standing idly by while the Anglo-Iranian Oil Company's inflexible directors foolishly surrendered their concession, an assertion that is only partly true. Early in the AIOC's dispute with Iran, British officials did, in fact, follow their traditional hands-off approach to the company, merely wanting to be kept informed of the financial terms of any new settlement, given the economic implications for Britain. Because of their concern for Britain's balance of payments, officials at Whitehall initially supported the Supplemental Agreement and were loath to see the AIOC give away any more than it already had. Consequently, they saw little need to meddle in the firm's affairs on this issue, even though some figures outside the Treasury, such

---

[49] Elm, *Oil, Power, and Principle*, 70–71; Bamberg, *History of the British Petroleum Company, Volume II*, 404–405.
[50] Quoted in ibid., 266.
[51] Dean Acheson, *Present at the Creation: My Years in the State Department* (New York: W. W. Norton & Company, 1969), 503.

2.1 The Iranian flag is raised over the general management offices of the Anglo-American Oil Company after the firm's nationalization, June 1951. At the entrance are members of the Iranian commission for nationalizing oilfields.

as Ernest Bevin, would have liked the government to exert more general control over it. Once the agreement and the Razmara leadership appeared to be in serious trouble, though, especially after Aramco and Saudi Arabia announced their fifty–fifty deal, Whitehall demonstrated greater interest in becoming more involved in the company's business than it ever had previously, more so even than during the Anglo-American dispute over sterling and dollar oil one year earlier.[52]

---

[52] Steve Marsh argues – but overstates his case, I think – that British officials strategically exploited the government's hands-off relationship with the company to its advantage in dealing with both Iran and the United States. See "Anglo-American Crude Diplomacy," 35–36. This interpretation leads him to contend, in his book, *Anglo-American Relations and Cold War Oil*, that the "conventional claim that the AIOC was to blame principally for British mishandling of the oil crisis" is wrong and that the British government "had

By October 1950, two months before Razmara pulled the Supplemental Agreement from the Majlis floor, the Foreign Office had seen enough. With the AIOC refusing payments to Iran until it signed a new deal, the country spiraled into a financial crisis, undermining the stability of the Razmara government. The Foreign Office began to take seriously Iranian calls for nationalization and, consequently, pressured the AIOC to "find something to offer" to secure passage of the Supplemental Agreement, even if the company found it "somewhat painful" to do so.[53] That Ernest Bevin took the lead in this matter is not surprising, given his desire for the AIOC to demonstrate greater concern for Iran's social welfare. But even the usually hard-headed director of the company, William Fraser, agreed that the AIOC would have to do more to get the Supplemental Agreement ratified, remarking that he "would not hesitate at finding further sums of even several million pounds if the right form and method could be devised."[54] These gestures proved to be too little too late, however.

While the AIOC, under pressure from the Foreign Office, did offer the Iranian government further incentives to adopt the Supplemental Agreement, the fact remains that the company did not alter the basic structure of the accord, which was a significant impediment to its ratification. Only one high-ranking figure at the company seemed to understand this fundamental point: Sir Frederick Leggett, the firm's labor advisor. He met with L. A. C. Fry of the Foreign Office's Eastern Department in February 1950 and said, "What was required was a fresh start, on the basis of equal partnership. Unless the company realized that, and were sincerely prepared to go forward in that direction, they might sooner or later find themselves without any installations in Persia."[55] He was no doubt correct, but, by the autumn of 1950, it seems that the Majlis would have found anything short of nationalization unacceptable.

At the beginning of 1951, the Foreign Office continued its efforts to influence AIOC policy, but it did not find support for its interventionism among Treasury officials. At a meeting in mid-January, Foreign Office representatives worried that the company now had to "fight for its life" in Iran. They said, "it might ... be good tactics" for the AIOC "to offer to renegotiate with the Persians, and meanwhile make preparations for giving

more responsibility than hitherto acknowledged," 4. The notion that the AIOC has been held primarily responsible for the debacle in Iran seems to be a straw man more than anything else.

[53] Minute by Wright, October 23, 1950, NA, FO 371/82376.

[54] Ibid.; Louis, *British Empire in the Middle East*, 642–647. Louis attributes Fraser's amenable attitude to his anticipation of a fifty–fifty agreement in Saudi Arabia, which is the most plausible explanation for his uncharacteristic change of heart, 646.

[55] Quoted in ibid., 650.

them short-term aid." These officials believed, moreover, that the AIOC should consider hiring more Iranians for high-level positions within the company to counter accusations of British or "foreign" control of Iranian resources. They speculated that this might involve creating an AIOC subsidiary in Iran and "offering the Persians a share in the control of a new company, and possibly a fifty–fifty share of its profits, on the Aramco model." Such an arrangement would mean scrapping the Supplementary Agreement altogether, as the company's labor advisor, Sir Frederick Leggett, recommended. The Treasury's Martin Flett responded that the Foreign Office's suggestions were "not something [the government] could dictate to the Company." Flett and his colleagues explained that the government "did not normally interfere in the Company's commercial activities, and that the Company must deal with the Persians as they saw fit." As a result, the Treasury was "reluctant to attempt to influence" the AIOC at that time.[56] Little more than a week earlier, another Treasury official wrote that the government should not "press" AIOC directors "to agree to any measure which they are not willing to take."[57] Although Ernest Bevin did not attend this meeting, he must have been agitated when he saw these remarks, since he complained bitterly about the government's lack of control over the company despite its majority shareholding position.[58]

Because of the importance of Anglo-Iranian to British national welfare, however, Treasury representatives did, in fact, leave room for greater government involvement in the company's affairs and eventually came around to the Foreign Office point of view. Even at the January meeting discussed above, Treasury representatives recognized the "political dangers of the situation" and therefore considered doing more to remedy it.[59] On a separate occasion, one Treasury official acknowledged that a major function of the department was to ensure that the compromises that British companies sought to make with oil-producing states were "not of the 'too little too late' variety," and that "by being inadequate" they did not "jeopardize both the interests of the companies themselves and [Britain's] national interests."[60] By March, around the time of Razmara's assassination, Treasury officials began expressing concern about the company's direction and what the British government could do about it. D. R. Serpell wrote to Martin Flett that he did "not feel confidence"

56 Record of Meeting at the Treasury, January 13, 1951, NA, FO 371/91522 and NA, T 236/2820.
57 Rudd to Reilly and Butler, January 4, 1951, NA, T 236/2820.
58 Louis, *British Empire in the Middle East*, 656.
59 Record of Meeting at the Treasury, NA, T 236/2820.
60 Rudd to Reilly and Butler, NA, T 236/2820.

in the way that the company handled its problems or the way it worked with government agencies. He added, "AIOC are now, it is clear, looking more to HMG for advice and assistance, and I should like to press again for urgent consideration of the way in which Persian and other oil problems – are to be dealt with." On the note itself, Flett, the avid anti-interventionist, commented, "I agree with him throughout."[61] Martin Flett reflected the general attitude of the British government when he wrote, "Our Middle East oil interests are of such paramount importance to us that we cannot simply leave these problems to be dealt with by the individual companies as purely commercial matters."[62] Less than a year removed from its conflict with the US government over sterling and dollar oil, Whitehall again found itself in the position of being forced to reconcile Britain's national interest with the AIOC's status as a semi-private company. And, yet again, concerns about national welfare trumped the historically laissez-faire attitude of the government towards the firm.

It is unusual that the Treasury, which stopped at nothing to defend sterling in the post-World War II era, took so much longer than the Foreign Office to recognize that active government involvement in the AIOC's dispute with Iran would be necessary to help save the economically vital concession. In November 1950, it was a member of the Foreign Office who, in response to a letter castigating the company board for its policies in Iran, wrote:

A recent survey of the UK oil balance of payments... reveals that we depend upon the British oil industry to an alarming extent to maintain our favourable overall balance of payments. The recent improvement in the latter balance has been primarily on the invisible account, to which oil has made by far the largest contribution. Our dependence on Persian and Venezuelan oil, not only for strategic but also for financial reasons, is only too apparent.

The official, P. E. Ramsbotham, explained that these concerns may not have been "sufficiently appreciated" by company directors and that the Foreign Office should advise them that, if they had "additional concessions up their sleeve," then they should be "offered immediately."[63]

One would have expected such statements to come from the Treasury at this time, but no one at the department said anything similar until the following spring. Clearly, Treasury officials viewed the principle of the government's non-intervention in Anglo-Iranian's commercial affairs as sacred. But would they have blindly followed this dogma at the expense

---

[61] March 15, 1951, NA, T 236/2821.   [62] Ibid.
[63] Statement by P. E. Ramsbotham, November 22, 1950, with a copy sent to Young at Treasury, NA, FO 371/82377.

of Britain's balance of payments? It seems that they believed in January that the company could still secure a deal with Iran that did not sacrifice too large a percentage of its profits or relinquish British management of the Iranian oil industry, a settlement that would benefit not only the company, but also Britain's balance of payments. That the AIOC board began "looking more to [the British government] for advice and assistance" certainly helped the Treasury get over its reluctance to become involved in company policy. In the end, what the disagreement between the Treasury and the Foreign Office really reveals is the differing opinions of the two departments about the degree to which both the stability of Iran and the company's concession were in danger – and whether company directors could rescue the concession without government help. Only when Treasury officials realized that the AIOC was jeopardizing both the concession and Britain's balance of payments by scuttling opportunities for a settlement did they adjust their rigid adherence to a hands-off approach to the firm. In April 1951, E. E. Bridges did not hesitate to remind the AIOC board of "the vast importance of the Company's operations to the economy of the United Kingdom, and indeed to the sterling area as a whole."[64] At the very least, the dispute between the Foreign Office and the Treasury in the winter of 1951 reminds us that the British government was not monolithic and that its decision-making on Iran was the product of interdepartmental debate.

In the spring and summer of 1951, the AIOC and the British government, which was now directly involved in the efforts to resolve the oil crisis, strove to reach an agreement with Iran that impossibly tried to reconcile the country's desire for nationalization with Britain's reluctance to relinquish control of Iran's oil industry. William Strang of the Foreign Office reported at the end of March that William Fraser "had declared that he was not afraid of 'nationalisation' and was prepared to consider any arrangement with the Persian Government which left management in the Company's hands – or indeed any proposal the Persian Government cared to make."[65] By the end of the summer, three missions, led respectively by the AIOC's deputy chairman, Basil Jackson, an American mediator, Averell Harriman, and a British government negotiator, Richard Stokes, had gone to Tehran to try to achieve some kind of modus vivendi. Jackson offered Iranian officials a form of nationalization that represented nothing more than window-dressing on a plan that left key areas of Iran's oil industry under British control, which the Iranian

64 Bridges to the AIOC, April 12, 1951, NA, T 236/5879.
65 "Record of a Meeting held in the Foreign Office," March 20, 1951, NA, FO 371/91525.

2.2 From left to right: Sir Donald Fergusson, Permanent Secretary to the Ministry of Fuel and Power, Richard Stokes, the Lord Privy Seal, and Sir Francis Shepherd, British Ambassador to Iran, at London Airport before flying to Tehran, August 1951.

government found objectionable.[66] Harriman, who had handled a host of complex problems in his long and diverse career in the US government, ostensibly went to Tehran as a kind of "honest broker," but he aimed to persuade Muhammad Mossadegh to adopt a more compromising position in advance of the Stokes mission.[67]

As for Stokes, he came armed with an eight-point memorandum that the British government hoped would finally end the impasse. Its basic features were as follows: first, the newly formed National Iranian Oil Company (NIOC) would take over the AIOC's assets for unspecified compensation. Second, Britain would establish a "purchasing organization" to manage the Iranian oil industry under the authority of the NIOC. Third, the purchasing organization would then agree to buy and market "large quantities" of Iranian oil over a "long period of years." And, finally, the purchasing organization would split the profits on the sale of Iranian

[66] Bamberg, *History of the British Petroleum Company, Volume II*, 422–430.
[67] Yergin, *The Prize*, 459–462.

2.3 Iranian Prime Minister Muhammad Mossadegh and Lord Privy
Seal Richard Stokes during the latter's mission to Iran, August
1951.

oil with the NIOC fifty–fifty.[68] Of course, like Jackson's proposal, the
eight-point memorandum left Britain virtually in control of Iranian oil,
which did not satisfy Iran's demand to manage its own petroleum industry
without interference from foreigners. Stokes and Harriman, moreover,
quickly discovered in conversations with Mossadegh and other influential
Iranians that the prime minister could not agree to any settlement that
left the British in Iran without risking his political and personal survival.
Consequently, Harriman realized that, no matter how much he cajoled
Mossadegh, his mission would end in failure, something to which he was

[68] "Memorandum by the British Delegation," August 11, 1951, NA, FO 371/91583.

not accustomed.[69] Stokes, because of his exasperation with Mossadegh, did not prove to be an ideal choice to lead the negotiations in the first place.[70] He left Tehran at the end of August in frustration, and the British government suspended its talks with Iran the following month. What became clear was that as long as both Britain and Iran were intent on maintaining control of Iranian oil, the two countries would continue to talk past each other and were unlikely to reach an accommodation.

The end of the AIOC as it had existed in Iran for half a century came with the eviction of its British staff in October 1951. While the British government considered the use of force to maintain a British presence at the company's refinery on Abadan Island – something it had threatened to do in the early months of the crisis – cooler heads prevailed. Instead, the AIOC complied with the Iranian government's orders to evacuate all of its British employees from the country by October 4, as described in the Introduction. The British ship *Mauritius* carried the firm's remaining staff from Abadan to safety in Iraq, a nation over which Britain still wielded considerable influence. But Britain's failure to maintain control over Iranian oil, and the enormous refinery that processed it, signified more than a blow to the nation's prestige. It also represented a strike to Britain's finances at a moment of profound economic weakness, the nation's third balance-of-payments crisis in five years. This crisis would further entrench British officials in the notion that some British oil company had to return to Iran to help protect Britain's balance of payments.

2.3 The balance-of-payments crisis of 1951 and the importance of British control over Iranian oil

In 1950, the British government had much to cheer about regarding the balance of payments. A worldwide economic recovery opened markets for British manufactured goods, and, in contrast to previous periods of rapid international economic growth, the relative price of primary products fell. In addition, the expansion of world trade and US private investment helped to alleviate the nagging postwar dollar shortage problem. As a result of the higher profits earned by British multinational corporations, particularly oil firms, the country's invisible earnings rose.[71] The upshot of these favorable trends was that, in 1950, Britain was able to run a trade

---

[69] Yergin, *The Prize*, 459–462.   [70] Louis, *British Empire in the Middle East*, 681.

[71] M. F. G. Scott, "The Balance of Payments Crises" in G. D. N. Worswick and P. H. Ady (eds.), *The British Economy in the Nineteen-Fifties* (Oxford: Clarendon Press, 1962), 205, 213.

surplus of £300 million, and, in the following year, the nation's reserves were three times higher than they had been at the nadir of the financial crisis in 1949.[72] Britain had, in fact, become a net creditor rather than a net debtor with the rest of the world.[73] Unfortunately, this return to equilibrium was short-lived and merely represented the calm before the storm.

The escalation of the Korean War, which had started in June 1950, precipitated a severe balance-of-payments crisis in Britain in 1951 that Winston Churchill described as a "'financial super-crisis'" that "threatened to destroy the value of sterling."[74] Rearmament in the United States, Britain, and elsewhere, as mandated by NATO, dramatically increased the demand for raw materials and drove up prices. The conversion of British domestic industries to military production reduced manufacturing exports, thereby forcing Britain to draw from its reserves to pay its rising import bill. Making matters worse, Marshall Plan aid ended in 1951, and the United States did not deliver on its informal promise to underwrite the balance-of-payments costs of Britain's ballooning military budget.[75] Real trouble came when the sterling area countries that benefited from the spike in the price of raw materials increased their imports of finished goods just as the price of their raw material exports started falling, further shrinking Britain's reserves.[76] In December 1951, the newly appointed Conservative Chancellor of the Exchequer R. A. Butler wrote, "If we lose even half as many dollars in the first half of 1952 as we have lost in the second half of 1951, the reserves will be well below danger point by the end of June ... We must, therefore, devote all our efforts to securing that steady increase in the reserves that alone will restore real confidence in sterling at the earliest possible moment."[77] Butler believed that Britain would have to maintain a surplus of roughly £300 million a year, either by increasing visible and invisible earnings or by reducing overseas payments to achieve this goal.[78] At the time, the loss of Iranian oil was estimated to have reduced the country's invisible income by £100 million.[79] With what appeared to be a current account deficit of £419

---

[72] Cairncross, *The British Economy since 1945*, 101.

[73] Scott, "The Balance of Payments Crises," 207.

[74] Peter Burnham, *Remaking the Postwar World Economy: Robot and British Policy in the 1950s* (New York, Palgrave Macmillan, 2003), 14.

[75] Cairncross, *The British Economy since 1945*, 99–104.

[76] Katz, "Sterling's Recurring Postwar Payments Crises," 220–221; Scott, "The Balance of Payments Crises," 213.

[77] Butler to MacEntee, December 14, 1951, NA, T 172/2122.

[78] Cabinet Conclusions, CM 57 (52), May 29, 1952, NA, CAB 128/25.

[79] Note of Meeting at Treasury, October 3, 1951, NA, POWE 33/1676. The number was reduced to £65 million at the end of the year when Anglo-Iranian provided a more accurate picture of the replacement cost of crude and products.

million, the balance-of-payments picture in 1951 looked bleak, causing the Treasury to write, "Persia is of decisive importance, and may indeed represent the difference between a just manageable position and a completely hopeless one."[80] It is impossible to understand fully British policy during the Iranian oil crisis without considering this economic context, as it undoubtedly motivated Britain to defend its income-generating assets abroad with an even greater sense of urgency.

As both the Iranian oil and British balance-of-payments crises reached critical mass during the spring and summer of 1951, Whitehall focused its attention on the connection between Iranian petroleum and Britain's financial wellbeing. The £100 million annually that British officials estimated they had forfeited to Iran as a result of its incapacitated oil industry represented 4 percent of Britain's entire balance of payments.[81] Considering all of the items that contribute to the sum total of visible and invisible trade, this number is significant. It is also important to keep in mind that, although 4 percent may seem like a small part of the overall balance-of-payments picture, Britain's reserve position was so delicate that policy-makers believed that the slightest adverse change on the debit side of the account augured trouble. As a result, one member of the Foreign Office wrote that Britain "should have to think very carefully before making large-scale concessions, either financial or of control" of Iranian oil.[82] The Persian Oil Working Party, the governmental committee that was established to deal with the AIOC's difficulties in Iran, drafted instructions for British negotiators that listed four objectives "of major importance" to Whitehall. One of these objectives was "safeguarding the United Kingdom balance of payments." The memorandum read: "Any loss of profit resulting from high payments to Persia will, of course, reduce the contribution to the balance of payments proportionately; but from the point of view of saving dollars the essential requirement is to keep oil flowing from Abadan under the control of a British company."[83]

For Whitehall, the Abadan refinery, the world's largest and Britain's greatest overseas investment, was the critical issue – even more than Iranian oil itself. After all, by 1952, the nation was able to make up the loss of Iranian crude by acquiring oil from other sterling sources. The

---

[80] HM Treasury, *United Kingdom Balance of Payments, 1946–1957* (London: Her Majesty's Stationery Office, 1959), 16; "Balance of Payments: Brief for Chancellor's Visit," August 28, 1951, BE G1/120. More recently compiled figures for the period show a less bleak picture. See Appendix 1.

[81] "Persian Oil and the Balance of Payments," June 9, 1951, BP 100738, Anglo-American meeting at the Foreign Office, April 2, 1951, NA, FO 371/91470.

[82] No. 1612 from the Foreign Office to Washington, March 31, 1951, NA, FO 371/91470.

[83] "Persia – Instructions to Negotiators," undated, but most likely written in May or June 1951, BP 100738.

Kuwait Oil Company (KOC), half-owned by the AIOC and half-owned by Gulf Oil, a major American multinational oil firm, greatly stepped up its production and provided a majority of the sterling area's substitute crude (see Table 4.1 on p. 207).[84] Replacing the petroleum products that came from Abadan proved to be much more difficult and costly. The Iranian refinery churned out roughly 20 million tons of chemicals annually, helping to satisfy a large portion of the Eastern Hemisphere's skyrocketing postwar demand by producing items such as heating oil, gasoline, airplane fuel, and bitumen, a chemical mainly used in asphalt road surfacing.[85] Since refinery-building was such a slow, expensive, material- and labor-intensive process, Anglo-Iranian and other British companies had to spend an exorbitant number of dollars to procure products from existing, American-controlled facilities, such as Saudi Arabia's Ras Tanura, to compensate for Abadan's shut-down. If British firms did not acquire petroleum products from dollar sources to replace the lost sterling output, they would have had to forfeit valuable markets that would have been impossible to win back. In May 1951, the Treasury estimated, based on Abadan's yield in the previous year, that the loss of Iranian products would have cost $504 million to replace.[86] Later, the department calculated that, in the second half of 1951, Abadan's shut-down bled $169 million from the sterling area's reserves.[87] The nationalization crisis clearly undermined Whitehall's efforts to equalize the sterling area's trade with the dollar world, explaining why the balance-of-payments issue greatly influenced British official thinking regarding Iran during this period.[88]

Britain was fortunate that it was able to replace Abadan's production at all, even from dollar sources. The world's refining capacity was pushed to its limits when Abadan stopped running, exerting considerable strain on existing facilities.[89] As discussed in chapter 1, petroleum products were considered a large enough drain on dollars that the British government allocated scarce dollar resources to British oil companies after World War II to build refineries for future dollar-saving. In that same spirit, Whitehall approved plans for Anglo-Iranian to begin construction on a facility in Aden, Britain's colony on the southern tip of the Arabian

---

[84] One consequence for Kuwait of its role in replacing Iranian crude was that its oil industry developed at a faster rate than expected and quickly produced enormous sterling revenues for the country.

[85] Unsigned memorandum, dated June 4, 1952, BP 118974.

[86] Reilly to Serpell, May 3, 1951, NA, T 236/3899.

[87] Meeting at the Treasury, February 24, 1954, NA, T 236/3900.

[88] See Appendix 2 for figures demonstrating the steep rise in the dollar cost of oil at the time.

[89] Unsigned memorandum, dated June 4, 1952, BP 118974.

2.4 An aerial view of the Abadan oil refinery.

Peninsula, to make up for the loss of Abadan.[90] With both the dramatic increase in Kuwait's crude production and the building of a new oil refinery in Aden, the British empire demonstrated an impressive ability to adjust to the difficulties that confronted it, solving problems in one area by exploiting the resources of another.

Maintaining British control over production at Abadan and in the Iranian oil fields was crucial for British officials because they recognized that Britain's economic interests did not always coincide with those of Iran. In fact, they were "diametrically opposed" in many cases, according to

[90] Spearing to Butler, "AIOC Refinery – Aden: Works Scheme Case," March 14, 1952, NA, POWE 33/1981. See BP 69123 for a correspondence between the AIOC's Basil Jackson and the Ministry of Fuel and Power's Victor Butler on this issue.

Allan Christelow, the former under-secretary of the British Treasury delegation to Washington and the former financial counsellor to the British Embassy there. In a paper prepared for Britain's negotiations with Iran in the spring of 1951, Christelow expressed his worry that the Iranian government would choose to develop its oil industry at a pace that showed no consideration for matters that Whitehall deemed important, such as fuel for the British navy and the stability of the British economy. He pursued this line of thinking further: "Put in extreme terms, what we want to do is to develop the Persian fields as rapidly as physically possible, the optimum being the exhaustion of the fields by the date of expiration of the concession in 1993." On the other hand, he maintained, Iran would want to develop its oil fields "at the rate which best suit[ed] general Persian development." Christelow then discussed the issue of pricing and profits, explaining that while both Britain and Iran would want to "maximise the price at which oil is sold to the rest of the world," it was in Britain's best interests to minimize the price of oil that it obtained from Iran by "maximising its share of the profits of the oil company operations." Iran would obviously want to do the opposite.[91] The consensus at Whitehall was that, if a British firm did not manage the Iranian oil industry, Britain's economic interests would be put in a vulnerable position.

Not only did fears about Iran's natural inclination to pursue its own interests motivate the British desire to control Iranian petroleum, but anxieties about Iran's inability to run its own oil industry also proved critical. In a Persian Oil Working Party memorandum on "The Persian Social and Political Scene," a section devoted to the "Persian Character" reads:

Although the Persians display a veneer of Western civilisation their character still derives from their long history of autocratic rule and from their Islamic background . . . The ordinary Persian is vain, unprincipled, eager to promise what he is incapable or has no intention of performing, wedded to procrastination, lacking in perseverance and energy, and amenable to discipline. Above all he loves intrigue, and readily employs prevarication and dishonesty whenever there is even a remote possibility of personal gain. Although in conversation an accomplished liar, he does not expect to be believed . . .[92]

In line with some of these sentiments, the Foreign Office expressed concerns about the inefficiency of the Iranian oil industry under "Persian management."[93] Similarly, Ernest Northcroft, the AIOC's representative in Tehran from 1945 to 1951, regretted that the European efficiency

[91] "The Persian Oil Negotiations," April 25, 1951, NA, T 236/4427.
[92] May 25, 1951, BP 100738.
[93] Persia (Official) Committee, PO (52) 3, January 25, 1952, NA, CAB 134/1147.

with which the company operated the Abadan refinery sometimes ignored "Persian susceptibilities."[94] Because AIOC board members considered Iranians to be inefficient, they were rarely given management positions at the company, though there were exceptions.[95] And because hardly any Iranians occupied management positions at the company, logic – circular as it was – dictated that Iran could not possibly hope to run its oil industry without Western help. The characterization of Iranians as unfit to manage their own industry owing to a variety of culturally determined personality flaws, which all added up to the larger trait of Iranian "inefficiency," indeed reflected the prevailing view of all Middle Easterners among many British officials. It is no wonder that Whitehall refused to relinquish control of Iranian oil, not only for the sake of Britain's economy but for the sake of Iran's as well.[96] After all, most British officials and company employees were also good paternalists, as those with an Orientalist worldview often were.[97] Thus, British policy-makers seriously considered the percentage of profits the AIOC could reasonably sacrifice to Iran in order to maintain control over the country's oil operations. In October 1951, Britain's ambassador in Tehran, Sir Francis Shepherd, wrote, "I think we should fight for retention by the Anglo-Iranian Oil Company, so far as possible, of the control of the industry they have built up. I would even go so far as to say . . . that from our point of view it might be worthwhile to sacrifice the 50/50 principle and go to say, 60/40 in order to retain the Anglo-Iranian Oil Company."[98]

During the previous June, the Persian Oil Working Party had discussed a memorandum in which the Ministry of Fuel and Power contemplated the pros and cons of such an idea in the context of Britain's balance of payments. The ministry calculated that at 50/50, Britain's trade account

---

[94] Shepherd to Furlonge, June 5, 1951, NA, FO 371/91545.

[95] In *The History of the British Petroleum Company, Volume II*, Bamberg writes, "For the Company . . . the efficiency and economy of its operations was a fundamental concern which it was reluctant to compromise by submitting to rigid regulations on employment" by the Iranian government, 360. Regarding the hiring of Iranians to management positions, Mustafa Fateh, whom the AIOC appointed assistant general manager of labor affairs at the Abadan refinery in January 1948, is the exception that proves the rule.

[96] Martin Flett wrote to R. J. Bowker at the Foreign Office on May 24, 1951, "If [the Iranians] are reasonable there should be no difficulty whatever in persuading them that the retention of control in UK hands is in their best interests as well as ours, and that to attempt to run so vital and complex an industry themselves will mean the ruin of the whole Persian economy," NA, FO 371/91540.

[97] For an indictment of the British attitude towards Iran at this time, see Richard Cottam's *Nationalism in Iran* (University of Pittsburgh Press, 1964), 273. Also see Wm. Roger Louis, "Musaddiq and the Dilemmas of British Imperialism" in James Bill and Wm. Roger Louis (eds.), *Musaddiq, Iranian Nationalism, and Oil* (Austin: University of Texas Press, 1988), 239.

[98] No. 1580 from Shepherd to the Foreign Office, October 23, 1951, NA, T 236/4443.

would have forfeited £15 million more than it would have under the Supplemental Agreement; at 60/40 (Iran/AIOC), £34 million would have been lost; and at 75/25, the figure jumped to £86 million. While the ministry believed that proceeding beyond 50/50 was risky, because "any situation in which the local government was taking more than 50%" would "make it very difficult to keep effective control in British hands," it decided that 60/40 "might be worth considering." The department also concluded that 75/25 sacrificed too much on the credit side of Britain's balance of payments to explore the idea seriously.[99]

Some officials worried about the effect on other concessionary agreements of the AIOC's return to Iran with a contract that undermined the fifty–fifty profit-sharing principle in Iran's favor. In June 1951, a representative of the Ministry of Fuel and Power's Petroleum Division told Anglo-Iranian's Neville Gass that some members of the Treasury believed that if the AIOC conceded more than 50 percent of its profits to Iran, other countries where the company had interests, such as Iraq and Kuwait, would demand similar terms. They argued that based on balance-of-payments considerations, "the stage could be reached where it would be less costly to forego Persian oil, if this were to make it possible to avoid a higher level of royalty payments to Kuwait and Iraq – rather than to agree to higher payments to Persia with corresponding payments also to Kuwait and Iraq."[100] This sentiment was confirmed in a note that the Treasury's N. M. P. Reilly sent to a colleague a few months later in which he wrote, "any settlement with Persia is bound to set in train a series of reactions which would almost certainly eventuate in other concessionary countries obtaining similar terms."[101] A year later, another Treasury official insisted that a "bad agreement with Persia" would lead to "the substitution of a similar bad agreement with Iraq," with the net effect on Britain's balance of payments being "very grave indeed."[102] Consequently, the Treasury concluded that, although a resumption of British control over Iranian oil was in Britain's best economic interests, if that control were gained by striking a deal with Iran that undermined Anglo-Iranian's other Middle Eastern concessions, then the effects suffered by Britain's balance of payments might demand that Britain forfeit Iranian oil altogether.

Policy-makers at Whitehall also refused to accept unfavorable terms because of the link they made between international confidence in sterling

99 "The Cost of Proceeding Beyond a 50/50 Split of Profits with Concessionary Countries," POWP (51)17, June 14, 1951, BP 100738.
100 Gass to Snow, June 6, 1951, BP 66900.
101 Reilly to Serpell, September 24, 1951, NA, T 236/4440.
102 Armstrong to Shuckburgh, December 18, 1952, NA, FO 371/98704.

and the ability of the British government to enforce the terms of British contracts around the world. In November 1951, the Treasury's Leslie Rowan explained the potential consequences for sterling of allowing Iran to appropriate Anglo-Iranian's interests with impunity:

The position of sterling depended to an extent . . . upon our invisible earnings. The oil industry accounts for a very large proportion of these earnings but they also arise from such things as banking, insurance, etc. Fundamentally they depend on the respect throughout the world for British skill and the integrity of contracts. If we were even to start to begin negotiations with Musaddiq on a basis which implied that we were prepared to see British interests exappropriated [sic] without compensation and to accept a settlement under which the exappropriating [sic] government became entitled to substantially better terms than a government which respected its contracts, the effects on our credit and standing throughout the world would be catastrophic. They would almost certainly nullify any measures which His Majesty's Government was proposing to take to re-establish the position of sterling.[103]

The Foreign Office's William Strang was equally concerned about this issue. He argued that, since Britain depended "so vitally for survival upon respect for foreign investment and the observance of commercial understandings," it was a "very serious matter that her vital interests may be attacked in defiance of international law by governments who can rely confidently upon the absence of an effective international remedy."[104] David Serpell at the Treasury wondered "where the loss of oil in present terms would end," comparing British acquiescence in Iran to "dropping a pebble into a pool of water – the ripples kept going out."[105] Whitehall could not back down: such a display of weakness would put all of the country's Middle Eastern interests at risk, the upshot of which would be not only direct and immediate damage to Britain's balance of payments, but indirect and long-term damage as well.[106] If the British government appeared soft in Iran, the larger effect on other British investments around the globe would create, policy-makers feared, an international lack of confidence in sterling that would do untold harm to the British economy. Consequently, the British government drew a line in the sand that it would not allow Iran to cross, a position that its US allies believed

---

[103] Unsigned Foreign Office Minute, November 6, 1951, NA, FO 371/91612.

[104] "Some Notes on the Persian Oil Dispute and its Implications," Foreign Office Minute, October 23, 1951, FO 371/91611.

[105] First meeting of Anglo-American talks on Iran at the State Department, April 9, 1951, NA, T 236/4425.

[106] "Balance of Payments Aspects of the American Proposals," undated and unsigned memorandum (most likely November 1951), NA, T 236/4443.

reflected a Victorian mentality that was out of touch with political trends in the post-World War II Middle East.

2.4   US anti-imperialism, anti-communism, and Anglo-American conflict, 1950–1953

While American missionaries traveled to Iran as early as the 1830s, official US involvement there did not begin until World War II. Seeking to establish its influence on behalf of the war effort, Washington must have been thankful that a century of private US contact created a "reservoir of good will" between Iran and the United States, forging a reputation for Americans in Iran that was "positive and warm."[107] In 1942, the US government started sending Lend-Lease aid to Iran to bolster the nation's economic and political stability, and, the following year, American financial and military advisors arrived at the request of Iranian officials who were anxious about the Anglo-Soviet occupation caused by the war. US policy-makers were more than happy to oblige the Iranian appeal for assistance, in part to safeguard American oil interests on the other side of the Persian Gulf in Saudi Arabia. According to Secretary of State Cordell Hull, these interests demanded that no single power, not even an ally as close as Britain, should be allowed to dominate Iran. Consequently, one of the chief US goals there was to preserve the country's independence.[108]

The perceived danger of communism after World War II, both domestic and international, gave American officials added incentive to remain involved in Iranian affairs. First and foremost, the Soviet Union's refusal to remove its troops from northern Iran six months after the end of the war, as delineated by the tripartite agreement that Moscow signed with both London and Tehran, unsettled the US government. This unease intensified when it became clear that Soviet leaders had used their army's presence in Iran's northern province of Azerbaijan to help support a revolt there. Furthermore, Iran's far-left Tudeh Party was growing in popularity, with American intelligence sources determining that it was receiving support from Moscow.[109]

---

107 James A. Bill, *The Eagle and the Lion: The Tragedy of American–Iranian Relations* (New Haven: Yale University Press, 1988), 16–17.

108 Ibid., ch. 1. Also see Mark Hamilton Lytle, *The Origins of the Iranian–American Alliance, 1941–1953* (New York: Holmes and Meier, 1987), ch. 7.

109 Francis J. Gavin, "Politics, Power, and US Policy in Iran, 1950–1953," *Journal of Cold War Studies* 1, 1 (1999), 65. For the most thorough discussion of the Tudeh Party, see Abrahamian, *Iran between Two Revolutions*, ch. 6.

While US-instigated pressure from the UN Security Council eventually forced the Soviet army to withdraw from Iran in 1946, communist actions in Europe and Asia throughout the rest of the decade persuaded Washington that the Soviet Union was bent on expanding its influence across the globe.[110] In contrast to its failed efforts in Iran, the Soviet government managed to keep its troops in Eastern Europe after World War II and turn the countries there into client states to create a buffer against any new incursions from Western Europe. At the same time, it tried to assert its authority over the Dardanelles straits between the Black and the Mediterranean seas, while the communist-led National Liberation Front was gaining strength in Greece. In 1948, Moscow blockaded non-communist West Berlin, attempting to hold that part of the city hostage by choking off all ground traffic. One year later, Mao Zedong's communist forces assumed control of China, and the Soviet Union successfully tested an atomic bomb. Finally, in 1950, the communist government of North Korea launched an invasion of Western-backed South Korea, sparking a land war in Asia. By the time of the Iranian oil nationalization crisis in 1951, the Cold War was in full swing, and the Truman Administration would not tolerate a Western defeat in a region as strategically important as the Middle East.

Consequently, when Saudi Arabian ruler Ibn Saud sought a more lucrative concession agreement with American-owned Aramco in 1950, the US government encouraged the firm's partners to satisfy his demands quickly. The result, as mentioned earlier, was a contract between Saudi Arabia and Aramco that split the profits on the sale of Arabian oil equally between the two parties. It is impossible to overstate the impact of the notion of fifty–fifty profit-sharing on the international oil industry, first when it appeared in Venezuela in 1943 and then when it arrived in the Middle East with the Aramco deal.[111] How much the landlord and the tenant – the oil-producing country and the foreign company that extracted, refined, and sold the petroleum – would receive on "rents" from the commodity's exploitation was a question that concerned issues not only of money, but also of power and pride. Until the emergence of fifty–fifty, there seemed to be no satisfactory guideline for the distribution of rents.[112] The elegance of fifty–fifty lay in the fact that by making partners of the landlord and tenant, this profit-sharing formula dealt

---

[110] Lytle, *The Origins of the Iranian–American Alliance*, chs. 9–10.

[111] Irvine H. Anderson details the fifty–fifty principle in the Saudi Arabian context in "The American Oil Industry and the Fifty–Fifty Agreement of 1950" in Bill and Louis, *Musaddiq, Iranian Nationalism, and Oil*, 145–163.

[112] For an analysis of rents and the impact of the fifty–fifty principle on the oil industry, see Yergin, *The Prize*, ch. 22.

with the intangible issue of national pride that accompanied the material bottom line. Assistant Secretary of State for Near Eastern, South Asian, and African Affairs George McGhee, a former oilman himself, phrased it best when he wrote that fifty–fifty "had an aura of fairness understandable to the ordinary man."[113]

Many American officials embraced the fifty–fifty principle because it fit well with their vision of American policy toward the colonial and semi-colonial world during and after World War II. This vision revolved around the twin themes of self-determination and capitalist development. "Self-determination of all peoples," one of the Fourteen Points that Woodrow Wilson advanced after World War I, was reiterated in the Atlantic Charter signed during World War II. Franklin Roosevelt, moreover, promoted an anti-colonial agenda over the objections of Winston Churchill throughout Second World War.[114] Washington's anti-colonial campaign continued in the postwar era, focusing particularly on the discriminatory sterling area. Of course, as in Woodrow Wilson's time, American anti-colonialism constituted a mixture of altruism and self-interest, the aim of which was not only freedom for African and Asian colonies, but also open markets for American exports. At the end of the decade, the United States launched the Point Four program to provide relief and development aid around the world. According to Dean Acheson, the program was designed to help "free peoples through their own efforts" to "produce more food, clothing, housing, and power to lighten their burdens," paving the way for the US government's more aggressive forays into Third World development during the 1960s based on ideas conceived by American economist and future national security advisor Walt W. Rostow.[115] Regarding the Middle East, George McGhee, an official sympathetic to non-Western nationalist movements – and one who well represented the development impulse at the Department of State during this time – asserted that "it was essential to assist the peoples of the Middle East to improve their living standards and social and political institutions and to acquire self respect and their proper place among the nations of the world."[116] For policy-makers such as McGhee, by providing oil producers with a larger share of the profits from the exploitation of their petroleum – and by

[113] George McGhee, *Envoy to the Middle World* (New York: Harper and Row, 1983), 335.

[114] Wm. Roger Louis, *Imperialism at Bay: The United States and the Decolonization of the British Empire, 1941–1945* (New York: Oxford University Press, 1978).

[115] Acheson, *Present at the Creation*, 265; W. W. Rostow, *The Stages of Economic Growth: A Non-Communist Manifesto*, third edition (Cambridge University Press, 1990).

[116] Hare to Rusk, December 19, 1949, Annex 1, "Statement by the United States and the United Kingdom Groups," Introductory Discussions, November 14, 1949, *FRUS, 1949, Vol. VI*, 61–64.

giving them a greater sense of control of their own destiny – the fifty–fifty principle embodied much of what the United States sought to accomplish in the developing world in the post-World War II era. US officials approached the Anglo-Iranian dispute over oil from this perspective.

In part, maintaining the fifty–fifty principle as the status quo in the Middle East motivated Washington's desire to put its stamp on any solution to the Anglo-Iranian oil dispute. To some degree this position was based on the dogmatic belief of US policy-makers that fifty–fifty represented the perfect solution to the problem of dividing rents. But to a larger degree these officials feared that allowing Iran to receive more than 50 percent of the profits would damage the position of all of the multinational petroleum firms in the region by triggering successive waves of renegotiations. Before Averell Harriman went to Tehran in the summer of 1951, American oil firms insisted that he take a "tough line" on fifty–fifty, worrying that if they eventually had to cede increasingly larger shares of their profits, then "the industry would in a fairly short time find itself without the necessary risk capital to undertake new expansion."[117] Indeed, according to George McGhee, Harriman insisted to Iranian officials that "they could not expect to get better terms than the other nations of the Middle East."[118] Even McGhee agreed that Britain and Iran should not break the fifty–fifty barrier because of the "jeopardy" in which such an agreement would place the firms that operated in the region.[119] Not surprisingly, the United States, the country that established the new status quo, did not want to see another party disturb it. Such an occurrence would have undermined its moral authority and undercut the financial position of its companies. Naturally, this is exactly how British officials felt after Aramco struck its deal with Saudi Arabia at the end of December 1950.

In the latter half of that year, when the British government and the Anglo-Iranian Oil Company anxiously awaited ratification of the Supplemental Agreement, US officials, led by George McGhee, pressed Whitehall and the firm to be more generous with Iran, especially because of the negotiations taking place in Riyadh. As early as January 1950, McGhee told AIOC representatives at a meeting at the State Department that "conditions had greatly changed in the Near East since most contracts were signed" and that "it was therefore necessary for oil companies to deal with the situation realistically by recognizing the legitimate

---

[117] No. 332 from the British Delegation at the United Nations to the Foreign Office, October 12, 1951, NA, T 236/4442.
[118] No. 2302 from Franks to the Foreign Office, July 25, 1951, NA, FO 371/91568.
[119] Ibid.

demands of oil producing states."[120] As the Supplemental Agreement languished in the Majlis that year, the British government and the AIOC clung to their belief that the accord was fair, given the standards of the Middle East at the time, causing the Department of State to grow frustrated with the inflexibility of the British position. Richard Funkhouser of the Office of African and Near Eastern Affairs wrote: "We have no doubt in our minds that Persian Gulf oil operations have been and continue to be *exceptionally profitable* from a commercial standpoint, particularly AIOC operations. It is sophistry to suggest oil companies can't pay and do much more."[121]

US officials had warned Britain that Aramco might sign a deal with Saudi Arabia that would render the Supplemental Agreement obsolete. In August 1950, the petroleum attaché to the US Embassy in Egypt, Albert F. Lager, told E. W. Noonan of the British Middle East Office in Cairo that he believed that "an increase in ARAMCO royalty" was "in the offing."[122] In November, Noonan pointed out that Whitehall had been alerted to the fact that Saudi Arabia had "just put forward demands so far reaching that if the Persians heard of them the Supplemental Agreement would never go through."[123] In the end, McGhee and his colleagues were right, and they did not hesitate to let their British counterparts know it. One can only conclude that complaints in London about not having been informed by US officials of the details of the new deal were merely a case of sour grapes.[124]

American policy-makers displayed a somewhat self-satisfied attitude toward Britain regarding both Aramco's success in Saudi Arabia and the AIOC's failure in Iran, one that was informed by a belief that the United States was a progressive force in world affairs and Britain was an obstacle standing in the way of progress. These officials saved most of their wrath for the company and its directors, but they also blamed Whitehall for either supporting the company or not doing enough to influence its policy, especially given the British government's majority ownership. Edward S. Crocker, the US Ambassador in Iraq, believed that the stability of the Middle East had been "dangerously and almost wantonly undermined by anachronistic policies pursued by AIOC

[120] Memorandum of conversation on discussions with Anglo-Iranian officials by Richard Funkhouser, January 24, 1950, *FRUS, 1950, Vol. V,* 15.
[121] September 14, 1950, *FRUS, 1950, Vol. V,* 97–99.
[122] Noonan to Nuttall, August 22, 1950, NA, FO 371/82375.
[123] Memorandum by E. W. Noonan on the Anglo-Iranian Oil Company, November 15, 1950, NA, FO 371/82377.
[124] One member of the Foreign Office commented, "Neither we nor the British Oil Companies in the Middle East were warned or consulted." Quoted in Louis, *The British Empire in the Middle East,* 597.

leadership, supported by portions of [the British government] and not effectively checked or controlled by [the Foreign Office]."[125] In a broad policy paper dealing with American and British interests in the Middle East, the Department of State's leading area representatives described AIOC policy as "reactionary and outmoded" and "responsible to a great degree" for "lowered Western prestige" in both Iran and the Middle East. It also characterized the company as "one of the greatest political liabilities" affecting Anglo-American interests in the region and bemoaned the fact that the Foreign Office had "scant influence" upon the AIOC despite its shareholding position.[126] The American Ambassador in Iran, Henry F. Grady, who shared George McGhee's sympathy for burgeoning nationalist movements in Africa and Asia, wrote at the end of October 1950 that, "had it really wanted to do so," the British government "would have more actively encouraged" the AIOC to "sweeten" the Supplementary Agreement.[127] Contrasting the experience of Whitehall and the AIOC in Iran with that of the US government and Aramco in Saudi Arabia, McGhee describes in his memoirs how the Aramco partners, initially reluctant to sign a fifty–fifty contract, became "convinced" of the appropriateness of a "share and share alike deal" after discussions with the Department of State about the shifting winds in the postwar Middle East. He then commends the Aramco leadership for its "high order of business statesmanship" and implies that the way that the US government and Aramco resolved matters in Saudi Arabia was a model to be emulated.[128] The British certainly got the message, as revealed in one Anglo-Iranian memorandum: "[US officials] felt very satisfied with their own policy, exemplified by the 50/50 profit-sharing agreement concluded in Saudi Arabia and thought that we, on the other hand, were being slow and were not keeping up with the development of feeling in Persia."[129]

It is important to note that the US government paved the way for the fifty–fifty deal between Aramco and Saudi Arabia by giving Aramco a tax credit for the extra revenues that the company would have to disburse under the new agreement. The AIOC's deputy chairman, Basil Jackson, commented on the implications of the policy: "while the Company and its landlord are both better off, this happy result has been obtained at the

---

[125] Crocker to the Department of State, March 29, 1951, *FRUS, 1951, Vol. V*, 292–293.
[126] Agreed Conclusions and Recommendations of the Conference of Middle East Chiefs of Mission, Istanbul, February 14–21, 1951, *FRUS, 1951, Vol. V*, 50–76.
[127] Grady to Acheson, October 31, 1950, *FRUS, 1950, Vol. V*, 612–613.
[128] McGhee, *Envoy to the Middle World*, 325.
[129] "Persia – Instructions to Negotiators" (second draft), undated (but most likely late May or early June 1951), BP 100738.

cost of the American taxpayer. This is the transaction which is held up to the world as a model of American generosity, but one wonders whether the people who really pay the piper would share this view if they realised just what has happened." Recounting that the United States had put pressure on Britain to do the same, Jackson argued that "such a system would hardly be received by the House of Commons, affecting as it would a corporation which was making millions, with approbation if some of the legitimate costs of operation were transferred to the hard-pressed British taxpayer."[130] Indeed, the US Congress held hearings on the propriety and legality of the government's deal with Aramco and Saudi Arabia, the upshot of which was the preservation of Aramco's tax break.

While British officials chafed at what they considered self-righteous utterances from across the Atlantic, by late 1950 and early 1951 many agreed with the negative American assessment of the AIOC board and took the kind of aggressive action regarding the company that American officials had advocated all along. Oliver Franks, the British Ambassador in Washington – who undoubtedly received an earful from US officials – wrote in April 1951:

The real trouble with the AIOC is that they have not got far enough past the stage of Victorian paternalism. This is an admirable attitude, but it just does not, or so it seems to me, make the grade in present circumstances. In fact, AIOC has done a great many very good things in Persia but to say "What a good boy am I" gets them nowhere either in Persia or in this country. Paternalism is out of fashion in this decade.[131]

That same month, Permanent Secretary to the Treasury Edward Bridges informed William Fraser that Whitehall would have to depart somewhat from the "procedure laid down" in the Bradbury letter that established the nature of the company–government relationship. He explained that the government's reluctance to interfere in the firm's negotiations with Iran was the "right policy in the situation as it existed in the past." However, given the changes that had occurred in Iran, as well as the "political, economic and strategic implications of the highest importance" of Iranian oil to Britain, rigid adherence to that policy was no longer feasible.[132] Bridges's colleague Martin Flett complained, "There have been occasions in the recent past when AIOC have kept HMG in ignorance of steps whose repercussions extended far beyond a narrow interpretation of their business interests."[133] In a demonstration of Whitehall's new

[130] Jackson to Heath Eves, March 21, 1951, BP 66255.
[131] Franks to Strang, April 21, 1951, NA, FO 371/91529.
[132] Foreign Office Minute, Strang to Morrison, April 3, 1951, NA, FO 371/91621.
[133] Flett to Brittain, March 6, 1951, NA, T 236/3451.

activist approach to the AIOC, British officials helped to decide the composition of the delegation that would represent the firm in Tehran later that April to negotiate a settlement.[134] Never one to mince his words, Basil Jackson decried the government's dealings with the company and wrote, "The only man who appears to me to follow a policy which one can even begin to understand is Attlee . . . It is pretty appalling to think that really great interests are dealt with at such levels by people who have no elementary comprehension of business principles, or any other for that matter!" Jackson was so disgusted with Whitehall's handling of the oil crisis that he even used his doctor to provide an excuse for not joining the Stokes mission that traveled to Iran at the end of the summer, a deception that he regretted he could not undertake more often.[135]

British officials were equally disgusted with the AIOC's leadership, prompting them to consider replacing William Fraser because, as the Treasury's Edward Bridges put it, he "was lacking in the wider political qualities that were necessary for the difficult period ahead."[136] William Strang wrote that the company's representatives had "never been very fertile in ideas or wide-ranging in their vision," and, agreeing with him, E. A. Berthoud thought that the British government might sell its company stock "to other British groups which would nominate new directors to the board and bring fresh life to that body."[137] Although neither of these extreme options was pursued, the mere consideration of them reveals how much the British government's conception of its relationship with the company had changed in only one year. Had Whitehall followed such a course much sooner, it might have averted the crisis in Iran. As discussed earlier, however, the evidence suggests that Whitehall did not want to interfere in the AIOC's negotiations with Iran before the latter part of 1950 because it believed not only that the Supplemental Agreement was reasonable for its time, but also that any further financial concessions by the company would have jeopardized the nation's balance of payments.

US officials were all too aware of the emphasis that the British government placed on the economic consequences of any unfavorable settlement with Iran. In November 1951, Dean Acheson articulated the British position with great precision in a letter to the Department of State

---

[134] Foreign Office Minute by Makins, June 1, 1951, FO371/91542; Foreign Office Minute by Strang, June 4, 1951, NA, FO 371/91541.
[135] Jackson to Wylie, September 4, 1951, BP 87230.
[136] Strang to Bridges, October 27, 1951, NA, FO 371/91607; Minutes of a meeting held in Sir Edward Bridges's room, October 23, 1951, NA, FO 371/91607.
[137] His comments were written regarding Nuttall to Flett, October 17, 1951, NA, FO 371/91621.

during a visit to London. He wrote that Britain's "overseas interests and the invisible items in her balance of payments are of overwhelming importance to her" and that the British argued that the country could not "recover from the course of action which [would] destroy the last vestige of confidence in British power and in the pound." Consequently, he said, "the cardinal purpose of British policy is not to prevent Iran from going Commie; the cardinal point is to preserve what they believe to be the last remaining bulwark of British solvency; that is, their overseas investment and property position." Acheson then described an encounter that he had with a British official who said that if the choice before the United States was that either "Iran goes Commie or [Britain] goes bankrupt," then he hoped that the secretary of state would agree that the former was "the lesser evil."[138]

US policy-makers thought that this characterization of the British position created a false dichotomy. They argued that Britain had an important stake in whether Iran fell under communist rule because the interests of all of Western capitalism were at risk. Therefore, Britain had to consider the larger implications of what Washington saw as an imperialistic foreign policy underpinned by narrow economic interests: "We fully understand the importance of the AIOC to the UK economy," officials at the Department of State wrote. "We would expect, however, because of the overriding importance to the UK, the US and the whole free world of continued peace and stability in the area and the continued flow of oil into world commerce, that the UK will not allow these objectives to be subordinated to commercial or balance of payments considerations."[139] Whitehall turned the argument around, asserting that the United States had just as much interest in protecting British access to Iranian oil as Britain did since "its loss would weaken the whole sterling position and might well affect the British rearmament effort" and, thus, the West's ability to fight communism. Furthermore, US taxpayers might be "compelled to replace British exchange losses," suggested one British official.[140]

The conflict between the Department of State's focus on the communist threat in Iran and Whitehall's aversion to signing a concession agreement that it believed would undermine the British economy lay at the heart of Anglo-American tensions over the oil crisis. The British boycott of Iranian oil, supported by the major American multinational oil companies, left Iran destitute. As a result, the overriding fear among

138 Acheson to the State Department, November 10, 1951, *FRUS, 1951, Vol. V*, 278–281.
139 "United States Views on Questions Raised During Discussions with the British on Iran," Burrows to the Foreign Office's Eastern Department, April 19, 1951, NA, FO 371/91471.
140 No. 1628 from Middleton to the Foreign Office, November 6, 1951, NA, T 236/4444.

US officials was that the continued lack of an oil settlement would either plunge Iran into the kind of economic chaos that would "inevitably lead to the loss of Persia to the West," or, at the very least, create political confusion for the communist-influenced Tudeh Party to exploit.[141] For their part, British policy-makers thought that the United States oversold the possibility that Iran would turn communist if they held out for an agreement that they considered reasonable. Understanding the political climate in the United States, the Foreign Office characterized the Department of State as "obsessed by their overriding fear of Communism, a fear aggravated by the attitude of Congress which would blame the State Department for any Soviet advance in the Middle East as they have done over China."[142] Because London did not take the communist threat as seriously as Washington did, it was prepared to "play'" with Iran for much longer than the United States, certain that Mossadegh would be "compelled to accept a satisfactory arrangement sooner or later."[143]

Whitehall was also aggrieved by the fact that the American government's "obsession" with communism led to what it perceived to be an insensitivity to Britain's energy and economic vulnerabilities. Victor Butler, an under-secretary at the Ministry of Fuel and Power, mirrored British statements made during discussions on the prospective Anglo-American petroleum agreement in 1944–1945 when he complained, "[George McGhee] seems to be totally unaware that the value of the Persian concessions to our economy is infinitely greater than the value of Middle Eastern concessions held by American oil companies is to the US economy. About 60% of the world's production of oil is produced in the USA whereas we have virtually no oil in the UK and not very much in the Commonwealth."[144] B. A. B. Burrows, a counsellor at the British Embassy in Washington, told members of the Department of State that British officials felt the US government was sometimes guilty of not paying "sufficient attention" to the "importance of protecting British interests."[145] Furthermore, Burrows's colleague, P. E. Ramsbotham, complained that the American fear of communism tended to make the United States "disregard the greater risks of repercussions of a bad settlement with Persia" in Britain's "other and more important

[141] Minute of a meeting in Washington, February 1, 1952, NA, FO 371/98608.
[142] Persia (Official) Committee: Comments on the State Department's Views of the Persian Oil Problem, PO (52) 3, January 25, 1952, NA, CAB 134/1147.
[143] "Meeting between British and American Representatives at the State Department," Memorandum by Roundtree, January 9, 1952, *FRUS, 1952–1954, Vol. VI*, 821–823.
[144] Butler to Bowker, February 13, 1951, NA, T 236/2821.
[145] Minutes of a meeting at the State Department, February 11, 1952, NA, FO 371/98608.

concessionary areas."[146] But a Foreign Office telegram to the British ambassador in Washington put the finest point on the difference between the British and American perspectives:

The main difficulty in reaching an agreed view with the United States Government about a possible basis for an oil settlement is the different weight which the two Governments attach to overseas investments. Such investments are our life blood. We are therefore bound to view with the utmost misgiving any proposals for a settlement with Persia which would put a premium on confiscation and not only encourage other governments to upset existing agreements but also put at risk all United Kingdom foreign investments on which we so largely depend for the vital invisible element in our balance of payments.[147]

The economic disagreements that emerged during the sterling–dollar oil controversy of the 1940s had come into full view once again over Iran.

Another source of tension between British and US policy-makers was their conflicting view of Iranian nationalism, a problem recognized by officials on both sides of the Atlantic.[148] After his visit to Iran in the summer of 1951, Averell Harriman asked in frustration why Britain could not accept Iranian nationalism as "real and substantial." He said that, based on his experience and that of his advisors, he "felt sure that the nationalist feeling in Persia was a real force and not just something quickly whipped up and quickly allayed," which the British had suggested.[149] Officials such as Harriman, George McGhee, and Henry Grady believed that Britain had to make sacrifices to placate a genuine and entrenched nationalist sentiment, rather than ignore it in the belief that it would eventually disappear. Early in 1952, Secretary of Defense Robert Lovett commented on what he considered the retrograde attitude of Anthony Eden, the new Conservative foreign secretary: "I have a feeling that a considerable amount of education is going to have to be done to overcome his tendency to live completely in the past and to forget or underestimate the enormous changes which have occurred since the war in the rest of the world."[150]

In contrast to the Americans, the British considered Iranian nationalism to be based not "on any real national fervour," but rather on an "attempt by the ruling classes to divert attention from their own

---

[146] Ramsbotham to Brook, May 22, 1953, NA, POWE 33/2087.
[147] No. 520 from the Foreign Office to Franks, January 26, 1952, NA, FO 371/98684.
[148] George Middleton wrote to the Eastern Department of the Foreign Office that "the main point of difference lies in differing assessments of the importance of Iranian nationalism as a political factor," November 19, 1951, NA, FO 371/91472.
[149] No. 3116 from Washington to the Foreign Office, September 26, 1951, NA, T 236/4441.
[150] Lovett to Eisenhower, January 24, 1952, *FRUS, 1952–1954, Vol. VI*, 859–861.

shortcomings by ascribing all ills to foreign domination."[151] William Strang argued that the National Front represented only a minority of Iranians and used "intimidation in silencing all voices of reason."[152] These views led officials at both Whitehall and the AIOC to criticize some US policy-makers for their approach not only to Iranian affairs but also to the developing world in general. Basil Jackson half-heartedly complimented Dean Acheson for his "pretty good job" as secretary of state, but lambasted the "tremendous number of young and relatively inexperienced do-gooders whose universal panacea for international unrest appears to be to spend money in the backward countries."[153] In the same vein, Francis Shepherd described Henry Grady as "desperately anxious to be the saviour of Persia in the same way that he believes himself to have been the saviour of Greece and, to a lesser extent, India."[154] When the Foreign Office's G. W. Furlonge looked back on US "efforts at mediation" in 1951, he took Shepherd's statement one step further, arguing that such efforts were shaped by the Department of State's Greece–Turkey–Iran desk's need for "Iranian love" and added that the attitude of McGhee, Grady, and others was influenced by their "sneaking admiration" for Mossadegh.[155] Because of Whitehall's frustration with what it perceived to be a wholly unrealistic attitude on the part of the Americans, Labour Foreign Secretary Herbert Morrison suggested to McGhee that British officials knew better how to handle Iran based on their "long experience of the Middle East and of the difficulties of dealing with the various countries in the area."[156]

These differing views of Iranian nationalism had two important consequences, the first of which was that the United States was able to maintain Iranian goodwill, thereby enabling US officials to play the role of honest broker between Britain and Iran. Loy Henderson, Henry Grady's successor as the American Ambassador in Tehran, asserted that if the United States were to become as "unpopular" as Britain in Iran, then the West might lose "its last chance of keeping Persia out of the communist camp."[157] The Truman Administration placed great weight on its role as neutral arbiter because it felt the oil crisis had to be resolved peaceably. US policy-makers thought that any hostile action by the British could lead to a Soviet invasion of the Middle East and possibly a global war

---

[151] British Delegation to the Foreign Office, October 12, 1951, NA, T 236/4442.
[152] No. 1755 from Strang to Washington, April 28, 1951, NA, FO 371/91528.
[153] Jackson's notes from his visit to the United States, November 2, 1949, BP 16987.
[154] Shepherd to Furlonge, May 14, 1951, NA, FO 371/91535.
[155] Furlonge to Stevens, January 24, 1957, NA, FO 371/127087.
[156] Quoted in McGhee, *Envoy to the Middle World*, 331.
[157] Middleton to Bowker, September 1, 1952, NA, FO 371/98697.

for which the United States and the West were militarily unprepared in 1951.[158] But US "neutrality" on the oil issue greatly upset British officials because Iran interpreted such neutrality as "disapproval" of Whitehall's policies.[159] The impression of US disapproval, the British believed, only fed Iranian obstinacy. Ernest Bevin wrote to Dean Acheson: "I must tell you that one of our main difficulties in dealing with this intractable problem has arisen from a belief persistently held by many Persians that there is a difference of opinion between the Americans and the British over the oil question."[160]

The second consequence of the divergence in the British and American views on Iranian nationalism was that by October 1951, when Muhammad Mossadegh appeared before the United Nations to plead Iran's case to the world, the US government thought that Britain would have to do more than simply "pay lip service" or "make a bow" to nationalization, as it had advocated for most of 1951.[161] In fact, American officials reached the conclusion that "no arrangement" was possible that would permit the return of AIOC to Iran "in any form" or that would allow another British firm to operate there. They were "convinced" that neither Mossadegh's government nor "any other" could "yield on this point." Consequently, the United States conceived a plan with the Iranian prime minister that had these features: (1) the sale of the Abadan refinery to a non-British, "preferably Dutch," foreign oil company; (2) NIOC control over "all aspects of production of crude oil"; (3) the elimination of all claims and counterclaims by both Britain and Iran; (4) AIOC purchase of a "major portion" of Iranian oil at prices that the company considered "financially attractive"; and (5) a financial arrangement between the AIOC, the new refinery owner, and the NIOC that would preserve the fifty–fifty profit-sharing principle, thereby protecting "existing arrangements in other oil producing countries."[162]

Mostly for financial reasons, Whitehall found the American proposal to be, on the whole, "quite unacceptable."[163] At a meeting at the Foreign Office, British officials argued that the scheme would "not satisfy" the

158 Gavin, "Politics, Power, and US Policy in Iran, 1950–1953," 62–74.
159 "Persia – Instructions to Negotiators," Persian Oil Working Party Papers, undated (probably late May/early June), BP 100738.
160 No. 2898 from Bevin to Acheson, NA, FO 371/91555.
161 For example, see "Anglo/US Talks on Persia in Washington (III)," April 13, 1951, BP 100557 and No. 1079 from Franks to the Foreign Office, April 10, 1951, NA, FO 371/91470.
162 Webb to the US Embassy in Britain, October 30, 1951, *FRUS, 1952–1954, Vol. X,* 249–255.
163 Minutes of a meeting held in the Secretary of State's room at the Foreign Office, November 1, 1951, NA, FO 371/91608.

nation's balance-of-payments requirements. In addition, they believed that the "effect on British credit and overseas interests would be very bad," and, given that the country's "balance of payments situation was extremely serious," it "could not afford to bear additional burdens."[164] Because Britain was in the midst of a major financial crisis, new Conservative Chancellor of the Exchequer R. A. Butler said that Whitehall would have to tell US officials that Britain's "economic viability was at stake," something that the United States government should have considered "more important" than either Iran's economic independence or its economic welfare.[165] Britain had used these arguments over the previous two years to defend its interests in Iran, so they must have sounded familiar to Washington. The United States had reached an impasse, unable to bridge the British and Iranian positions after months of effort.

US officials grew concerned about Britain's weakening position in the Middle East and the consequences for Western interests in the region. In a draft study written at the end of 1951, the National Security Council concluded that the United States needed to review and restate its policy in the Middle East because of Britain's "declining ability" to "maintain and defend" those interests. The study's authors believed that the "decline of British capabilities" was "in important measure a reflection of the nationalist aspirations of the Middle Eastern states – accompanied and intensified by the desire to end what they regard as unjust exploitation."[166] In May 1952, the Department of State's Policy Planning Staff described the "general picture" in the Middle East as one of "continuing weakness." While acknowledging Britain's primary responsibility for the region's security, members of the staff feared that the nation's capabilities were "wholly inadequate to defend the Middle East against Soviet aggression." Thus, the United States would have to "provide more assistance and bring its influence to bear" to stabilize the region.[167] In a phone conversation with Harry Truman three months later, Henry Byroade, who succeeded George McGhee as the Assistant Secretary of State for Near Eastern, South Asian, and African Affairs, expressed the bigger fear that Britain's "general economic and financial situation," coupled with its "deteriorating political position" in the Middle East, would lead to a "general withdrawal" from the area. Such an outcome, he assessed, would leave the United States with "some very fundamental decisions" as to how to fill the vacuum in order to

---

[164] Ibid.   [165] Ibid.

[166] "Draft Study by the National Security Council," December 27, 1951, *FRUS, 1951, Vol. V*, 257–264.

[167] "Memorandum Prepared by the Policy Planning Staff," May 21, 1952, *FRUS, 1952–1954, Vol. IX*, 232–233.

protect US interests there. At the end of the conversation, Byroade referred to Iran, specifically, characterizing the situation as "extremely serious." Truman responded that, "if it proved impossible to get together with the British" on the issue, then the United States "would have to see what [it] could do unilaterally."[168] The US government never had to resort to such measures.

By late 1952, US disillusionment with Muhammad Mossadegh, the British realization that a communist coup in Iran was a legitimate possibility, and a dramatic increase in American military strength led to a convergence of US and British policies. In October 1951, Winston Churchill had brought his Conservative Party to power in Britain after a campaign in which he castigated the previous government for its weakness during the oil crisis. A Victorian in mind, body, and soul, the new prime minister seemed even less willing to bargain with Mossadegh than had his predecessor. Nonetheless, British and US officials came together to draft a proposal dealing with terms of arbitration for compensating the AIOC in January 1952. Mossadegh's rejection of this proposal and future ones caused Washington to lose all patience with the prime minister, about whom the Department of State was developing serious doubts.[169] Furthermore, Mossadegh's position within his own country weakened as he took extraordinary measures to consolidate his authority – after briefly resigning from office during a power struggle with the Shah in July. Mossadegh's growing number of opponents, both outside the National Front and within the party itself, criticized these moves and complained about his failure to bring an end to the nation's economic difficulties. The prime minister's eroding base of support led him to rely more and more upon the Tudeh Party, which had taken to the streets on his behalf during his week-long absence from power in July.[170] Churchill had seen enough to persuade him that Iran could, in fact, succumb to communism, as US officials had argued all along.[171] At the same time, by mid-1952, the massive arms buildup spurred by the recommendations of National Security Council Paper 68 (NSC-68) two years earlier put the United States in a position to take more risks in the Middle East. As a result, the Truman Administration pursued a more aggressive approach toward

---

[168] Memorandum of Conversation, August 8, 1952, *FRUS, 1952–1954, Vol. IX*, 262–263.
[169] Oliver Franks reported to the Foreign Office that the Department of State "continued to feel that Musaddiq's Government was most undesirable and they had strong doubts whether it was possible to negotiate with him. They also agreed with us that his régime was an ineffective barrier against Communist penetration, but they now feared that any change would probably be for the worse," January 21, 1952, NA, FO 371/98684.
[170] Heiss, *Empire and Nationhood*, ch. 6.
[171] Louis, "Musaddiq and the Dilemmas of British Imperialism," 242.

Mossadegh, feeling confident that it could handle the potential military consequences of such a policy.[172] The United States was no longer a neutral party in the dispute between Britain and Iran, a shift in mindset that culminated in the Anglo-American overthrow of Mossadegh and the installation of the Shah as the nation's ruler.

The Anglo-American plan to topple Muhammad Mossadegh had begun to be conceived during Truman's last months as president, but it was not executed until well into the Eisenhower Administration's first year in office.[173] Given that during the run-up to the 1952 presidential election the Eisenhower campaign criticized Truman's failure to "contain" communism and announced its intention to implement a foreign policy that would "roll it back" around the world, one might assume that Mossadegh's overthrow was the result of Eisenhower's vision of a more aggressive role for the United States in international affairs. Reading back the administration's future efforts to destabilize governments unfriendly to US interests might also lead to this conclusion. The documentary record reveals, though, that by the autumn of 1952, had any further attempts to negotiate a settlement with Mossadegh failed, the Truman Administration was prepared to use covert action or direct force to prevent a communist government from establishing itself in Iran.[174] Truman and his advisors simply left office before they got their chance to carry out the developing Anglo-American plan.

With little skill and much luck, the plan just barely succeeded in removing Mossadegh from office in the summer of 1953. After a major bungle in July triggered the Shah's flight from Iran and forced the Anglo-American choice for prime minister, the anti-communist, nationalist General Fazlullah Zahidi, to go underground, US-organized mobs flooded the streets in mid-August to demonstrate on behalf of the army-backed Shah. In no time, Mossadegh was arrested, Zahidi became prime minister, and the Shah returned to rule the country. All that was left to do was resume the flow of Iranian oil to the West. But, for British officials, matters were not quite so simple. They demanded that bringing Iranian oil back on line had to do as little damage to sterling as possible, a policy that led them to take positions that would continue to hamper

---

[172] Gavin, "Politics, Power, and US Policy in Iran," 74–76.

[173] There is no doubt that it was a joint effort. Wm. Roger Louis discusses the heavy British involvement at the planning stages in "Musaddiq and the Dilemmas of British Imperialism," 253–255, a point confirmed by a classified Central Intelligence Agency history of the coup by Dr. Donald N. Wilbur, entitled "Overthrow of Premier Mossadeq of Iran, November 1952–August 1953," CS Historical Paper No. 208, written in March 1954, published in October 1969, and reported by the *New York Times* on April 16, 2000.

[174] Gavin, "Politics, Power, and US Policy in Iran," 79–80.

Anglo-American relations as the two countries tried to restart the Iranian oil industry with a consortium of multinational oil firms.

2.5   The Consortium Agreement, sterling, and British policy, 1953–1954

Two different considerations inspired the idea of a consortium of several oil companies from several different countries producing and marketing Iranian oil: first, that Iran, even without Mossadegh as prime minister, would never again allow the AIOC or any other British company to assume a dominant position in the Iranian petroleum industry; and second, that multinational participation in Iranian oil represented good, common-sense, risk management. The United States had argued for a much-reduced role for the AIOC in Iran since the end of 1951, which the British had refused to accept. Two years later, Whitehall and the company board were forced to acknowledge that there was "no practical probability that [the AIOC would] be able to get back 100% into Persia."[175] The idea of having other firms participate in Iranian oil to distribute risk was not new either. As early as 1945, US officials and oil company executives believed that, because the Soviet Union posed a threat to the Middle East and Iran, Britain and the AIOC should consider American involvement in the Iranian petroleum industry. They argued that the AIOC's "concessionary security" would be "substantially increased by the establishment of sound American interest in the country," a point that Basil Jackson thought "reasonable" if the Soviet threat were indeed real.[176] It was no doubt dangerous for Britain to have had so many of its eggs in one basket, as one Treasury official recognized when he commented on the country's "dangerous dependence" on Iranian oil.[177] Consequently, the "main objective" of the consortium plan, according to Royal Dutch-Shell director Sir Francis Hopwood, was "to protect the world oil industry against the serious consequences" of Iranian oil falling into "undesirable hands."[178]

While Whitehall accepted the idea of a consortium, it wanted to ensure that any new arrangement would do no further harm to Britain's balance of payments, given the damage already perpetrated by the crisis itself. The Treasury's William Armstrong told a group of American oil representatives that these concerns "remained a basic principle of

175 Foreign Office Minute by Belgrave, December 22, 1953, NA, FO 371/110046.
176 No. 172 from Jackson to Fraser, January 25, 1945, BP 70986.
177 Working Party on the Oil Expansion Programme, Meeting on October 24, 1950, GEN.295/67th, NA, T 236/2885.
178 Hopwood to Fraser, March 2, 1954, NA, FO 371/110048.

policy."[179] After the AIOC had been evicted from Abadan in October 1951, the Ministry of Fuel and Power considered a consortium arrangement in which the firm would be a 60 percent shareholder in a crude-producing company and an 80 percent shareholder in a refining company. The two firms would be registered in Britain and purchase oil from Iran in sterling, splitting the profits equally with the Iranian government, the upshot of which would be that Britain would "suffer very little loss" to its balance of payments.[180] But the two points that Whitehall deemed virtually non-negotiable were the currency with which the consortium paid Iran for its oil and the nationality of the operating (or Group Services) companies, both of which would affect the sterling area's balance of payments.

Whitehall wanted the consortium to pay for Iranian petroleum in sterling for practical reasons and for the advantages that would accrue to the Empire-Commonwealth.[181] Iranian oil, like almost all Middle Eastern oil, was sold in the Eastern Hemisphere either to sterling area members or to non-dollar, non-sterling countries that had easier access to pounds. Therefore, purchasing oil from Iran in dollars or anything else would represent a drain on the sterling area's balance of payments because Britain would have to convert pounds into foreign exchange. Britain also wanted the consortium to conduct its business in sterling because the currency would benefit from the increase in value that would come with its widespread use.[182] In 1947, the Foreign Office wrote to its representatives stationed around the globe: "We must maintain confidence in our currency and make sure that as many countries as possible are willing to take sterling from other countries as well as from the sterling area in payment for their current exports: this is necessary if we are to keep our own economy running, and to avoid a heavy blow to world trade."[183] British officials also argued that they could not "justify to other oil-producing countries in the sterling area any arrangement under which Persia received more favourable treatment than they, only a

---

[179] Meeting at the Treasury, February 24, 1954, NA, T 236/3900.

[180] Note by the Ministry of Fuel and Power for the Persian Oil Working Party, POWP (51) 24–30, October 30, 1951, NA, T 236/2827.

[181] In *Oil, Power and Principle*, Mostafa Elm argues that Britain insisted that the consortium pay Iran in sterling "to compel Iran to import items from the sterling area even when such items were not competitively priced," 323. The documentation presented here demonstrates that sterling recycling explains only part of why Britain insisted on payment in pounds.

[182] In 1951, the Treasury wrote that the AIOC "must deal in sterling to help preserve sterling's position in international trade," Memorandum for "Lord Privy Seal's Mission to Persia," undated (most likely July), NA, T 236/4437.

[183] Telegram No. 54, August 16, 1947, BE/OV44/16.

fraction of whose oil [could] be sold for dollars."[184] Iran's use of sterling had also historically provided a good outlet for sterling area exports, a boon for the pound and the Empire-Commonwealth. For products that it could not buy in the sterling area, though, Iran needed dollars, which Britain had once provided under the Memorandum of Understanding signed during the war but suspended during the oil crisis. For the sake of the balance of payments, it wanted to avoid signing a similar accord under a new oil settlement, but rather agree to one that was not nearly as generous.

Whitehall was concerned with dollar expenditure in Iran, both by the country itself and by the US companies that would operate as part of the consortium.[185] Consequently, it sought to establish financial relationships with the Iranian government and the consortium's American firms that would favor sterling. British officials wanted a new currency deal with Iran that allowed the country to convert only 40 percent of its sterling into dollars and gold and to purchase in dollars only products that were unavailable in the sterling area. They also raised the possibility of not permitting Iran to convert sterling to pay down dollar debts.[186] The Treasury's William Armstrong explained to the US Treasury representative in London, "we [have] to proceed at present on the basis that sterling was not yet convertible and that we could not tell when convertibility would come."[187] Plus, Whitehall felt that Iran could not receive better foreign exchange terms than "either of the other great oil producing Middle Eastern countries," Iraq and Kuwait, both of which were members of the sterling area.[188]

With the US firms, Whitehall revisited the issues raised during the controversy over sterling and dollar oil at the end of the 1940s. Updating and restarting the Abadan refinery was going to cost dollars since American materials and engineering firms would have to be used. For this reason, and because the taxpaying, Iranian subsidiaries of the US firms would be registered in the United States, the American oil coming out of Iran would have a higher dollar content than other Middle Eastern

[184] No. 2925 from the Foreign Office to Washington and Tehran, June 23, 1954, NA, T 236/4701.

[185] The consortium's American members included Standard Oil of New Jersey, Standard Oil of New York, Standard Oil of California, Gulf, and Texaco. Royal Dutch-Shell and the Compagnie Française des Petroles (CFP) also participated.

[186] No. 281 from Makins to the Foreign Office, undated (most likely mid-June 1954), NA, T 236/4700.

[187] Armstrong's note for the record, April 21, 1954, NA, T 236/4699.

[188] "Persia: Currency Arrangements," discussing proposals set out in OME (54) 9, March 9, 1954, NA, T 236/4699.

oil, according to Armstrong.[189] In addition, the shift in production from countries such as Iraq, Kuwait, and Saudi Arabia back to Iran would also cost the sterling area dollars, the greatest problem being the transfer of currency from sterling area countries, Iraq and Kuwait, to Iran.[190] If Britain were going to allow the US companies to sell Iranian petroleum in the sterling area – and to sell it for sterling to third countries – officials at Whitehall felt that something had to be done to compensate for these dollar costs.

Treasury officials and representatives of the US companies conducted negotiations to resolve these issues. For all intents and purposes, they constituted a sequel to the discussions on sterling and dollar oil discussed in chapter 1. The Treasury made various demands of the companies, the most controversial of which concerned where the firms would obtain the sterling to pay the cost of their operations in Iran. Rather than allow the US companies to use sterling earned from sales of Iranian oil to pay these costs, Treasury officials wanted them to obtain sterling from Britain in exchange for dollars.[191] US representatives threatened to walk out before they met what they considered to be such an unreasonable demand.[192] They were already reluctant to become involved in Iranian oil, as they had been throughout the crisis, because of fears of "trespassing" on the "preserves" of other companies, worries about what might happen to their own concessions, and anxieties about not having the markets to absorb so much extra petroleum in a period of oil glut. They had only agreed to participate in the consortium because the US government encouraged them to do so in the belief that American involvement would help achieve a settlement.[193] Britain backed down, allowing the firms not only to use sterling revenues to maintain their operations in Iran but also to convert sterling earned in sales outside the Empire-Commonwealth into dollars.[194]

The British government's desire to maintain strict control over the flow of currency in and out of the sterling area meant that it would work

[189] "Persian Oil Settlement: US Companies' Currency Problems," Note of a meeting held in the Treasury, March 25, 1954, NA, T 236/3901.
[190] "Persian Oil Settlement: Effect on the Balance of Payments," Appendix I, "Factors affecting Balance of Payments Result," March 6, 1954, NA, T 236/3900; Raeburn to Armstrong, June 19, 1954, NA, T 236/3902.
[191] "Persian Oil Settlement: US Companies' Currency Problems," Note of a meeting held in the Treasury, March 25, 1954, NA, T 236/3901.
[192] Catherine R. Schenk discusses these issues in "Exchange Controls and Multinational Enterprise."
[193] No. 474 from Makins to the Foreign Office, March 22, 1954, FO371/110049; Makins's record of conversation with Eugene Black, December 13, 1951, FO371/91617; Foreign Office Minute by Dixon, May 15, 1953, NA, FO 371/104616.
[194] Schenk, "Exchange Controls and Multinational Enterprise," 31–32.

assiduously to have the consortium's operating companies registered in the United Kingdom. The Foreign Office explained that Iran's ability to exchange sterling for dollars – and the ability of the American companies to accept pounds for the sale of Iranian oil in the sterling area and to third countries – were the two main concerns: "If we are to permit use of sterling in this way we feel we must at least have control of foreign currency and especially dollar expenditure of Group Services companies. This is the purpose of making companies British. We do not see how this purpose could be secured in any other way ... certainly at this stage we do not regard the position as expendable."[195] Whitehall also did not want the companies registered in Iran for fear of rendering them vulnerable to Iranian law and Iranian exchange and trade controls, neither of which might consider the best interests of the companies or of sterling.[196]

Issues other than exchange control also motivated Whitehall's demand that the operating companies be registered in Britain. The Treasury's A. K. Potter believed that "no other country outside the USA would be in as good a position as the UK to afford the company diplomatic support in a dispute with Persia." Registering the companies in the United States to secure future American diplomatic support was out of the question, though, because of the currency issues involved. Potter argued that another benefit of making the firms British was that it would "predispose" them to "order British goods and employ British nationals as much as possible."[197] Furthermore, a firm registered in the United Kingdom would be subject to British taxation, providing a boost to the balance of payments. And finally, there was the issue of prestige. The Foreign Office's L. A. C. Fry wrote: "The oil industry in Persia was begun and developed to a very high point of efficiency by a British Company ... the fact remains that the House and British public opinion at large certainly expect that, when the industry is started again, the British should have an unmistakable part in it."[198]

As British officials anticipated, Iranian representatives to the consortium negotiations were not pleased with the idea of either receiving sterling for Iran's oil or having the operating companies registered in the United Kingdom.[199] Dr. Ali Amini, the Iranian finance minister and the

[195] No. 378 from the Foreign Office to Stevens, April 20, 1954, NA, FO 371/110061.
[196] No. 366 from Stevens to the Foreign Office, April 23, 1954, NA, FO 371/110061.
[197] Potter to Armstrong, December 17, 1953, NA, T 236/3900.
[198] Foreign Office Minute, May 11, 1954, NA, FO 371/110062.
[199] In "Notes on Possible Oil Settlement," the section on "Payments in Sterling" opens, "The Persians will strongly resist any arrangement that appears to leave them dependent on the will of London for their supplies of dollars and other currencies," March 6, 1954, BP 79661.

chairman of the Iranian delegation to the talks, raised his concerns with Jersey Standard's Orville Harden, a member of the consortium's negotiating team. Regarding the currency question, the US oilman remarked that in the case of the group's British interests, "there could be no question" about payment for Iranian oil in sterling. As for the US companies, he explained that, because the "outlet for dollar oil in the Eastern Hemisphere was very limited," they had no choice but to sell Iranian petroleum for sterling to maintain the product's competitiveness. Plus, the British government would certainly not wreak havoc on the sterling area's balance of payments by converting the sterling that the American companies earned on Iranian oil into dollars, just so that Iran could receive dollars for its petroleum.[200]

The currency issue was settled much more easily than that of the nationality of the operating companies. Abdullah Entezam, Iran's foreign minister, argued that the country would resist "any form of foreign domicile," especially British, and that "belligerents" would attack a British-registered consortium as a "reconstitution of the Anglo-Iranian Oil Company in a new guise," possibly undermining the whole settlement."[201] At the consortium negotiations, Harden explained that, to keep dollar expenditure "within proper limits," Whitehall insisted that the Group Services companies be registered in Britain. Another member of the Iranian delegation wondered why the official home of the companies could not be in Iran or anywhere else for that matter if "satisfactory currency arrangements were worked out." According to Royal Dutch-Shell's John Louden, another member of the consortium negotiating team, Whitehall felt that such an arrangement would not provide "the necessary jurisdiction" to manage the dollar drain.[202] Harden added that the US companies had agreed to support the British position on this issue in order to secure the conversion facilities and oil outlets that the British government provided to enable the American firms to sell Iranian oil in the sterling area and to third countries.[203] In the end, he told Ali Amini that he would have to take the matter up with the British ambassador.

US Treasury Secretary George Humphrey was livid about what he thought were the unreasonable limitations that the British government was putting on Iran's ability to convert sterling to dollars. The Foreign Office's Roger Makins recounted the pointed remarks that Humphrey made to him in a conversation at the end of June 1954:

[200] "Notes of a Second Meeting Held on 17 April, 1954 at the White Palace," BP 94788.
[201] No. 398 from Stevens to the Foreign Office, April 27, 1954, NA, FO 371/110061.
[202] "Notes of Fourth Meeting Held on 22nd April, 1954," BP 94788.
[203] "Notes of Seventh Meeting Held on 28th April, 1954" and "Notes of Eighth Meeting Held on 2 May, 1954," BP 94788.

The situation was that the Anglo-Iranian Oil Company had lost their concession in Persia and had no hope at all of getting it back... If after all that the United States Government and the United States oil companies had done to save the situation in Persia, we were to try to insist on controlling Persia's commercial policy, there would be an outcry in Congress which would destroy all chances of success in the wider plans for international economic cooperation which we had in mind. He thought that this attempt to dictate to the Persians where they should buy was just as out of date and unacceptable to the Persians as the idea that any British company could resume control of oil operations in Persia.[204]

Two weeks later, Humphrey continued his critique. According to Makins, he said:

if the US were not allowed to trade with Persia on even terms after all they had done to bring about an oil settlement he would regard it as "unfair" and would consider that we were exacting "our pound of flesh"... he wanted to assure me that there would be a lingering feeling of resentment and that if we squeezed the last ounce out of them on this occasion they would remember it and be equally hard traders when the next occasion came along... while they might have to lump it they would not like it and would remember it for next time.[205]

To justify the restrictions, Makins informed Humphrey that, as a result of the crisis in Iran, Britain had spent $500 million on American oil and the AIOC had lost valuable markets to competitors. He also explained that restarting the flow of Iranian oil would cost the sterling area reserves a net of $40 million in the first year and $55 million by the third year of the new contract. But Humphrey was "incredulous," unable to see, given the large amount of money that the US companies would pay to the AIOC, how the sterling area would sustain that kind of dollar loss.[206]

In interdepartmental memos, British Treasury officials accused Humphrey of simply not understanding the issues involved.[207] Responding to criticisms of Britain's sterling convertibility policy on Iran, members of the Foreign Office told US representatives that Iranians "themselves had more than once described the arrangements as fair and just."[208] The Treasury's E. W. Playfair wrote that American policymakers were "out to pick on" Britain "wherever" they could, and he described the attitude across the Atlantic as a "normal reflection of the Washington mood," calling it a "twang on the harp of colonialism."[209]

---

[204] No. 291 from Makins to the Foreign Office on June 28, 1954, NA, T 236/4701.
[205] No. 1462 from Makins to the Foreign Office, July 13, 1954, NA, T 236/4701.
[206] No. 291 from Makins to the Foreign Office, June 28, 1954, NA, T 236/4701 and Makins to Humphrey, July 3, 1954, NA, FO 371/110009.
[207] Playfair to Petch, July 13, 1954 and Playfair to Petch, July 14, both T 236/4701.
[208] No. 2907 from the Foreign Office to Washington, June 22, 1954, NA, FO 371/110009.
[209] Playfair to Rowan, June 23, 1954, NA, FO 371/110009.

British officials were sensitive to the fact that members of the US government viewed their foreign economic policies as regressive, whereas they considered them to be a legitimate defense of the sterling area's economic interests. It was a clash driven by modern-day economic interests, but also influenced by deeply rooted perceptions of one another. George Humphrey, who was a key player during the Suez crisis of 1956, did, in fact, exact his revenge "when the next occasion came along."

US officials were no less angry about the demands that the Anglo-Iranian Oil Company made in terms of its percentage share of the consortium and the compensation that Iran and the other consortium members owed the firm for giving up its former concession. Fraser wanted the AIOC's stake in the new corporation to be no less than 50 percent, and he wanted Iran to give the company 110 million tons of free oil, valued at $1,460 million, over a period of twenty years. In addition, Fraser thought that the consortium members should pay the AIOC the equivalent of $1,270 million to participate in Iranian oil. Commenting on these figures, US Secretary of State John Foster Dulles remarked that Anglo-American efforts to resolve matters in Iran "appeared to be obstructed by a totally unrealistic attitude on the part of the AIOC." He said that Fraser's proposals "would be completely unacceptable to any Persian Government," as they already were to the American oil companies that had agreed to join the consortium.[210] Frustrated and upset, Dulles told British officials that "a turning point had been reached, not only in the oil dispute, but in the policy of Anglo-American solidarity in Middle Eastern affairs," and that if they could not come to an agreement over Iran, then he thought that the United States would have to take its "own line" in the region "more often" and rely on its "own judgment in dealing with Middle Eastern countries and problems."[211] Roger Makins was greatly concerned about the feeling in Washington at this point and wrote to the Foreign Office: "I can only say that if negotiations do break down there will be no sympathy or support in any American heart for what will universally be regarded as the obstinacy and unreasonableness of the AIOC, and that nobody here believes that Her Majesty's Government could not bring their influence to bear on the company."[212] Recognizing that the AIOC board was once again jeopardizing the British national interest because of its intransigence over Iran, Whitehall intervened to handle the question of compensation on behalf of the company.[213] The

[210] No. 348 from Washington to London, March 17, 1954, BP 79661.
[211] No. 349 from Washington to London, March 17, 1954, BP 79661.
[212] No. 449 from Makins to the Foreign Office, March 17, 1954, NA, PREM 11/726.
[213] No. 1152 from the Foreign Office to Washington, March 25, 1954, NA, PREM 11/726.

result was that a settlement between the consortium and Iran was finally reached at the end of the summer.

The oil crisis concluded in October 1954, when the Majlis and the Iranian Senate ratified the consortium agreement. The new accord created a holding company, Iranian Oil Participants Ltd (IOP), which would be registered and headquartered in Britain. Under the IOP were two operating companies that would run the oil industry in the southern part of the country where the AIOC formerly had its concession. The operating companies, with two Iranian directors on both boards, would manage the oil fields and the Abadan refinery for the National Iranian Oil Company, the owner of the assets. While the two companies were incorporated in the Netherlands, they were registered and headquartered in Iran. Iranian Oil Services Ltd, which provided supplies, engineering services, and non-Iranian staff for the operating companies, represented the third arm of the consortium and was incorporated in Britain and had its headquarters in London. The AIOC, renamed British Petroleum later that year, would have a 40 percent stake in the consortium, with Shell receiving 14 percent, the five American firms 8 percent each, and the Compagnie Française des Petroles 6 percent. Regarding compensation, Iran would pay the AIOC £25 million ($70 million) in ten equal installments, and the consortium members would give the firm an initial payment of £32.4 million ($90.7 million) over the first year and then an amount of crude oil equivalent to £182 million ($510 million). Iran and the consortium would split the profits on Iranian oil fifty–fifty.[214] All transactions would be settled in sterling and Britain would be able to maintain exchange control through the IOP and reap the balance-of-payments benefits that came with having Iranian Oil Services Ltd registered in the United Kingdom.[215] Whitehall, moreover, maintained its right to convert only 40 percent of sterling held by Iran into dollars.

Despite forfeiting 60 percent of its interest in Iranian petroleum, the AIOC emerged from the oil crisis in good shape. The firm's ability to develop other sources of crude, especially in Kuwait, meant that regaining 100 percent of what it had lost in Iran would have overloaded the company with more supply than its markets could absorb, a problem that it had already been trying to resolve.[216] Also, the firm would no longer have to depend so heavily on a single processing plant for its products, diversifying a refinery-building program that had begun in the late 1940s and continued with its project in Aden. In addition, the terms that the

---

[214] Bamberg, *The History of the British Petroleum Company, Volume II*, 507–509.
[215] No. 845 from the Foreign Office to Tehran, August 3, 1954, NA, FO 371/110070.
[216] Bamberg, *History of the British Petroleum Company, Volume II*, 510–511.

AIOC and the other consortium partners secured in their new agreement with Iran left the British company better off than if Muhammad Mossadegh had accepted one of the proposals that the group offered in the desperate months of early 1953. Had Iran settled with the consortium a year earlier, its partners would have been forced to serve merely as the country's purchasing and distributing agents rather than managing the country's oil industry as it did in the post-Mossadegh era.[217] Finally, the AIOC escaped from the crisis without having to split the profits on its worldwide operations, a much greater financial sacrifice than the 60 percent share of Iranian oil that it relinquished in 1954.

Ultimately, the Iranian oil crisis did not cause the economic imbroglio in Britain that many officials at Whitehall feared, either during the crisis itself or afterwards. In fact, at the end of 1952, the British government had to reduce its projected annual dollar-loss estimates on oil from $350 million in 1951 to $120 million for 1953. According to one economic historian, Britain's overall gold and dollar reserves rose "practically without interruption" from September 1952 to June 1954.[218] The improvement in the dollar balance on petroleum was the result not only of Britain's ability to obtain sufficient amounts of crude from sterling area oil producers Iraq and Kuwait, but also of the country's improved refining capacity, embodied mostly by the AIOC's new facility in Kent.[219] That said, Britain's invisible earnings fell from £330 million to £260 million in 1953–1954, to a large degree because of "heavy," one-time payments that the AIOC had to make to Kuwait and Iraq in accordance with new concession agreements precipitated by the renegotiations in Iran and Saudi Arabia.[220]

While one might expect that the increase in annual disbursements to Middle Eastern oil producers would result in an interminable detriment to the sterling area's balance of payments, the Treasury's A. H. M. Mitchell argued that Whitehall should anticipate the sterling area's "net oil receipts to start rising again" once the "heavy initial cost" of restarting the Iranian oil industry was met and "the arrears of increases in tax payments and oil royalties to the Middle East" had been "cleared off."[221] On the other hand, Peter Vinter at the Treasury wrote that it was "far from easy to obtain estimates of the impact on the balance of payments of the settlement with Persia and of the revenue negotiations which are still

[217] Ibid.   [218] Scott, "The Balance of Payments Crises," 218.
[219] Minute by Ramsbotham, December 29, 1952, and Potter to Norris, December 19, 1952, both NA, FO 371/99168.
[220] Kahn to France and Gilbert, October 14, 1955, NA, T 234/266.
[221] Mitchell to Kahn and Rickett, August 16, 1955, NA, T 236/4602.

proceeding, or are about to begin, with Iraq and Kuwait."[222] Such uncertainty meant that the British government would have to remain vigilant about its access to Middle Eastern oil at prices that it deemed reasonable, especially if the "over-riding duty which faced the Government," according to R. A. Butler, "was the restoration of a long-term balance in payments between the sterling area and the rest of the world."[223]

Donald Fergusson once feared that, if oil-producing countries ever thought that the British government was diverting companies, such as the AIOC, from the dual objective of satisfying the welfare of their firms and the welfare of their oil-producing hosts "in the interest of the British Exchequer or British balance of payments or other British economic policies which ran contrary to their own interests there would be trouble."[224] Indeed, trouble occurred in Iran, in part, because policymakers at Whitehall believed that Britain's and Iran's economic interests were not complementary. For them, the process of renegotiating the 1933 concession contract, or its successor, the Supplemental Agreement, was a zero-sum game between Britain and Iran in which the stability of sterling was at stake. A paper by Standard Oil of New Jersey on the lessons of the AIOC's experience in Iran includes a section that accuses the company of being "too much influenced by the British tradition of Colonial government" and asserts that the "London management certainly did not regard the Persian Government as its 'operating partner.'"[225] Indeed, many at Whitehall, along with the AIOC's leadership, did not view Iran as a legitimate partner when it came to the exploitation of that country's oil. The Treasury's Allen Christelow wrote:

In a world where primary resources become ever scarcer and ever more important we cannot continue to agree that economic development of the rest of the world may rightly be handicapped or frustrated because a primitive people who are admitted sovereign power over a given resource choose to limit or forbid or mismanage development of that resource. The United Kingdom, given its own lack of primary resources, must inevitably be one of the first countries called upon for the unpopular task of challenging any such thesis. We therefore need to move from a stage where stigmatization as imperialism of such measures as we take for the development of scarce real resources is not allowed to pass unchallenged but where our moves are put in their proper light as measures necessary for

222 "Balance of Payments Prospects in 1955," November 9, 1954, NA, T 229/826.
223 Cabinet Conclusions, CM 57 (52), May 29, 1952, NA, CAB 128/25.
224 Fergusson's commentary on Bridges's "Note for Record," February 8, 1949, NA, T 236/4748.
225 Ramsbotham's comments on "Some Observations on the Anglo-Iranian Experience: Indicated Policies to Lessen Possibility of Repetition," March 13, 1952, NA, FO 371/98709.

the allocation of the resources of the world in accordance with the needs of the maximization of real income for the world.[226]

At a time when strengthening the pound was a primary goal of Britain's external economic policy, Whitehall would not allow nations that produced sterling oil, or controlled its transportation from East to West, to undermine that goal. It also refused to be labeled "imperialist" for doing so.

[226] "The Persian Oil Negotiations," April 25, 1951, NA, T 236/4427.

3 The Suez crisis: a sterling rescue operation gone wrong

> ... oil was vital to our life ... if faced by the alternative of strangulation or war we should have to choose the latter. Egypt would be playing a very dangerous game if ever she tried to interfere with our supplies of oil.
>
> Ivone Kirkpatrick, Permanent Under-Secretary of State, British Foreign Office[1]

> If we could achieve a quick and satisfactory settlement of [the Suez Canal] issue, confidence in sterling would be restored; but, if a settlement was long delayed, the cost and the uncertainty would undermine our financial position.
>
> Harold Macmillan, Chancellor of the Exchequer[2]

The Suez Canal, which connects the Red Sea with the Mediterranean, was one of Britain's two most important links to sterling oil. While one-third of the oil that traveled to Western Europe from the Middle East came from pipeline outlets on the shores of Syria and Lebanon, two-thirds came through the Egyptian waterway.[3] Designed by European engineers, financed by European capital, and built on the backs of Egyptian laborers, the Suez Canal opened to traffic in 1869. Less than a decade later, Britain and France appropriated the canal's operating company after the Egyptian Khedive, with no small encouragement from European lenders, plunged the nation into bankruptcy.[4] Even before the invention of the internal combustion engine or the discovery of oil in the Persian Gulf region, the canal was a vital part of facilitating both British trade with Africa, Asia, and the Middle East and the defense of the empire. It was so important to British interests that when a

---

[1] No. 1437 from the Foreign Office to Cairo, regarding a meeting between I. Kirkpatrick and the Egyptian Ambassador to the United Kingdom, May 25, 1956, NA, FO 371/118863.

[2] Cabinet Conclusions, CM 64 (56), September 12, 1956, NA, CAB 128/30.

[3] The Middle East produced 180 million tons of oil a year, of which 118 million traveled west of Suez: 75 million through the canal and 43 million through pipelines. See "Financial Consequences to the United Kingdom of the Oil Operation: Case for Dollar Aid," Rickett to Bridges and Petch, September 19, 1956, NA, T 236/4842.

[4] Britain owned 44 percent of the shares in the Suez Canal Company.

proto-nationalist revolt occurred in Egypt in 1882, Britain invaded the country in part to protect the canal's smooth operation.

The invasion turned into a full-fledged British occupation that, within little more than ten years, an Egyptian nationalist movement challenged until the last vestiges of British authority were finally removed from Egypt. After gaining ground in the first decade of the twentieth century, Egyptian nationalists succumbed to British political suppression during World War I but resurfaced in the wake of the armistice to demand Egyptian independence. The country's dominant political party, the Wafd, which competed with the monarchy for control of the Egyptian government, negotiated intermittently with London during the interwar period to end British rule. In 1936, the two sides finally signed a treaty that, in return for granting Egypt its independence, permitted Britain to keep its forces in the Suez Canal zone until 1956. But in a moment of extreme vulnerability during World War II's North African campaign, the British government helped to sabotage its future position in Egypt by surrounding the royal palace with tanks, demanding that the king, Farouk, either appoint an Anglo-friendly cabinet to head the government or abdicate the throne. To save himself, the king complied with the British ultimatum, a humiliation that, in part, precipitated the monarchy's eviction from Egypt by revolutionary army officers in 1952.

One of the key orchestrators of that revolution, Colonel Gamal Abdel Nasser – who, like his co-conspirators, was also motivated by the ignominious defeat of the Egyptian military during the first Arab-Israeli war – ascended to the country's leadership in 1954. That year, after a long and arduous negotiation process, Egypt and Britain signed a treaty that mandated the removal of British forces from the Suez Canal zone within twenty months. In exchange, Britain won the right to reoccupy the waterway if any outside power attacked any member of the Arab League or Turkey.[5] While British military planners had concluded that the advent of the hydrogen bomb rendered the Suez base obsolete anyway, because of the critical role that the installation played in the strategic framework of the British empire, the decision to abandon it was freighted with significance no less than that of the decision to leave India seven years earlier.

During the period that Britain and Egypt struggled to reach the defense arrangement that led to the departure of British forces from Suez, the

---

[5] Organized in 1944, but not formally begun until March 1945, the Arab League was to some extent inspired by the British government's desire for the Arab states to develop political unity based on the economic integration that it helped them to achieve during World War II. No mission unified its members more than trying to prevent the establishment of a Jewish state in Palestine. The founding members of the League included Egypt, Transjordan, Iraq, Syria, Lebanon, Saudi Arabia, and Yemen.

Iranian oil crisis festered, worrying officials in London about the impact of events in one country on the other. They recognized that nationalistic Iranians and Egyptians viewed each other as brothers in arms, resisting a British imperialism manifest in British control over both the Abadan refinery and the Suez Canal. Iranian success in nationalizing its oil industry, the Foreign Office feared, would "encourage nationalistic claims in other spheres," with the canal topping the list.[6] The Cabinet feared that the Anglo-Iranian Oil Company's eviction from Abadan Island would "embolden" Egypt to "take drastic action to end the military treaty and possibly to bring the Suez Canal under Egyptian control."[7]

The economic consequences for Britain would be disastrous if the Suez Canal and the pipelines from the Persian Gulf were closed to Middle Eastern oil. To gain access to it, Britain would have to send an insufficient number of tankers on the much longer – and more costly – water route around much of the perimeter of Africa. Furthermore, as happened during the Iranian oil crisis, the country would also have to spend valuable dollars to obtain additional petroleum from the Western Hemisphere. Even with these compensatory measures, Britain would still not be able obtain all of the oil that it needed, and petroleum rationing would have to begin. Disruption of the normal functioning of the Suez Canal was a nightmare scenario for Britain.

The British government confronted that possibility when Egyptian President Gamal Abdel Nasser nationalized the canal at the end of July 1956, ostensibly to pay for a major development project that, for political reasons, Britain and the United States no longer wanted to finance. International confidence in sterling was already low in mid-1956 as a result of fears about rising wages in the United Kingdom. The nationalization of the Suez Canal further eroded confidence in the pound as holders of the currency questioned Britain's future ability to trade through the canal, particularly in oil. Worsening sterling's fortunes was its return to de facto convertibility the previous year, which facilitated flight from the currency. Treasury and Bank officials, especially Chancellor of the Exchequer Harold Macmillan, worried that if the government did not take decisive action, the extreme pressure on the pound would force Britain to devalue. The upshot of a second devaluation in less than a decade, officials believed, would have been nothing less than the end of sterling's reserve role.

More importantly, policy-makers in London argued, if Nasser were allowed to succeed in keeping Egyptian control of the Suez Canal, his

---

[6] Foreign Office Minute by Bowker, April 6, 1951, NA, FO 371/91470.
[7] "Cabinet Conclusions," CM 60 (51), September 27, 1951, NA, CAB 128/20.

prestige and influence in the Middle East would rise to such a degree that he would be able to turn all of the oil-producing states against Britain, doing untold damage to sterling. The most senior officials, including Macmillan, Prime Minister Anthony Eden, and Foreign Secretary Selwyn Lloyd, repeated this argument so often that they built the level of anxiety about Nasser and the threat that he posed to Britain's oil interests in the Middle East to a fever pitch. In the end, it seemed that only a military invasion designed to install and preserve international control of the Suez Canal – and to humiliate the Egyptian president in the process – would suffice. But, as the British government learned in Iran, Britain's declining military and economic power meant that its range of options was constrained by what the United States would sanction; and just as in Iran, US officials rejected the use of force in Egypt.

Nonetheless, without informing the Eisenhower Administration of its plans, Britain invaded the Suez Canal zone in 1956 in collusion with France and Israel (both of which also had axes to grind with Nasser) to wrest control of the waterway from Egypt. The operation coincided with the last week of the US presidential election as well as the Hungarian Revolt, suppressed by the Soviet Union while events in the eastern Mediterranean distracted the United States and much of the rest of the world. It is impossible to overstate the anger in Washington over what Eisenhower considered a betrayal by the country's closest allies, not least because of concerns about the effect of the invasion on Western prestige in the Middle East and the possibility that it would provoke a larger war with the Soviet Union. The poor timing of the operation further infuriated the Eisenhower Administration, which conveyed its displeasure to Britain by denying it access to oil from the Western Hemisphere and by refusing to help rescue sterling until Britain withdrew its troops from the Suez Canal zone.

Why did the British government choose to invade Egypt when it knew that the operation was unlikely to succeed without US support and that the support was not likely to come? The British decision to employ force in Egypt was, in part, an act of desperation meant to save sterling when it appeared that the currency would sustain damage from which it would never recover, at least in terms of its widespread international use. Both Labour and Conservative governments had worked assiduously since the end of World War II to reestablish the strength and stability of the pound. In 1956, Anthony Eden's government was closer than ever to realizing the goal shared by Conservative, Treasury, and Bank officials of reintroducing sterling into the wider world. Nasser's nationalization of the Suez Canal threatened to prevent Britain, directly and indirectly, from obtaining Middle Eastern oil, access to which could make or break the nation's reserve position. In the autumn of 1956, another upsurge of nationalism in the Middle East had threatened not only sterling's international restoration, but its viability. The Conservative government – with Harold Macmillan as a prime mover – would not allow such an outcome. The irony, of course, is that, by using force in Egypt without securing US support first, Britain almost caused the very outcome that it sought to prevent.

3.1   De facto sterling convertibility, declining confidence in the pound, and the continuing importance of oil to the British balance of payments, 1954–1956

While the British government negotiated settlements in Iran and Egypt, the Bank of England and the Treasury considered new measures that would bring sterling closer to convertibility. Spurred by the Conservative victory in October 1951, a group of officials at both the Treasury and the Bank had already tried to make sterling convertible from late 1951 to mid-1953 through plans known as Operation "ROBOT" and "The Collective Approach."[8] But because of strong opposition both inside and outside Britain, neither of the proposals – both of which were based on flexible exchange rates within fixed boundaries – was implemented.[9] Nonetheless, in March 1954, Whitehall helped clear the path toward convertibility by unifying the bilateral and transferable account areas, meaning that almost all countries transacting in sterling outside the dollar and sterling areas were treated alike for exchange control purposes and, thus, eliminating the so-called "57 varieties" of sterling described in chapter 1.[10] The result was that three kinds of sterling emerged:

---

[8] Named for the plan's advocates, Leslie Rowan (RO), George Bolton (BO), Executive Director of the Bank of England, 1948–1957, and Otto Clarke (OT), an under-secretary in the Overseas Finance Division of the Treasury.

[9] For detailed descriptions of ROBOT and "The Collective Approach" see PEC (52) 18 "Steps Towards Convertibility," Memorandum by a Group of Officials on 30th August, 1952, Cabinet Committee on Preparations for Commonwealth Economic Conference, NA, T 236/3369. Also see Schenk, *Britain and the Sterling Area*, 114–124, and, most recently, Burnham, *Remaking the Postwar World Economy*. Burnham argues that ROBOT was not merely a "Bank plan to achieve sterling convertibility," but rather, "a bold, almost revolutionary, step in the external field which would have transformed the international political economy (through the abolition of the fixed rate system, the International Monetary Fund, and the European Payments Union)," 2. Going further, he later writes that "it was an attempt to breakout of postwar constraints and remake the world economy in an effort to check the relative economic and political decline of Britain," 5. Finally, he posits that, "at heart, Robot was about the future direction of British, and by implication, global capitalism," 17.

[10] John Fforde, *The Bank of England and Public Policy, 1941–1958* (Cambridge University Press, 1992), 526.

(1) that used by members of the sterling area; (2) that used by non-members outside the dollar area – called non-resident, external, or transferable sterling; and (3) that used by members of the dollar area.[11] Ideally, unification would ease the trauma of an eventual move to full convertibility by providing a transitional step along the way. Also, because of the strength of the exchange markets at the time, Britain would not be making this leap from a position of weakness, which, since the convertibility debacle of 1947, officials believed was critical for success. The hope was that the reduction in restrictions on external sterling that came with unification would make the currency easier to manage, thus increasing its use and raising its value. It was clear that, despite official attempts to play down the significance of unification to fend off any blows to confidence, convertibility was in the offing.[12]

A combination of pressures from the marketplace, Bank officials, and sterling area members compelled the Treasury to make sterling de facto convertible by 1955. The market for transferable sterling grew robust when non-resident traders found a way to acquire it cheaply by repatriating their profits on sterling securities and exchanging them for other currencies – mostly dollars – at a discount. Consequently, there were two different rates for sterling: the official, resident rate, and the lower, transferable rate. After the unification of the bilateral and transferable account areas at the beginning of 1954, the value of transferable sterling increased, as British economic planners had hoped. But the rate eventually fell, and the Bank persuaded the Treasury that payments to the sterling area in "cheap" sterling were weakening the currency, more so than the sterling area's balance-of-payments difficulties at the time. Concurrently, Australia informed Britain that it wanted to sell gold in the transferable market, where it fetched a better price, revealing a frustration with sterling area controls that was not unique to Australia and suggesting that sterling area members were growing restless on the issue of convertibility.[13] With transferable sterling in a free fall in February 1955, the Treasury allowed the Bank to support the unofficial rate, raising the rate of transferable sterling to that of resident sterling. Holders of transferable sterling were then able to obtain dollars at the official rate, and, thus, sterling was unofficially convertible for all non-residents outside the

[11] Catherine R. Schenk, "Finance and Empire: Confusions and Complexities: A Note," *The International History Review*, 18, 4, (1996), 869–872.
[12] Schenk, *Britain and the Sterling Area*, 124–126.
[13] Australia cooperatively sold £20 million worth of gold to the Bank of England to bolster the sterling area's central reserves during the Suez crisis one year later. See Harold Macmillan, *Riding the Storm, 1956–1959* (London: Harper&Row, 1971), 117.

dollar area, or de facto convertible on current account transactions.[14] While a drain on the reserves would no doubt follow, the argument at Whitehall was that the loss would not be as great as it would have been had cheap sterling transactions been allowed to persist.[15]

De facto convertibility may have stemmed the tide of reserve losses due to business in cheap sterling, but continuing balance-of-payments problems and declining confidence in the pound undermined Britain's financial stability throughout 1955. Current account difficulties that year were triggered by a growth in demand and additional inflationary pressure caused by large wage hikes, an income tax cut, and an increase in retirement pensions, all occurring during the first third of the year. The mixture of higher demand and rising prices at home led to a dramatic increase in imports. Dock and railway strikes, moreover, broke out in May and June, which, together with the balance-of-payments and inflation trouble, undermined confidence in sterling. Rumors spread that Whitehall would devalue the currency. As a result, speculators fled the pound, contributing to a £144 million drain from the sterling area's reserves in July, August, and September. That Chancellor of the Exchequer R. A. Butler denied rumors of an impending devaluation at the end of July did not seem to matter, although his eventual success in persuading the market that he had no intention of devaluing sterling helped bring the crisis to a close at the end of the year.[16]

Late in 1955 and well into 1956, Treasury and Bank officials sought to restore confidence in the pound by improving the sterling area's reserve position. They believed that they would have to accomplish this goal by developing consistent trade surpluses in Britain, maintaining that the condition of Britain's balance of payments was "fundamental" to the proper functioning of the sterling area and the whole sterling system. The system's survival, they added, depended "above all else on the avoidance of current account deficits by the UK."[17] Why target Britain as opposed to the Rest of the Sterling Area? Since it was likely that RSA countries would run balance-of-payments deficits based on lower primary product prices and development spending, they would draw on their sterling balances and deplete £100–150 million annually from sterling area reserves. Adjusting for the £50 million that the Bank and Treasury estimated that

---

[14] Officially, Britain would still exert exchange control over the American account (dollar) area, but, in practice, transfers between it and the transferable account area were allowed. The Treasury would also continue to regulate capital transactions between all three areas. See Fforde, *The Bank of England and Public Policy*, 505.

[15] Ibid., 126–128; Dow, *The Management of the British Economy*, 85–86.

[16] Scott, "The Balance of Payments Crises," 219–220.

[17] "Draft Conclusions," Sterling Area Working Party, June 6, 1956, NA, T 236/4303.

the RSA would acquire in gold and dollars, officials thought that Britain would have to increase its annual surpluses by £100 million just to keep the reserves stable. Therefore, if confidence in sterling were to be preserved during a bad trade year, the country would have to run average annual surpluses of £250–300 million to create a buffer against speculation and other negative effects.[18] "Without a sufficient surplus," Harold Macmillan wrote in February 1956, "we shall be unable to meet our commitments to maintain our currency and our position as the center of the sterling system or to retain our position as a world power."[19]

Oil, as always, loomed large, acting as a source of strength as well as weakness for Britain's balance of payments. Britain was earning £200 million a year on oil transactions, mostly as a result of the extremely profitable operations of British Petroleum and Royal Dutch-Shell.[20] Of course, because Britain imported all of its oil, three-quarters of it from the Middle East, the possibility of not having access to it represented a kind of Sword of Damocles hanging over the pound, something of which British planners were acutely aware.[21] Not only did Britain's "actual and potential" military and foreign aid commitments eliminate the prospect of the country's "being any more free from strain and crisis" than it had been in 1945, officials lamented, but Britain's continued dependence "on external supplies of vital foods and raw materials, in particular of oil from the Middle East," contributed to the nation's susceptibility to crisis. Consequently, a top secret Cabinet study on the future of Britain in world affairs distinguished two major political and military objectives for the government: (1) avoiding global war; and (2) protecting the country's "vital interests overseas, particularly, access to oil."[22] This access, and, concomitantly, the value of sterling, depended on the smooth operation of the Suez Canal and the pipelines that carried oil from the Persian Gulf to the Mediterranean. Given that "the maintenance of the international value of sterling" was considered "a matter of life or death" for Britain, and that Treasury officials focused on improving *Britain's* – as opposed to the sterling area's – balance of payments to maintain this value, the

[18] "Problems of the Sterling Area: Report by a Working Party of the Treasury and the Bank of England," June 25, 1956, NA, T 236/4304.
[19] "Balance of Payments Prospects," Note by the Chancellor of the Exchequer, CP (56) 55, February 27, NA, PREM 11/1324.
[20] "Overseas Investment Policy," a Paper by the Treasury, July 25, 1956, NA, FO 371/120799.
[21] "Economic Effects of the Middle East Crisis," Draft Passage for a speech by Macmillan, amended on September 11, 1956, NA, T 236/5649.
[22] "The Future of the United Kingdom in World Affairs," Policy Review of the Cabinet Office, PR (56) 3, June 1, 1956, NA, CAB 134/1315.

nation's ability to acquire Middle Eastern oil through the Suez Canal had become more critical than ever.[23]

3.2   Anglo-American defense planning, the Aswan High Dam project, and the nationalization of the Suez Canal, 1954–1956

Ever since Britain withdrew its support from Greece and Turkey in 1947, the US government worried about Britain's ability to pull its weight in defending the Middle East against Soviet influence. The Iranian oil crisis deepened this concern and prompted US officials to conclude that Britain's economic weakness and the deterioration of its political position in the region would likely demand increasing US involvement to protect Western interests. By the mid-1950s, with nationalism growing stronger – and with the British position, if anything, becoming weaker – US anxiety about the security of its interests in the area heightened even more. In July 1954, the National Security Council wrote: "In the Near East the current danger to the security of the free world arises not so much from the threat of direct Soviet military attack as from a continuation of the present unfavorable trends. Unless these trends are reversed, the Near East may well be lost to the West within the next few years." One of those trends, the paper noted, was Britain's dissipating influence in the region, the result of "distrust and hatred" among states in the area "replacing the former colonial subservience."[24] And there was no greater symbol of British decline in the Middle East that year than the government's agreement with Egypt to abandon its Suez base, signed in July.

US planners believed that a Middle East defense organization, revolving around the "Northern Tier" states of Turkey, Pakistan, Iran, and Iraq – and underpinned by US aid – could help secure the region. The idea was not new. The United States had attempted two similar efforts, the Middle East Command and the Middle East Defense Organization, which failed because they suffered "the stigma of being under direct Western control," the drafters of a National Intelligence Estimate assessed.[25] To some degree, the new organization had already begun to coalesce when Western allies, Turkey and Pakistan, signed a security agreement in April 1954. Subsequently, the United States sought to "encourage when appropriate the adherence of Iraq and Iran" to the

---

[23] Ibid.
[24] "United States Objectives and Policies with Respect to the Near East," July 23, 1954, *FRUS, 1952–1954, Vol. IX*, 525–532.
[25] Ibid.; "National Intelligence Estimate," June 22, 1954, *FRUS, 1952–1954, Vol. IX*, 516–519.

pact, "avoiding pressure but endeavoring to create political conditions" that would "make adherence possible and attractive."[26] Important to US officials was that any "Northern Tier" organization be viewed as an "indigenous movement," not linked formally with the Western powers or defense organizations, "except through the participation of Turkey," until a later date.[27] Nonetheless, they recognized that future British support would be "an important factor in determining the success of the 'northern tier' concept" – although they would eventually resent the nature of British participation.[28] While supporting the notion of a Middle Eastern regional defense organization based on the Northern Tier, a group of US ambassadors warned that Egypt was "likely to be displeased" with the idea and would "resent any Middle East arrangement in which it does not play a leading role." Consequently, they encouraged that "it be made clear to Egypt that the 'Northern Tier' concept" did not "reduce the importance of Egypt."[29]

The US-inspired regional defense organization, eventually known as the Baghdad Pact, came into existence in piecemeal fashion in 1955. In February, Iraq, still very much a British client state, reached an accord with Turkey and established the Baghdad Pact's core. A veteran of Middle Eastern politics, Iraq's prime minister, Nuri al-Said, had hoped that, by joining the organization, he could assert his leadership in the region with British support. Britain itself became a member in April 1955, seeking to maintain influence in the Arab world through Iraq and possibly other potential participants, such as Jordan and Lebanon. In defending its membership to Egypt, the Foreign Office claimed that the government's object was "solely to be able to help in the defence of the Middle East from a position where this defence must strategically be organized" and not "to acquire a position of domination in Iraq or over any other Arab state," an assertion that Egypt never believed.[30] The pact expanded in the fall of 1955 when Pakistan and Iran joined in September and October, respectively. Noticeably absent from the accord was the United States, a disappointment to Britain because it wanted the Eisenhower Administration to contribute more to Anglo-American defense in the Middle East. Indeed, Under Secretary of State Herbert Hoover, Jr., said that during conversations between US and British officials on the defense of the Middle East "two British objectives had become apparent": first, the

[26] "United States Objectives and Policies with Respect to the Near East," July 23, 1954, *FRUS, 1952–1954, Vol. IX*, 525–532.
[27] Ibid.   [28] Ibid.
[29] "Paper Approved by the Chiefs of Mission Conference at Istanbul, May 11–14," May 14, 1954, *FRUS, 1952–1954, Vol. IX*, 506–512.
[30] Shuckburgh to Kirkpatrick, February 22, 1956, NA, FO 371/118861.

British "desired to assure themselves of command responsibility in the area in the event of difficulties"; and, second, they "expected the United States to foot the bill required to place the area in some posture of defense."[31] The authors of a National Intelligence Estimate also seemed troubled by Britain's attitude regarding regional defense, believing that Britain remained "deeply concerned with protecting as much as possible of its own special interests and influence in the area." As a result, the Baghdad Pact would reflect not just "military concern over the Soviet threat" but also Britain's "over-all political and economic interests in the area."[32]

Growing US discomfort over what the Baghdad Pact had become under British stewardship prevented the United States from joining the organization, although the US government still provided military assistance to individual members. In a conversation with the president, Dulles said that the "trouble" with the Baghdad Pact was that "the British have taken it over and run it as an instrument of British policy," inviting a "tremendous amount of criticism."[33] Britain, US officials believed, put too much weight on Nuri al-Said and Iraq, which Gamal Abdel Nasser saw as a threat to his bid for unofficial leadership of the Arab world. It was fast becoming clear that in the competition for the hearts and minds of Arabs, Nasser was more influential than al-Said, and US policy-makers did not want to lose a country as strategically important as Egypt by appearing to favor Iraq in any way. Moreover, Washington believed that, by alienating Egypt, US membership in the Baghdad Pact might jeopardize Washington's ability to play a significant role in reducing Arab-Israeli hostilities. Dulles even requested that the British government delay asking Jordan and Lebanon to become members of the new defense organization for fear of alienating Nasser. Anthony Eden, frustrated by what he saw as mixed messages from the United States and wanting to emphasize Britain's clout in the Middle East, asked Jordan and Lebanon to join anyway, only to be rebuffed by them early in 1956.[34] Nasser, who viewed Iraq's participation in the British-led defense organization as a betrayal of the Arab League's authority in collective Arab security, persuaded both countries not to join the Baghdad Pact, demonstrating that the

---

[31] "Memorandum of Discussion at the 247th Meeting of the National Security Council, May 5, 1955, *FRUS, 1955–1957, Vol. XII*, 54–55.

[32] "NIE 30–55," June 21, 1955, *FRUS, 1955–1957, Vol. XII*, 77–89.

[33] "Memorandum of a Telephone Conversation Between the President and the Secretary of State, Washington, April 7, 1956, 9:10 a.m.," *FRUS, 1955–1957, Vol. XII*, 270.

[34] Ovendale, *Britain, the United States and the Transfer of Power in the Middle East*, ch. 5, considers Anglo-American relations regarding the Middle East in the context of the Baghdad Pact.

Egyptian prime minister had indeed become a potent force in the Arab world.[35]

Part of Nasser's hostility to the Baghdad Pact grew out of an evolving neutralist foreign policy that took shape in the middle of 1955. As Egypt's treaty with Britain revealed, Nasser did not oppose the cooperation of formerly subjugated countries with their erstwhile masters.[36] But he was averse to joining their defense organizations. In his view, alliances such as the Baghdad Pact reflected the interests of their stronger Western members, which sought to dominate such organizations and manipulate their weaker signatories. The Arab states could better protect their own interests, he thought, by establishing an Arab defense pact, even if they still procured arms from the West.[37] Taking place within two months of the Turko-Iraqi accord, the Bandung Conference was held in Indonesia in April 1955, further energizing Nasser's neutralist thinking. At this gathering of African and Asian countries that represented more than one billion people, Nasser realized the potential for the Afro-Asian world to achieve the dignity and independence that it desired as it confronted the globe's colonial and imperial powers. He recognized that the collective strength of these nations, aligned with neither the West nor the Soviet Union, lay in the age-old strategy of playing the great powers off one another. As head of a country that connected the African continent with the Middle East, Nasser was well positioned to become a leading figure in the non-aligned world, and he came into his own at Bandung.[38]

Nasser's aversion to the Baghdad Pact also stemmed from his adherence to Pan-Arab nationalism. This and positive neutralism would form the twin pillars of Egyptian foreign policy for more than two decades. Nasser's Pan-Arab philosophy was based on the notion that the Arab people constituted a "nation," or a distinct cultural group, that had been artificially divided into separate states by Britain and France.[39] Egypt's Free Officers, who overthrew the country's British-supported monarchy in 1952, redrafted the Egyptian constitution early in 1956 to reflect that

[35] Brief for Shuckburgh for talks in Washington, January 7, 1956, NA, FO 371/118861; M. E. Yapp, *The Near East since the First World War* (London: Longman, 1991), 405–406.
[36] Ali E. Hillal Dessouki details the evolution of Nasser's foreign policy, demonstrating that the popular image of him as the anti-Western revolutionary is too simplistic. See "Nasser and the Struggle for Independence" in Wm. Roger Louis and Roger Owen (eds.), *Suez 1956: The Crisis and its Consequences* (Oxford: Clarendon Press, 1989), 34–37.
[37] Ibid., 36.
[38] Robert Stephens, *Nasser: A Political Biography* (New York: Simon and Schuster, 1971), 158.
[39] See Bassam Tibi, *Arab Nationalism: A Critical Enquiry*, second edition, edited and translated by Marion Farouk Sluglett and Peter Sluglett (New York: St. Martin's Press, 1990), ch. 6.

the Egyptian people "consciously perceive of [Egypt's] existence as part of the great Arab whole, and correctly acknowledge its responsibility and duty within the common Arab struggle for the victory and glory of the Arab nation."[40] For Nasser, Iraq's membership in the Baghdad Pact was an obstacle to Arab unity, undermining his ability to reconstitute and reinvigorate the Arab nation to be strong enough to challenge the powers that sought to control it. And the Baghdad Pact looked suspiciously like an attempt at British control. Officials at Whitehall, on the other hand, viewed Nasser's Pan-Arab nationalism as the single greatest threat to Britain's oil interests in the Middle East – and by extension, to sterling.

Nasser first put his neutralist foreign policy into practice in October 1955 when he accepted a generous offer from the Soviet Union to supply Egypt with arms, much to the dismay of the United States and Britain. He considered the move an act of necessity for the defense of his country. At the end of February 1955, Israel had launched a deadly raid on Egyptian-controlled Gaza in retaliation for a series of border incidents over the previous months, dramatically revealing Egypt's military weakness. Meanwhile, France disturbed the delicate balance of power in the Middle East by selling weapons to Israel to punish Egypt for its support of the nascent revolution in Algeria as well as nationalist movements in Tunisia and Morocco. The arms-control regime that the United States, Britain, and France had carefully maintained in the Middle East since the first Arab-Israeli war was now broken.

To match Israel's arms buildup, Egypt asked the United States for aid, but the Eisenhower Administration would not sell it weapons at a price that it could afford. In contrast, the Soviet Union not only offered to exchange numerous fighter jets, tanks, and bombers for Egypt's large stocks of unsold cotton, but it also said that it would accept cotton as payment for the construction of the enormous dam that the government was planning to build on the Nile at Aswan in Upper Egypt. Nasser, who had previously shown his anti-communist credentials by jailing hundreds of Egyptian communists, was forthcoming with the United States and Britain about the deal, informing them that he would have to accept it unless they proposed something similar. They did not, so he took the Soviet offer. To help the West save a little face, though, Nasser agreed to announce publicly that Egypt would receive its new cache of arms from Czechoslovakia rather than the Soviet Union. Regardless, the world knew that Egypt was acquiring weapons from the Soviet Union, and the West was jolted into the realization that a communist power had just taken a significant step toward becoming a major player in the Middle East.

---

[40] Quoted in Stephens, *Nasser: A Political Biography*, 183.

As for Nasser, what became known as "the Czech arms deal" lifted his prestige to new heights in both the Arab and the non-aligned worlds. Just as important, it increased his popularity within Egypt itself.[41]

After initially responding to Nasser's bold stroke with anger, British and American officials resumed their cautious courtship of the Egyptian prime minister to capitalize on his influence in the region. They considered Nasser to be the linchpin of any effort at reconciling the Arab states and Israel, and they believed that he could potentially play an important role in keeping the Soviet Union at bay in the Middle East. Nasser well understood his value to Britain and the United States, and, as a result, the Soviet arms deal appeared to be a successful application of positive neutralism: suddenly, Britain, with US support, wanted to help finance the construction of the Aswan High Dam, the largest civil engineering project in the world, expected to provide electricity and irrigation to many parts of Egypt. British Prime Minister Anthony Eden believed that if a European consortium could secure the project, it "would be of immense value in restoring the prestige of the West and particularly of the older European powers in the Arab World generally."[42] Providing aid in the construction of the dam would also be a way of demonstrating Britain's long-term interest in the welfare of the Egyptian people without actually helping Nasser himself, he thought.[43] In the end, Whitehall made the offer "largely in the hope of improving" British relations with Egypt and "keeping the Egyptians from falling further under Communist influence."[44] For its part, the Department of State thought that the United States "should have one more good go-around with [Nasser] in an endeavor to reach an understanding."[45]

Funding the dam was a financially complex and expensive affair, one that British and US officials began to think was not worth their while once Nasser seemed unwilling to play by their rules. A consortium of British, French, and German firms agreed to undertake the project, as long as Western governments would guarantee their compensation if Egypt could no longer pay its share of the $1.3 billion cost.[46] Afraid of the financial consequences to Britain of an Egyptian default, Anthony Eden

[41] Kyle, *Suez*, 62–78; Mohammed Heikal, *Cutting the Lion's Tail: Suez through Egyptian Eyes* (London: André Deutsch, 1986), 71–83.

[42] "Cabinet Discussion of the Aswan Dam Project, October 20, 1955," Document 2.3 in Gorst and Johnman, *The Suez Crisis*, 40–41.

[43] Kyle, *Suez*, 77.

[44] "High Aswan Dam," Memorandum by the Foreign Office, ME (0) (56) 35, June 12, 1956, NA, CAB 134/1298.

[45] Hoover to Dulles, October 29, 1955, *FRUS, 1955–1957, Vol. XIV*, 677–679.

[46] According to estimates from the International Bank for Reconstruction and Development (IBRD), now known as the World Bank.

approached the United States to help pay for the dam. He was anxious to secure financing for the project as soon as possible because British intelligence sources suggested that Nasser was more intimately linked with the Soviet Union than he had acknowledged – or than anyone had previously realized. Policy-makers in Britain and the United States wanted to overthrow the troublesome Egyptian leader, as they had Muhammad Mossadegh. But they feared that the Soviet Union would gain an even greater foothold in Egypt while they pondered how to remove him from power.[47]

In mid-December 1955, Nasser received an Anglo-American proposal to fund the Aswan Dam that involved US and British grants, loans from the International Bank of Reconstruction and Development, and US foreign aid – all on the condition that the Soviet Union would not participate in the project. The offer did not stay on the table very long, as events in the Middle East took a decidedly anti-British turn. In January, Jordan refused to join the Baghdad Pact, and, two months later, it delivered yet another blow to British prestige in the region by dismissing Sir John Glubb, the British officer who had long commanded the renowned Arab Legion. Then, anti-British hostilities broke out on Bahrain, an island close to Britain's oil-producing protectorates on the Persian Gulf, and Anthony Eden lost his patience with Nasser, whom he blamed for all of these events. The US government grew tired of Nasser as well, especially when, after months of discussions with him, he revealed that he had no desire to make peace with Israel.[48] A memorandum by the Foreign Office about the Aswan High Dam proposal read:

The effect we desired has not been achieved. Colonel Nasser has since shown less disposition to co-operate with the West, and has drawn closer to the Communist bloc. The British offer has come in for hostile criticism in Parliament and in the Press. Our friends in the Middle East, inside the Baghdad Pact and elsewhere, are increasingly puzzled at this Anglo-American offer to Egypt (especially since we have to tell them that our aid must be limited by the need to husband our slender resources).[49]

Nasser's "conduct" had become "so obviously hostile" to Anglo-American interests, that British and US officials decided "to let the Aswan Dam negotiations 'languish'" without telling him that they intended to cancel their offer.[50]

---

[47] Kyle, *Suez*, 82–99.   [48] Ibid.
[49] "High Aswan Dam," Memorandum by the Foreign Office, ME (0) (56) 35, June 12, 1956, NA, CAB 134/1298.
[50] Ibid.

On July 19, John Foster Dulles officially withdrew the Anglo-American offer, which prompted the newly titled "President" Nasser to nationalize the Suez Canal, an act that he claimed would enable Egypt to build the Aswan High Dam without external aid (although the revenue from the Suez Canal alone could not have financed anything but a portion of the dam's cost). British officials disliked how Dulles handled the matter. While they believed that it was necessary for Britain and the United States to inform Nasser that the two countries were no longer interested in funding the project, they did not agree on the timing: they wanted additional discussions with the White House before making a definitive statement to him. Dulles thought that he had to act quickly because the Aswan venture was unpopular in the United States, and Congress was ready to reject support for it. Nasser knew that Britain and the United States no longer wanted to finance the dam, so he intentionally held back Egyptian counter-proposals to their offer in an effort to force their hand. Anticipating what Dulles would tell Egyptian Ambassador Ahmed Hussein on July 19, Nasser was prepared to nationalize the Suez Canal so that he would not have to rely solely on the Soviet Union's help to build the dam. After all, Britain had just removed its last troops from the canal zone in mid-June, as required by the Anglo-Egyptian Treaty, and he did not want to replace one master with another.[51]

Nasser announced the nationalization of the Suez Canal in a speech in Alexandria on July 26, 1956, the fourth anniversary of the Free Officers' deposition of King Farouk. Before he spoke, some of his ministers raised the issue of Mossadegh's failure in Iran, worrying that Egypt would be similarly unsuccessful. Nasser replied that there was a significant difference between the canal and oil: Mossadegh faced the problem of not being able to sell Iranian crude, which prevented Iran from capitalizing on nationalization. If Egypt allowed ships to pass freely through the waterway, and it received support from its Afro-Asian allies, Nasser believed that its chances of success were good.[52] Indeed, Egypt succeeded in ways that he could never have predicted.

While senior officials at Whitehall objected to Egyptian control over the Suez Canal for fear that Egypt could block British access to Middle Eastern oil at any moment, what particularly worried them was Nasser's growing prestige and influence in the region as a result of nationalization. On August 1, Harold Macmillan, the most hawkish member of the Cabinet on the subject of Nasser and Suez, told John Foster Dulles and

[51] Kyle, *Suez*, 127–134; Heikal, *Cutting the Lion's Tail*, 112–129.
[52] Heikal, *Cutting the Lion's Tail*, 112–129.

3.1 Egyptian Prime Minister Gamal Abdel Nasser is celebrated upon his return to Cairo from Alexandria after nationalizing the Suez Canal Company, August 1956.

a group of US officials that appeasing the Egyptian president would start a "chain reaction" that would "ultimately lead to the loss of the entire British position in the Middle East." Ultimately, he warned, "even the oil reserves in Kuwait might be lost." Macmillan continued by insisting that Britain had to meet this "danger" immediately, if it did not want to be destroyed as a "first class power" and reduced "to a status similar to that of Holland." "No one wanted to see another Munich," the chancellor added, concluding that the British people "would rather die fighting than slowly bleed to a state of impotence."[53] Indeed, officials believed that the dollars and gold that would begin to flow out of the British reserves as a result of Nasser's action would wreck the pound as an international currency and destroy Britain's capacity to play an important role in world affairs.[54]

---

[53] "Memorandum of a Conversation, 11 Downing Street, London," August 1, 1956, *FRUS, 1955–1957, XVI*, 108–109.

[54] George Bolton, executive director of the Bank of England, wrote, "I feel that the situation created by the Egyptian Government imperils the survival of the UK and the Commonwealth, and represents a very great danger to sterling," "Sterling and the Suez Canal Situation," Memorandum by Sir George Bolton, August 1, 1956, BE/G1/124.

Dulles countered this intemperate language with sober comments about what he thought was the most appropriate way for Britain and the United States to deal with the nationalization of the canal. He considered any one nation's control of the waterway to be "unacceptable," and the fact that Egypt was in charge certainly made matters worse. Nonetheless, he thought that only "if all other methods failed" should force be used to open the canal; it was "the last method to be tried." The secretary of state maintained that military action would require the support of world opinion, and, if Britain resorted to force without this sanction, the result would be "disastrous." Dulles predicted that the repercussions of an invasion would include "the loss of Western influence in all the Moslem countries" as well as the flow of Soviet arms into the Middle East, if not direct Soviet intervention in the region. Unless Britain first made "genuine efforts to reach a satisfactory solution by negotiation," he doubted whether the United States "would be able to associate" itself with a British attack on Egypt. The primary goal, the secretary of state maintained, should be "to bring world opinion to favour the international operation of the Canal" before falling back on the use of force. Unlike Dulles and his associates, many at Whitehall viewed efforts "to reach a satisfactory solution by international consultation" as a "matter of form," window dressing hung to justify the inevitable invasion that would be necessary to neutralize Nasser and ensure the free flow of oil to Britain and Western Europe.[55]

US officials knew that Britain preferred to use force to solve the Suez problem. Much like during the Iranian oil crisis, they criticized Whitehall for what they believed was its obsolete approach to the Afro-Asian world. When learning of the British government's desire to "initiate hostilities at an early date" to "break Nasser," President Eisenhower, who consistently opposed any British military action in Egypt, commented that such an approach was "out of date." He also thought that the British view of Nasser was grossly exaggerated, writing to Eden that he was "making of Nasser a much more important figure than he is."[56] Already fed up with Britain over its handling of Iran, Secretary of the Treasury George Humphrey exclaimed: "it looked as though they were simply trying to reverse the trend away from colonialism, and turn the

[55] Ibid. See also "Memorandum of a Conversation between Prime Minister Eden and Secretary of State Dulles, 10 Downing Street, London," August 1, 1956 in *FRUS, 1955–1957, XVI*, 98–99 for a similar conversation.
[56] Eisenhower to Eden, in No. 1839 from Makins to the Foreign Office, September 8, 1956, NA, FO 800/740.

clock back fifty years."[57] In fact, Eisenhower had dispatched John Foster Dulles to London in an effort to calm British thinking on the matter, particularly because of "how impossible it would be to obtain Congressional authorization for participation by the United States" in an armed intervention.[58]

Of course, the British government did not view the defense of the country's vital interests in the Middle East, especially oil and its connection to sterling, as imperialistic. Earlier in the year, the Foreign Office's assistant under-secretary, Evelyn Shuckburgh, sent Ivone Kirkpatrick, the permanent under-secretary of state, notes on Whitehall's approach to Nasser: "we are determined to defend the essential elements of our position in the world, including strategic bases and other assets which are essential not only for our own survival but for that of other free peoples. This includes protection of our vital oil requirements. If this is imperialism, then Nasser might as well know that we are imperialists."[59] The last remark echoes the comment that Allen Christelow made during the Iranian oil crisis that Britain should challenge the "stigmatization as imperialism" the measures that Britain took "for the development of scarce real resources" (see p. 140). Key US officials obviously believed that "imperialism" was an appropriate way of categorizing the attitude at Whitehall. They considered Britain's reaction to the nationalization of the Suez Canal to be anachronistic, just as they did Britain's behavior toward Iran only a few years earlier. The British approach, they thought, had severe repercussions for all of the countries of the industrialized West, and with so much at stake, they could not abide it. In contrast, the hawks at Whitehall thought that aggressive action would probably be necessary precisely because there was so much at stake, especially for Britain's vulnerable economy.[60] British officials were willing to conform to the US view, however, hoping that Nasser's intractability would compel the United States to recognize that only by using force could they ensure the safety of Western interests in the Middle East. And British military planners continued to prepare for an invasion of the Suez Canal zone, not only to preserve the option, but also as if it were an inevitability.

In the meantime, the British government turned to financial pressure to punish Egypt for its actions, and, as with Iran, it exploited Egypt's use of

---

[57] "Memorandum of a Conference with the President, White House, Washington," July 31, 1956, *FRUS, 1955–1957, Vol. XVI*, 62–68.

[58] Ibid.

[59] Shuckburgh to Kirkpatrick, February 22, 1956, NA, FO 371/118861.

[60] There was not complete agreement at Whitehall about the use of force. For dissenting views, see Kyle, *Suez*, 200–206.

sterling. On July 27, the day after Nasser announced the nationalization of the Suez Canal, Whitehall froze Egypt's sterling accounts in London and extended rigid controls over Egyptian use of sterling, thereby neutralizing 60 percent of the country's total reserves.[61] The United States also imposed sanctions on Egypt, although not nearly as stringent as Britain's, disappointing British policy-makers.[62] Whitehall justified its measures by explaining that Nasser's canal policy had "very serious economic implications not only for the United Kingdom but for the Commonwealth, Europe and the world as a whole," one that demanded an immediate response from London.[63] This attempt to undermine Egypt's financial position backfired, though, and hurt Britain as much as, if not more than, Egypt itself. With British exports to Egypt drying up, other countries, such as Japan, were able to capture British markets. China resorted to settling a trading debt with Egypt in Swiss francs, which damaged sterling because the francs were obtained with pounds.[64] India began trading with Egypt in rupees, and South Africa was prepared to do business with it in dollars.[65]

Furthermore, "considerable resentment" among sterling area members emerged over how Britain was taking advantage of its position as the currency group's banker. According to the Treasury, the loyalty of sterling area members was strained, as was their confidence in sterling.[66] Worst of all, Middle Eastern countries were losing confidence in sterling as a reserve currency. The Treasury's Denis Rickett, the former economic minister at the British Embassy in Washington, wrote: "If Egypt's sterling balances can be frozen in this way, they are asking, what is to prevent the same thing happening to our sterling balances?"[67] The idea of an oil producer, such as Kuwait, abandoning the sterling area, and taking with it £200 million from its account in London, was too frightening to contemplate. One Treasury official concluded that the effectiveness of

---

[61] "Suez Canal: Financial and Economic Measures: Draft Memorandum for Tripartite Discussion," ME (0) (SC) (56) 24, August 27, 1956, NA, CAB 134/1302.

[62] Economic Committee (Washington), EC (W) (56) 26th Meeting, September 21, 1956, NA, CAB 134/1218.

[63] No. 315 from the CRO to the High Commissioners in Canada, Australia, New Zealand, South Africa, India, Pakistan, Ceylon, and the Federation of Rhodesia and Nyasaland, August 2, 1956, NA, T 236/4635.

[64] Treasury Memorandum by Moberly, undated (received in the Foreign Office Registry on October 1, 1956), NA, FO 371/118948.

[65] "Effect on Egypt of Current Financial Measures of 27th July," ME (0) (EM) (56) 7, October 8, 1956, NA, CAB 134/1300.

[66] Treasury Memorandum by Moberly, undated (received in the Foreign Office Registry on October 1, 1956), NA, FO 371/118948.

[67] Rickett to Maude, August 16, 1956, NA, T 236/4635.

Whitehall's financial measures had "not been very great" and "had been achieved at a substantial cost to the UK economy."[68]

Along with pressure from Britain on the economic front, John Foster Dulles spearheaded attempts at finding a solution to the Suez dispute on the political front in an effort to slow any Anglo-French momentum toward military action. He convened the First London Conference (there would be two more) during the third week of August, inviting representatives from twenty-four countries, all of whom attended except for those from Egypt and Greece. The former resented its status as a mere invitee, viewed in the same light as the other participants, and the latter was angry at Britain over its Cyprus policy. On August 23, the conference produced a proposal, largely conceived by Dulles, signed by eighteen nations representing the signatories of the 1888 Suez Canal Treaty, the canal's main users or countries whose economies greatly depended on the canal.[69] The proposal provided for a Suez Canal Board on which would sit representatives from a wide geographic distribution of nations and on which Egypt would have a permanent seat. Egypt would also reap all of the profits from the canal's use, and any interference in its operation would be considered a threat to peace. When delegates from five nations, led by Australian Prime Minister Robert Menzies, brought the proposal to Nasser, he rejected it out of hand, explaining that he would accept nothing less than Egyptian ownership, management, and operation of the Suez Canal. He was happy to negotiate agreements dealing with tolls, non-discrimination, and future development of the waterway, but only if Egyptian control over it underpinned any discussion.[70] Nasser said, "I have read a statement by Sir Anthony Eden, or it may have been by Mr. Dulles, that he didn't trust Gamal Abdel Nasser. I must confess that I don't trust them either."[71]

On September 15, less than a week after the conclusion of the failed Menzies mission, Britain tried to demonstrate to the world that Egypt could not efficiently run the Suez Canal by encouraging the Suez Canal Company's non-Egyptian staff to quit. After nationalization, Britain,

---

[68] Treasury Memorandum by Moberly, undated (received in the Foreign Office Registry on October 1, 1956), NA, FO 371/118948.

[69] Known as the Convention of Constantinople, the treaty was designed to protect the freedom of transit for warships through the waterway. At the same time, the Convention also deprived Egypt of most of its rights to regulate shipping through its own territory, internationalizing the canal for all time, even beyond the end of the Suez Canal Company's concession in 1968. See D. A. Farnie, *East and West of Suez: The Suez Canal in History, 1854–1956* (Oxford: Clarendon Press, 1969), 336–342.

[70] Kyle, *Suez*, 192–199, 219–222.

[71] Quoted in Heikal, *Cutting the Lion's Tail*, 151. For Heikal's account of Nasser's discussions with Menzies, see 148–153.

France, and Egypt had all implored the firm's mostly British and French employees to stay in their jobs to maintain the free flow of shipping through the canal. Egypt paid their salaries with canal dues that were not deposited in blocked accounts in London and Paris, a figure that, at the time, Harold Macmillan estimated to be almost half of the total dues received.[72] To make the point that Egypt could not manage the waterway without Western help – while simultaneously protecting European interests – the British government conceived two plans: "Pile-Up" and "Convoy." The first would create a log-jam in the canal and the second would alleviate the bottleneck by having British and French pilots ready to guide ships through it. But the chaos that Britain had expected never ensued because Egyptian replacement pilots were able to perform their duties without difficulty, as canal pilots were not the elite corps of highly skilled workers that British officials had apparently imagined them to be. Unlike the Panama Canal, which rose by three locks to eighty-five feet above sea level, the Suez Canal was essentially a big ditch that did not require extraordinary skill to navigate.[73] In the month and a half after nationalization, Egyptian pilots had studied the work of the British and French staff and had learned their jobs well.[74] The prejudices that British officials revealed during the Iranian oil crisis were on display once again: in this case, Britain's misplaced notions of Western efficiency and Eastern inefficiency led to a victory for Nasser. For Britain, Operation "Pile-Up" represented another failed attempt to pressure Egypt into accepting international control of the waterway and left the fate of sterling and the British economy in the Egyptian president's hands.

At the end of September, John Foster Dulles continued his efforts to forestall Britain and France's march toward war with a scheme called the Suez Canal Users Association (SCUA).[75] His idea was to establish a club of canal users that would guide member ships through the waterway and collect the tolls themselves. Rather than hiring Egyptian pilots, the club would use its own staff, thus allowing SCUA participants to circumvent the Egyptian government and deny it the fruits of nationalization. If successfully executed, Dulles thought that the plan would compel Nasser to

---

[72] Macmillan believed that Egypt was receiving roughly £15–16 million annually. See "Possible Future Action," Memorandum by the Chancellor of the Exchequer, Cabinet Egypt Committee, EC (56) 41, September 5, 1956, NA, CAB 134/1217. In his memoirs, Macmillan wrote that Egypt received 35 percent of canal dues. See *Riding the Storm, 1956–1959*, 109.

[73] Farnie, *East and West of Suez*, 528.   [74] Kyle, *Suez*, 249–250.

[75] Dulles had originally called it CASU for Cooperative Association of Suez Canal Users, but the name was changed because CASU meant something obscene in Portuguese. For an amusing account of the name change, see Selwyn Lloyd, *Suez 1956: A Personal Account* (London: Jonathan Cape, 1978), 145.

work with canal users to devise a mutually agreeable scheme for international management of the waterway. Both Eden and Macmillan hoped that SCUA would involve the United States in something that would end in failure as a result of "Egyptian obstruction" and therefore justify a British invasion of the canal zone.[76] Dulles intended nothing of the sort, illustrating just how far the American and British agendas had diverged that autumn. While the secretary of state managed the crisis with greater concern for staving off a conflagration before the presidential election, British policy-makers worried more about oil and the viability of sterling and, therefore, sought an immediate end, one way or another, to Egyptian control over the Suez Canal.[77]

SCUA, as initially conceived, somewhat resembled Britain's successful effort to isolate Muhammad Mossadegh by preventing Iran from selling its oil, but in mid-October, Dulles changed the nature of the scheme, further upsetting British officials who were already annoyed by his delaying tactics. Nasser, who well understood why Mossadegh had failed in his stand against the West, said that it was "out of the question that there could be any discussion of tolls being paid to SCUA."[78] Dulles told Selwyn Lloyd that he wanted an "interim system" by which 90 percent of the tolls paid to the users' club would go to Egypt. Given that the secretary of state had already acknowledged that SCUA had no "teeth," that any obstruction of its duties should not be used as a pretext for force, Lloyd viewed the United States as a "broken reed" as "far as pressure on Nasser was concerned."[79] It was clear to the foreign secretary and the rest of the Cabinet that Britain and the United States were working at cross-purposes. Dulles's behavior in September and October, while understandable based on the difficult task that Eisenhower had given him, merely hardened the longstanding view at Whitehall that Britain could not count on the United States to help protect its economic interests.[80] Referring, no doubt, to the Iranian oil crisis, one member of the Foreign Office wrote: "Our hand is weakened by the American tendency in disputes between us and Middle Eastern States, to take a middle position instead of supporting us."[81]

---

[76] Harold Macmillan "regarded the establishment of this users' organisation as a step towards the ultimate use of force. It would not in itself provide a solution. It was very doubtful whether the canal could be operated effectively under such an arrangement as this." See Cabinet Conclusions, CM 64 (56), September 12, 1956, NA, CAB 128/30, and Kyle, *Suez*, 223–224.

[77] The best discussion of the conflict in British and US aims is Robert R. Bowie, "Eisenhower, Dulles, and the Suez Crisis" in Louis and Owen, *Suez 1956*, 189–214.

[78] Heikal, *Cutting the Lion's Tail*, 169.   [79] Lloyd, *Suez 1956*, 168–169.

[80] See Bowie, "Eisenhower, Dulles, and the Suez Crisis" for a helpful examination of Dulles's role.

[81] Foreign Office Minute by Walmsley, July 24, 1956, NA, FO 371/120812.

The users' club was discussed in the UN Security Council, where Lloyd gave a speech outlining six principles regarding use of the Suez Canal. For Britain, the most important of the principles was his third, which reiterated the point that "the operation of the Canal should be insulated from the politics of any country." Among Lloyd's other principles was the guarantee of "free and open transit through the Canal without discrimination," as well as "respect for Egyptian sovereignty."[82] The Security Council unanimously approved all six. Because of the strong statement that the unanimous vote conveyed to the international community, there was a sense that progress was being made. Eisenhower apparently believed as much. At a press conference on October 12, the election-conscious president optimistically – and perhaps naively – told reporters that "a very great crisis" had been averted.[83] Since Egypt still controlled the Suez Canal, the British government could not agree with Eisenhower's assessment. With British and French troops massing in the Mediterranean, the productive atmosphere of the Security Council lulled US officials into a sense of false security.

Britain and Egypt were never going to see eye-to-eye on who should control the Suez Canal. In fundamental ways, Britain's dispute with Nasser over the canal mirrored its conflict with Mossadegh over Iranian oil. Whitehall wanted to maintain British, or at the very least Western, control over the waterway, in large part because of the enormous impact of its operation on sterling and the British economy. It did not trust Nasser not to use the canal to hold sterling hostage by preventing Middle Eastern oil from passing through it. Nor did it trust him not to use his newfound prestige to turn Middle Eastern oil producers against Britain. Indeed, officials believed he was already trying to do so. The Foreign Office's C. R. A. Rae wrote: "Nasser has shown that no reliance can be placed upon his word, or on his protestations of friendship . . . He has consistently abused this friendship and his radio openly proclaims his intention to subvert the British position in the Middle East and Africa."[84] Given that the Suez Canal was carved out of Egyptian soil, "an integral part of Egypt," Nasser said, the Egyptian government believed that it had every right to manage the waterway and to reap the rewards of its use. It would not be told otherwise by colonial powers desperately trying to maintain their influence in the region.[85] As the Suez dispute dragged on, sterling's position grew more and more uncertain, and Treasury and Bank of England officials began to ponder the worst. With or without US help, the hawks at Whitehall needed to put Nasser in his place to

[82] Lloyd, *Suez 1956*, 159.   [83] Quoted in ibid., 160.
[84] Foreign Office Minute, October 5, 1956, NA, FO 371/119153.
[85] Quoted in Heikal, *Cutting the Lion's Tail*, 151.

reestablish British authority in the Middle East. By doing so, they also hoped to preserve, among other things, the viability of sterling.

3.3   Speculation against sterling and the march toward war

Sterling was particularly sensitive to confidence movements because of its widespread use, and the nationalization of the Suez Canal only exacerbated an already ebbing faith in the currency. Declining confidence in sterling had nothing to do with Britain's trade performance. The nation had recovered from the severe balance-of-payments deficit of the latter half of 1955 to post a surplus of £140 million in the first half of 1956, helping add £100 million to sterling area reserves. Rather, downward pressure on the pound came from fears among sterling holders that uncontrolled wage increases would undermine Britain's ability to compete in the world market. Uncertainty about the status of the Suez Canal further heightened concerns about the currency. Not only did governments shed sterling as a result, but some importers of British goods also delayed payments to their suppliers for two to three weeks at a time because they anticipated that Whitehall would devalue sterling, thereby reducing the relative cost of British imports.[86] Harold Macmillan and his advisors were so worried about confidence in the pound that at a press conference at the end of August he decided to keep "to the minimum" any discussion of the importance of oil and the canal to Britain: "It is really too dangerous, and there are too many sterling balances which could easily be withdrawn."[87]

The main problem for Britain was the prolonged nature of the Suez crisis since uncertainty about control of the canal bred uncertainty about sterling, primarily because of concerns about access to oil. Of course, the British economy was dependent on a range of commodities that passed through the canal, including all of the nation's imports of natural rubber, jute, and jute goods; half of its imports of zinc ores, lead, wool, cotton yarns, and fabrics; and more than a quarter of its cotton, hardwood, hides, skins, leather, carcass meat, dairy products, and vegetable oils.[88] But in terms of value and overall importance to the normal functioning

---

[86] Economic Committee (Washington), EC (W) (56) 26th Meeting, September 21, 1956, NA, CAB 134/1218. Such a delay, or lag, in payments represented one half of a trade effect known as "leads and lags." The other half, the lead, represented the demand by exporters to the sterling area to be paid immediately, before the pound lost any of its value.

[87] Macmillan to Eden, August 29, 1956, NA, PREM 11/1135.

[88] "British Use of the Suez Canal: Note by Officials," Part I, "The Extent to which We Rely on the Canal," Cabinet Committee on the Suez Canal, CM (57) 70, March 19, 1957, NA, PREM 11/2012.

of the British economy, nothing compared with oil. As Macmillan pointed out, "any interruption of oil supplies would be by far the most serious consequence" of the Suez crisis, and as long as the crisis persisted, sterling-holders feared that Britain's artery to Middle Eastern petroleum could be blocked at any moment.[89] They knew that Britain's inability to procure oil through the canal would greatly deplete the sterling area's reserves due to dollar expenditure on replacement oil from the Western Hemisphere as well as the balance-of-payments damage caused by a reduction in exports. The Treasury estimated that the dollar cost of rerouting tankers, both around the Cape of Good Hope and from the United States and Latin America (assuming that the pipelines from the Persian Gulf to the Mediterranean continued to operate) would cost Britain $515 million a year – a staggering figure.[90] Concerns about the potential for such losses translated into a steady flight from the pound, a trend facilitated by sterling's de facto convertibility.[91] The measure taken the previous year to encourage the currency's use was producing the opposite effect.

Treasury and Bank officials believed that the strain on sterling could not continue without Whitehall resorting to drastic measures. By the end of September, the reserves would have lost between $250 and $300 million in only two months if the British-controlled oil firm Trinidad Leaseholds had not been sold to the Texas Company and if special receipts from Australia had not come in. According to Leslie Rowan, the reserves had dropped near the $2 billion mark – the minimum amount of gold and dollars that Bank and Treasury officials estimated that the sterling area had to have to stay afloat, based on outstanding debts that might demand repayment at a moment's notice.[92] Denis Rickett wrote that "if matters were to get worse," the drain "could not be dealt with by any technical measure," but "only by some fairly far-reaching decision of policy,"

[89] "The Egypt Crisis and the British Economy," Memorandum by the Chancellor of the Exchequer, August 27, 1956, NA, PREM 11/1135.
[90] This figure included $303 million for additional supplies from the Western Hemisphere, $110 million in lost earnings on the sale of Middle Eastern oil, $112 million to hire additional dollar tankers, and a saving of $10 million as a result of reduced sales of Middle Eastern oil to Britain. See "Financial Consequences to the United Kingdom of the Oil Operation: Case for Dollar Aid," Rickett to Bridges and Petch, September 19, 1956, NA, T 236/4842.
[91] Edward Bridges wrote to Harold Macmillan: "It is already clear that our balance of payments and therefore our gold and dollar reserves are going to be under considerable strain over the next month or so, even if the [Suez] Conference reaches a successful conclusion. But if there is no clear-cut conclusion to the Conference and negotiations drag on for some time, our balance of payments position may come under even greater strain," August 8, 1956, NA, T 236/4188.
[92] Rowan to Macmillan, September 21, 1956, NA, T 236/4188.

including the resurrection of restrictive, bilateral sterling relationships or, worst of all, devaluation.[93] For policy-makers at Whitehall and the Bank of England, another devaluation amounted to financial suicide and was a measure to be avoided at all costs. The devaluation of 1949 "dealt the sterling system a blow" from which it had not recovered, according to the executive director of the Bank of England, George Bolton.[94] Expressing his concerns about the British economy in 1955, future executive director of the Bank, Maurice Henry Parsons, wrote: "World confidence in our ability to manage our affairs and to manage an international currency would be so shaken [by a devaluation] that I doubt whether sterling could ever recover from the shock."[95] With either a return to bilateralism or devaluation, the project to restore the international prestige of sterling was finished.

Leslie Rowan argued that sterling's troubles, as they pertained to the Middle East, transcended the Suez crisis and involved the larger Arab-Israeli conflict. He wondered "whether there would be complete confidence [in sterling] until not only the Suez problem, but the other sources of uncertainty in the Middle East had been resolved."[96] Investors flee unstable political and economic environments, and the British economy's overwhelming dependence on a commodity that came from such a volatile region did not inspire confidence in sterling. Rowan also feared that private financiers would refrain from putting money into sterling area countries that sympathized with Nasser, such as India, prompting those countries to use their sterling balances to fund development and shrink the reserves accordingly. Overthrowing Nasser and reorienting Egyptian policy "away from Russia" was an essential first step toward renewing faith in the pound, but such action would not do enough to save sterling, Rowan argued. Britain needed to implement a plan to "relieve the mutual fear" between Israel and its Arab neighbors so that they would be "free to concentrate on economic development." The result, he said, would be "calm" in the region and fewer opportunities for "Russian interference and intrigue," and, by implication, a revitalization of sterling. Rowan concluded: "unless something like this is done, both soon and successfully, sterling will be in the greatest danger and our other resources – IMF,

---

[93] "Possible Action if the Drain Continued," Rickett to Bridges, September 29, 1956, NA, T 236/4188.

[94] "The Foreign Exchange Market," Memorandum by George Bolton, NA, T 236/4189.

[95] Parsons to Bolton and the Governor, August 11, 1955, BE/G1/99. Sterling's devaluation in 1967 proved Parsons's assumption correct in terms of sterling's status as an international reserve currency.

[96] Economic Committee (Washington), EC (W) (56) 26th Meeting, September 21, 1956, NA, CAB 134/1218.

dollar securities, etc. – will not do much to put off the day."[97] To save the pound, either Nasser's influence had to be checked or the Egyptian president had to be removed altogether, a sentiment shared by the Cabinet's top three officials.

Anthony Eden, Selwyn Lloyd, and Harold Macmillan – hawks, all of them – made clear why they thought it would have been a mistake for Britain to negotiate any further with Nasser. Eden argued that additional discussions with Egypt would have produced an agreement "dressed up to look fairly reasonable," but one that "did not mean much." Worse still, "This would have lulled people at a time when I thought they should be alerted. It would have reassured the world about a dictator whose intentions were, I was sure, predatory." Signing a superficial accord that did not guarantee international control of the Suez Canal, Eden thought, "would have been false to everything I had learned in thirty years of foreign policy." It would not have "insulated the canal from the control of one man," he concluded, and, by forfeiting de facto international control, Britain would have been "laying up certain trouble for the future."[98] Lloyd, who was famously loyal to Eden, wrote: "our prestige in the Middle East would fall still further as inconclusive negotiations dragged on. Nasser would be seen to have won," which would have set a "dangerous precedent," in terms of his ability to seize with impunity something of vital interest to the world. On the other hand, "restoration of the Canal to international control would be a sufficient defeat for him."[99] Macmillan, the most aggressive of the three regarding Nasser – particularly because of the financial stakes, as he perceived them – saw two choices facing Britain with starkly different outcomes: imposing international control over the Suez Canal by force, so that the dispute was "settled in such a way as not to threaten [Britain's] oil supplies" or "to surrender altogether, not only the Canal, but Western prestige in the Middle East."[100]

Referring to Sarajevo in 1914, Eden wrote, "We are all marked to some extent by the stamp of our generation." Britain's appeasement of Hitler at Munich in 1938 represented just such a stamp.[101] When Nasser nationalized the Suez Canal, it was the twentieth anniversary of Germany's reoccupation of the Rhineland, and Lloyd, Macmillan, and Eden all compared the Egyptian leader to the German dictator to justify cutting him down, both during the crisis and in their memoirs. Lloyd wrote that Britain had learned its "lesson over Hitler," that his "appetite

[97] Rowan to Macmillan, September 21, 1956, NA, T 236/4188.
[98] Anthony Eden, *Full Circle: The Memoirs of Anthony Eden* (Cambridge: The Riverside Press, 1960), 588.
[99] Lloyd, *Suez 1956*, 194, 190.   [100] Macmillan, *Riding the Storm*, 130, 149.
[101] Eden, *Full Circle*, 576.

had grown with eating – the rape of Austria, Munich, the absorption of Czechoslovakia, Poland and the dream of world conquest resulting in 20 million dead." "If Nasser was not checked," he argued, "the prospect in the Middle East was grim."[102] Recalling a speech he had made in the United States in September 1956, Macmillan described how "Hitler had established his position by a series of carefully planned moves" and told his audience, "I feel that all of us who went through those years . . . are determined to see that this shall not happen again."[103] Eden's language mirrored that of the chancellor: "As my colleagues and I surveyed the scene in these autumn months of 1956, we were determined that the like should not come again . . . There might be other mistakes, there would not be that one." Therefore, the prime minister concluded, "Intervention by the Western powers, with all its risks, was clearly to be preferred."[104]

Although desperate to stop Britain's financial losses, Treasury officials worried about the potential costs for sterling of taking military action against Nasser without US support. Permanent Secretary Edward Bridges could not have made this point any clearer when he wrote to Harold Macmillan:

Very broadly it seems to us that unless we can secure at least US support and a fairly unified Commonwealth, then it is not possible to predict either the exact timing or the magnitude of the strains which are likely to come upon our currency. At the worst, however, the strains might be so great that, whatever precautionary measures were taken we should be unable to maintain the value of the currency . . . What this points to therefore is the vital necessity from the point of view of our currency and our economy of ensuring that we do not go it alone, and that we have the maximum US support.[105]

Even as far back as April, several months before Nasser nationalized the Suez Canal, members of the Treasury considered the aid that Britain would need from the United States if either the canal or the oil pipelines from the Persian Gulf were obstructed. One official commented that consultation with the United States was "clearly vital" because "only close United States cooperation [could] lead to any sort of solution of the difficulties which could arise" from a disruption in oil supplies.[106]

Leslie Rowan's depiction of the obstacles that Britain and sterling would face if it invaded Egypt without US support made such action seem very risky indeed. Rowan forecast that, without backing from the

[102] Lloyd, *Suez 1956*, 192–193.   [103] Macmillan, *Riding the Storm*, 131–132.
[104] Eden, *Full Circle*, 578–579. It is worth noting that the leader of the opposition Labour Party, Hugh Gaitskell, compared Nasser to both Mussolini and Hitler in August 1956, as Macmillan relished pointing out in *Riding the Storm*, 131.
[105] Bridges to Macmillan, September 7, 1956, NA, T 236/4188.
[106] Rampton to Armstrong, April 12, 1956, NA, T 236/4841.

United States, Britain would need "all the help [it] could get" from the International Monetary Fund. But he recognized that such help would hardly be forthcoming if the US government found itself at odds with the British because of the influential US position at the IMF. He also figured that it would be next to impossible to activate the Anglo-American Financial Agreement's waiver clause – the provision that allowed Britain to default on its interest payments, but not the principal, during times of severe economic difficulty – or to obtain oil and tankers from the United States, if Britain sacrificed American goodwill by going it alone.[107] On September 15, Macmillan himself wrote in his diary that although it was "absolutely vital to humiliate Nasser," and to "do it quickly," if Britain did not secure US support, the country would "have no chance of getting out of [its] financial ruin."[108] The chancellor never discussed the Treasury's warnings or his own concerns with the Cabinet. Moreover, despite his understanding of the financial dangers of military action against Nasser, he remained Whitehall's staunchest advocate for such an operation.[109] Given his position as the Cabinet minister responsible for the nation's finances – not to mention his personal influence at Whitehall – his role in the decision to internationalize the Suez Canal by force is important to explore.

At the end of September 1956, Macmillan spent a critical ten days in the United States, during which he had discussions with the most senior officials in the Eisenhower Administration. On the morning of September 25, he met with Eisenhower himself, and, much to the amazement of Roger Makins, the British Ambassador in Washington and a note-taker during this conversation, the two hardly mentioned Suez. The subject did arise once, though, and, according to Macmillan: "I made it quite clear that we could *not* play it long, without aid on a very large scale – that is, if playing it long involved buying dollar oil." When the chancellor discussed the meeting with Eden, he told the prime minister that Eisenhower "seemed to understand this point," adding that he had the "feeling" that the president was "really determined, somehow or other,

---

[107] "Economic and Financial Measures in the Event of War with Egypt," undated memorandum by Leslie Rowan, attached to a letter dated September 11, 1956, NA, T 236/4188.

[108] Quoted in Alistair Horne, *Macmillan, 1894–1956: Volume I of the Official Biography* (London: Macmillan, 1988), 418.

[109] That few others saw the Treasury papers is argued by Lewis Johnman in "Defending the Pound: The Economics of the Suez Crisis, 1956." According to him, Guy Millard, Anthony Eden's private secretary, who dealt with the prime minister's paperwork on Suez, said, "I'm not sure Eden saw the Treasury warnings. I didn't see them. Macmillan saw them, but he was a hawk," suggesting that Macmillan prevented those warnings from reaching the prime minister's desk, 179.

to bring Nasser down."[110] Macmillan repeated this assessment in his memoirs, but Makins would later contradict the chancellor's account, claiming that there was "no basis at all for Harold's optimism." Makins added, "Yes, the Americans were willing to see Nasser put down, *but* what they would not contemplate were military operations – especially ahead of the election."[111]

In two other meetings, one with John Foster Dulles that afternoon and another with George Humphrey the next day, Macmillan found further reason to be optimistic. While Dulles was angry with Britain and France for taking the Suez case to the United Nations without first consulting with the United States, he said that the administration "was prepared to do everything it could to bring Nasser down." Furthermore, Dulles acknowledged that Britain "might have to use force" to do so. At the very least, he asserted, the threat of force was vital to coerce Nasser into making concessions. He even cryptically mentioned using "other means of pressure," to accomplish this goal, possibly referring to covert action. Regardless, Dulles did not want anything to disturb the "present situation in the Canal," especially before the presidential election on November 6, asking Macmillan to "hold things off" until it was over. Dulles responded similarly to the chancellor's request for financial aid to help reinforce Britain's reserves. He said that the administration could try to rework the Anglo-American Financial Agreement, but not until after the election.[112] The following day, George Humphrey, who had spoken with Dulles on the phone on the subject of amending the Loan, echoed the secretary of state's remarks about postponing any action on the Loan until after the first week of November. Macmillan and Humphrey never directly referred to Suez, and the former wrote in his memoirs that he had surmised that the secretary of the treasury "had no very strong feelings about it." Encouraging to the chancellor was Humphrey's "emphatic" statement that "America must see the United Kingdom through any of her troubles," which left Macmillan feeling that, in the secretary, Britain was "likely to find a useful as well as a powerful friend." He acknowledged in his memoirs: "In this I was soon to be proved tragically wrong."[113]

Once Macmillan returned to London, he is reported to have told his colleagues in an oft-quoted remark that "Ike will lie doggo until after

[110] Horne, *Macmillan*, 420–422. Also see Macmillan to Eden, September 26, 1956, NA, PREM 11/1102.
[111] Macmillan, *Riding the Storm*, 135; Horne, *Macmillan*, 422. Makins's comments are from an interview with Horne.
[112] Macmillan to Eden, September 26, 1956, NA, PREM 11/1102; quoted in Kunz, *The Economic Diplomacy of the Suez Crisis*, 104–105.
[113] Macmillan, *Riding the Storm*, 137–138.

the election."[114] Eden himself later wrote that the chancellor "found the American attitude reassuring in a number of respects."[115] Did Macmillan simply hear what he wanted to hear during his meetings with Eisenhower, Dulles, and Humphrey? Did he willfully misrepresent his conversations to Eden and the rest of the British Cabinet? Perhaps most importantly, did the chancellor's positive gloss critically influence Anthony Eden's decision to invade Egypt?[116] Macmillan's opinions concerning Eisenhower and American sensibilities did, in fact, carry some weight because of his warm relationship with the president – stretching back to the North African campaign of World War II – and because the chancellor was himself half-American.[117] Nonetheless, given Eden's own hawkish attitude regarding Nasser, it seems that only a definitive report from Macmillan that the United States would sabotage any attempt by Britain to regain control of the canal by force might have slowed the prime minister's momentum towards war. Furthermore, Macmillan and Eden were both guilty of thinking that Dulles, who seemed to find the use of force against Nasser less objectionable than Eisenhower, controlled US foreign policy rather than the genial, golf-playing president – a common misconception at the time.[118] With or without Macmillan's misinterpretations, Eden certainly knew that the Eisenhower Administration would respond unfavorably to what was being planned.[119] Otherwise, he would not have

---

[114] Quoted in Horne, *Macmillan*, 434.   [115] Eden, *Full Circle*, 551.

[116] About Macmillan's conversation with Eisenhower, Alistair Horne writes, "The effect that Macmillan's version of this crucial meeting – coming from the strong man of the Cabinet – was to have upon the feverish Eden, then just returning from Paris where the French had applied the strongest pressures to act without more delay, can hardly be exaggerated; and it was to be further reinforced by what Macmillan had to say in person on his return to London," *Macmillan*, 422.

[117] Eisenhower said that he had "always thought most highly of Macmillan," describing him as a "straight, fine man" and "the outstanding one of the British" with whom he served during World War II. Memorandum of a Conference with the President, November 20, 1956, *FRUS, 1955–1957, Vol. XVI*, 1166–1169.

[118] Eden fixated on a remark that Dulles uttered not long after the nationalization of the Suez Canal that "a way had to be found to make Nasser disgorge what he was attempting to swallow." David Dutton, *Anthony Eden: A Life and Reputation* (London: Arnold, 1997), 390–391; Horne, *Macmillan*, 423–424. Robert R. Bowie accuses Britain and France of selectively hearing comments from the secretary of state that favored their approach, which Bowie maintains Dulles made to persuade them to stay astride the United States. See "Eisenhower, Dulles, and the Suez Crisis." For an analysis of the British perspective on Dulles, see Wm. Roger Louis, "Dulles, Suez, and the British" in Richard H. Immerman (ed.), *John Foster Dulles and the Diplomacy of the Cold War* (Princeton University Press, 1990). See Fred I. Greenstein, *The Hidden-Hand Presidency: Eisenhower as Leader* (New York: Basic Books, 1982) for a corrective to the misconception that Eisenhower let Dulles run US foreign policy.

[119] Eisenhower wrote to Eden during the second week of September, "The use of military force against Egypt under present circumstances might have consequences even more serious than causing the Arabs to support Nasser. It might cause a serious

allowed the position of British ambassador in Washington to go unfilled during the month leading up to the Suez invasion; nor would he have refused to see the recently returned former ambassador, Roger Makins, until the operation had already begun.[120] Eden and his French and Israeli counterparts, moreover, timed the invasion to occur just before the presidential election so that the United States would be less able to thwart their plans. Would they have done so if they did not expect an adverse reaction from across the Atlantic? In his memoirs, Macmillan blames himself for the Cabinet's misreading of Eisenhower and Dulles: "We altogether failed to appreciate the force of the resentment which would be directed against us. For this I carry a heavy responsibility . . . I believed that the Americans would issue a protest, even a violent protest in public; but that they would in their hearts be glad to see the matter brought to a conclusion."[121] In the end, the criticism that Macmillan receives for how he portrayed his September meetings in Washington seems a bit overdone.[122]

More justifiable, perhaps, are the assaults on Macmillan for not having financially prepared Britain for war. In October, the Treasury debated whether Britain should borrow from the International Monetary Fund (IMF) to support the nation's reserves. Together, its gold tranche of $236 million and its first credit tranche of $325 million would have provided a much-needed buffer against any further depletion of Britain's gold and dollars.[123] To maintain confidence in sterling, though, Treasury officials

misunderstanding between our two countries because I must say frankly that there is as yet no public opinion in this country which is prepared to support such a move," September 8, 1956, NA, FO 800/740.

[120] Makins said, "absolutely nobody wanted to see me . . . I couldn't understand why. Selwyn didn't want to see me – Anthony didn't want to see me – even Harold." He recalled that when Macmillan finally agreed to see him after Britain's invasion fleet had left on October 28, "I think I did give him a jolt by telling him what Suez would do to Anglo-American relations," quoted in Horne, *Macmillan*, 431, 434. The former ambassador also had no doubt that he would have resigned had he remained at his post. After all, he had written to the Foreign Office almost two months earlier: "As it looks from Washington, to attempt [military action in Egypt] without full American moral and material support could easily lead to disaster . . . A go-it-alone policy of military intervention would obviously deal [Anglo-American relations] a body-blow," No. 1849, September 9, 1956, NA, FO 800/740.

[121] Macmillan, *Riding the Storm*, 157.

[122] Kunz, *The Economic Diplomacy of the Suez Crisis*; Johnman, "Defending the Pound: the Economics of the Suez Crisis, 1956"; Edmund Dell, *The Chancellors: A History of the Chancellors of the Exchequer, 1945–1990* (London: HarperCollins, 1996). This is particularly true of Kunz, one of Macmillan's most vociferous critics. She writes that the chancellor's "sense of complacency . . . seems incomprehensible or perhaps even discreditable," 108.

[123] "Economic and Financial Measures in the Event of War with Egypt," undated memorandum by Leslie Rowan, attached to a letter dated September 11, 1956, NA,

generally felt that Britain was better off borrowing from the IMF when it did not appear that Whitehall felt compelled to do so. C. F. Cobbold, the Governor of the Bank of England, agreed, arguing that an approach to the IMF would be "regarded on a second view as a sign of weakness" and would consequently erode confidence in sterling, especially in Europe.[124] Thus, on the advice of the governor and his Treasury advisors, Macmillan stayed away from the Fund until it was too late. In fact, Cobbold, Rowan, and Makins – who had just become joint permanent under-secretary of the Treasury – decided with Macmillan at the outset of the Suez operation that, only if the military campaign was successful and "the political situation improved," would it be "appropriate" for Britain to ask for a stand-by credit from the IMF.[125]

Unfortunately for Britain, Macmillan's decision not to draw the country's gold or credit allotments left sterling vulnerable to attack during the Suez invasion. France, having borrowed from the IMF in mid-October, was better prepared for a run on the franc once military operations were underway. Of course, hindsight is twenty-twenty, and had Britain been successful in reestablishing international control of the Suez Canal and toppling Nasser in the process, people might have returned to sterling in large numbers. The fact remains that the prospects for such an outcome were not good, and the chancellor should have prepared Britain for the worst by insulating the nation's reserves. That said, he cannot be solely blamed for not going to the IMF when others discouraged him from doing so.

Macmillan's decision not to inform the Cabinet of the Treasury's warnings about the financial dangers of invading the Suez Canal zone without US assistance has rightly earned him the condemnation of historians for negligence and incompetence but has also led, unfortunately, to unprovable conspiratorial insinuations and allegations. Lewis

---

T 236/4188. A member of the IMF paid a subscription to the organization in gold and its own currency, 25 percent in the former and 75 percent in the latter, also known as its quota. If a member's reserve position was threatened, it could draw its gold tranche – the difference between the Fund's holding of a member's currency and its quota – without condition. A member could also draw on its quota in quarterly credit tranches, the first of which the IMF granted liberally, with the promise that the member would work to ameliorate the cause of its financial troubles in a reasonable period of time. Any further drawing was made under a standby arrangement, which was a line of credit extended over a specified period of time, usually twelve months, on the assurance that the member would follow macroeconomic policies that ideally would meet agreed upon performance targets. Britain's total quota was $1,300 million.

[124] Rowan to Makins, October 26, 1956, NA, T 236/4188. Coincidentally, Cobbold, who could not have known about the plot to invade Egypt, made this statement three days before the Suez operation began.

[125] Note for the Record by Leslie Rowan, October 31, 1956, NA, T 236/4188.

Johnman accuses Macmillan of "deliberately misleading" Eden and his colleagues and implies that he did so to manufacture the kind of failure that would drive Eden out of office and position the chancellor for the premiership.[126] Diane Kunz argues that, at the very least, "Macmillan's performance as chancellor during the Suez crisis must be assessed as incompetent" and leaves open the possibility that he had more Machiavellian intentions.[127] The Cabinet, which did not unanimously support the action against Egypt, might have been swayed from participating in the venture if Macmillan had apprised its members of the enormous financial risks involved. He should have, no doubt, shared more of the information at his disposal.

We can never know for certain the motives behind Macmillan's actions in the month and a half leading up to the Suez invasion. However, we can arrive at a less conspiratorial assessment of his intentions, by locating his behavior in a pattern of foreign policy aggressiveness at Whitehall – particularly among Treasury officials – regarding the defense of sterling through British control of Middle Eastern oil. British policy-makers did not think that Britain could regain or maintain its prominence in international affairs without restoring the strength and stability of the pound. Exploiting petroleum from the Middle East had become a critical part of that project, whether using it to displace dollar oil or ensuring that Britain could acquire it cheaply and pay for it with sterling. Many in London had no qualms about disrupting Anglo-American relations when they believed that Britain's vital economic interests were at stake, as was the case in the sterling–dollar oil controversy and in the Iranian oil crisis. Admittedly, Edward Bridges, Leslie Rowan, and other members of the Treasury bucked this trend when it came to using force to retake the Suez Canal, fearing the financial consequences of doing so without US support. Macmillan, on the other hand, did not. As other British officials had before, the chancellor believed that US policy-makers did not fully appreciate the vulnerability of sterling or understand the measures and the risks that the British government had to take to protect it. Macmillan wrote in his diary: "The more we can persuade [the Americans] of our determination to risk everything in order to beat Nasser, the more help we shall get from them . . . We shall be ruined either way; but we shall be more inevitably ruined if we are humiliated [by Nasser]."[128] In his view, even a disastrous run on the pound precipitated by an all-or-nothing gambit was

---

[126] Johnman, "Defending the Pound," 179.
[127] Kunz, *The Economic Diplomacy of the Suez Crisis*, 107. Politicians and others have made such accusations since the crisis.
[128] Quoted in Horne, *Macmillan*, 415.

more tolerable than the "slow strangulation" of the British economy that Nasser would induce by turning Middle Eastern oil producers against Britain.[129]

Context is also crucial to consider when assessing Macmillan's decision-making during the Suez crisis. First, the government had made sterling de facto convertible only a year and a half earlier, a move that was supposed to pave the way for the currency's complete international restoration. Instead, not only was the pound more susceptible to attack than it had been previously, but the sterling restoration project that members of the Treasury, the Bank, and the Conservative Party had pursued since the end of World War II was on the verge of unraveling. Second, Britain was only a few years removed from the Iranian oil imbroglio, a devastating event that had already significantly diminished British prestige in the Middle East. The chancellor and other hawks did not think that Britain could sustain any more damage to what remained of that prestige and still exercise the kind of influence over the region's oil that would be necessary to protect sterling and the British economy. The chancellor's unflagging dedication to this belief, reinforced by Eden, Lloyd, and others, contributed to his zeal and poor judgment.[130] Desperate times called for desperate measures, and, as Macmillan would later tell John Foster Dulles, Britain's plot to retake the Suez Canal was "the last gasp of a declining power," adding that, "perhaps in two hundred years," the United States would know how Britain felt.[131]

That is not to say that the British government's invasion was either prudent or excusable – or that Macmillan should not be held accountable for his mistakes. But by recognizing the postwar predilection among British officials for apocalyptic forecasts regarding sterling's viability without British access to Middle Eastern oil – as well as Whitehall's defiant attitude toward the United States on the subject of the pound and petroleum in the postwar era – one can explain Macmillan's behavior during the Suez crisis without resorting to conspiracy theories.[132] One can also

[129] Cabinet, Confidential Annex, CM (56) 63rd Conclusions, September 6, 1956, NA, PREM 11/1100.
[130] Ivone Kirkpatrick, the permanent under-secretary of state at the Foreign Office, wrote to Makins in Washington, "If Middle East oil is denied to us for a year or two our gold reserves will disappear. If our gold reserves disappear the sterling area disintegrates . . ." Quoted in Horne, *Macmillan*, 416.
[131] "Memorandum for the Record by the Secretary of State," December 12, 1956, *FRUS, 1955–1957, Vol. XXVII*, 677–678.
[132] In *Macmillan: A Study in Ambiguity*, Anthony Sampson also rejects the Machiavellian view of Macmillan, writing: "Macmillan was clearly genuinely carried away by Suez, and shared Eden's defensive emotions. He certainly saw the operation as a gamble; but he was convinced that the danger was as great if Britain did nothing. The actual

understand why the Cabinet agreed to such a risky operation in the first place. Two weeks before the launch of the Suez invasion, C. F. Cobbold said that Britain "should regard a further devaluation of sterling as a disaster to be fought with every weapon at [its] disposal."[133] The non-resolution of the Suez Canal question and the steady deterioration of sterling that it produced made devaluation an increasingly greater possibility, compelling Macmillan and his colleagues to interpret the governor's remark literally.

3.4   Operation "Musketeer," Anglo-American discord, and sterling's collapse

The Suez invasion, known as Operation "Musketeer," began on October 29, 1956, with an Israeli foray into the Sinai Desert. Justified as retribution for Nasser's part in enabling and encouraging Palestinian *fedayeen* raiders to attack Israel from Egyptian soil, the move was designed to serve as a pretext for an Anglo-French occupation of the Suez Canal zone. On October 30, Britain and France sent notes to Egypt and Israel demanding that the two sides separate and retreat to a distance of ten miles from the canal. The note to Egypt contained an additional passage requesting that it allow Anglo-French forces to occupy "temporarily" positions along the waterway to protect shipping. It also threatened that, if Egypt did not signal compliance to their requests within twelve hours, they would send troops anyway. Of course, the international community did not – as British and French leaders had wanted – view the intervention as an impartial, selfless act meant to help keep the peace. Instead, the world saw the Anglo-French maneuvering for what it was: a transparent scheme to impose by force international control of the Suez Canal. John Foster Dulles described the ultimatum to Egypt as being "about as crude and brutal as anything" he had ever seen.[134]

Operation "Musketeer" was an unmitigated failure. After Anglo-French air forces began dropping bombs on Cairo on October 31, Eisenhower appeared on television to broadcast his opposition to the attack. He completely dissociated the United States from the action and threw his support behind the United Nations. American, international, and British domestic antagonism towards Operation "Musketeer" precipitated a loss of $50 million from Britain's reserves during the first two days

outcome of the Suez war could not have been predicted by anyone, for the situation was confused and criss-crossed with emotion and miscalculation," 122.

[133] Cobbold to Macmillan, October 17, 1956, NA, T 236/4188.
[134] Quoted in Kyle, *Suez*, 361.

of November.[135] Regardless, in violation of United Nations resolutions calling for an end to hostilities, Britain and France deployed more than 1,100 paratroopers near Port Said on the Mediterranean side of the canal. Their ability to control the northern part of the waterway did not have nearly the impact on Egypt, however, as Nasser's ability to block the canal had on them: he sank ships, including a 10,000 ton freighter filled with rocks and cement, in the canal, thereby preventing them from obtaining oil through it.[136] Making matters worse, Syria sabotaged the pumping stations that propelled Iraqi petroleum by pipeline to the Mediterranean. Although Aramco's Tapline still functioned, Saudi Arabia denied British and French ships access to oil from it. Thus, by November 7, Britain was virtually cut off from Middle Eastern petroleum. Treasury officials estimated that if oil consumption continued at existing rates, the country might have to spend $800 million a year to obtain it from the Western Hemisphere. That first week of November, Britain's reserves lost $85 million, prompting C. F. Cobbold to describe sterling as a "major casualty" of the Anglo-French operation and to conclude that "radical treatment" would be necessary to save the currency.[137]

The atmosphere at the Treasury and the Bank throughout November was one of crisis, a mood reflected by Harold Macmillan from the outset. After witnessing the drubbing that sterling endured during the first week of November, the staunchest advocate of "Musketeer" became its most fervent opponent. The chancellor lost his nerve. Eden, Lloyd, and others were prepared to continue with the military action until Macmillan told the Cabinet on November 6 – inaccurately it turns out – that Britain's reserves had lost an extraordinary £100 million ($280 million) during the week from a run on sterling allegedly organized by the United States.[138] According to Lloyd, Macmillan told him earlier that day, "in view of the financial and economic pressures we must stop," and the foreign secretary cites Macmillan's remarks as a fundamental reason for Eden's

---

[135] On November 3, 1956, *The Economist* wrote, "This is a gambler's throw; upon it the Prime Minister has hazarded not only his own political future and that of his Government, but, vastly more important, his country's position, interest, and reputation in the world." Protestors took to the streets in London, eventually organizing a mass demonstration in Trafalgar Square near all of the major government offices; Rickett to Rowan, November 2, 1956, NA, T 236/4188.

[136] *The Economist*, November 10, 1956; Farnie, *East and West of Suez*, 729; Yergin, *The Prize*, 490.

[137] Note of a meeting at 11 Downing Street, November 7, 1956, and Makins to Macmillan, November 9, 1956, both NA, T 236/4189.

[138] Horne, *Macmillan*, 440. Diane Kunz argues that there is no evidence for Macmillan's assertion that sterling sales occurred primarily in New York in early November, nor that anyone at the Treasury or the Bank even mentioned New York as a source of trouble until November 20. See *The Economic Diplomacy of the Suez Crisis*, 132.

3.2 Block ships sunk by Egypt at the entrance of the Suez Canal at Port Said.

announcement of a cease-fire that evening.[139] Eden himself pointed to the influence of Britain's economic troubles on his decision to halt "Musketeer" while also maintaining the fiction, as Lloyd did, that the primary impetus for the Cabinet's acceptance of a cease-fire was Britain's containment of the Israeli–Egyptian conflict.[140] Indeed, given that Eden's reluctant decision to comply with UN demands came in the wake of Macmillan's grim report on the state of the reserves, it is difficult to believe any explanation that does not emphasize financial motives.

Much like his overwhelming support for "Musketeer," Macmillan's dramatic about-face has been the source of debate and puzzlement among his contemporaries and historians alike.[141] Most troubling is the

---

[139] Lloyd, *Suez*, 209.   [140] Eden, *Full Circle*, 624.

[141] Macmillan wrote, "Many commentators and historians, then and now, have given a number of diverse, sometimes contradictory, sometimes inaccurate reasons which induced the Government to take so grave a decision . . . I have often been reproached for having been at the same time one of the most keen supporters of strong action in the Middle East and one of the most rapid to withdraw when that policy met a serious check," *Riding the Storm*, 163.

chancellor's gross exaggeration of Britain's reserve losses in the first week of November. Nobody knows how he arrived at the figure of £100 million, especially since the following day the Treasury reported the drain as being less than a third of that amount. Could he actually have been so careless as to mistake pounds for dollars? Diane Kunz argues that Macmillan seemed to want to scare the Cabinet into ending the doomed operation and knew that, as a figure who commanded attention for both his financial acuity and his hawkish credentials, making a case based on catastrophic economic figures would be the best way to persuade his colleagues to give up the game.[142] Macmillan himself disingenuously writes in his memoirs that the nation's financial straits did not cause his change of heart but instead perpetuates the scarcely believable myth, first advanced by Eden and later supported by Lloyd, that the Cabinet agreed to a cease-fire because Britain had achieved what it had set out to do in Egypt.[143]

The question nonetheless remains why the chancellor turned so abruptly. His official biographer, Alistair Horne, writes that "the weight of opinion among his eminent contemporaries" indicated that the flight from sterling proved to be "quite categorically" of "decisive" influence.[144] As we have seen, one of those contemporaries, Selwyn Lloyd, believed that Britain's financial difficulties did, in fact, give Macmillan cold feet. But the foreign secretary hypothesizes that the nature of the American reaction to "Musketeer" is really what made the difference. Lloyd wrote: "I think that he was emotionally affected when he was told that the administration of his close wartime friend, Eisenhower, through the mouth of George Humphrey... whom Macmillan also regarded as a friend, was obstructing our drawing from the International Monetary Fund."[145] Two things must have crossed the chancellor's mind at the time: first, that he had egregiously misperceived how Eisenhower, Dulles, and Humphrey would respond to Britain's deception; and, second, that Britain would not only not receive US support for its invasion of Egypt – the worst that Macmillan and his advisors had anticipated – but that it would also have to contend with its opposition. After processing the potentially catastrophic consequences for sterling of proceeding with "Musketeer" in the face of concerted American obstruction, it is not surprising that Macmillan had a change of heart. He knew the operation was a gamble in the first place, and it had clearly not paid off.

---

[142] Kunz, *The Economic Diplomacy of the Suez Crisis*, 132–133.
[143] Macmillan, *Riding the Storm*, 163–166.   [144] Horne, *Macmillan*, 443.
[145] Lloyd, *Suez 1956*, 210–211.

The poor timing of the Anglo-French plot further intensified the animus within the Eisenhower Administration toward Eden and his Cabinet. Dulles could not have been clearer with Macmillan about postponing any British plan to retake the Suez Canal by force until after the presidential election – that is, if Whitehall were unwisely to pursue what the secretary of state and his colleagues viewed as an ill-advised course in the first place. The British government proceeded with "Musketeer" anyway, doing so before November 6 in the hope that the president would be too hamstrung by domestic politics to stop it. Most inconvenient for Eisenhower was the fact that his campaign had highlighted the president's success in maintaining world peace. Thus, the administration looked foolish as American voters prepared to go to the polls while the closest allies of the United States waged an unpopular war in the Middle East.[146] The Suez invasion also squandered a golden opportunity for the United States to showcase Soviet aggression in Eastern Europe by diverting the world's attention from the Soviet Union's suppression of the Hungarian Revolt at the end of October 1956, and, instead, directing it towards the Western assault on Egypt. Worst of all, the British government had, as John Foster Dulles said, "kept [the United States] deliberately in the dark about its plans." He characterized October 30, 1956 as "the blackest day" that had "occurred in many years" in US relations with Britain and France.[147]

While the timing of "Musketeer" sharpened the edges of the Eisenhower Administration's response to the operation, the core of its anger derived from a general and longstanding frustration in government circles with British policy toward the non-Western world. Much like the previous July, when Eden, Macmillan, and Lloyd first threatened to use force against Egypt to internationalize the Suez Canal, the events of late October and early November resurrected the issue of Britain's anachronistic foreign policy among US officials. At a White House meeting on October 30, Eisenhower characterized the British action in Egypt as "in the mid-Victorian style" and wondered if the "hand of Churchill" was at work. Dulles said that he had been "greatly worried for two or three years over [the United States's] identification with countries pursuing colonial

---

[146] Eisenhower's aggravation concerned more than appearances. His desire to ease Cold War tensions was genuine, and he and his advisors believed that the Anglo-French action could have escalated into a larger conflict with the Soviet Union. See Robert A. Divine, *Eisenhower and the Cold War* (New York: Oxford University Press, 1981) for a discussion of Eisenhower's efforts to achieve détente with the Soviet Union during his second term in office.

[147] Memorandum of Conversation, Department of State, October 30, 1956, *FRUS, 1955–1957, Vol. XVI*, 875–877.

policies not compatible with [US foreign policy]."[148] While the Truman and Eisenhower Administrations never liked the sterling area, they had, in fact, grudgingly accepted the British empire for the sake of international stability and the benefit of having allied military bases across the globe. Nonetheless, they had hoped that the empire would come to an orderly end in the near future. As discussed previously, the problem with the sterling area and the empire for US policy-makers was that they both violated American ideals of free trade and self-determination, undermined American economic interests, and subverted the West's moral authority in the fight against communism. Since the end of World War II, Washington had grown increasingly disturbed by what it viewed as Britain's somewhat reckless and neo-colonial pursuit of its economic interests at the expense of the welfare of the United States and the rest of the free world. The Eisenhower Administration's outrage at Britain's attempt to resolve the Suez crisis by military means represented, to a large degree, the culmination of a decade's worth of Anglo-American tension over economic and strategic issues, especially as they pertained to the Middle East and oil.[149]

Eisenhower, Dulles, and Humphrey did not express their anger with words alone. They used all of the economic weapons at their disposal to compel Britain to reverse its course, refusing to discuss financial aid or replacement oil with British officials until they agreed to a cease-fire and withdrew their troops from Egypt.[150] The administration pursued this policy not only to penalize Britain for what it viewed as the country's disloyalty and irresponsible action, but also to protect US interests in the Middle East, which it feared would be damaged by any open association with Britain or France. Consequently, Eisenhower and his team prevented the Middle East Emergency Committee (MEEC) – an organization established to ensure the flow of oil to Western Europe if the Suez Canal were blocked – from convening. They also refused to authorize representatives of the US petroleum industry to work with their counterparts across the Atlantic to organize oil supplies for Europe by waiving the anti-trust regulations that made such cooperation

[148] Memorandum of a Conference with the President, White House, October 30, 1956, *FRUS, 1955–1957, Vol. XVI*, 851–855.
[149] Regarding Suez, Eisenhower sent a note to Anthony Eden saying, "I must say that it is hard for me to see any good final result emerging from a scheme that seems certain to antagonize the entire Moslem world," October 30, 1956, *FRUS, 1955–1957, Vol. XVI*, 874–875.
[150] Kunz, *The Economic Diplomacy of the Suez Crisis* is, by far, the most comprehensive work on this subject.

illegal.[151] Eisenhower quipped that "those who began this operation should be left to work out their own oil problems – to boil in their own oil so to speak."[152]

Two days after Eden had announced his acceptance of a cease-fire, the new British Ambassador in Washington, Harold Caccia, reported that Britain would probably still be unable to borrow from either the International Monetary Fund or the Export-Import Bank of the United States (EXIM), the latter of which lends money to foreign countries to buy American goods. Even though Britain was allowed to draw its gold tranche from the IMF automatically, the United States could keep the matter from coming up at the IMF board meetings, obstructing Britain's access to its own resources. Caccia wondered if Britain could even secure a majority of the voting board members without US support.[153] Whitehall would also have to abandon any hope of activating the waiver clause of the Anglo-American Financial Agreement. According to Caccia, George Humphrey told Viscount Harcourt, Britain's economic minister in Washington, that "for the United States to offer financial aid to the United Kingdom and France in the light of [their] actions in the last ten days would be totally unacceptable politically in the United States for some considerable time."[154]

The Eisenhower Administration's unequivocal denunciation of the British adventure at Suez, and its refusal to provide Britain with access to either oil or money until it retreated from Egypt, helped make November a disastrous month for sterling. Britain's reserves lost $279 million in November, reducing the nation's total gold and dollar holdings to $1,965 million, or just below the $2,000 million threshold considered necessary for the sterling area to function properly (see Table 3.1). This drain – which would have been worse by $122 million if the Treasury had not sold some of Britain's US short-term Treasury bonds and other dollar securities – followed on the heels of an $84 million loss in October.[155]

[151] Foreign Office Minute by Wright, November 11, 1956, NA, FO 371/120833, No. 819 from the British Delegation in Paris to the Foreign Office, November 21, 1956, NA, FO 371/120834; *The Economist*, November 10, 1956, 524.
[152] Memorandum of a Conference with the President, October 30, 1956, *FRUS, 1955–1957, Vol. XVI*, 873–874.
[153] No. 2273 from Caccia to the Foreign Office, November 8, 1956, NA, T 236/4189. C. F. Cobbold wrote to Macmillan and Makins, "It would be most unfortunate to have a debate in IMF Board with no, or with lukewarm, American support. This would prejudice further approach to IMF and might easily damage rather than restore confidence. So would a gold tranche drawing by itself, even if we could get it without opposition," November 16, 1956, NA, T 236/4189.
[154] No. 2272 from Caccia to the Foreign Office, November 8, 1956, NA, T 236/4189.
[155] The British government's portfolio of dollar securities had a total market value of approximately $850 million, including stock in Shell Oil, Standard Oil of New Jersey,

Table 3.1 *United Kingdom reserves, August 1956–April 1957, in million dollars*

	EPU settlement[a]	Direct dollar balance	Special payments or credits	Change in reserves	Reserves at end of period
1956					
August	−51	−68	−10	−129	2,276
September	−334	−94	+180[b]	+52	2,328
October	−28	−63	+7	−84	2,244
November	−28	−285	+34[c]	−279	1,965
December	−49	−169	+386[d]	+168	2,133
1957					
January	−17	−36	+4	−49	2,084
February	+20	−20	+63	+63	2,147
March	+17	−27	+72	+62	2,209
April	−6	+11	+106[d]	+111	2,320

Source: The Economist, May 4, 1957.
Notes: [a] Relates to balance in previous month. [b] Includes $177 million from sale of Trinidad Oil. [c] Includes $30 million from official sale of US government bonds. [d] Balance of drawing of $561 million from IMF, defense aid of $6 million and year-end installments of $181 million on US and Canadian postwar loans. [e] Including the return of $104 million of deferred loan interest.

Had the Texas Company not acquired British-owned Trinidad Lease-holds for $173 million – as mentioned previously – the third quarter shortfall would have totaled $230 million.[156] Britain, moreover, still had to pay $175.5 million to service the American loan, transfer $70 million to the European Payments Union (EPU), disburse $7.5 million for the quarterly installment of the Canadian wartime loan, and compensate the United States $5 million for a small Marshall aid loan, an array of debits that would plunge the reserves well below the $2 billion mark.[157] When

Standard Oil of Indiana, General Motors, Eastman Kodak, and Amerada. See Rowan to Macmillan, November 13, 1956, NA, T 236/4189.
[156] The Chancellor's Parliamentary Statement on "Gold and Dollar Reserves and Economic Situation," December 4, 1956, NA, T 234/79 and Makins to Macmillan, November 30, 1956, NA, T 236/4190.
[157] Cabinet Conclusions, CM 95 (56), December 1, 1956, NA, CAB 128/30. Of the $175.5 million owed to the United States and Canada, $103.8 million represented the interest and $71.7 million represented the principal. *The Economist* quotes the EPU repayment as $50 million for settlement of Britain's November deficit and $3 million for its regular monthly payment to EPU creditors, December 8, 1956, 902. I don't know how Macmillan and Makins arrive at the figure of $70 million, but it is clear that they round the $175.5 million up to $180 million in the documents.

Roger Makins reported the financial statistics for November to Macmillan, he informed the chancellor that by the end of the year the reserves could be "well within" $200 million of the lowest figure reached in the postwar years, which was $1,340 million in September 1949 when Britain devalued sterling.[158]

Partly as a consequence of a flight from sterling by the major US petroleum firms, the latter third of November proved particularly devastating for Britain's reserves. To resolve the sterling–dollar oil dispute discussed in chapter 1, Whitehall agreed to allow the American oil companies victimized by British discrimination to sell oil for sterling as long as they reduced the dollar content of their oil to levels comparable to those of British Petroleum and Royal Dutch-Shell. Consequently, firms such as Standard Oil of New Jersey, Standard Oil of New York, Standard Oil of California, and the Texas Company would become some of the largest private holders of sterling. Like others who feared the currency's imminent devaluation, they sold as much of it as they could to minimize potential losses. According to C. F. Cobbold, Britain's reserves would have lost $8 million and $40 million on November 20 and 21 respectively as a result of sterling sales in New York, if Britain had not sold US Treasury short-term securities to compensate for its capital deficits. Fortunately for Britain, the market was closed on the 22nd, but when it reopened on the 23rd, the country would lose another $20 million because of what the governor described as near "panic" in New York about sterling, citing American petroleum companies as the prime movers against the pound.[159] That week, the Treasury's concerns about allowing the US majors to sell oil for sterling six years earlier were validated.

While American oil companies fled the pound, Macmillan told the Cabinet that he and his colleagues might have to "face the grave choice of deciding whether to mobilize all of [Britain's] financial resources in order to maintain the sterling/dollar rate at its present level, or to let the rate find its own level with the possible consequence that sterling might cease to be an international currency." He added that the latter of the two choices "would lead almost inevitably to the dissolution of the sterling area" and would be a "severe blow to the prestige of the United

[158] Makins to Macmillan, November 30, 1956, NA, T 236/4190. The highest the reserves had reached in the postwar era was $3,867 million at the peak of the Korean War primary products boom in June 1951; the lowest the reserves had dropped since the devaluation in 1949 was $1,662 million in April 1952 during the Iranian nationalization crisis, *The Economist*, December 8, 1956, 902.

[159] Makins to Macmillan, November 22, 1956 and Makins to Macmillan, November 23, 1956, NA, T 236/4190.

Kingdom."[160] Treasury and Bank officials knew after the first week of November that a crisis was at hand, and they demonstrated an immediate and unanimous preference for maintaining sterling's rate of $2.80 rather than devaluing the currency or allowing it to float. The mission to prop up sterling cut across government departments and party lines, as revealed in a speech by then Shadow Chancellor of the Exchequer Harold Wilson: "I am sure that the whole House will agree with the Chancellor that it is the duty of all of us to put first the strength of sterling, which is not a party asset, or a Government asset, but a national asset and, indeed an asset for the whole sterling area and world trade." He then pledged Labour's support for "any appropriate measures" that Macmillan chose to bolster Britain's reserves.[161]

Because Britain would have to maintain the pound's value by allowing gold and dollars to flow *out* of its reserves in a demonstration of confidence, the government would also have to abandon the principle of keeping the reserves above $2 billion, a figure that C. F. Cobbold said should no longer be viewed "in any sense as a Rubicon."[162] He and others expected that Anglo-American relations would eventually improve, thereby providing Britain with access to financial aid and oil from the Western Hemisphere. He also hoped that petroleum would once again flow through the Suez Canal within three to six months. If the Treasury and the Bank could maintain the $2.80 sterling rate at least until Britain resumed its amicable relationship with the United States, then sterling might be able retain its international status and the sterling area would survive.[163] Since devaluation represented a point of no return for the currency, avoiding such a measure was worth pushing Britain's reserve position to the limit. In addition, because a confidence crisis, not a trade imbalance, was causing the drain on Britain's reserves, British officials knew that neither devaluing sterling nor allowing it to float would solve the nation's financial problems.[164] The Treasury's A. W. France wrote,

[160] Cabinet Conclusions, CM 85 (56), November 20, 1956, NA, CAB 128/30. Lewis Johnman writes that Macmillan made this statement in front of the Cabinet on October 26, *before* the Suez invasion, a grave error because Johnman deals with the chancellor's comments in the context of the decision to attack Egypt instead of the decision to reverse course. See "Defending the Pound," 172–173. Unfortunately, this error also found its way into Keith Kyle's *Suez*, 335.

[161] Harold Wilson's statement before the House of Commons, December 4, 1956, NA, T 236/4309/1.

[162] Memorandum by George Bolton, November 7, 1956, and Makins to Macmillan, November 9, 1956, both NA, T 236/4189.

[163] Makins to Macmillan, November 9, 1956, and a note by Makins on a talk by Cobbold on November 19, 1956, both NA, T 236/4189.

[164] Rowan to Makins, November 28, 1956, NA, T 236/4190. Rowan also points out that if Britain devalued sterling, the rest of the non-dollar world would probably not "follow

"The policy is to hold the rate, and to throw in all we have to do so. This is clearly right: few things could be more damaging to our reputation and our prospects than a devaluation."[165]

Britain would not have to struggle too long to hold the rate because by early December, the Eisenhower Administration, upon receiving word from London that Britain would withdraw from Egypt without condition, told British officials that it would help the government mobilize the financial aid necessary to restore confidence in the pound.[166] George Humphrey, the member of the administration most critical of Britain at the end of the Iranian oil crisis – and the cabinet official described by Harold Caccia as the "most intransigent" and the "most vindictive" regarding Britain's invasion of Suez – proved both encouraging and helpful as the United States became convinced of the sincerity of Britain's intention to leave Egypt.[167] "Profoundly shocked" by Britain's reserve losses, Humphrey said that "nobody was more interested in the maintenance of sterling" than he and the US Treasury and later added that "when the green light was given" Britain "could look forward to 'massive support.'"[168] Of greatest importance, though, was Humphrey's contribution to Harold Macmillan's speech on the state of the economy before Parliament on December 4. The treasury secretary suggested that Macmillan declare in his statement that financial support from the United States would be "promptly available" and that the Eisenhower Administration planned to recommend to the US Congress changes in the language of the Loan Agreement such that Britain could use the waiver clause as the signatories had originally intended. Thus, the chancellor was able to remind the world of the various tools at his disposal to defend the pound, communicating not only the government's intention but also its ability to maintain the $2.80 rate.[169] Because Britain's reserve losses were based on confidence movements, it is impossible to exaggerate the importance of Humphrey's contribution to this speech.

The combination of Macmillan's strong statement before Parliament and the International Monetary Fund's acceptance of Britain's application for support would help to restore some confidence in sterling.

sterling down" as it did in 1949, making imports more expensive, driving up prices and wages, and thereby creating inflationary problems that would make matters worse rather than better.
165 France to Rowan, November 20, 1956, NA, T 236/4189.
166 The public announcement of the Anglo-French withdrawal came on December 3, 1956.
167 No. 2335 from Caccia to the Foreign Office, November 23, 1956, NA, T 236/4190.
168 No. 2347 from Caccia to the Foreign Office, November 26, 1956, and No. 2396 from Caccia to the Foreign Office, December 3, 1956, NA, T 236/4190.
169 No. 2396 from Caccia to the Foreign Office, December 3, 1956, NA, T 236/4190.

Indeed, *The Economist* remarked that the chancellor's effort to "impress foreigners" that the attack on sterling was "irrational" was executed "as sensibly and, on the whole, as effectively as could have been expected."[170] Macmillan left no doubt about the government's willingness to "use to the maximum every means at [its] disposal to maintain sterling as a sound and stable currency and means of payments and exchange," including borrowing from the IMF and using its portfolio of dollar securities as collateral for a loan from the United States.[171] The following week, the British Treasury announced that it had arranged with the IMF a drawing of its gold tranche and its first credit tranche, totaling $561.5 million, as well as the right to draw the $738.5 million left in its quota over the following twelve months if Whitehall deemed such action necessary. That the IMF interpreted its articles of agreement in such a "liberal spirit" was a testament to the return of normal relations between Britain and the United States – as was the $500 million line of credit that the Export-Import Bank extended to Britain a week later. Macmillan's efforts to prove to the world the British government's ability to maintain sterling's value produced an immediate and favorable response in the marketplace, with the pound achieving its best rate in two months. Most encouraging for Bank and Treasury officials, though, was that sterling would hold its rate against the dollar even after the excitement over Macmillan's initial moves wore off.[172] The increase in Britain's reserves to $2,133 million in December 1956 and to $2,320 million by April 1957 reflected both the dollar infusion that Britain received from the IMF and the United States and the greater confidence in sterling that the aid fostered.[173]

Because the Suez Canal could be closed for a period of anywhere between three and six months, the injection of dollars into Britain's reserves was vital to help pay for shipments of oil from the Western Hemisphere. Of course, these shipments could not begin until the Eisenhower Administration reactivated the Middle East Emergency Committee, which, as with its decision to help Britain rescue sterling, it did once Britain informed US officials that it would unconditionally withdraw from Egypt.[174] The MEEC reconvened on December 3 and began the monumental task of coordinating the work of a number of different

---

170 December 8, 1956, 851.
171 Parliamentary Debates (*Hansard*), Fifth Series, Vol. 51, House of Commons, Official Report, Second Session of the Forty-First Parliament, Session 1956–7 Comprising Period from 26th November to 7th December, 1956, 1052.
172 *The Economist*, December 15, 1956, 987–988, and December 22, 1956, 1072.
173 *The Economist*, May 4, 1957.
174 On November 30, 1956, the United States government issued a press release announcing Eisenhower's approval for the secretary of the interior to authorize fifteen American oil companies to coordinate their efforts to help alleviate Western Europe's oil supply

companies from the United States, Britain, France, and elsewhere to bring oil to Western Europe, an effort known simply as the Oil Lift. The major companies were able to work closely together without concern for anti-trust laws – because of a special exemption – helping them to overcome the transportation difficulties associated with the Suez Canal's closure. By acting in concert with one another, the oil firms were able to use a relatively small number of tankers much more efficiently to haul petroleum both around the perimeter of Africa and across the Atlantic Ocean. Once the Texas oil industry – which to a large extent consisted of small independent companies resentful of the multinationals for import- ing cheap foreign oil into the United States – finally agreed to increase production in mid-February 1957 (after a price hike by the majors and threats from the Eisenhower Administration to intervene), the lift was an enormous success. The operation was aided by an unusually mild winter as well as measures taken by Western European countries to deal with the oil shortage, which in Britain included cutting imports of gasoline, diesel oil, and heating oil, levying a tax on gasoline and other light oils, and rationing.[175]

As the Oil Lift got underway, so did the task of clearing and reopening the Suez Canal. A team supervised by the United Nations began this project after British and French troops withdrew from Egypt in Decem- ber. The job was scheduled to finish on April 8, 1957, one month earlier than planners had initially anticipated, but Nasser would not allow work- ers to remove the final blockships from the waterway until Israel aban- doned the Sinai Peninsula. Although Israeli forces left Egypt on March 6, prompting Nasser to give the United Nations permission to complete its work, the Egyptian government and the Suez Canal's main users still needed to reach an agreement regarding its operation – and Whitehall forbade British ships to use the canal until a settlement had been nego- tiated. In mid-March, Egypt released what London and Paris – and, to some degree, Washington – viewed as too unilateral a declaration regard- ing the operation and control of the waterway. The document did not mention the six principles crafted by Selwyn Lloyd and supported by the UN Security Council, included no statement on cooperation between Egypt and the canal's main users, and left no room for any organization to collect dues other than the Egyptian Canal Authority. On April 24, however, when Nasser's government announced to the United Nations

problem. See No. 2383 from Caccia to the Foreign Office, November 30, 1956, NA, FO 371/120836.

[175] James Bamberg, *British Petroleum and Global Oil, 1950–1975* (Cambridge University Press, 2000), 92–96; Yergin, *The Prize*, 493–494; Statement by the Minister of Fuel and Power on Oil Supplies, November 20, 1956, NA, POWE 17/88.

the opening of the canal to normal traffic, it also submitted a declaration that greatly expanded upon the document released in March, including provisions for international arbitration on critical issues such as toll increases, a promise of structural improvements to the canal in accordance with changes in navigational requirements, and a statement regarding cooperation between the Canal Authority and its users. Whitehall, knowing that it could not stop British ships from using the waterway for too long, capitulated, and British Petroleum sent its first tanker through the Suez Canal on May 20. At the same time, Syria began to repair the IPC's pipeline pumping stations and Saudi Arabia allowed Britain to lift petroleum from Aramco's Tapline outlet in Lebanon, helping to return international oil flows back to their previous patterns and greatly helping to relieve pressure on Britain's reserves.[176]

In the end, how much did Britain's limited access to sterling oil during the Suez crisis cost the nation's balance of payments? No one at the Treasury seemed to know. Leslie Rowan wrote that it was "virtually impossible" to make any assessment regarding the effect of Suez on Britain's trade accounts because it was "quite impossible to arrive at any definite figure." All he could say for certain was that Britain's net earnings from oil would "temporarily turn into a deficit, maybe a large one."[177] A week and a half later, Rowan was more optimistic, writing that the interruption of oil supplies from the Middle East may have been "somewhat less damaging to the balance of payments" than he and his colleagues had originally feared, although he provided no figures to support this judgment.[178] Notwithstanding Rowan's doubts about the Treasury's ability to attach specific numbers to the impact of the Suez crisis on the balance of payments, by comparing oil transactions in the trade accounts from January to June 1956 with the same transactions in those accounts from January to June 1957 – the period in which Britain experienced the brunt of the Suez Canal closure – we can appreciate how the disruption in the flow of oil from the Middle East affected Britain's balance of payments.[179] First, visible trade on petroleum earned £13.1 million less for Britain in January to June 1957 than during the same period in 1956. Second, the country's invisible income from the operations of British and semi-British oil companies, namely British Petroleum and Royal Dutch-Shell, was £30.8 million less from January to June 1957 than during the same period in 1956. This decline is not

---

[176] Kyle, *Suez*, 543–546; Bamberg, *British Petroleum and Global Oil*, 96–99.
[177] Rowan to Rickett, February 4, 1957, NA, T 236/4355.
[178] Rowan to Makins, February 15, 1957, NA, T 236/4355.
[179] See Appendix 2 for the complete figures.

surprising given that Shell and BP, the latter of which still acquired most of its oil from the Middle East, supplied 50 percent of Western Europe's petroleum imports, amounting to 5 million tons a month under normal conditions.[180] Thus, taking Britain's invisible and visible trade together, it appears that the Suez crisis contributed to a deficit of almost £44 million in Britain's balance of payments.[181] While this is not a staggering figure, Britain's reserve position was weak enough for such a deficit to be meaningful.

What really hurt Britain's reserves during the Suez crisis, however, was the country's need to purchase more expensive dollar oil from the Western Hemisphere and the speculation against the pound that occurred in the second half of 1956. Comparing petroleum imports in April–May 1956 with those in April–May 1957, *The Economist* noted that while the country only imported 3 percent more oil during the latter period, it spent one-third more on it, a change caused by purchases of high-priced oil from across the Atlantic as well as an overall rise in the cost of petroleum resulting from Suez-related demand increases.[182] In fact, Britain spent $127.7 million more dollars on oil in January–June 1957 than in the same period in 1956, a significant amount given sterling's precarious position.[183] The greatest dollar losses were precipitated by the flight from the pound associated with the uncertainty over Nasser's control of the Suez Canal, the US condemnation of the Anglo-French invasion of Egypt, and the closure of the waterway itself – draining $279 million from the reserves in November alone. Whitehall's efforts to bolster sterling's position by trying to wrest control of the Suez Canal away from Nasser, and hoping, in the same stroke, to diminish his influence in the Middle East, backfired in the most extraordinary way. Nonetheless, the balance of payments and dollar deficits that occurred as a result of the canal's blockage serve to remind us why officials at Whitehall remained so vigilant about protecting British access to Middle Eastern oil, the cheapest in the world, and why, among other reasons, Eden, Macmillan, Lloyd, and others would advocate an operation as risky as "Musketeer" in the first place.

---

[180] "Suez Emergency – Dollar Costs," unsigned and undated memorandum (most likely prepared in mid-August 1956), NA, T 236/4841 and "Middle East Crisis: Oil," memorandum by J. H. Rampton, November 6, 1956, NA, T 236/5648.
[181] Oil Account Transaction Tables, United Kingdom Balance of Payments, NA, POWE 33/1845.
[182] *The Economist*, June 29, 1957, 1179.
[183] Oil Account Transaction Tables, United Kingdom Balance of Payments, NA, POWE 33/1845.

3.5   Consequences

As Gerold Krozewski notes, the devastating effect of the Suez crisis on sterling precipitated changes in the British government's external economic policy.[184] The severe damage done to the pound's reputation – at a point of no return on the road to *de jure* convertibility – rattled British officials. Having just endured a devastating reserve crisis, they worried about the sterling area's largest balance holders, namely Nigeria, the Gold Coast, and Malaya, drawing upon their balances for development upon achieving independence. Studies initiated by Whitehall revealed that the problem of the sterling balances continued to be an albatross around Britain's neck, exposing the contradiction between Britain's economic relationships with its colonies and the Conservative government's larger goal of liberating the pound into the wider world. In response to these findings, British officials drastically limited loans to the colonies from the London market, redirected capital exports to promising areas of investment outside the empire, and ended the policy of providing protection for colonial finance.[185]

But the impact of the Suez crisis transcended mere sterling policy. In fact, it is no exaggeration to say that the crisis was the kind of rare transformative event that serves as a historical reference point, dividing the postwar era into distinct periods. The world that was born in 1945 reached maturity after the crisis, with economic and political trends set in motion by World War II becoming much more clearly defined in its wake. Suez demonstrated once and for all that the old colonial powers were finished. And from the ashes of their African and Asian empires emerged a plethora of new states, energized by varieties of nationalism that found inspiration in Nasser's humiliation of Britain and France – a feat that also certified Arab nationalism as the most dominant force in the Middle East. The United States and the Soviet Union competed for the allegiance of the newly independent nations in the rush to fill the power vacuum left by the demise of European imperialism in its Victorian form. While they did not establish formal colonies themselves, the United States and the Soviet Union constructed new empires of informal influence in place of the old ones through a range of political, economic, and military activities. This transition certainly began before 1956, as the US experience in Southeast Asia and other examples reveal. However, there can be no doubt that the shape that the postwar world would take appeared much sharper after Suez than it did beforehand.

[184] Krozewski, *Money and the End of Empire*, 195.   [185] Ibid.

The Suez crisis may not have directly triggered the surge of British decolonization in Africa and Asia during the late 1950s and 1960s, but it was a critical catalyst in the process. To begin, sterling's freefall exposed Britain's economic weakness for the world to see, a vulnerability that the United States exploited to its strategic and political advantage.[186] The raw display of US power in compelling Britain to abandon Egypt by holding the pound hostage revealed to British officials and colonial nationalists alike the extent to which internal and external forces circumscribed Britain's ability to defend its interests. To some degree, the Iranian oil crisis had already uncovered the emerging limitations to British influence in both the Middle East and beyond – but not in the dramatic way that the debacle at Suez did. In part, this was because the near unanimous hostility to the Suez operation fostered the rise of the United Nations as a significant actor in international politics, providing anti-colonial critics a forum in which they could denounce Britain's unprovoked act of aggression. By 1960, the UN General Assembly had evolved into a courtroom in which the burgeoning anti-colonial movement would put British imperialism on trial before the world.[187] In addition to the external pressure on Britain that Suez exacerbated, the crisis had a psychological impact on the colonial policy of Harold Macmillan, a prime mover in the post-Suez process of decolonization.[188] The British public, which had become profoundly disillusioned with its government as a result of Eden's Suez subterfuge, gave Macmillan a mandate to wind down the empire by electing the Conservative Party by a wide margin in October 1959.[189] Taking all of these effects together, we can say that the Suez crisis had its greatest influence on decolonization by accelerating postwar economic and political trends to such an extent that an urgency emerged – both in London and on the colonial periphery – to end the empire.

Something similar can be argued about Suez's effect on the Anglo-American relationship. That Britain could not take significant action in the world or the Middle East without first consulting the United States was becoming clear by the early 1950s. US influence in the region was already on the rise, starting with the US intervention in the eastern Mediterranean in 1947 and continuing with the US role in resolving the Iranian oil crisis. As British sway in the Middle East started to

---

[186] C. F. Cobbold told Macmillan: "Whatever longer-term effects Suez may prove to have on the economy, it has certainly had the immediate effect of laying bare to the public eye, both at home and abroad, some of the weaknesses of which we have long been conscious," December 20, 1956, BE/G1/99.

[187] Wm. Roger Louis, "Public Enemy Number One: Britain and the United Nations in the Aftermath of Suez" in Louis, *Ends of British Imperialism*, 695–697.

[188] Hyam, *Britain's Declining Empire*, 239.   [189] Ibid., 239–240, 244.

wane – illustrated not only by the Greek and Iranian episodes but also by Britain's historic agreement with Egypt in 1954 to abandon the Suez base – US officials began to consider the United States an equal partner with Britain in the region, at least in terms of policy-making, if not in military responsibility. Britain, however, saw itself as first among equals, given its long experience and military leadership in the Middle East. Thus, Whitehall reserved the right to defend British economic interests even when those interests did not coincide with US definitions of Western interests. This contradiction in how Britain and the United States perceived their respective roles and concerns reached a breaking point over Suez, which accelerated the mutually reinforcing trends of British decline and US ascendance in the region. After Suez, Britain had no choice but to defer to the United States in the Middle East. As Cobbold wrote to Macmillan in December 1956: "There is no point in trying to 'keep up with the Jones' in political and military affairs when it is obvious that it will so destroy our economic strength as to make us useless (or a liability) as an ally, and unable even to look after ourselves."[190]

The United States quickly asserted its leadership in the Middle East through the Eisenhower Doctrine, the promulgation of which was the direct result of the Suez crisis. Addressing a joint session of Congress on January 5, 1957, the president asked for a resolution that committed US economic and military aid – and, in the last resort, American troops – to any country in the Middle East seeking to repel communist-supported insurgents.[191] On New Year's Day, Eisenhower and Dulles had met with Congressional leaders at the White House to brief them on the new policy, telling them that Britain and France were too weakened by Suez to serve as a counterweight to the Soviet Union in the region. The United States had to fill the vacuum left by the two European powers, the president said, before the Soviet Union did so first. Dulles added that the administration had not previously pursued such a strategic framework because of Britain's past primary responsibility for regional defense. But the increased role that the United States would play in the Middle East, Eisenhower emphasized, should not detract from the "importance of Britain and France continuing as strong powers."[192]

The president reinforced this point to British officials at the Bermuda Conference in March 1957, a series of meetings convened on the island of Bermuda for US and British officials to discuss a range of strategic

[190] C. F. Cobbold to Macmillan, December 20, 1956, BE/G1/99.
[191] Editorial Note, *FRUS, 1955–1957, Vol. XII*, 437–439.
[192] "Notes on Presidential-Bipartisan Congressional Leadership Meeting," *FRUS, 1955–1957, Vol. XII*, 432–437.

3.3 From left to right: British Foreign Secretary Selwyn Lloyd, US President Dwight Eisenhower, British Prime Minister Harold Macmillan, and US Secretary of State John Foster Dulles at the Bermuda Conference, March 1957.

issues. The conference gave Macmillan – who had become prime minister on January 9 after Eden resigned due to illness – an opportunity to repair any lingering damage to the Anglo-American relationship wrought by the Suez betrayal. Once referring to Britain and the United States as "more than allies – blood brothers," Macmillan would have delighted in an entry in Eisenhower's diary on March 21, written at the end of a day of Bermuda discussions on the Middle East: "The meeting was by far the most successful international meeting that I have attended since the close of World War II."[193] The president attributed some of the success to an "atmosphere of frankness and confidence that was noticeable throughout the day."[194] What benefited the Anglo-American relationship, both at Bermuda and afterwards, was the clear division of responsibility delineated for Britain and the United States in Middle Eastern security. When Macmillan told Eisenhower that, "despite recent events," he felt that Britain "still had an important role to play" in the region, the president agreed, replying that he "wished to assure the British that the US wants

---

[193] Macmillan to Eden, February 8, 1956, NA, PREM 11/1324; "Diary Entry by the President," March 21, 1957, *FRUS, 1955–1957, Vol. XXVII*, 718–719.
[194] Ibid.

if anything to build them up again in the Middle East."[195] With US encouragement, Britain would spend most of the post-Suez era focusing its resources and energy on defending the Persian Gulf. Although Washington viewed Britain's relationships with Kuwait and the other Persian Gulf principalities as – in the words of one British official – the "legacy of an outdated colonialism," the United States nonetheless wanted Britain to maintain its influence in the area to help limit "the exploitation of Arab nationalism by the Communist powers to the detriment of, among other things, the supply of oil to the West."[196] While Iraq and Jordan remained British spheres of influence in the aftermath of Suez, Iraq fell out of the Western orbit after its revolution in 1958, and Jordan gravitated toward the United States in the 1960s.

Britain's role in Kuwait was particularly important to Dulles and Eisenhower. At Bermuda, the secretary of state told British officials that "it seemed to him important that the United Kingdom should have more power" in Kuwait. Eisenhower added that "the preservation of the Kuwait oil reserves" should be Britain's "first objective" in policing the Persian Gulf and said that "it would be wise for the United Kingdom to regard all aspects of policy in the area from the point of view of holding Kuwait and its oil."[197] For his part, Macmillan described Kuwait as the "greatest" of oil producers in a region that contained many of them – and believed that it could produce enough oil "for all Western Europe for years to come."[198] British officials, especially at the Treasury, certainly did not need the extra encouragement to maintain their focus on this, the most important of the Gulf sheikhdoms to Britain – not only because of its vast supply of oil, but also because of the money that the oil generated.

[195] Memorandum of a Conversation, Mid-Ocean Club, Bermuda, March 21, 1957, *FRUS, 1955–1957, Vol. XXVII*, 712–718.
[196] "Anglo-American Discussions on Middle East Policy," OME (57) 27 (Revise), April 12, 1957, NA, CAB 134/2339. Ray Takeyh explores Britain's role in the Middle East under the Eisenhower Doctrine, calling it "America's attempt to reintegrate Britain back into the regional political order," *The Origins of the Eisenhower Doctrine: The US, Britain, and Nasser's Egypt, 1953–1957* (New York: St. Martin's Press, 2000), xvi–xvii.
[197] Minutes of the Second Plenary Meeting of the Bermuda Conference, BC(P), 2nd Meeting, March 21, 1957, NA, PREM 11/1838.
[198] Ibid.

4   Kuwait's surplus oil revenue: the benefit and threat to sterling

> The expenditure of [Kuwait's] large sterling revenue unless properly directed is capable of inflicting the most serious damage on the sterling area.
>
> British Foreign Office[1]

> We must realise, of course, that we can in no sense dictate our wishes to the Kuwaitis: we can only proceed by gaining their confidence that we have the best advice to offer. We must also do nothing to make the Kuwaitis believe that we are anxious about sterling or about the possible effect on sterling of any investment policy that they might adopt.
>
> J. E. Lucas, British Treasury Office[2]

Britain's involvement in the Persian Gulf began during the first part of the nineteenth century, when to help defend India, it established treaty relations with many of the sheikhdoms on the eastern and northeastern flanks of the Arabian Peninsula. Generally speaking, these treaties stipulated that the British government would maintain regional peace in return for the sheikhdoms' promise to cease pirating and end their participation in the slave trade. By the end of the century, most of the Persian Gulf principalities, including Bahrain, the Trucial States (now the United Arab Emirates), and the Sultanate of Muscat and Oman (now Oman), had become British protectorates under the sway of the British Government of India.[3] While the change in status meant that the

---

[1] "Instructions Given to Burrows, on His Appointment as Political Resident in the Persian Gulf," July 25, 1953, NA, FO 371/104272.

[2] Memorandum on "Kuwait Investment Policy," May 17, 1961, NA, T 236/6527.

[3] Britain preferred to refer to the sheikhdoms as "states in special treaty relations with Britain." In 1949, the British government officially designated them "Protected States," which is legally different from the classification "Protectorate," the status of two of Britain's three territories in southern Arabia (excluding the Crown Colony of Aden). According to Glen Balfour-Paul, "the difference between a Protectorate and a Protected State was that, while both (unlike Colonies) remained foreign territory, in a Protectorate the Crown reserved the power to make laws for its 'peace, order, and good government,' whereas in a Protected State the sovereignty of the ruler was recognized and such rights as the Crown exercised had to be acquired by treaty." See *The End of Empire in the Middle East: Britain's Relinquishment of Power in Her Last Three Arab Dependencies* (Cambridge University Press, 1991), 102.

sheikhdoms submitted to British authority in areas such as defense and foreign affairs, the ruling families believed that peace and stability were worth the price of deference to Delhi. Besides, they had not been formally annexed, and the British did not usually interfere in the domestic affairs of the states unless requested to do so by the rulers themselves – although the level of interference depended on the individual sheikhdom. In part because of its ambiguous relationship with the Ottoman empire, Kuwait was not asked to join its neighbors under the British umbrella until 1899, when increasing great power activity in the region led Britain and the sheikhdom to sign a treaty that gave London control over its foreign affairs. Fifteen years later, Kuwait would become a protectorate like the others, essentially turning the Persian Gulf into a "British lake."[4]

The discovery of oil in the Gulf ensured that the protectorates would remain valuable to Britain long after India left the empire – and no territory would be worth more than Kuwait.[5] Suspicions about the existence of oil led the American-owned Eastern Gulf Oil Corporation to seek a concession there during the 1920s. But neither Whitehall nor Kuwait's ruling family, the al-Sabah, would allow a non-British firm to negotiate a contract to drill for oil.[6] The US government put enough pressure on Britain, however, to ensure that Gulf would not be left out of a petroleum deal with the sheikhdom. As a result, when the Anglo-Iranian Oil Company signed a concession agreement with Kuwait in 1934, it did so in partnership with the American firm as the Kuwait Oil Company (KOC), incorporated a year earlier. While the KOC – which was equally owned and financed by its two parent companies – consented to pay Kuwait in

[4] Rosemarie Said Zahlan, *The Making of the Modern Gulf States: Kuwait, Bahrain, Qatar, The United Arab Emirates and Oman* (London: Unwin Hyman, 1989), 12. Qatar, another Gulf principality, became a British protectorate in 1916 and was the most loosely administered of the group. Eventually, the discovery of oil in the Persian Gulf, post-World War II geopolitical considerations, and Indian independence would transfer authority over the sheikhdoms from the Government of India to the Foreign Office, which supplied political agents to each territory, who were in turn overseen by the Political Resident at Bahrain. See Robert J. Blyth, "Britain versus India in the Persian Gulf: The Struggle for Political Control, *c.*1928–48," *The Journal of Imperial and Commonwealth History*, 28, 1 (2000), 90–111.

[5] For this reason, Kuwait is the subject of focus in this chapter, to the exclusion of the other oil-producing protectorates were Bahrain, Qatar, Abu Dhabi, and Dubai. Bahrain's resources were exhausted relatively quickly, so it never accumulated the wealth that the others did.

[6] Rosemarie Said Zahlan writes that the phrase "Kuwait is the Al Sabah and the Al Sabah is Kuwait" has often been heard in Kuwaiti circles in reference to the fact that the ruling family's leadership is an "integral part of the modern state," *The Making of the Modern Gulf States*, 79. The same has been true of the state's oil revenues.

Indian rupees, the official Gulf currency, the sheikhdom was later persuaded to accept sterling for its petroleum, much to Britain's benefit.[7]
Striking oil in 1938, the firm had to suspend drilling operations because
of World War II, and it took another eight years before the KOC finally
delivered its first commercial oil shipment. Before long, though, Kuwait
was well on its way to becoming one of the most prolific petroleum
producers in the world.

By the early 1950s, British authorities began to grow concerned about
what the al-Sabah were going to do with their expanding surplus wealth.
At the time, a large amount of sterling oil had dropped out of the market
as a result of the Iranian oil crisis, and the KOC dramatically expanded
production to fill the void. Furthermore, partly as a result of events in
Iran, the sheikhdom secured a fifty–fifty agreement with the KOC in
1951. Thus, the combination of burgeoning production and a lucrative petroleum contract caused the state's revenue to rise much more
quickly than anyone had previously anticipated. British officials felt a
paternalistic obligation to ensure that the country's ruler, Sheikh Abdullah, did not waste his excess earnings on items they deemed frivolous
or on development plans they considered ill-advised. Most importantly,
the Treasury and the Bank of England wanted to make certain that the
bulk of the sheikhdom's assets remained within the sterling area to protect Britain's balance of payments. After meeting with some resistance,
British officials eventually persuaded Abdullah to establish a London-
based board, chaired by a trusted advisor, to handle the bulk of Kuwait's
investments. For its part, the Treasury intended to ensure that the board,
which included an official from the Bank of England among its membership, did nothing to harm sterling.

Whitehall grew increasingly anxious about Kuwait's investment policy
by the mid to late 1950s, as the pace of decolonization within the British
empire accelerated. Several years after gaining independence in 1947,
India began to run down a significant portion of its sterling balances
to pay for economic development, thereby draining gold and dollars
away from the sterling area's reserves. British officials feared that the
empire's largest sterling holders, Ghana, Nigeria, and Malaya, which
all achieved independence by the end of the 1950s, would follow the
pattern established by India. Thus, the long-term stability of Kuwait's
enormous balances became increasingly more important to compensate

[7] The rupee came into use in the Persian Gulf in the nineteenth century when the British
Government of India administered the protectorates and when complementary trade
existed between them and India. Kuwait would adopt its own currency, tied to sterling,
in April 1961. See Cocker to Ashe, November 8, 1949, NA, T 236/5188.

for the reserve losses precipitated by the spending practices of recently liberated members of the sterling area.[8]

Around the time that British officials began to wrestle with the potentially detrimental effect of decolonization on the value of sterling, they believed that the internal and external threats to an Anglo-friendly regime in Kuwait were growing increasingly dangerous. Of greatest concern was the spread of Pan-Arab nationalism across the Middle East. Nasser's victory over the British at Suez enhanced his prestige and increased the popularity of his anti-imperialist, Pan-Arab ideology in the region. A significant number of foreign workers, who were crucial to the operation of the Kuwaiti oil industry, brought this ideology with them to the sheikhdom and found receptive ears among other foreign workers as well as native Kuwaitis. At the very least, British officials thought that nationalistic fervor within the sheikhdom might force the al-Sabah to conceive policies detrimental to British interests, especially once Kuwait gained independence. London's woes continued in 1958 when Iraq, Kuwait's neighbor to the north and Britain's longtime client state, experienced a violent revolution that reverberated with anti-British hostility. After Kuwait achieved full independence in 1961, Whitehall wound up sending British troops back to the sheikhdom in response to Iraqi threats to annex it. British officials had been served notice that a vital source of sterling oil – and one of the largest holders of sterling in the world – was surrounded by forces antagonistic to British interests.

Arab leaders from Baghdad to Damascus to Cairo accused the al-Sabah of being both British lackeys and selfish with their vast wealth. These criticisms first appeared in the early 1950s, and they began to influence the direction of Kuwait's investment policy as the decade unfolded. By the late 1950s, the al-Sabah wanted greater freedom to make investment decisions. Led by the younger and more independent finance minister, Sheikh Jabir, Kuwait sought to diversify its portfolio and invest more of its income in the Arab world to improve the ruling family's image among its Arab brethren, especially after Iraq's annexation threats. British officials acquiesced to the al-Sabah's demands, fearing that if they did not, the sheikhdom might go the way of Iraq. They also recognized that Britain and Kuwait would both benefit, image-wise, from the latter's investment

---

[8] In 1958, those balances totaled £260 million, which was roughly 10 percent of the £2,838 million held by the Rest of the Sterling Area at the time. As RSA balances were run down, Kuwait's holdings would represent an increasingly greater proportion of the RSA's total balances. See "The Persian Gulf States and the Sterling Area: Note by the Treasury," November 10, 1959, NA, T 236/5181, and Schenk, *Britain and the Sterling Area*, 53.

in sound projects in the Arab world and gave their blessing to a fund designed to help finance Arab development.

In the 1960s, Whitehall became even more concerned about Kuwait's investment practices as a result of the severe trade account problems that Britain endured in the era of currency convertibility launched by the nations of Western Europe in 1958. In fact, in every year except two between 1961 and 1968, Britain's balance-of-payments difficulties threatened to exhaust the nation's cache of gold and foreign currency reserves in the nation's Exchange Equalisation Account – the mechanism through which the Bank of England maintained the international value of sterling.[9] Because Kuwait's relationship to the sterling area was much like that of a major shareholder to a company, British officials feared that any significant movement by Kuwait out of sterling would exacerbate declining confidence in the currency and sought to prevent such activity. They recognized, however, that they had to allow small to moderate transfers into gold and other currencies to avoid giving the ruling family the impression that sterling was not worth holding and thereby trigger the larger transfers that they were trying to avoid in the first place. Despite all of the worries at Whitehall, Kuwait never shifted large enough quantities of money out of the sterling area to damage British interests. Even after Britain devalued the pound in 1967, Kuwait still kept a majority of its finances in sterling.

In some ways, this chapter differs from the three that have preceded it. First, while Whitehall remained concerned about how British access to sterling oil – and how much British companies had to pay for it – could help or harm the nation's balance of payments during the late 1950s and 1960s, in the case of Kuwait, British officials were more concerned about the effect on sterling of the sheikdom's investment decisions. Second, with much of its focus on the Middle East in the post-Suez era, this chapter considers the Anglo-American relationship at a time when the United States had taken Britain's place as the dominant power in the region. The clarity of their respective positions led to an equally clear division of labor in terms of the Anglo-American protection of Western interests – as outlined at the Bermuda Conference in the spring of

---

[9] J. H. B. Tew, "Policies Aimed at Improving the Balance of Payments" in F. T. Blackaby (ed.), *British Economic Policy*, 1960–74 (Cambridge University Press, 1978), 304. The Treasury and the Bank of England established the Exchange Equalisation Account at the Bank in 1932, depositing in it large amounts of sterling and foreign exchange, which Bank authorities used to stabilize the pound's value by buying and selling currencies in the international marketplace. In general, the total amount of gold and dollars in the account reflected the balance-of-payments position of the entire sterling area. See "Draft Paper by the Treasury on the Sterling Area," sent to the Bank of England in March 1957, BE/OV 44/10.

1957 – with successive US administrations counting on Britain to police the Persian Gulf.[10] Ironically, given the problems that afflicted Anglo-American relations as they pertained to the Middle East during the post-war era, it was only when the Wilson government informed US officials that Britain would have to abandon the Gulf that strains reemerged.

Nonetheless, the driving force here is the same as that of the previous three chapters: how the link between sterling and Middle Eastern oil shaped aspects of British imperial and foreign relations after World War II. And also similar to those three chapters, the predominant issue is one of control. Indeed, much like the flow of dollar oil into the sterling area, the operation of the Iranian oil industry, and the question of authority over the Suez Canal, Britain sought to control or, at the very least, influence the direction of Kuwait's investments for the benefit of sterling. In this chapter, however, while Britain's exertion of financial control over Kuwait created some tension in the Anglo-Kuwaiti relationship, whatever stresses emerged were never allowed to reach the point of crisis. The combination of the codependent nature of the Anglo-Kuwaiti relationship and the acceptance among British officials that nationalism in the Middle East was a genuine and powerful force that had to be reconciled led to the abandonment of the heavy-handed approach that Britain used in Iran and Egypt during the first half of the 1950s. These policy-makers certainly did not abandon their preoccupation with the connection between Middle Eastern oil and the value of sterling after the Suez debacle. But the stability of Britain's relationship with Kuwait

---

[10] At the Bermuda Conference in 1957, John Foster Dulles said that it seemed "important that the United Kingdom should have more power" in Kuwait just in case "things went wrong in Saudi Arabia and Iraq," Minutes of Second Plenary Meeting, BC (P), March 21, 1957, NA, PREM 11/1838. Miriam Joyce covers Kuwait in the context of Anglo-American relations in *Kuwait 1945–1996: An Anglo-American Perspective* (London: Frank Cass, 1998). Of course, this does not mean that Britain and the United States did not have disagreements regarding the Persian Gulf states; only that such a dialogue did not produce flare-ups comparable with those over Iran and the Suez Canal or conflicts that dealt with the link between sterling and Middle Eastern oil. One example of such a disagreement is the Anglo-American dispute over the Buraimi Oasis in the mid-1950s, which concerned a clash between Oman and Saudi Arabia – British and American spheres of influence, respectively – regarding jurisdiction over the potentially oil-rich territory. In "Anglo-American Rivalry in the Middle East: The Struggle for the Buraimi Oasis, 1952–1957," *The International History Review*, 14, 1 (1992), 71–91, Tore Tingvold Petersen argues that the Anglo-American dispute over Buraimi constituted an important aspect of a larger Anglo-American competition for influence in the Middle East. His argument is overstated, but Buraimi was, in fact, more than a minor point of contention between Britain and the United States. Also see Tore Tingvold Petersen, "Crossing the Rubicon? Britain's Withdrawal from the Middle East, 1964–1968: A Bibliographical Review," *International History Review*, 22, 2 (2000), 318–340, for a discussion of Anglo-American relations in the context of the Middle East in the mid to late 1960s.

suggested an attitude at Whitehall of lessons learned and, more importantly, reflected the economic and political realities that Britain faced in the post-Suez era.

4.1   A new oil agreement, expanding production, and Whitehall's anxiety over rapidly rising sterling revenues in Kuwait

In the late 1940s, the ruler of Kuwait, Sheikh Ahmad, began to express dissatisfaction with the terms of the Kuwait Oil Company's concession. His cousin and successor, Sheikh Abdullah, who acceded to the throne in 1950, complained that Kuwait was receiving much less income from oil than other producers in the region, especially after Saudi Arabia secured a fifty–fifty profit-sharing agreement in December 1950. Furthermore, Iraq was discussing the same sort of deal with the Iraq Petroleum Company (IPC).[11] Sheikh Abdullah believed that the difference between Kuwait's oil revenue and that of its neighbors "seriously impaired his dignity and prestige" both among his own subjects and in the Persian Gulf. With Iran's move towards nationalization depicting in sharp relief the unwelcome consequences of not quickly reaching an agreement with an unhappy petroleum producer, the Gulf Oil Company was "firmly of the opinion" that the KOC should satisfy the Kuwaiti ruler's demands.[12] As a result, the sheikhdom and the KOC quickly and amicably reached an agreement based on the fifty–fifty principle that took effect on December 1, 1951.[13]

A critical aspect of the new deal was that Kuwait agreed to let the KOC pay for its oil in sterling, a condition upon which Whitehall insisted to protect Britain's reserves. Initially, the renegotiated concession called for Kuwait to receive payment in Indian rupees. But such a provision would have increased the Indian sterling balances that the British government was working to reduce.[14] Although Sheikh Abdullah was amenable to the idea of accepting half of the KOC's payments in sterling, he believed that Kuwait was entitled to receive the other half in dollars, given the American nationality of Gulf Oil.[15] Because the KOC was officially British,

[11] An agreement was reached on August 13, 1951 and signed on February 3, 1952.
[12] "The Problem in Kuwait and a Suggested Solution," unsigned and undated (most likely March or April 1951) Treasury Memorandum, NA, T 236/5865.
[13] Bamberg, *The History of the British Petroleum Company, Volume II*, 334–344.
[14] The Treasury estimated that it would have to purchase £60 million worth of rupees from India in 1952 to fulfill the KOC's obligations under the new concession agreement. See Bancroft to Reilly, September 29, 1951, NA, T 236/5866.
[15] "Oil Production and Negotiations in the Persian Gulf," Memo by C. M. Rose, February 4, 1952, NA, POWE 33/1969.

though, a status that Whitehall secured when the firm was incorporated, if Gulf were to pay Kuwait in dollars, the British government would have to supply some of those dollars in exchange for the firm's sterling earnings, a drain on Britain's reserves. On the other hand, if Gulf paid Kuwait in sterling, dollars would flow into the reserves as a result of Gulf's need to convert dollars into pounds. Some of the dollars earned by the sheikhdom, moreover, would inevitably leave the sterling area through the "Kuwait gap," an exchange control loophole that allowed for a robust free market in dollars, the only such market in the sterling area other than Hong Kong.[16] Britain was already losing dollars this way on income that Kuwait earned from the American Independent Oil Company (Aminoil), which, since 1948, had operated a concession in the Neutral Zone between Kuwait and Saudi Arabia that paid Kuwait roughly $1.6 million a year.[17]

To prevent further petroleum-related dollar losses, Whitehall sent a Treasury official to the Persian Gulf to deal with the currency aspects of the KOC's new agreement with Kuwait. He explained to Abdullah that the sheikhdom could not receive dollars for its petroleum from the KOC without violating sterling area practice. He also informed the sheikh of the important advantages that Kuwait derived from being a member of the currency area, such as privileged access to London's capital market. On other occasions, British officials told Abdullah and the ruling family that Kuwait could sell oil freely for pounds in the sterling area, in addition to the fact that it could more easily sell oil for sterling than dollars in the Transferable Account Area.[18] In the end, the ruler agreed to accept

---

[16] Kuwaitis could buy dollars for sterling at a discounted price, purchase dollar securities in the United States, and then turn around and sell those securities for sterling at a premium in the London market to sterling area residents. This practice was tolerated because British authorities believed that "a gap of reasonable proportions seemed a not undue price to pay" to keep Kuwait in the sterling area. The Treasury closed the Kuwait gap in 1957 when the cost of the gap to Britain's reserves became too high. For information on the Kuwait gap, see "Hong Kong and Kuwait," SAWP (56) 11, March 1, 1956, OV44/31, "Kuwait Gap Closed," *The Economist*, July 13, 1957, and Simon Smith, *Kuwait, 1950–1965: Britain, the al-Sabah, and Oil* (Oxford University Press, 1999), 75–77. For an analysis of the importance of parallel foreign exchange markets in developing countries, see Catherine R. Schenk, "Closing the Hong Kong Gap: The Hong Kong Free Dollar Market in the 1950s," *The Economic History Review*, 47, 2 (1994), 335–353.

[17] The Neutral Zone was created to preserve the grazing rights of nomadic desert tribes; "Oil Production and Negotiations in the Persian Gulf," Memo by C. M. Rose, February 4, 1952, NA, POWE 33/1969, and "Sterling Balances of Kuwait," Note by the Treasury, NA, T 236/4293. The sterling area gained no advantage from Aminoil's dollar payments to Kuwait because the Persian Gulf protectorates were exempt from contributing dollars to the central pool. See "Note on the Sterling Area," Reilly to Burrows, January 30, 1956, NA, T 236/3932.

[18] "Note on the Sterling Area," Reilly to Burrows, January 30, 1956, NA, T 236/3932.

4.1 From left to right: Ruler of Kuwait Sheikh Abdullah, AIOC Chairman Sir William Fraser, and the sheikh's private secretary exit Britannic House, Anglo-Iranian's headquarters in London, June 1953.

sterling for the sheikhdom's oil in return for assurances that the British government recognized his right to convert sterling into Indian rupees as his requirements demanded, and that the British government would supply dollars "for any goods essential for the benefit of his state and not available in sterling."[19] To sweeten the deal, the Treasury also allowed Abdullah, his family, and "a few of the most senior sheikhs" to make capital transfers of sterling abroad to purchase property without consulting Britain.[20] The importance to Whitehall of Abdullah's capitulation on the currency question cannot be exaggerated: "Our economic interest in the Persian Gulf, to which we must look increasingly for supplies of

---

[19] The British government formalized the arrangement in a letter to Sheikh Abdullah on November 26, 1951. See "Exchange Control in Kuwait," Note by the Treasury, June 22, 1960, and "Oil Production and Negotiations in the Persian Gulf," Memo by C. M. Rose, February 4, 1952, both NA, POWE 33/1969.

[20] Mackay to Milner-Barry, May 20, 1960, NA, T 317/118.

Table 4.1 *Iranian oil production versus Kuwaiti oil production and revenue, 1946–1955*

Year	Iranian production (thousand barrels)	Kuwaiti production (thousand barrels)	Kuwaiti revenue (thousand pounds)
1946	146,819	5,931	200
1947	154,998	16,225	
1948	190,384	46,500	3,425
1949	204,712	90,000	2,950
1950	242,457	125,722	3,100
1951	123,512	204,910	7,500
1952	7,800	273,433	34,850
1953	9,400	314,592	60,161
1954	21,500	347,319	69,302
1955	120,562	398,493	100,498

Sources: US Office of Naval Petroleum and Oil Shale Reserves, *Twentieth Century Petroleum Statistics*, 9, and Y. S. F. al-Sabah, *The Oil Economy of Kuwait* (London: Keegan Paul International, 1980), 52.

sterling oil, demands that we keep the Gulf as dependent as possible on sterling."[21]

Just as Kuwait began to earn more money for each barrel of oil that it sold, its production dramatically increased as well, a tandem of changes that led to skyrocketing petroleum revenues for the sheikhdom. The jump in production began in 1951 – during the early stages of the Iranian nationalization crisis – when the Anglo-Iranian Oil Company collaborated with the world's other major multinational oil firms to prevent Iran from selling its petroleum in the international marketplace. To replace Iranian crude, Gulf and the AIOC dedicated significant amounts of capital and technical resources to expand Kuwait's production. The result was a rise in output from 125.7 million barrels in 1950 to 273.4 million barrels in 1952 (see Table 4.1). By 1955, when Iranian oil was just coming back on line, Kuwait had expanded production to a staggering 398.5 million barrels, making it the largest petroleum producer in the Middle East and the third largest in the world behind the United States and Venezuela.[22] The sheikhdom's revenues followed suit. In 1951, the

---

[21] "Proposed New Currency in the Persian Gulf," Annex to the note of a meeting to discuss Persian Gulf currency held in the Foreign Office, January 17, 1952, NA, T 236/4286.

[22] US Office of Naval Petroleum and Oil Shale Reserves, *Twentieth Century Petroleum Statistics*, 37th edition (Dallas: DeGolyer and MacNaughton, 1981) and Stephen Hemsley Longrigg, *Oil in the Middle East: Its Discovery and Development*, third edition (London: Oxford University Press, 1968), 223–224.

last year of the original 1934 concession, Kuwait earned £7.5 million, whereas in 1955, it earned £100.5 million, a remarkable 1,340 percent increase in four years (see Table 4.1). The al-Sabah would use this revenue to wrap themselves in luxury and transform their nomadic city-state in the desert into a society with all of the trappings of modernity. How Kuwait's ruling family would use its extraordinary wealth began to preoccupy British officials primarily because it was denominated in sterling.

The subject of a British financial advisor for Kuwait arose as early as 1944, when the sheikhdom's oil industry was just getting off the ground.[23] At the time, policy-makers worried about the mismanagement of Kuwait's finances and wanted a British official in place to ensure that the state obtained the most benefit from its oil revenue. Because authorities in London did not expect the sheikhdom to earn in excess of £5 million per year by 1955 – or £20–25 million by 1958 – they figured that most of Kuwait's income would be ploughed into administration, social services, and development or, as one Bank of England official phrased it, "squandered in a number of mad ways."[24] No one envisioned that its revenue would grow to a level that could potentially threaten the financial stability of the sterling area. Once it became clear that Kuwait's earnings would reach such a point, Whitehall put extra pressure on Abdullah to accept a British advisor to increase Britain's influence over the sheikhdom's finances.[25]

Sheikhs Ahmad and Abdullah both refused to take on senior British advisors because they fervently protected their independence regarding Kuwait's internal affairs.[26] As a result, until 1951, the principal official link between Whitehall and the rulers was the political agent stationed in the sheikhdom. He is described by Jill Crystal as having been nothing more than a "background figure" whose two main duties were to serve as a liaison between the government and the KOC and to deal with expatriate legal issues.[27] Instead, Ahmad and Abdullah relied primarily on the advice of H.T. Kemp, the rulers' representative to the KOC in London. The duties that Kemp performed, however, transcended his

[23] Smith, *Kuwait, 1950–1965*, 16.
[24] Donaldson to Hay, October 27, 1947, NA, FO 371/61446; Loombe to Playfair, December 22, 1948, NA, T 236/4152.
[25] "An Account of Kuwait's Sudden Access to Wealth, of Her Majesty's Government's Relations with Kuwait and of the Present Problems in Kuwait," Annex B, Ross to Serpell, June 8, 1953, NA, POWE 33/1927.
[26] "Anglo-American Discussions on Middle East Policy," Brief by the committee, OME (57) 27 (Revise), April 12, 1957, NA, CAB 134/2339.
[27] Jill Crystal, *Oil and Politics in the Gulf: Rulers and Merchants in Kuwait and Qatar* (Cambridge University Press, 1990), 66–68.

role with the oil company, and his position became more influential as the state bureaucracy expanded.[28]

Eventually, Whitehall persuaded Abdullah to accept two junior British advisors in 1951.[29] After discussions with the sheikh and members of the Foreign Office, Kemp chose Colonel G. C. L. Crichton, an official who served in the Government of India, to provide Abdullah with fiscal advice as a member of Kuwait's finance department. While the Foreign Office was initially pleased with his appointment, a paper written two years later described him as "inadequate for his job" because of his lack of financial expertise.[30] The other advisor, an "experienced engineer" named General W. F. Hasted, was selected by Crichton to serve as controller of development in Kuwait's Public Works Department. The Foreign Office was dissatisfied with Hasted as well, lamenting his lack of financial control and administrative acumen and complaining that he was ill-suited to provide Crichton with the kind of guidance that he needed.[31] Neither could exert the kind of influence over Abdullah that the British government desired.[32] Given the disappointment in London with both Crichton and Hasted – whose sub-par performances were not entirely of their own making – officials at Whitehall continued to plead with Abdullah to accept a senior British advisor, but to no avail.[33]

The British government rejected the idea of annexing Kuwait to protect its economic interests despite not being able to achieve the quality of financial control that it sought. Representatives from the Foreign Office,

[28] Smith, *Kuwait, 1950–1965*, 19, 25.

[29] Smith and Crystal disagree as to why Abdullah accepted these advisors. Smith maintains that it is difficult to establish the sheikh's motivations but speculates that his "initial delay and subsequent acceptance" can be "ascribed to his need to reconcile the al-Sabah to the presence of British personnel in the internal administration of Kuwait." He does not support Crystal's argument that Abdullah accepted British advisors to increase his own strength relative to that of family members who were growing increasingly powerful as they became more involved in the burgeoning Kuwaiti government. See Smith, *Kuwait: 1950–1965*, 24, and Crystal, *Oil and Politics in the Gulf*, 68. In the end, the decision appears connected to the ruler's desire to launch a substantial economic development program.

[30] "Her Majesty's Government's Position in and Policy towards Kuwait," Foreign Office paper, April 15, 1953, NA, POWE 33/1927.

[31] Ibid.

[32] "An Account of Kuwait's Sudden Access to Wealth, of Her Majesty's Government's Relations with Kuwait and of the Present Problems in Kuwait," Annexe B, Ross to Serpell, June 8, 1953, NA, POWE 33/1927.

[33] The British government eventually upgraded the status of the political agent in Kuwait, giving him the authority to speak on its behalf and increasing the size of his staff. The potential for Kuwait to inflict "the most serious damage" on the sterling area had become too great for Whitehall to let the diplomatic machinery that regulated Anglo-Kuwaiti relations remain unchanged. See "Instructions Given to Burrows, on his Appointment as Political Resident in the Persian Gulf," July 25, 1953, NA, FO 371/104272.

Treasury Office, Ministry of Fuel and Power, Board of Trade, Commonwealth Relations Office, and the Bank of England all agreed that "it was not practicable to impose control [over Kuwait] by taking over executive authority and attempting to run the state as a British territory." They believed that to do so would violate Britain's treaty relations with the sheikhdoms and would unleash a flurry of criticism from India, Pakistan, and other countries. Therefore, they concluded, the government would have to "accept that executive authority [would] rest in the hands of the Kuwaitis" and "concentrate on building up the authority of British officials employed by the Kuwait authorities in an advisory capacity." Furthermore, the government would have to improve the means by which it was able to persuade Abdullah to accept its advice.[34]

The central problem for Whitehall, of course, was its inability to install the kind of senior advisor that would hold sway over Abdullah and the rest of his family, a state of affairs that greatly worried British officials. Rupert Hay, the Political Resident in the Persian Gulf, characterized as "frightening" the al-Sabah's acquisition of so much sterling without receiving the proper guidance on what to do with it.[35] First, the Foreign Office worried that the "riot of spending" that occurred in Kuwait during the early to mid-1950s would cause an inflationary spiral. Second, the department fretted that the al-Sabah, whom many viewed as Oriental spendthrifts, seemed little concerned with the possibility that their money might run out.[36] The Gulf states in general, one Treasury official asserted, would be better served by using their royalties to "reduce their dependency on a wasting asset" rather than squandering their wealth on "riotous living."[37]

British officials were concerned that what they perceived as inefficient allocations of revenue by the al-Sabah, whether to themselves, the growing state bureaucracy, or "wasteful [development] schemes," would leave less surplus revenue to be invested in ways that they thought would best promote Kuwaiti and sterling area interests.[38] Ideally, Whitehall wanted the ruling family to invest the "major portion" of its income in sterling securities and spend the remainder on "those goods and services which [could] most conveniently be provided by the other countries

---

[34] "Persian Gulf: Kuwait," Record of a meeting held at the Foreign Office, April 16, 1953, NA, POWE 33/1927.

[35] Hay to Furlonge, November 13, 1951, NA, FO 371/91300.

[36] Draft Foreign Office paper on "Her Majesty's Government's Position in and Policy towards Kuwait," April 15, 1953, NA, POWE 33/1927.

[37] Clarke to Hedley-Miller, April 19, 1951, NA, T 236/4286.

[38] "Administration of Finance in Kuwait," Memorandum by D. R. Serpell, March 1, 1952, POWE 33/1927.

of the sterling area."[39] If the al-Sabah sought to finance development projects outside Kuwait, they were to be encouraged to do so in the Commonwealth.[40] What British officials feared most was "indiscriminate spending or lending abroad" on the part of the sheikhdom because of the havoc it could wreak on Britain's balance of payments.[41]

Much like during the Iranian oil and Suez crises, British authorities were alarmed at the degree to which "Oriental" control over important "British" assets could harm Britain's economic interests. In the case of Kuwait, they worried about what they considered the ruling family's extravagant spending habits, which reflected both an objective reality and British stereotypes about Arab monarchs. The profligate Oriental ruler was a trope that stretched back to at least the nineteenth century and assumed its most vivid form for British and French officials in the shape of Khedive Ismail, the Egyptian head of state who, with great encouragement from British and French financiers, bankrupted his country through what they viewed as unnecessarily lavish spending on public works projects and personal luxuries.[42] Use of the words "riot," "indiscriminate," and "mad" to describe the actual or potential spending behavior of Kuwait's rulers also conforms to typical European conceptions of Arabs and Muslims as having uncontrolled and excessive personalities. Throughout the 1950s and 1960s, paternalistic policy-makers at Whitehall would try to influence the al-Sabah's financial decisions in such a way that they could rein in what they viewed as the ruling family's inveterate Oriental impulse to waste money. Success in this effort, they believed, would safeguard both Kuwaiti and sterling area interests.

British officials were also concerned about saving both Kuwait and Britain from predatory development firms that regarded the sheikhdom as a place of unlimited wealth and opportunity. From the perspective of C. E. Loombe, an advisor at the Bank of England and a future member of the Kuwait Currency Board, the sheikhdom was a "paradise for contractors, architects and swindlers," many of whom saw Kuwait as "easy game for large profits."[43] Included in this group were five British companies that monopolized development contracts in Kuwait, operating

[39] "Her Majesty's Government's Position in and Policy towards Kuwait," Foreign Office paper, April 15, 1953, NA, POWE 33/1927.
[40] "Investment of Kuwait's Surplus Oil Royalties," draft brief by Waterlow, July 14, 1953, NA, FO 371/104341.
[41] "Her Majesty's Government's Position in and Policy towards Kuwait," Foreign Office paper, April 15, 1953, NA, POWE 33/1927.
[42] David Landes, *Bankers and Pashas: International Finance and Economic Imperialism in Egypt* (Cambridge, MA: Harvard University Press, 1958).
[43] Memorandum by Loombe, February 10, 1953, NA, POWE 33/1926.

on a non-competitive, "cost-plus 15 percent" basis that General Hasted believed produced both efficiency and speed.[44] The dominance of the "Big Five," as they were collectively called, greatly benefited Britain's balance of payments since their work was conducted in sterling. But this dominance would backfire by provoking enough Kuwaiti resentment to cause the sheikhdom to do more business with non-British companies.[45] The condition that all British firms had to enter into partnerships with Kuwaiti merchants clearly did not do enough to ease the anxiety among more nationalistic elements in the sheikhdom that Britain had too much influence over its economic life. The Foreign Office acknowledged that 'the system is obviously open to abuses [by British companies]. Criticism is bound to arise, whether justified or not, and there is reason to believe that British firms have regarded the present arrangement as an excellent opportunity to make a good thing out of Kuwait."[46]

The loudest voice in opposition to the privileged position of the British companies – and a major impediment to Whitehall's efforts to assert greater authority over Kuwait's finances – was Sheikh Fahad, Abdullah's powerful half-brother. A full-fledged empire-builder, Fahad made his presence felt throughout the state's expanding bureaucracy, heading both the country's municipality and health departments, becoming heavily involved in the finance and public works departments, and eventually leading the sheikhdom's yet-to-be-established development board. It was in public works, the department responsible for Kuwait's development program, that he initially caused Britain the most trouble. Fahad tried to assert his authority over it, hoping to transfer contracting jobs to Kuwaiti businesses, not only for nationalistic reasons, but also to enlarge his patronage network. As a result, he obstructed Crichton's and Hasted's work in every possible way, including canceling ongoing projects and getting into fistfights with supporters of reform.[47] By early 1953, Fahad succeeded in relegating Hasted from his position as controller of

---

[44] The five firms were Richard Costain, Holland, Hannen and Cubitt, John Howard, C. and D. William Press, and Taylor Woodrow.

[45] A brief for a meeting between Winston Churchill and Abdullah read: "If, as seems probable, the Arab firms were Syrian or Lebanese, there would, in addition to the loss of British trade, be harm to the sterling area, since the diversion of Kuwait's sterling to Syria and the Lebanon would create very serious balance of payments difficulties for us," "An Account of Kuwait's Sudden Access to Wealth, of Her Majesty's Government's Relations with Kuwait and of the Present Problems in Kuwait," Annexe B, Ross to Serpell, June 8, 1953, NA, POWE 33/1927.

[46] "Her Majesty's Government's Position in and Policy towards Kuwait," Foreign Office paper, April 15, 1953, NA, POWE 33/1927.

[47] Crystal, *Oil and Politics in the Gulf*, 68–69.

development to a smaller advisory role and, much to Britain's dismay, he put a Syrian engineer in Hasted's place.[48]

Fahad resented what he considered the British government's meddling in Kuwaiti affairs. During a conversation with the Persian Gulf's Political Resident B. A. B. Burrows and Kuwait's Political Agent C. J. Pelly in September 1953, he reminded them in blunt language that the Anglo-Kuwaiti Treaty of 1899 gave the British government "no right to interfere in the internal affairs" of the sheikhdom.[49] Fahad then listed examples of occasions in which he believed that Whitehall violated the spirit of the treaty, including a letter from Winston Churchill prodding Abdullah to appoint a financial advisor. Later, he complained about the government's "constant attempts to divert contracts and purchases" to Britain.[50]

Neither Fahad's obstructions nor his comments sat well with British officials. The sheikh clearly viewed himself as a nationalist, as illustrated by his use of the slogan "Kuwait for the Arabs," while the British viewed him as a self-interested demagogue resistant to "any measures calculated to put the administration into order."[51] For his part, Pelly thought that Fahad suffered from "a mixture of megalomania and Anglophobia."[52] What bothered British officials most, though, was the sheikh's ability to frustrate Crichton and Hasted's attempts to exert British authority over Kuwait's finances. In a brief for a meeting between Winston Churchill and Abdullah in the summer of 1953, British officials complained: "[Crichton and Hasted's] influence . . . has been limited by the emergence of 'nationalist' elements in Kuwait who, working upon the native pride and independence, are determined to keep executive control in Kuwaiti hands, resist any invasion by the British advisers into executive matters."[53] It is worth noting that policy-makers at Whitehall, who were in the process of planning Muhammad Mossadegh's overthrow, viewed Fahad in the same light as they viewed the Iranian prime minister: as a disingenuous nationalist who stirred the emotions of his followers in

---

[48] "Her Majesty's Government's Position in and Policy towards Kuwait," Foreign Office paper, April 15, 1953, NA, POWE 33/1927.

[49] The Foreign Office thought differently: "Our special position in the Persian Gulf States and their obscurity and primitive character have long enabled us to exercise a considerable influence on internal affairs and the Rulers have looked to us for advice: thus we have acquired, so to speak, a traditional right to interfere," ibid.

[50] Pelly to Greenhill, October 4, 1953, NA, FO 371/104330.

[51] "Her Majesty's Government's Position in and Policy towards Kuwait," Foreign Office Paper, April 15, 1953, NA, POWE 33/1927 and Fry to Burrows, October 8, 1953, NA, FO 371/104330.

[52] Pelly to Greenhill, October 4, 1953, NA, FO 371/104330.

[53] "An Account of Kuwait's Sudden Access to Wealth, of Her Majesty's Government's Relations with Kuwait and of the Present Problems in Kuwait," Annexe B, Ross to Serpell, June 8, 1953, NA, POWE 33/1927.

a way that damaged his country's interests, at least as Britain defined them. Whether Fahad was a legitimate nationalist, a corrupt bureaucrat, or both, is not as important as the fact that his resistance to British control represents the most glaring example of the growing movement within the al-Sabah family to achieve greater independence from Britain.

In a more defensive and subtle way, Abdullah also resisted Britain's efforts to influence how the sheikhdom used its oil revenues, as demonstrated by his constant refusals to appoint a senior British advisor as well as his initial reluctance to accept British proposals for a London-based investment board. In February 1952, Deputy Under-Secretary of State Roger Makins led a mission of Treasury and Bank of England representatives to Kuwait to "secure the Ruler's acceptance" of the establishment of three different boards to deal with finance, investment, and development. Makins faced the daunting task of explaining to Abdullah why it was important to the sterling area – and, thus, to Kuwait, as a member and one of its largest sterling holders – that he invest his surplus revenues safely.[54] He told Abdullah that the British government was impressed with his development plans and recommended that he select "trusted advisers" to allocate funds for normal government expenses and development. But, Makins said, large sums of money would remain even after the state had funded both the government and development. Therefore, British officials thought it best for the sheikh to authorize a "small committee in London," including "one of his most trusted counselors from Kuwait," to invest this money in sterling securities, rather than allow it to sit in a low-interest account at the British Bank of Iran and the Middle East.[55]

Abdullah had suspicions about Makins's visit from the beginning. First, he wanted to know why Whitehall found it necessary to use an "exceptional procedure and send a special mission" to discuss the sheikhdom's finances when it could have accomplished the same goals through the

---

[54] Makins wrote to the Foreign Office: "It was hard enough to explain to Nuri al-Said [the Iraqi prime minister] the working of the sterling area, but I cannot adequately describe to you the difficulty of doing so to Abdullah Selim," No. 24 from Pelly to the Foreign Office, following from Makins, February 21, 1952, NA, POWE 33/1926.

[55] Originally named the Imperial Bank of Persia, this medium-sized institution conducted most of its business in Iran from its establishment in 1889 until 1940. It changed its name to the British Bank of Iran in 1935, then to the British Bank of Iran and the Middle East in 1949, and finally to the British Bank of the Middle East (BBME) in 1952 when it left the country amidst the tensions of the oil nationalization crisis. The BBME became a "major force" in Middle Eastern banking, in part by introducing modern banking practices to the Persian Gulf protectorates. It was the first and only bank in Kuwait from 1941 to 1952, and it eventually became a member of the Hong Kong Bank Group in 1960. See Geoffrey Jones, *Banking and Empire in Iran: The History of the British Bank of the Middle East*, 2 volumes (Cambridge University Press, 1986 and 1987).

political resident and the political agent, in whom he had "the fullest and most complete confidence."[56] Moreover, Abdullah wanted further clarification as to why his unused balances on deposit at the British Bank of Iran and the Middle East represented a danger to sterling, Britain, and other sterling area countries. The challenge for Makins was to provide the sheikh with the answers he desired without suggesting that the British Bank of Iran and the Middle East lacked competence or integrity or that the sheikh himself would use his excess revenues irresponsibly, an issue about which Abdullah was sensitive. After all, the sheikh claimed he was happy with the 0.75 percent interest that he earned on his account with the British Bank, and Makins could not say with any legitimacy that the sheikh's deposits were in any danger. The deputy under-secretary tried to elucidate the differences between central and commercial banks to persuade Abdullah to move his sterling deposits to the Bank of England. He also struggled in vain to explain how the wise investment of his enormous sterling balances would breed confidence in sterling and consequently bolster the respective positions of every member of the sterling area.[57]

It was not just his lack of understanding about the nuances of the sterling area, but a genuine skepticism about the British government's motives that caused Abdullah to keep Makins at bay. The ruler worried about the "extent of control" that Whitehall sought for the proposed investment committee, and he doubted the need for such a committee altogether. Makins recognized the sheikh's concerns, and, as a result, he was careful not to justify the creation of the investment board with arguments that linked the fate of the British economy to the use of Kuwait's excess sterling revenue. Regardless, Abdullah surely knew that the British government would not have badgered him so relentlessly about his finances if significant British interests were not at stake. As a result, he trusted H. T. Kemp much more than anyone at Whitehall, and, not surprisingly, the sheikh turned to Kemp for advice. Upon learning that Abdullah had consulted Kemp about the mission's recommendations, Makins concluded that it was pointless to continue pursuing the matter with the ruler until British officials met with Kemp. Once they sat down with him, they hoped to persuade him to advise the sheikh to adopt the government's proposals.[58]

[56] Makins to Eden, February 22, 1952, NA, POWE 33/1926.
[57] No. 24 from Pelly to the Foreign Office, following from Makins, February 21, 1952, and No. 25 from Pelly to the Foreign Office, following from Makins, February 21, 1952, both in NA, POWE 33/1926.
[58] No. 25, Pelly to the Foreign Office, February 21, 1952, NA, POWE 33/1926.

Eventually, Whitehall's persistence paid off. While Abdullah remained skeptical about a London-based investment board for months, at the end of October 1952, he finally relented. There is no documentary evidence to explain why Abdullah finally accepted the British government's recommendations, but it is almost certain, as Simon Smith relates, that Kemp was a "decisive" part of the process.[59] Through conversations with Kemp, the sheikh probably recognized that even if Whitehall's proposals had been designed with British interests in mind, his interests and Britain's interests were not necessarily mutually exclusive.

Before the proposed Kuwait Investment Board (KIB) was constituted, Abdullah established certain guidelines for it to follow. First, the board had to invest in securities backed by the British government, also known as gilt-edged securities. Second, Kuwait's portfolio had to obtain a higher overall rate of interest than that which it was receiving at the British Bank of the Middle East (so much for being happy with 0.75 percent). And, finally, the board had to maintain a high level of liquidity for the country's investments. The question of liquidity was extremely important to Abdullah because he believed that he was "required to hold his surplus revenues in trust for his successors, to be drawn upon in emergencies or when the oil reserves [were] exhausted." Not all of these guidelines were officially documented, but, for a while, the investment board followed them closely, with adjustments occurring as circumstances allowed or necessitated.[60]

The Kuwait Investment Board was officially launched on February 23, 1953, and, as one might expect, H. T. Kemp was its first chairman. Sitting alongside him were C. P. L. Winshaw, a partner in the law firm that handled the ruling family's affairs, Lord Kennet, a director at the British Bank of the Middle East, and Lord Piercy, an official from the Bank of England. No native Kuwaitis served on the committee, which, according to a note by the Treasury, stemmed from the "lack of sufficient experience" among the members of the ruling family and the sheikhdom's leading merchants.[61] Abdullah never insisted on Kuwaiti participation, though, and G. W. Bell, Kuwait's political agent from 1955 to 1957, later surmised that the sheikh would have been "most unwilling for any leading merchant or any member of his family" to "become familiar with the State's financial affairs which he feels he must keep strictly under his own control."[62] As for the board's size, it could have no more than

[59] Smith, *Kuwait, 1950–1965*, 43.
[60] "Sterling Balances of Kuwait," Note by the Treasury, October 17, 1956, NA, T 236/4293.
[61] Ibid.   [62] Bell to Riches, February 28, 1957, NA, CAB 134/2339.

five members, and Abdullah and his successors retained the power of removal and appointment.[63] All the money that the committee invested was held in an account at the Bank of England, which provided "special facilities" to the rulers of Kuwait, including the "services and advice" of the British government's official stockbroker, with whom the board was encouraged to consult. Abdullah ensured that the board invested his money "with due regard to liquidity," so that "as far as may be practicable" funds would be "readily available" if and when he and his successors needed them. Finally, the committee met in Britain's capital to maintain the "day-to-day contact with the London market" that the sheikh demanded.[64]

Although no official representative of the British government sat on the Kuwait Investment Board, the Treasury certainly hoped to exert great influence over it nonetheless. When British officials initially discussed the idea of an investment committee, the Foreign Office's C. M. Rose explained why they could not be directly involved:

We feel it is important to avoid any suggestion that His Majesty's Government are controlling the Ruler's use of his money, not only because of the risk to His Majesty's Government of accepting such a grave responsibility but also because any direct official representation would be difficult to sell to the Ruler and would be liable to criticism, both in Kuwait and elsewhere.[65]

Still, the Treasury did not want the board to be completely independent of the British government, and department Under-Secretary D. R. Serpell hoped that "means would be found" by which Whitehall could "exert enough influence behind the scenes to prevent market investment (or disinvestment) in a way directly damaging" to British interests.[66] At a meeting with Bank and Foreign Office officials two months later, he explained that while the Treasury was "quite content" to use the "method of advice and gentle persuasion" with Kuwait on its finances, it "regarded as essential" that "proper control" of the sheikhdom's revenue "should actually be achieved." He added that "direct intervention" by the British government might eventually be necessary to accomplish this goal, and he

---

[63] Official document signed by Abdullah and C. J. Pelly constituting the Kuwait Investment Board, February 23, 1953, Document II, NA, FO 371/104340.

[64] "General Directive from His Highness Shaikh Sir Abdulla Al-Salem Al-Sabah, KCMG, CIE, to the Investment Board," February 23, 1953, Document III, NA, FO 371/104340. It is important to note that the KIB had no jurisdiction over Kuwait's dollar revenues, which were first handled by the National City Bank of New York and then by the Chase Manhattan Bank as well. See "The Economy of Kuwait, 1950–1968," FCO Research Department, October 1969, NA, FCO 51/93.

[65] Rose to Serpell, January 28, 1952, NA, POWE 33/1926.

[66] Serpell to Flett, January 29, 1952, NA, T 236/4287; Serpell to Rose, January 23, 1952, NA, POWE 33/1969.

"hoped that there was no misunderstanding on this point."[67] As has been demonstrated throughout this book, when British economic interests were at stake, Treasury officials were almost always willing to go farther to defend those interests than their colleagues in other departments, regardless of the diplomatic consequences.

The composition of the Kuwait Investment Board, the kinds of investments it made, the nature of its control over the sheikhdom's excess sterling revenue, and even its location would all change by the late 1950s and early 1960s. When the board was first established, it invested one-third of Kuwait's total revenues in short-term, gilt-edged securities.[68] Soon, its members would consider other types of financial instruments, and development projects outside Kuwait would eventually absorb a greater share of the revenue available for them to invest. But Whitehall did not decrease its efforts to exert as much influence as possible over how Kuwait used its oil income. Because of the steady increase in the size of the sheikhdom's sterling balances, as well as the political movements that would convulse both the Middle East and the British empire, London would become more anxious than ever about the fate of Kuwait's excess sterling.[69]

4.2 Sterling convertibility, decolonization, development, and the growing importance of Kuwait's sterling balances to the sterling area

At the end of December 1958, the British government capitalized on an extremely favorable economic climate to make sterling *de jure* convertible, formalizing the changes that it had initiated in 1954–1955.[70] Britain ran a higher balance-of-payments surplus in 1958 than at any time since the end of the war. In addition, Britain's reserves climbed to almost $3,100 million (see Appendix 3), raising the ratio of the country's reserves to its net external sterling liabilities to a postwar peak.[71] The dollar gap between the United States and Western Europe, moreover, finally

---

[67] Memorandum of conversation by Ross, March 17, 1952, NA, T 236/4287.
[68] "The Oil Revenues of Kuwait," by H. S. Lambert, May 18, 1955, NA, T 236/5871.
[69] The sterling balances of the Persian Gulf protectorates reached £70 million at the end of 1954, £135.8 million at the end of 1955, and £157.2 million near the end of 1956. Separate figures for Kuwait's balances are not available, but it is safe to say that the sheikhdom's balances represent most of these totals. See "Sterling Balances of Kuwait," Note by the Treasury, October 17, 1956, NA, T 236/4293.
[70] "Economic Survey, 1959," Economic Survey Working Party, NA, CAB 134/1909.
[71] In 1958, the ratio was 28 percent, whereas in 1952 it was 18 percent. See P. L. Cottrell, "The Bank of England in its International Setting, 1918–1972" in Richard Roberts and David Kynaston (eds.), *The Bank of England: Money, Power and Influence, 1694–1994* (Oxford: Clarendon Press, 1995), 130.

closed as a result of US direct foreign investment, US military spending in the region, and the recovery of its economies, a shift demonstrated by the redistribution of global monetary reserves from the United States to the rest of the world.[72] The time was ripe for sterling convertibility, spurring Treasury and Bank of England officials to proceed with their plan to unify the transferable and official sterling rates. Dubbed Operation "Unicorn," the plan made sterling convertible on current account transactions for all non-sterling area residents, including members of the American account area. Britain orchestrated this move with Germany and France, the Continent's economic leaders, and the rest of Western Europe followed suit, finally allowing the Bretton Woods system to operate as its framers had intended fourteen years earlier.[73] While the Treasury continued to regulate the current account transactions of sterling area residents, as well as all capital transfers denominated in sterling, the currency was, for all intents and purposes, convertible. Conservative Party, Treasury, and Bank officials had achieved their collective goal of reintroducing the pound to the world beyond the sterling area as part of their effort to reestablish the international prominence of the currency.

Gerold Krozewski argues that the changes in the monetary and financial relationships between Britain and the colonies that led British officials to make sterling convertible in 1958 help to explain British decolonization in the late 1950s and 1960s. In the wake of World War II, the empire and sterling area served the primary purpose of helping Britain to recover economically from the consequences of total war. But changes in empire trade and capital flows during the 1950s – due in part to postwar international economic trends – reduced economic complementarity between the center and the periphery, rendering obsolete the empire's convalescing function. By the mid to late 1950s, it had become clear that Britain and the colonies would both benefit from looking beyond each other's markets to meet their respective economic needs. Furthermore, British policy-makers in the Conservative Party, the Treasury, and at the Bank had, since the end of the war, sought to reorient the focus of British economic relations toward Europe because of the benefit they believed would accrue to sterling and the British economy (the Macmillan government's application for British entry into the European Community in July 1961 demonstrated as much). With the Conservative Party's ascension to power in 1951, British officials could take the necessary steps to accomplish this objective, such as limiting capital flows to the colonies

---

[72] From 1948 to 1958, the United States's share of global monetary reserves dropped from two-thirds to one-half. See Eichengreen, *Globalizing Capital*, 113–114.

[73] Ibid., 106–113.

and directing them toward non-imperial growth areas. Convertibility signified a crossing of the Rubicon of sorts, as there was no returning to the old sterling area relationships once it was achieved. Thus, in 1958, Britain's economic destiny was set and maintaining the empire no longer made economic sense, an argument that helps to explain the timing of decolonization in the late 1950s and early 1960s.[74] Krozewski is careful, however, to note that there are "geographic limitations" to his thesis, specifically colonies or territories that did not achieve independence because of their particular strategic or economic importance to Britain, such as Cyprus, Aden, and Hong Kong, or those that "stood on the margins of the imperial sterling area," such as the West Indies, Kenya, and Rhodesia.[75] The Persian Gulf sheikhdoms fit into the first category, with their relatively late independence in 1971, in part because of their combined strategic and economic value.

Krozewski's argument, while an important addition to our understanding of the process of decolonization, needs expansion to provide a more complete picture of the unraveling of the British empire. Given that decolonization involved British decision-making about a wide range of territories that spanned the globe, making broad generalizations about the process is loaded with pitfalls, but nonetheless a worthwhile exercise because generalizations can indeed be made. Imperial historians usually employ multi-causal approaches to explain the why, the how, and the when of decolonization – with economics, international politics, and colonial nationalism constituting a sort of holy trinity of categories of inquiry.[76] In pondering why the British empire ended when it did, Ronald Hyam gets to the heart of the matter when he writes: "The really significant historical question to ask is how the imperial power had got psychologically to the point where it was prepared to open the door to self-rule when nationalist leaders knocked and asked."[77]

---

[74] Krozewski, *Money and the End of Empire.*   [75] Ibid., 205–206.

[76] Darwin's *The End of the British Empire*, while almost two decades old, still provides the best survey of the main arguments. Also see Darwin, *Britain and Decolonization*; Hyam; *Britain's Declining Empire*; Louis, "The Dissolution of the British Empire"; Louis, "Suez and Decolonization: Scrambling out of Africa and Asia," in Wm. Roger Louis (ed.), *Ends of British Imperialism: The Scramble for Empire, Suez and Decolonization* (London: I. B. Tauris, 2006), 1–31; and Louis and Robinson, "The Imperialism of Decolonization." J. D. B. Miller's *Survey of Commonwealth Affairs: Problems of Expansion and Attrition, 1953–1969* (London: Oxford University Press, 1974) deals with decolonization in the context of the evolution of the British Commonwealth.

[77] Hyam, *Britain's Declining Empire*, 403. Hyam's emphasis on the role of metropolitan policy-makers at the expense of colonial nationalists is inherent in this question. He is right to focus his lens here because, in the final analysis, officials in London decided how and when to dismantle the empire.

To find the origins of the forces that caused British officials to open that door, one need not look much farther than World War II, in many ways the Big Bang that set these forces in motion.[78] The imperative to exploit the colonies on behalf of the war effort led to an imperial intrusiveness in colonial life that helped spur local nationalist movements. As previously discussed, these policies persisted after the war to speed economic recovery, further invigorating peripheral nationalisms and paving the way for demands for self-rule. By realigning international economic relationships through the simultaneous destruction and expansion of the European and US economies, respectively, the war accelerated changes in imperial economic relations that, in turn, dissolved the economic ties that held the empire together, as Krozewski explains. Regarding international politics, the war thrust the United States, the Soviet Union, and the United Nations into leading global roles that limited Britain's political and strategic options in the context of the Cold War.[79] After all, Victorian imperialism hindered the West in the fight against communism by creating an image problem for Britain – and by extension the United States – that the Soviet Union and colonial nationalists both exploited, particularly in the UN General Assembly in the wake of Suez. With officials at Whitehall focusing on maintaining and improving Britain's international prestige, the empire had become a liability that they needed to shed.[80] Underlying everything, of course, was Britain's economic weakness, which shaped British strategic decision-making in such a way that directly and indirectly accelerated the process of decolonization. In the end, we can reasonably argue that the successive decisions by British officials to acquiesce when colonial nationalists demanded independence were political, strategic, and economic ones imposed on Whitehall by political and economic forces that, by the late 1950s, had to be accommodated.

In the late 1950s and 1960s, the decolonization process accelerated to a pace that many British officials, especially at the Colonial Office, had neither anticipated nor welcomed. Prior to Suez, Anthony Eden and Secretary of State for the Colonies Alan Lennox Boyd had envisioned a gradual, possibly decades-long, transition in which economic and political development, supervised by colonial officials, would pave the way for an orderly and harmonious end to the British empire – one that preserved British influence in the newly independent states. By the beginning of the 1960s, though, Malaya (1956), the Gold Coast (1957), Singapore (1958), and Nigeria (1960), the sterling area's largest

---

[78] Darwin, *The End of the British Empire*, 118–120.
[79] This is Hyam's basic argument in *Britain's Declining Empire*.   [80] Ibid., 408–410.

balance holders other than Kuwait and Hong Kong, had all achieved independence, a change that British officials felt could have harmful repercussions for sterling.

Before the dramatic rise in the oil revenues of the Persian Gulf protectorates, the Overseas Sterling Area (OSA) experienced two periods of significant growth in the size of its balances. The first occurred during World War II, when, as previously mentioned, Britain had to borrow heavily from the Empire-Commonwealth to fund the war effort. India emerged as the sterling area's largest balance holder by far, but as a result of an agreement with Britain to reduce its holdings, trade account deficits, and development spending, its sterling accumulations diminished significantly by the mid-1950s. The second major increase in the OSA's balances occurred when the Korean War drove up the global price of raw materials. Within the empire, the greatest beneficiaries of this commodities boom were Malaya, one of the world's biggest exporters of rubber and tin, Ghana, a center of cocoa production and gold mining, and Nigeria, a significant producer of palm oil, tin, and cocoa.[81] Thus, the bulk of the OSA's balances shifted from independent members in South Asia to dependent members in Southeast Asia and West Africa (see Table 4.2).

According to Catherine Schenk, not only did these balances move geographically, but they changed character as well. Seeking to challenge the long-held notion that the colonial balances were volatile, and, hence, an albatross around the neck of the British economy, she argues that the colonial balances were stable overseas assets used predominantly for reserve purposes and should not be equated with the more liquid, "extraordinary wartime accumulations" of the Independent Sterling Area (ISA).[82] This stability, she asserts, was not a coincidence but the result of "the deliberate functioning of the sterling area."[83] Gerold Krozewski disagrees, believing that Schenk "has given insufficient emphasis to the political volatility of the colonial sterling balances."[84] For the purposes of this study, whether Schenk or Krozewski makes the better argument is not relevant: what matters most is what British officials *themselves believed*. And the documentary record shows that makers of sterling area policy in London did, in fact, worry about the instability of the colonial balances. Indeed, as Treasury and Bank officials contemplated the onset of postcolonial development in the mid-1950s, they did not distinguish

---

[81] In 1950, Malaya received $350 million (gross) of the $1,285 million that the sterling area earned that year. Karl Hack, *Defence and Decolonisation in Southeast Asia: Britain, Malaya and Singapore, 1941–1968* (Richmond: Curzon Press, 2001), 23.

[82] Schenk, *Britain and the Sterling Area*, 19.

[83] Ibid., 18.   [84] Krozewski, *Money and the End of Empire*, 198.

Table 4.2 *Sterling balances in Africa and Asia, 1945–1960 (in million pounds)*

Year	India, Pakistan & Ceylon	India[a]	East, Central & West Africa	West Africa[a]	Far East	Malaya[a]
1945	1,358		205		142	
1946	1,314		217		193	
1947	1,218		253		198	
1948	957		314		195	
1949	790		346		201	
1950	820	804	436	253	284	164
1951	837	730	551	329	399	252
1952	668	694[b]	612	351	430	283
1953	660	697[b]	675	400	438	282
1954	672	691[b]	773	488	426	305
1955	728	687	765	507	465	364
1956	570	412	748	480	498	369
1957	371	254	701	462	479	361
1958	248	156	683	454	517	376
1959	281		660		607	
1960	236		595		695	

Sources: J. D. B. Miller, *Survey of Commonwealth Affairs*, 297 and Schenk, *Britain and the Sterling Area*, 50–53.
Notes: [a] Fourth quarter totals. [b] Indicates a statistical discrepancy between sources.

between the World War II and Korean War accumulations of sterling – at least not when discussing their potential to be transferred into dollars and gold in large amounts over a short period of time.[85]

In the summer of 1956, as Britain was negotiating the terms of Malayan independence, British policy-makers started expressing anxiety about the future of the sterling area in the context of decolonization and development. The Sterling Area Working Party, the committee of Treasury and Bank officials formed in 1955 to examine and recommend sterling area policy,[86] registered its concerns:

[85] "The Sterling Area Working Party's Report: Origin of the Inquiry," final report published June 25, 1956, BE/OV44/33. Schenk argues that the sterling balances alone "would never be sufficient to meet the aspirations for development in the colonies and so it was obvious that the colonies even after independence would continue to rely on international investors." See "Finance and Empire: Confusions and Complexities: A Note," 870. Treasury and Bank of England officials nonetheless worried about the run-down of those balances for development purposes, as the evidence demonstrates.

[86] The committee was established at the end of 1955 "because it was felt that strains were developing in the [sterling area] which made a fresh examination desirable." See "The Sterling Area Working Party's Report: Origin of the Inquiry," final report published June 25, 1956, BE/OV44/33.

The main conclusion of the report therefore is to underline the increased burden which is likely to fall on the United Kingdom current balance in the next ten years or so as a result of economic and political development in the Commonwealth and sterling area. If the United Kingdom is to maintain her position as the leader and financial centre of the sterling area she must be ready to meet this additional strain.[87]

That British officials were anxious about a rapid reduction in the post-colonial sterling balances is not surprising. After all, India's holdings had diminished by 50 percent by the end of 1956, and, since the beginning of the decade, the "main determinant" of the size of India's balances "tended to be development expenditure." The same was true for Pakistan and Ceylon. All three of these countries experienced a one-third decline in their reserves from 1955 to 1958 because of the "unanticipated rising costs of development" (see Table 4.2). Regardless of the fact that a "precipitous run-down" in the sterling balances of Malaya and Ghana did not occur after they gained independence, Treasury and Bank officials still worried that the two former colonies might follow the pattern set by India, Pakistan, and Ceylon: "We can do nothing to prevent these trends, which are the reflection of perfectly legitimate internal policies in RSA countries. But there are risks too (and equally unavoidable) of foolish policies as untried governments come to power."[88]

Spending by Middle East sterling holders also emerged as a potential threat to Britain's reserves. Egypt had £128.3 million remaining in balances amassed as a result of British borrowing during World War II, and those funds, which were gradually released to Egypt based on agreements signed after the war, were expected to be turned over in their entirety by 1963.[89] Meanwhile, Iraq, where Britain's longtime influence was waning, had built up £115.4 million in balances. Because Iraq was spending most of its oil income – adding only £1.2 million to its holdings in 1955 on £75 million in total earnings that year – it would almost certainly exploit its London account to pay for economic development. Iran, the petroleum industry of which had just begun to resume normal operations after the nationalization crisis, would find itself in a similar position in a

---

[87] "The Sterling Area Working Party's Report," attached to a note from Cobbold to the Treasury on July 12, 1956, NA, T 236/4303.
[88] Schenk, *Britain and the Sterling Area*, 25, 42; "Minutes of the Sixth Meeting of the Cabinet Official Committee on the Middle East," ME (0) (56), June 11, 1956, NA, CAB 134/1297; "Problems of the Sterling Area," SAWP (56) 24, May 4, 1956, BE/OV44/32.
[89] Egypt's balances totaled £390 million in 1945 and peaked at £470 million in 1947. See Rodney Wilson, "Economic Aspects of Arab Nationalism" in Michael J. Cohen and Martin Kolinsky (eds.), *Demise of the British Empire in the Middle East: Britain's Responses to Nationalist Movements, 1943–1955* (London: Frank Cass, 1998), 67–68.

Table 4.3 *Sterling balances of the Persian Gulf territories, 1950–1958 (in million pounds)*

Year	Balances[a]
1950	0
1951	3
1952	15
1953	38
1954	70
1955	136
1956	169
1957	203
1958	260

Source: Schenk, *Britain and the Sterling Area*, 51.
Note: [a] Fourth quarter.

few years time.[90] In 1956, D. S. Laskey, the private secretary to Britain's Secretary of State for Foreign Affairs, expected that the Middle Eastern sterling holders other than Kuwait would exhaust all of their oil revenues and run down balances totaling roughly £300 million. "The dangers of this situation," he wrote, "are obvious."[91]

According to the Sterling Area Working Party, one way to meet the "additional strain" caused by the economic development of Independent Sterling Area members and other sterling holders was to lock up the growing revenues of the sterling area's Persian Gulf territories. Treasury and Bank officials believed that if they could help channel the accumulations of the protectorates (see Table 4.3) into loans and investments denominated in sterling, then the balances "could prove a source of strength" to the currency, an "invaluable" asset in the phase of decolonization that was beginning to unfold in Africa and Asia.[92] Thus, the end of empire in Africa and Asia led to a renewal of imperial will in a critical part of the Middle East.

Several months later, the working party stressed the importance of keeping the Middle East's oil-producing countries in the sterling area to

[90] "Minutes of the Sixth Meeting of the Cabinet Official Committee on the Middle East," ME (0) (56), June 11, 1956, NA, CAB 134/1297.
[91] "Development and the Sterling Balances," Minute by D. S. Laskey, NA, FO 371/120829.
[92] "Sterling Balances – IV: General Conclusions to Parts I to III," SAWP (56) 17, March 26, 1956, NA, T 236/3933.

compensate for the potential spending practices of the newly independent colonies. The group then advocated funneling the balances of the sterling area's oil producers – after their liquidity requirements had been met – into high-grade, long-term investments in the sterling area, unless such investments conflicted with their interests.[93]

With its enormous surplus revenues, Kuwait "occupied a position of special importance" for British officials.[94] The incomes of the other Persian Gulf protectorates did not approach the scale of Kuwait's, while Iraq was expected to plough much of its revenue into development. A Treasury note written in October 1956 describes Kuwait's balances, which totaled £157 million that year, as a "source of strength to sterling at a time when the balances of other RSA countries [were] either being run down or [were] not growing."[95] But the balances might also constitute a source of weakness, the note's authors explained, if Abdullah's investment policy "over-emphasize[d] liquidity."[96] As a result, the Treasury recommended that the sheikh "should adopt a more flexible investment policy, the effect of which would be to make available to the London market fresh savings which could be used to finance less liquid forms of investment."[97]

The Treasury and the Cabinet listed equities and long-term investment in the sterling area as possibilities, as well as "sound" investment in the Middle East, if such investment did not "absorb any significant proportion" of Kuwait's surplus revenues.[98] The Cabinet's Official Committee on the Middle East hoped Abdullah would become interested in financing large development programs in the Commonwealth, especially in India, where an "immense gap" existed between the demand for capital and the sterling area's available financial resources.[99] The committee also suggested that Kuwait could fund projects in the colonies, such as the Volta river scheme in the Gold Coast, while the Colonial Office advocated persuading the ruler to invest in colonial government loans, particularly in Muslim territories.[100] Concerned about appearances, though, Treasury

[93] "Draft Conclusions," June 6, 1956, NA, T 236/4303.
[94] "Minutes of the Sixth Meeting of the Cabinet Official Committee on the Middle East," ME (0) (56), June 11, 1956, NA, CAB 134/1297.
[95] "Minutes of the 28th Meeting of the Cabinet Official Committee on the Middle East," ME (0) (56), November 1, 1956, NA, CAB 134/1297; "Sterling Balances of Kuwait", Note by the Treasury, October 17, 1956, NA, T 236/4293.
[96] "Sterling Balances of Kuwait," Note by the Treasury, October 17, 1956, NA, T 236/4293.
[97] Ibid.   [98] Ibid.
[99] "Minutes of the Sixth Meeting of the Cabinet Official Committee on the Middle East," ME (0) (56), June 11, 1956, NA, CAB 134/1297.
[100] "Minutes of the 28th Meeting of the Cabinet Official Committee on the Middle East," ME (0) (56), November 1, 1956, NA, CAB 134/1297.

officials concluded that any change in the sheikhdom's investment policy "should be presented on its financial merits and should not be capable of being misrepresented" as an attempt by the British government to "divert the ruler's surpluses to its own purposes."[101]

One way to persuade Abdullah to invest Kuwait's balances in a way that benefited Britain without prompting criticism from the sheikhdom's nationalist elements – or from other Arab states – was to persuade him to fund projects in the Arab world. While the Treasury believed that "few opportunities for sound investment" existed in the Middle East, it thought that pipeline projects in the region would provide the ruler with an outlet for his surplus revenue that would benefit not only him, but also the countries through which the pipelines traveled, as well as Western Europe, "without adding to the strain on sterling."[102] The Official Committee on the Middle East discussed this idea in addition to the possibility of having Abdullah finance a Syrian refinery project, something that its members considered "very desirable." They figured that if he were "to invest at all in Middle East development, the Syrian project provided a good starting point," and, thus, they should "encourage the Ruler to participate."[103] Nothing came of these suggestions, but after independence, Kuwait did, in fact, establish a fund to invest in such projects and others to promote economic development in the Arab world.[104] Whether the ruler financed projects in the colonies, the Commonwealth, or the Arab world, what mattered to the Treasury was that Kuwait's balances were invested "in such a way as to contribute to the strength and stability of the sterling area."[105]

There does not seem to be any evidence that definitively reveals whether the Treasury and the Bank of England directly influenced the decisions of the Kuwait Investment Board. At a meeting of the Cabinet's Official Middle East Committee, someone pointed out that the British government "could not *properly* seek to influence the Ruler's investment

[101] "Sterling Balances of Kuwait," Note by the Treasury, October 17, 1956, NA, T 236/4293.

[102] "Minutes of the 19th Meeting of the Cabinet Official Committee on the Middle East," OME (57), May 23, 1957, NA, CAB 134/2338.

[103] "Minutes of the Seventh Meeting of the Cabinet Official Committee on the Middle East," ME (0) (56), June 13, 1956, NA, CAB 134/1297.

[104] In a meeting at the Treasury, one official said that "investment in Arab projects" was an idea "which had been discussed very frequently in the past but had come to nothing because the ruler insisted on security and liquidity." See the Minutes of a meeting regarding "Kuwait Investment Policy" on May 5, 1960, NA, T 236/6314.

[105] "Sterling Balances of Kuwait," Note by the Treasury, October 17, 1956, NA, T 236/4293.

Table 4.4 *Kuwait's sterling investments, 1955–1961*
(in million pounds)

Year[a]	Government bonds	Treasury bills and cash	equities	Private bonds	Total
1955	61.5	33.5	2.2		97.2
1958	133.1	44.2	18.4	10.0	205.7
1960	154.2	28.9	22.3	6.0	211.4
1961	148.3	79.2	31.4		258.9

Source: Lucas to Mackay, June 14, 1962, NA, T 317/121.
Note: [a] All figures are for March 31, except 1961, which is for June 31.

policy."[106] But this does not mean that Treasury or Bank officials did not try to do so anyway. One board member, Lord Piercy, provided a direct link to the Bank of England, and because the board convened in London, one can be fairly certain that representatives of the Bank and the Treasury voiced their opinions to the KIB, albeit emphasizing the mutual interests of Britain and Kuwait. To Britain's economic benefit, the board, having concluded that Abdullah's liquidity requirements were being satisfied, had already begun to invest a greater proportion of Kuwait's sterling revenues in equities (see Table 4.4).[107] Given that a shift in the board's investment practices toward less liquidity had already taken place, it is nearly impossible to assess whether lobbying efforts by Treasury and Bank representatives, if they occurred, had any effect. Finding evidence of KIB investment in the sterling area would go some way toward proving that they did.

The extent of "British" control over Kuwait's investments began to come under fire in 1956, a reflection of the rising internal and external pressures on the Anglo-Kuwaiti relationship. A younger generation of sheikhs and a burgeoning native intelligentsia had begun to emerge, demanding not only greater Kuwaiti control over the state's investments but also greater independence from Britain altogether. Nasser's stunning victory over the British and French at Suez helped unleash a wave of nationalism across the Middle East that precipitated shifts in the foreign and domestic policies of every government in the region, sometimes causing wholesale regime changes. Even before Nasser's triumph in the summer and autumn of 1956, one member of the Foreign Office

---

[106] My emphasis. "Minutes of the Sixth Meeting of the Cabinet Official Committee on the Middle East," ME (0) (56), June 11, 1956, NA, CAB 134/1297.
[107] Ibid.

considered "political and extreme" nationalism a greater threat to British and Western interests in the Middle East than communism or "direct Soviet penetration" into the region.[108] In trying to protect British economic interests in Kuwait, officials at Whitehall would have to contend with the various forces that militated against those interests. They would do so as chronic balance-of-payments problems continued to afflict Britain and threaten the stability of sterling.

4.3 Arab nationalism, the threat to Britain's interests in Kuwait, and Anglo-American intervention in the Middle East

The Suez crisis presented the Anglo-Kuwaiti relationship with the first genuine test of its durability. Pro-Egyptian and anti-British activities, such as fundraising for the Egyptian army and the publication of anti-imperialist articles in weekly newspapers, started to occur in Kuwait with greater frequency during the first part of 1956.[109] The level of this activity increased substantially following the nationalization of the Suez Canal. On the evening of August 14, after Nasser called for a general strike throughout the Arab world to protest the First Suez Canal Conference in London, 4,000 people gathered at one of Kuwait's leading reformist institutions, the National Cultural Club, to discuss a plan of action. While most of the speakers that night were Palestinian, the attitude of the "general population" to the Suez Canal's nationalization, according to one member of the Political Agency, was one of "general satisfaction that an Arab brother had made a strong gesture against the West."[110] During the first week of November, anti-British feeling surged among Egyptian and other Arab workers employed in the sheikhdom, at first in response to the Anglo-French ultimatum to Egypt on October 30 and then to the invasion of the canal zone itself. Various nationalist groups hung anti-British banners, circulated anti-imperialist pamphlets, recruited volunteers to serve in the Egyptian armed forces, and organized fundraising drives, strikes, demonstrations, and a boycott of British and French goods.[111] In one pamphlet distributed before the Suez invasion, entitled "An Awakening Call to the Free Arabs of the Gulf,"

---

[108] "Development and the Sterling Balances," Minute by D. S. Laskey, NA, FO 371/120829.

[109] Joyce, *Kuwait 1945–1996*, 32–33.

[110] Confidential Annex to Kuwait Diary No. 8 covering the period July 31–August 26, 1956, A. K. Rothnie, August 27, 1956, NA, FO 371/120551.

[111] Confidential Annex to Kuwait Diary No. 11 covering the period October 28–November 28 by G. W. Bell, Political Agency, Kuwait, November 28, 1956, NA, FO 371/120551.

nationalists exclaimed: "We Arabs of the Gulf must unite our ranks and revolt against the Imperialist everywhere until he loses his consciousness and control of his nerves . . . The Imperialist will try to stay as long as he can manage . . . taking away the wealth of their countries to the British Isles so that the traders of death may enjoy our wealth."[112]

Despite what seemed to be an emerging threat to Britain's position in Kuwait, British interests were never in jeopardy during the Suez crisis because the ruling generation of the al-Sabah viewed the sheikhdom's survival as tied to its relationship with Britain. B. A. B. Burrows, the Political Resident in the Persian Gulf, described in early 1957 why he believed Britain's short-term position in Kuwait was secure: "The factor that makes almost all Kuwaitis hesitate to sever their connexion with us . . . is that our protection of [the sheikhdom] is essential to its continued independent existence; in other words the realization that our protection is preferable to incorporation in Iraq or Saudi Arabia."[113] As a result, the ruling family went out of its way to demonstrate its loyalty to its British patrons. In a conversation with A. K. Rothnie of the Political Agency during the previous summer, Abdullah described Nasser's decision to nationalize the Suez Canal as the "devilry of a military minded man." Members of the al-Sabah reassured Rothnie that their police and security forces "would be able to maintain order and protect the lives and property [of British citizens] within the state."[114]

The security forces did not seek to maintain order as much as they sought to stifle the growing protest movement. They used rifle butts to disperse the 200 "hard core" pro-Nasser demonstrators that remained at the National Cultural Club after most of the crowd had gone home on the evening of August 14. Two nights later, the police used staves to break up a group of protestors in the capital's central square, an action that probably caused more damage than it prevented.[115] In November, Abdullah and the sheikhs in charge of security continued to reassure the Political Agent, G. W. Bell, that they would maintain public order, and, indeed, security forces continued to break up crowds of activists wherever they gathered.[116] Abdullah and like-minded members of the al-Sabah had signaled to both London and their subjects that a major change in the political status quo would not be tolerated.

---

[112] Included in a note from Southwell to Riches, October 2, 1956, NA, FO 371/120551.
[113] Burrows to Bell, January 3, 1957, NA, FO 371/126917.
[114] Confidential Annex to Kuwait Diary No. 8 covering the period July 31–August 26, 1956, A. K. Rothnie, August 27, 1956, NA, FO 371/120551.
[115] A coffee shop was destroyed, and 112 people went to the hospital: 100 outpatient and 12 overnight. See ibid.
[116] Confidential Annex to Kuwait Diary No. 11 covering the period October 28–November 28 by G. W. Bell, Political Agency, Kuwait, November 28, 1956, NA, FO 371/120551.

There would be no change in the economic status quo either, at least not in the areas that mattered most to Britain. During the Suez invasion, the ruler did not participate in a boycott of British imports and refused to cancel British contracts, skillfully arguing that "merchants were free to take what actions they thought best vis-à-vis British goods and customers."[117] Since Treasury officials were deeply troubled over the reported loss of confidence in sterling among Middle Eastern countries as a result of Britain's decision to block Egypt's sterling balances, they must have breathed a collective sigh of relief when Kuwait did not do further damage to the pound during the currency's traumatic November by transferring large amounts of its sterling reserves into gold and dollars. Given that the sheikhdom held so much sterling, such a move would have been detrimental to its own interests, which, along with its dependence on British defense, probably helped keep the ruler in check.

B. A. B Burrows nonetheless worried about the political pressure that was mounting on Abdullah, particularly as a result of Britain's actions regarding Suez. Even though the ruler and the older generation of sheikhs were "unusually virile and resilient," the political resident remarked, they must have been "deeply distressed" at a British Middle East policy that made the state's connection to Britain very difficult to maintain. He feared that Kuwait's ruling clique might succumb to "reformist-nationalist" pressures and sever the sheikhdom's ties with Britain, an action he thought would not only damage British interests, but also sacrifice the position of the sheikhs and Kuwait's independence in the process.[118] Consequently, Burrows believed that Whitehall should consider "expressing sympathy for some of the internal aspirations" of the nascent political movement in Kuwait as well as persuade Abdullah and the more conservative members of his family to pursue political and economic reform.[119] In large part to protect British interests, British officials had tried blunting political extremists in Egypt and Iran earlier in the century by coopting moderate reform movements and serving as handmaidens for political development.[120] In both cases, Whitehall failed to prevent anti-British political groups from taking power, at least in the long run, and eventually resorted to heavy-handed measures to preserve British influence in both countries, salvaging some of what it

[117] Ibid. Radio broadcasts from Cairo transmitted anti-British propaganda across the Gulf.
[118] Burrows to Bell, January 3, 1957, NA, FO 371/126917, and Burrows to Lloyd, January 24, 1957, NA, FO 371/126915.
[119] Burrows to Lloyd, January 24, 1957.
[120] John Darwin, *Britain, Egypt, and the Middle East* (New York: St. Martin's Press, 1981); Abrahamian, *Iran between Two Revolutions*, chs. 2 and 3. For a useful, albeit whiggish, interpretation of Britain's role in Egyptian political development see John Marlowe, *Anglo-Egyptian Relations, 1800–1956*, second edition (London: Frank Cass, 1965), chs. 9–13.

had lost in Iran, but not in Egypt. When Kuwait's younger generation of sheikhs began to agitate more forcefully for political change, the old guard would accommodate their demands. The reform that occurred, however, dealt less with internal governance than with the greater independence of Kuwait from Britain, especially in the financial realm. However, there would be no MI6 intervention or military invasion as there had been in Iran in 1953 and Egypt in 1956.

While Britain and the United States agreed on the importance of preserving their mutual oil interests in Kuwait, British officials continued to recognize, as they had since the end of World War II, that the nature of Britain's stake in Middle Eastern petroleum was different than that of the United States. In contemplating potential challenges by Middle Eastern oil-producing states to concession agreements based on the fifty–fifty principle, the Treasury wrote in September 1958 that, other than France, only Britain had "such a strong economic interest" in making sure that existing agreements were maintained. The US government, on the other hand, was only concerned with protecting the investments of American oil companies, and, unlike Britain, only had a "marginal economic interest in ensuring that the profitability of that investment [was] not reduced." Consequently, the Treasury argued, the United States would risk prejudicing its political influence in the Middle East by intervening in a sovereign country's affairs only if the threat of nationalization emerged.[121] In response to the question "Should we in the next decade regard Middle East oil as a vital interest of the United Kingdom or as a collective Western interest?" the Treasury wrote:

The UK has a special interest [in oil] . . . going beyond security of supplies. Nearly 40% of Middle East production accrues to British Companies by virtue of their shareholdings in the area (nearer 50% including oil obtained by Shell on favourable long-term contracts), and the Companies' operations, including the sale of Middle East oil to other countries contribute greatly to the strength of our economy and balance of payments. This financial and economic interest will not always coincide with the simpler concern of most of our friends and allies for continued access to supplies. In a serious dispute with Middle East countries involving earnings rather than supplies, it would be difficult for the UK to mobilise their support, and we certainly could not count on it if we sought to institute counter-measures that could themselves provoke an interruption of supplies.[122]

121 "The Fifty/Fifty Principle in Oil Agreements," Note by the Treasury, September 23, 1958, NA, T 236/5645.
122 "Oil Aspects of Future Overseas Policy," September 25, 1959, NA, T 236/5640.

The Treasury was growing anxious about the possibility of Middle Eastern oil producers renegotiating their existing concession agreements because Iran and Saudi Arabia had signed contracts with petroleum companies that abandoned the fifty–fifty profit-sharing principle in 1957 and 1958. Enrico Mattei, the independent Italian oilman who famously coined the derisive expression the "Seven Sisters" in reference to the world's major oil firms, reached an agreement with the Shah of Iran in 1957 that gave the country 75 percent of the profits that his company, Ente Nazionale Idrocarburi (ENI), earned on the sale of Iranian oil. The deal allowed Mattei to achieve some measure of revenge upon the majors for their having shut him out of the consortium agreement with Iran in 1954. Along with the ENI concession, the Arabian Oil Company, a Japanese firm backed by the Japanese government, signed a 56–44 deal with Saudi Arabia in favor of the kingdom. In addition, Standard Oil of Indiana secured a contract in Iran in 1958 with terms similar to that of ENI's – except that the former had to provide more cash up front. Ever since Aramco achieved its historic agreement with Saudi Arabia in the last days of 1950, US and British officials strove to preserve the stability of relations between Middle Eastern countries and the foreign companies that exploited their oil based on the fifty–fifty principle. Now, they had to ask, where would it all end?[123]

No group was more concerned with the answer to this question than the officials at the British Treasury, especially in 1958. Throughout the postwar era, the Treasury sought to take advantage of the benefits that accrued to Britain's balance of payments as a result of both the enormous profitability of the British oil firms and the fact that they allowed the country to save dollars on petroleum imports. In 1958, the department was offered another reminder of the impact that the trade in Middle Eastern oil could have on Britain's current account – in a positive way. In October, Britain earned a balance-of-payments surplus of £426 million, the largest in the postwar era (see Appendix 1). Much of this improvement was due to lower import prices. But a significant rise in invisible income over the previous eighteen months, in large part because of the recovery of oil earnings from the Suez crisis, also played an important role.[124] When it became clear how much oil had contributed to Britain's improved trade position in 1958, the Treasury's Mary Hedley-Miller

---

[123] Yergin, *The Prize*, 503–508. At the end of the 1940s, J. Paul Getty's Pacific Western and Aminoil, both independent American oil firms, negotiated agreements with Saudi Arabia and Kuwait, respectively, to drill for oil in the Neutral Zone that offered terms better than fifty–fifty. But the scale of their operations did not compare with those of Aramco or the other major multinationals, ibid, 437–445.

[124] *The Times* (London) and the *Financial Times*, October 13, 1958, NA, T 236/4606.

emphasized the economic risks for Britain if the concessionary status quo on Middle Eastern oil was disturbed. Making herself abundantly clear, she characterized the invisible income from Britain's involvement in the petroleum trade as "the most important single item in the calculation" of the nation's current account surpluses in the previous few years, helping the country to maintain sterling as an international currency as well as compensating for the economic strain that would be caused by a run-down of the sterling balances.[125]

Various departments at Whitehall examined "as a matter of urgency" the future of the oil concession arrangements in the Middle East. The Ministry of Fuel and Power even convened a working party to explore how Britain "might forestall pressure for wider reaching modifications of existing concessions" as a result of the agreements struck in Iran and Saudi Arabia in 1957 and 1958.[126] One member of the Political Agency in Kuwait, however, advised Leslie Rowan that dealing stubbornly with the sheikhdom on this issue would not serve Britain's interests:

> We must, I am sure, look at the situation in Kuwait quite hard headedly. Our fundamental objective is to ensure, as far as we can, that Kuwait's oil flows to us and the sterling area not for one year but for the next twenty. This will not be secured by panic measures. We must go along with the Kuwaitis even if their ways are unpalatable to us. The Ruler is a very shrewd man and our best and most reliable friend in the Sabah family; he has his finger on the pulse of the sentiment of his people; the ultimate folly would be violently to oppose him. If we want to preserve our stake in Middle East oil we must come to terms with Arab aspirations.[127]

In the case of Kuwait, those who favored accommodation would win the day: only two weeks earlier, Britain witnessed the consequences of not coming to terms with Arab aspirations in Iraq.

On July 14, 1958, Kuwait's northern next-door neighbor experienced a thundering revolution that shook the country's political landscape and laid bare its deep-seated bitterness toward Britain.[128] The king, the crown prince, and other members of Iraq's British-installed royal family, the

---

[125] Oil contributed £142 million to a £275 million surplus in 1956; £184 million to a £273 million surplus in 1957; and £254 million to a £485 million surplus in 1958. See Hedley-Miller to Taylor, August 8, 1958, NA, T 236/5645.

[126] Taylor to Legh, August 20, 1958, NA, T 236/5645.

[127] Peter (last name not given) to Rowan, July 27, 1958, NA, T 236/5645.

[128] Hanna Batatu, *The Old Social Classes and the Revolutionary Movements of Iraq: A Study of Iraq's Old Landed and Commercial Classes and of its Communists, Ba'thists, and Free Officers* (Princeton University Press, 1989) is the classic work on the social aspects of political movements in Iraq during this period. See Robert A Fernea and Wm. Roger Louis (eds.), *The Iraqi Revolution of 1958: The Old Social Classes Revisited* (London: I. B. Tauris, 1991) for a variety of perspectives on the revolution itself. Marion Farouk-Sluglett and Peter Sluglett, *Iraq since 1958: From Revolution to Dictatorship* (London: I. B. Tauris, 1990), covers the political fallout in the decades that followed the revolution.

Hashemites, were shot to death in the courtyard of their palace, while the nation's veteran prime minister, Nuri al-Said, was captured the next day trying to escape. He was eventually dragged through the streets of Baghdad, torn to pieces, and immolated. Nuri's brutal murder provided a cathartic release for a nation fed up with its government, one that had ruled the country for decades on behalf of a class of wealthy merchants and large landowners, most of whom were Sunni Muslims, a national religious minority. Most Iraqis viewed the prime minister and the king as little more than agents of British imperialism, a collaborationist elite that used British power to perpetuate an unjust political and economic system that was manipulated to protect British interests. Nuri's decision to play a central role in the Western-oriented defense organization, the Baghdad Pact, only reinforced the image of him as a British puppet out of touch with political trends in the Arab world.[129] British officials were aware that they relied too heavily on an unpopular leader to help maintain Britain's position in Iraq. Nonetheless, they had hoped that oil-driven economic development would diffuse the country's escalating socioeconomic tensions fast enough to prevent the kind of political upheaval that eventually brought down the monarchy.[130] But time ran out, and the price that London paid for its inertia was the further erosion of its influence in the Middle East, reinforcing to both US and British policy-makers the importance of Britain's stake in the Persian Gulf.

The Iraqi revolution was one of three crises in July 1958 that tested how the post-Suez, Anglo-American relationship under the Eisenhower Doctrine would deal with significant Middle East events of mutual concern. The pro-Western governments of King Hussein in Jordan and President Camille Chamoun in Lebanon were both greatly disturbed by what happed in Iraq and consequently worried about the stability of their own respective positions. With Lebanese rebels celebrating the Iraqi regime's overthrow in the streets of Beirut, Chamoun pled for Western help, threatening to turn to the Soviet Union out of desperation if he did not receive it. Eisenhower sent US forces to Lebanon to support Chamoun's government, framing the decision in the larger context of the US position in the Middle East by arguing that the United States "had to act or get out" altogether.[131] US officials sought to keep Britain from intervening in Lebanon – contrary to British wishes – for the twofold reason that, first, they did not want France to think it was being left out

---

[129] Wm. Roger Louis, "The British and the Origins of the Iraqi Revolution" in Fernea and Louis, *The Iraqi Revolution of 1958.*

[130] Ibid.

[131] Salim Yaqub, *Containing Arab Nationalism: The Eisenhower Doctrine and the Middle East* (Chapel Hill: University of North Carolina Press, 2004), 219–224, Eisenhower quoted on 224.

of an exclusive, Anglo-American operation; and, second, they wanted British forces to remain available to intervene in Iraq or Jordan, if necessary. Indeed, having already foiled a coup plot against him in June and facing the possibility of an imminent uprising, King Hussein, like Chamoun before him, asked for Anglo-American assistance. Britain sent troops to Amman on July 17, and, despite Harold Macmillan's and Hussein's impassioned requests for the United States to participate directly in a joint operation, the US government provided only logistical and rhetorical support. For its part, the Eisenhower Administration seemed loath to approach Congress to sanction a Jordanian mission, especially after having had to twist arms to gain approval for US military efforts in Lebanon. Furthermore, fearing how broader Anglo-American activities in the region – which Macmillan expected to include Iraq and Kuwait – would be received on the Arab street, the administration wanted to limit the scope of US intervention. Ultimately, the division of labor that the US government sought between Britain and the United States to contain the multiple crises proved sufficient to preserve friendly governments in Lebanon and Jordan. As for Iraq, stability prevailed after the revolution, leading the United States and Britain to conclude that meddling in another Arab nation would do more harm than good to Western interests in the Middle East. Finally, US officials counseled the Macmillan government out of any intervention in Kuwait, which, in the end, proved unnecessary.[132]

US and British management of the Middle East crises in July 1958 clarified the nature of the post-Suez, Anglo-American relationship as it pertained to the Middle East and also marked the beginning of a new US strategy for the region. First, any lingering doubt that Britain had become a junior partner to the United States in the area had vanished. Eisenhower and Dulles did as they saw fit while Macmillan was forced to follow the US lead. When Britain wanted to act, it consulted with the United States before doing so, and it restrained itself when US officials advised as such. Second, the transparent vulnerability of conservative allies in the region forced the Eisenhower Administration to recognize the futility of a policy of trying to defeat Nasserism. Relying solely on weak reeds seemed self-defeating, especially when occasionally working with Egypt could serve Western interests. Dulles himself acknowledged the unhelpfulness of conflating radical and moderate forms of Arab nationalism, the goals of which did not always overlap. As Salim Yaqub persuasively argues, US officials consequently abandoned the Eisenhower Doctrine's "underlying political strategy" of confronting Nasserist Arab nationalism

[132] Ibid., 226–246.

in favor of a more accommodating approach.[133] NSC 5820/1, approved by Eisenhower on November 4, 1958, embodied this shift in US policy, describing "the most dangerous challenge to Western interests" as arising not from "Arab nationalism per se but from the coincidence of many of its objectives with many of those of the USSR." The document's overriding policy guidance was for the United States to "establish an effective working relationship with Arab nationalism while at the same time seeking constructively to influence and stabilize the movement." Put another way, it advised that the US government reconcile nationalist aspirations in the Middle East with Western interests, the most important of which, the document's drafters noted, was the continued availability of oil to the United States and its NATO allies.[134]

NSC 5820/1 had implications for Anglo-American relations as well, pointing to the further evolution of the relationship between Britain and the United States in the post-Suez era. It codified the United States's "major responsibility for providing Free World leadership" in the Middle East while also supporting a "continued substantial British position in the Persian Gulf and Arabian Peninsula with particular reference to the Sheikdoms." Although it recommended that the United States "seek to retain the existing Western military position to the maximum extent feasible," it nonetheless advised that officials be prepared to "make appropriate revisions," if necessary, to "assure the achievement" of US objectives in the region. Moreover, the extent to which the United States should make efforts to achieve and maintain harmony with Britain – and to a lesser degree other allies – depended on compatibility with US goals: the United States should "reserve the right to act alone," the NSC argued.[135]

On July 19, 1960, Eisenhower approved an updated version of NSC 5820/1 – NSC 6011 – which acknowledged the contradiction between the US objectives of "maintaining friendly relations with the Arab countries" and "giving appropriate support to vital British interests in the area." It noted that "Arab nationalism may be expected to bring increasing pressure on the British position in the various UK dependencies on the Arabian Peninsula," thus, making the two goals progressively incompatible.[136] With the United States forecasting the decline of British influence in the Middle East and leaving itself the option of restructuring the region's strategic framework, US officials sought to groom a junior partner to succeed Britain in the area. NSC 6010, approved by

[133] Ibid., ch. 8.
[134] National Security Council Report, "NSC 5820/1," *FRUS, 1958–1960, Vol. XII*, 187–199.
[135] Ibid.
[136] National Security Council Report, "NSC 6011," *FRUS, 1958–1960, Vol. XII*, 262–273.

Eisenhower on July 6, 1960, selected Iran to fill the role. That Iran was already engaged in a "campaign to woo the Persian Gulf Sheikhs," as part of its mission to fulfill what the Shah considered the nation's destiny as the "logical heir to present British influence" in the area, made it the perfect candidate.[137] Thus, as Douglas Little rightly notes, NSC 6010 sowed the seeds of the future US strategy – which would not achieve full bloom for another decade – that depended on regional powers to defend Western interests in the Gulf as Britain's influence in the area waned.[138]

Since the Iraqi revolution represented a steep drop on the graph of British decline in the Middle East, it is important to consider how the decisions made by Iraq's new military dictatorship impinged on sterling. Wanting to avoid the mistakes of Muhammad Mossadegh seven years earlier, the country's prime minister, Abd al-Karim Qasim, did not nationalize the Iraq Petroleum Company. Rather, he allowed the firm to continue its operations as negotiations took place over the terms of its concession (British Petroleum had a 23.75 percent stake in the IPC). Discussions dragged on for years, though, and by the end of the 1960s – and three coups later – Iraq would expropriate almost all of the IPC's original holdings.[139] Britain's balance of payments on oil never suffered as a result of the 1958 revolution, whereas Iraq ended up losing a great deal of potential oil revenue because the IPC did not invest in new exploration and production owing to the uncertainty of its position.[140] Qasim took more drastic steps regarding Iraq's membership in the sterling area. Almost immediately, he expressed his intention to withdraw. In an official statement released in mid-1959, the minister of finance explained that by abandoning the sterling area Iraq was helping to fulfill one of the major objectives of the July 14 revolution: the nation's "complete economic independence." He also celebrated the fact that Iraq would be "free to use its foreign balances in such a manner as [would] suit its interests" and proclaimed that the Iraqi dinar would gain "new strength" from a currency cover that would include gold and "a collection of the strongest international currencies" rather than sterling alone.[141]

On the whole, the British Treasury did not think that Iraq's decision to leave the sterling area would adversely affect the currency group, either directly or indirectly by causing the Persian Gulf protectorates to follow its lead. Department officials believed that if Iraq maintained its pattern of

137 National Security Council Report, "NSC 6010," *FRUS, 1958–1960, Vol. XII*, 680–688.
138 Little, *American Orientalism*, 136–137.
139 Bamberg, *British Petroleum and Global Oil, 1950–1975*, 163–171.
140 Yergin, *The Prize*, 535.
141 "Unofficial Translation of an 'Explanatory Note' about Iraq's Withdrawal from the Sterling Area Issued by the Ministry of Finance," June 23, 1959, BE/OV23/25.

trade and payments, its abandonment of the sterling area would probably make "no difference" either to Britain's current account or its reserves, although any switch of a large portion of its sterling reserves into other currencies or gold might cause a tremor in the sterling area.[142] Ultimately, the Treasury was proven correct, as Iraq's action did not seem to have any adverse economic impact on Britain or the Empire-Commonwealth. Assessing the reaction of the Persian Gulf states, the Treasury concluded that Iraq's departure from the sterling area "had little effect" on their attitudes. Even if Kuwait was encouraged to diversify its reserves, such a move had been "a potential threat all along," the Treasury wrote, because of the sheikhdom's expressed desire to establish its own currency. Most important, all of the Persian Gulf states viewed Iraq's decision as motivated by sheer politics, not economics, given how much stronger sterling had grown in 1958 and 1959.[143]

Much as during the Suez crisis, Abdullah and his like-minded family members did not give British officials any reason to worry that Kuwait would do anything rash with its sterling holdings after the Iraqi revolution. In June 1959, Bank of England Advisor C. E. Loombe met with Abdullah's uncle and acting ruler, Abdullah Mubarak, and reported that the sheikh had said that Iraqi policy-makers must have been "out of their minds to break with sterling" when the currency was strong, Britain's gold and dollar reserves "were higher than ever before," and restrictions on convertibility were being lifted.[144] A week later, the ruler seconded his uncle, saying that Iraqi officials "were being ill-advised to weaken their link with sterling." After his conversations with the two sheikhs, Loombe concluded that as long as Abdullah remained alive, any "substantial change in Kuwait's attitude toward sterling was unlikely." The problem, of course, was that his successor "might have different ideas."[145]

Indeed, in the wake of the Iraqi revolution in 1958, and Egypt's unification with newly radicalized Syria to form the United Arab Republic (UAR) that year, British officials grew more concerned about nationalism in Kuwait. Not long after the overthrow of the monarchy in Iraq, a

---

[142] "Iraq and the Sterling Area," Note by the Treasury, Cabinet Official Committee on the Middle East, OME (58) 58, December 19, 1958, NA, CAB 134/2343; Ford to Johnston, September 22, 1958, BE/OV23/24. That said, even before the revolution, the Treasury's Michael Johnston worried that Iraq's withdrawal from the sterling area "would be a blow to the reputation of sterling and to the prestige of the United Kingdom in the world at large," Chadwick to Johnston, April 12, 1957, NA, T 236/4796.

[143] Note by the Overseas Department, July 13, 1959, BE/OV23/25.

[144] Loombe to Stevens, Parsons, and the Governors, June 25, 1959, BE/OV23/25; Loombe was also in Iraq's Ministry of Finance from 1941 to 1945.

[145] Ibid.

delegation representing the leaders of Kuwait's various reform clubs visited Baghdad as guests of the government, prompting the managing director of the Kuwait Oil Company, C. A. P. Southwell, to write: "There is no doubt that the young nationalist group in Kuwait has received a tremendous boost by the success of the Iraq revolution."[146] He warned that the nationalist movement was "growing every day" and was "much stronger" than people realized, fearing that "even the sheikhs" were "bound to bow to the tide and accept the inevitable changes" that the burgeoning movement would foster in Kuwait.[147] While one should never underestimate the potential for an oil executive, British or American, to exaggerate political threats to ensure that his government will protect his company's interests, future events would bear out Southwell's assessment.

The comments of the KOC's managing director were probably also influenced by a separate conversation that took place a couple of weeks earlier between another company official and Sheikh Fahad, Abdullah's half-brother who had so irked British officials earlier in the decade. Apparently, Fahad had complained that Britain "seemed to regard the Arab lands as a place in which to wield [its] influence," blaming Whitehall for what had happened in Iraq.[148] British policy-makers "called upon the Hashemites and Nuri and his henchmen to do too much, to put up an all-out opposition to Arab nationalism," he pronounced. "This was more than any Arab government could be expected to do: some concessions ought to have been made to it." Fahad then turned to the subject of Kuwait. "[Britain] should be very careful not to upset people," he said ominously, and continued by warning that, while there was "no real anti-British feeling" in Kuwait, "any unwise action could bring about an anti-British movement." The head of the Foreign Office's Eastern Department, D. M. H. Riches, believed that the sheikh was not just speaking for himself but "probably reproducing much of the ruler's thought" as well.[149]

In his "Valedictory Despatch" upon leaving Kuwait, Political Agent A. S. Halford seemed to have learned a major lesson from the British experience in Iraq. He wrote:

I have no doubt that, if the interests of Arab nationalism and our interests came into direct collision, Arab nationalism would prove the stronger. And here is the first moral we should draw: we should never allow ourselves to be forced into the position where British and Arab nationalist interests can come into conflict with each other. This, of course is easier said than done, but it is worth making a big

---

[146] Southwell to Walmsley, September 15, 1958, NA, FO 371/132532.   [147] Ibid.
[148] Foreign Office Minute by Riches, NA, FO 371/132547.   [149] Ibid.

effort, even at the risk of some loss of so-called prestige, to avoid precipitating a crisis, to paper over the cracks, to demonstrate that Britain's interest in Kuwait is not solely materialistic.

Halford ultimately concluded:

The essential consideration must be, however, that in the course of nature Kuwait, because of her cohesive political identity, backed by great wealth, must some day achieve complete independence . . . I submit that we must accept this necessity and be prepared to meet it before it becomes too urgent and a cause for dissension between us.[150]

British officials understood that the al-Sabah, caught between the hammer of Baghdad and the anvil of Cairo, were in a difficult position. Revolutionary Iraq, which reached out to the Soviet Union, lay across Kuwait's northern border, and Egypt, although not geographically close, nonetheless stirred up trouble by using the airwaves to inundate the Arabian Peninsula with Arab nationalist propaganda. A dispute between Iraq and Egypt over the former's refusal to join the UAR meant that Kuwait had to perform a somewhat tricky balancing act of trying to impress Egypt, the undisputed leader of the Arab world, without offending Iraq, the greatest immediate threat to its security. To survive, the al-Sabah would have to make an effort to demonstrate their solidarity with their Arab brethren, and British officials knew that in whatever way the ruling family chose to do so, Whitehall would have to "play along."[151] Abdullah was too important to the internal stability of Kuwait – and, thus, to British economic interests – not to support his efforts to establish stronger relations with other Arab states.[152]

Consequently, when the sheikh asked the British government to relax the restrictions on his ability to conduct relations with other Arab countries, it obliged. Whitehall sent him a letter on October 23, 1958, officially permitting him to deal with Arab countries on matters that he believed would promote Kuwait's interests. But the letter also reinforced the terms of the 1899 treaty that structured the Anglo-Kuwaiti relationship, directing Abdullah to consult British officials before entering into any commitments.[153] The sheikh tested Whitehall's credibility almost

[150] Halford to Lloyd, August 13, 1959, NA, FO 371/140084.
[151] For example, S. J. Aspden of the Political Agency's Commercial Office advised the Board of Trade in London to accept that Kuwait's participation in the Arab boycott of Israel had "come to stay." He lamented that it would be "impossible to do very much" to help British firms that would be blacklisted or threatened as a result. Aspden to O'Brien, February 10, 1958, NA, FO 371/132810.
[152] Halford to Lloyd, June 11, 1959, NA, FO 371/140083.
[153] "Text of Her Majesty's Government's Letter of Assurance," October 23, 1958, NA, FO 371/132547.

immediately by informing the Political Agency that he wanted Kuwait to join the Arab League and to accept consuls from other Arab states. To indicate his seriousness on these issues, he reminded Political Agent A. S. Halford of what happened to Arab leaders, such as Nuri al-Said, who did not properly represent their constituents when "confronted by ideas" that symbolized the general "aspirations of Arab peoples."[154] Selwyn Lloyd told the Political Resident in Bahrain that both he and Harold Macmillan felt that as long as the "fundamental features" of the Anglo-Kuwaiti relationship were preserved, they were prepared "to accept [Abdullah's] judgment" if he thought such action was at that point "inevitable."[155] Regardless, given that the sheikhdom had already participated in Arab League activities as a non-member, such as boycotting Israel and sending representatives to its Petroleum Committee and its Economic Council, Kuwait's membership in the League would hardly signify a dramatic departure.[156]

Pressure was building in Kuwait for greater financial independence as well, something that caused far more concern in London than Abdullah's forays into Middle Eastern diplomacy, especially at the Treasury. This pressure came as no surprise to Political Agent J. C. H. Richmond, who wrote: "Kuwait is emerging from a semi-colonial status and Arab nationalist sentiments reinforce their natural desire for complete freedom to deal with their own money. They are sensitive to jibes from other Arabs that it is used to support a tottering British empire."[157] Those jibes did not come just from "other Arabs." Kuwaiti reformists roundly criticized the sheikhdom's investment policy, calling the sterling balances "direct loans" to the British government and implying that its investment in sterling securities served Britain's interests far more than Kuwait's.[158] The Treasury worried that if these attacks prompted the ruling family to diversify Kuwait's reserves, or to hold its surplus oil revenues in some form other than sterling, there would be "serious

---

[154] No. 10 from Halford to the Foreign Office, January 5, 1959, NA, FO 371/140118.
[155] No. 184 from the Foreign Office to Bahrain, January 30, 1959, NA, FO 371/140118. Also see "International Status of Kuwait," Draft Cabinet Paper by Walmsley, January 28, 1959, NA, FO 371/140104.
[156] "Kuwait: International Relations," Foreign Office Minute by King, February 17, 1959, NA, FO 371/140119. The sheikhdom joined the Arab League two years later, soon after it had gained independence.
[157] Richmond to Beaumont, May 24, 1960, NA, FO 371/148997.
[158] Such criticism emerged during the Suez crisis, with younger, nationalistic members of the al-Sabah joining the chorus. However, at the time, the Treasury did not find any evidence that critics of the British-influenced Kuwait Investment Board "influenced the ruler." See "Sterling Balances of Kuwait," Note by the Treasury, October 17, 1956, NA, T 236/4293.

consequences."[159] "Apart from the drain on the central reserves of the sterling area," the Treasury explained, "any move to weaken the link between Kuwait and sterling would be likely to affect confidence in sterling as an international currency and to weaken the benefits UK trade derives from its worldwide use."[160] The problem for Whitehall was that the methods at its disposal to prevent such an outcome, such as blocking Kuwait's balances, for example, would most likely damage confidence in sterling among the currency's largest holders. British officials, moreover, felt that they should not oppose small to moderate Kuwaiti moves out of sterling because such opposition would suggest that the currency was unstable and could precipitate the kind of massive transfer out of sterling that British officials were seeking to avoid.

An expanding Kuwaiti merchant class also sought to reduce Britain's influence over the state's financial affairs, and Whitehall appeased this group for fear of undermining the Kuwaiti government's faith in sterling. Because the sheikhdom did not offer nearly enough investment outlets for the increasing wealth that Kuwaiti residents accumulated as a result of the burgeoning oil industry, the native elite sought to pursue investment options beyond Kuwait. But whereas the ruling family could freely transfer sterling into other currencies to purchase property outside the sterling area – as a result of the deal that Britain struck with Abdullah in 1951 to persuade him to accept sterling from the KOC – other Kuwaitis could not. Adhering to the sterling area's normal exchange control guidelines, the Political Agency in Kuwait "consistently refused" applications from private citizens who wanted to purchase property in other currency areas, which fomented resentment in the merchant class.[161] J. C. B. Richmond determined in May 1960 that a policy change had "become necessary." Alistair Mackay at the Treasury agreed, believing that narrow restrictions on the flow of private funds abroad might cast "doubt in the minds of the ruling few in Kuwait on the advantages of Kuwait's links with sterling generally."[162] Indeed, only ten days earlier, Fakhri Shehab of Kuwait's Department of Finance and Economy urged Richmond "to approve freely" Kuwait's applications for the transfer of sterling – and to "show no anxiety."[163] "This would be the best guarantee," he said, of

---

[159] "The Persian Gulf States and the Sterling Area," Note by the Treasury, November 10, 1959, NA, T 236/5181.
[160] Ibid.
[161] "Exchange Control in Kuwait," Note by the Treasury, June 22, 1960, and Mackay to Milner-Barry, May 20, 1960, both NA, T 317/118.
[162] Mackay to Milner-Barry, May 20, 1960.
[163] Richmond to Beaumont, May 10, 1960, NA, FO 371/148997. The Political Agency ended up approving proposals for two transfers by the Kuwaiti government, £500,000

Kuwaitis retaining "confidence in their links with sterling" and limiting their transfers to a "moderate scale." Shehab warned that showing anxiety or questioning relatively minor moves into other currencies could rouse Kuwaiti suspicions and encourage a much wider departure from sterling.[164]

In July 1961, a month after Kuwait achieved independence from Britain, the sheikhdom inherited exchange control responsibilities from the Political Agency, and Abdullah's nephew, Sheikh Jabir al-Ahmad al-Sabah, the powerful and nationalistic president of the Department of Finance and Economy, took charge of the new exchange control regime.[165] No figure gave British officials more pause regarding Kuwait's future economic policies than Jabir, who at one time or another was characterized as "tough," "ambitious," "suspicious-minded," and "Anglophobe."[166] A Treasury background paper described him as "the dominant personality in Kuwait," one who exercised more influence than the ruler himself. Indeed, H. T. Kemp reported that the Kuwait Investment Board was starting to receive instructions "in the first person" from Jabir instead of in the name of the ruler, as had been the usual practice.[167] Furthermore, Jabir was "much less attached to the British connexion and much more interested in forays into independence" than the more conservative Abdullah, Fakhri Shehab informed British representatives.[168] As head of the sheikhdom's currency board, Jabir's decision to back the new Kuwaiti dinar, introduced in April, with more gold than sterling seemed to demonstrate the sheikh's desire to "assert Kuwait's financial and economic independence" of Britain, an impression reinforced by his appointment of three Kuwaiti Finance Department officials to advise on investments outside the United Kingdom.[169] "The view of the Treasury, Bank of England and Foreign Office," the Treasury's J. E. Lucas wrote,

to purchase shares in the Arab Bank and £2.5 million for investment in Switzerland. See Lucas to Mackay on May 4, 1960, NA, T 236/6314.

[164] Ibid.

[165] Cranston to Beaumont, May 21, 1961, NA, FO 371/156860 and Lucas to Mackay, February 8, 1961, NA, T 236/6315.

[166] "A Note on Some of the Sabah Family," by M. S. Berthoud, December 1, 1965; Lucas to Sharp, September 16, 1965, NA, T 317/685.

[167] Beaumont to Richmond, May 4, 1960, NA, T 317/685.

[168] "Kuwait: Shaikh Jabir," Note by the Treasury, September 20, 1965, NA, T 317/844; Beaumont to Richmond, May 4, 1960, NA, T 236/6314.

[169] The cover for the Kuwaiti dinar was 50 percent gold, 40 percent sterling, and 10 percent dollars. When the new currency was being considered a year earlier, Fakhri Shehab said that it was "the fear of possible restriction on freedom of exchange or devaluation" that led Kuwait to want to hold "a good part of their currency backing in other currencies or gold, especially the latter." Furthermore, "other countries were . . . offering attractive terms," Shehab continued, and "Kuwaitis wished to be free to invest according to their own best interests." See Richmond to Beaumont, May 10, 1960, NA, FO 371/148997.

"is that . . . some further effort is now required if we are to maintain the maximum British influence in Kuwait's investment policy and serve Kuwait's and our own interests in this matter."[170]

Fortunately for Britain, Kuwaiti authorities remained deferential to British officials on matters concerning investment outside the sterling area. Haider Shehabi, the head of the Financial Section of the Department of Finance – and the figure who oversaw the day-to-day operations of the state's exchange control – consulted W. P. Cranston, who had become the counsel-general at the British Embassy, on issuing permits for Kuwaiti investments in other currency areas. Shehabi and his colleagues wanted Cranston's view on certain applications to ensure that they did not "start something which might cause difficulties" for Britain or the sterling area.[171] Echoing sentiments expressed by other British officials over the previous two years, Cranston explained that he and others recognized that Kuwait's private citizens needed access to investment outlets beyond the sheikhdom and added that Britain was prepared to deal with the resulting currency transfers, "provided that the investments were not so large and sudden as to disrupt markets and cause a dislocation in the sterling area." Shehabi assured him of Kuwait's commitment to this principle, telling him that transfers outside the sterling area would be "graduated on a rising scale" so that their effects "could be judged progressively." Cranston then concluded his discussion with Shehabi by reminding him that, because the Kuwait government was its "own control authority," he and his associates were "free to issue permits as they wished."[172] Given the "delicacy" of its relations with Kuwait, the Treasury's J. E. Lucas observed, Britain could not "afford to be too obstructive," and, thus, he backed the overall tone of Cranston's meeting with Shehabi. But in typical Treasury fashion, he believed that Whitehall should submit tighter guidelines for Kuwait to follow than those suggested by Cranston.[173]

---

[170] "Kuwait Investment Policy," Treasury Memorandum by Lucas, May 17, 1961, NA, T 236/6527. At least one British official, J. C. B. Richmond, possessed a sober-minded view of Jabir: "I think it is understandable that Shaikh Jabir's attitude . . . should be less attached to the British connexion than the Ruler. He is younger, has been in touch with a wider international circle of people and, as President of the Finance Department in direct charge of Kuwait's finances, must, somewhat naturally, feel that he should put Kuwait's money where it is of greatest advantage to the State. This need not mean that he is anti-British or that he plans a major departure from the long standing links with sterling so long as sterling stays sound." See Richmond to Beaumont, May 10, 1960, NA, FO 371/148997.

[171] Cranston to Mackay, July 10, 1962, NA, T 317/119.   [172] Ibid.

[173] Lucas to Clowser, July 18, 1962, NA, T 317/119.

Kuwait's ability to disrupt Britain's economy and Britain's capacity to defend Kuwait from outside threats ensured that neither country would do anything to offend the other to the degree that would disturb the stability of the Anglo-Kuwaiti relationship. Time and again, British officials affirmed that they would respect Kuwait's progress toward greater financial independence as long as that progress did not undermine sterling. In fact, they were reluctant to impede Kuwaiti efforts in this direction because they thought that to do so *would* undermine sterling. Kuwait, on the other hand, desperately needed Britain's military support. Viewed as self-serving with their vast wealth, the al-Sabah were not very well liked in the Arab world, which, of course, included their immediate neighbors, the competing monarchy in Saudi Arabia and the revolutionary regime in Iraq. Ironically, Britain, the country that kept Kuwait in a state of political dependence for more than sixty years, represented the most reliable guarantor of Kuwait's newly acquired independence. Therefore, beyond the fact that the sheikhdom's own economic interests compelled it to help maintain the stability of sterling, the al-Sabah's need for British military support prevented the family from pursuing economic policies detrimental to Britain. The Political Resident in the Persian Gulf, W. H. Luce phrased it best when he wrote, "Our strongest asset in maintaining our position in the Persian Gulf is that its Rulers and most of their people still want us to protect them."[174]

And nothing served notice to the al-Sabah of Kuwait's dependence on British military support more than Iraq's threat to annex the sheikhdom soon after it gained independence in mid-June 1961. With virtually no legal basis, Abd al-Karim Qasim claimed Iraqi sovereignty over Kuwait and, according to British intelligence reports – the accuracy of which has since been debated – the prime minister began to prepare his troops for an invasion of the newly independent state. While members of the Arab League rejected Qasim's assertions and denounced his behavior, the organization did not seem ready to intervene in the event of an Iraqi attack. Meanwhile, Britain's new Treaty of Friendship with Kuwait guaranteed Britain's military support if the al-Sabah requested it.[175]

As this new crisis with Iraq unfolded, Harold Macmillan's government made every effort to consult with US officials in the Kennedy Administration (which took power six months earlier) on future action. British Foreign Secretary Sir Alec Douglas Home wrote to US

---

[174] Luce to the Earl of Home, November 22, 1961, NA, FO 371/156670.
[175] The guarantee can be found in Clause (d) of the Anglo-Kuwaiti exchange of letters on June 19, 1961 that abrogated the 1899 treaty and granted Kuwait its independence. See NA, FO 371/162893.

Secretary of State Dean Rusk on June 28 to tell him that Britain had "an absolute obligation" to intervene in Kuwait if it was attacked. The foreign secretary also said that he wanted British and US officials to act in closest cooperation and endeavored that he and Rusk be in touch as frequently as Selwyn Lloyd and John Foster Dulles were during July 1958 – when the Lebanese, Iraqi, and Jordanian crises erupted.[176] The following day, Home wrote to Rusk again, telling him that he hoped that Britain could "count on full political support from the United States Government" if it sent forces to Kuwait at the ruler's request, characterizing US backing as "absolutely essential."[177] The foreign secretary preferred that Britain would not have to intervene and noted the advantages of another Arab government, such as Saudi Arabia, initiating action rather than the British. Rusk replied to Home on June 29, conveying the US government's appreciation of Britain's obligation to Kuwait and informing him that it was "prepared to render the full political support" that Britain requested, which the National Security Council approved that day, along with logistical help, if necessary.[178]

After receiving a request from the ruler of Kuwait for military intervention to defend the country against an Iraqi attack, Britain sent 5,000 troops there on July 1.[179] Not only had the British government received US consent for the operation, but the United States also directed the Solant Amity naval force – consisting of two destroyers, three amphibious vessels, and 463 marines – toward Bahrain in support of the British mission.[180] Ultimately, the US government recalled Solant Amity as a result of the successful British military buildup and Iraqi statements regarding a peaceful settlement.[181] Once Kuwait was secure, the British government immediately sought a way to extract its troops, fearing that, in the words of W. H. Luce, "the longer we stay here the more isolated from the rest of the Arab world Kuwait will become."[182] Just as bad, he thought, Britain might be "drawn into physical support of the Sabah family against a rising tide of Arab nationalist agitation."[183] Consequently, British officials conferred with their counterparts in Washington to find a non-British, non-US, solution to the problem of securing Kuwaiti independence – possibly through the United Nations (although Kuwait was not yet a member) – once Britain withdrew its forces.[184]

[176] *FRUS, 1961–1963, Vol. XVII*, 168.   [177] June 29, 1961, in ibid., 171–172.
[178] Editorial Note, ibid., 172.
[179] Joyce, *Kuwait 1945–1996*, 102–106; Sluglett and Sluglett, *Iraq since 1958*, 82; Smith, *Kuwait 1950–1965*, 117–121.
[180] Home to Rusk, July 2, 1961, *FRUS, 1961–1963, Vol. XVII*, 176–177.
[181] Editorial Note, ibid., 178.
[182] Luce to Stevens, July 16, 1961, NA, CAB 134/2345.   [183] Ibid.
[184] Telegram from the Department of State to the Embassy in the United Kingdom, July 12, 1961, *FRUS, 1961–1963, Vol. XVII*, 184–185.

With the passage of a Saudi-proposed resolution on Kuwait by the Arab League Council on July 20, an "Arab solution" to the Kuwait problem was found that satisfied both the British and US governments. The resolution required that Kuwait ask for the withdrawal of British troops "as soon as possible" and called on Iraq "not to use force in connection with Kuwait."[185] It also admitted Kuwait to the Arab League and committed the organization to "take 'practical assistance' to safeguard Kuwait's independence," which took the form of a multilateral force led by Saudi Arabia.[186] British troops were, thus, able to leave the sheikhdom on September 19.[187] In a telegram to the Department of State, John Jernegan, the US Ambassador in Iraq, wrote that Kuwait's dependence on British forces for its defense should be "no more than [a] desperate last resort" and that Kuwait had to "become [the] genuine concern of other Arab states."[188] He also argued: "The West can no longer afford [the] present policy of reliance on British military protection, which seems to be [the] most attractive one to greedy, short-sighted Shaikhs [sic]. Under [present] circumstances it behooves us to seize [the] initiative while time (now very short) remains."[189] National Security Council staff member Robert Komer agreed, arguing that "Kuwait's independence can only be assured if Ruler uses his fantastic oil revenues to buy support from other Arab leaders, particularly Nasser and Jordanians."[190] This focus on a non-British means of securing Western interests in the Gulf represented another step in the growth of the US defense strategy – begun by the Eisenhower Administration – to compensate for Britain's waning influence in the region.[191]

What helped pave the way for the presence of Arab League troops in Kuwait was a tour of Arab capitals by Sheikh Jabir, who used the opportunity to "polish up [the country's] image" around the Arab world.[192] But the lukewarm response that Sheikh Jabir received on his mission jolted the al-Sabah into an appreciation of their unfavorable standing in Arab circles. According to J. C. B. Richmond, state leaders reacted to Jabir with "hostility and jealousy," expressing to the sheikh their belief that Kuwait used its newfound wealth "selfishly" rather than for the benefit of Arab unity and progress.[193] Consequently, Sayyid Ahmad Sayyid Omar, the head of the Department of Finance's Investment Committee,

[185] Strong to Talbot, July 24, 1961, *FRUS, 1961–1963, Vol. XVII*, 197–199.
[186] Ibid.   [187] Little, *American Orientalism*, 137.
[188] Telegram from the Embassy in Iraq to the Department of State, December 28, 1961, *FRUS, 1961–1963, Vol. XVII*, 374–375.
[189] Ibid.
[190] Komer to Bundy, December 29, 1961, *FRUS, 1961–1963, Vol. XVII*, 378–380.
[191] Little, *American Orientalism*, 136–137.
[192] Richmond to Home, January 4, 1962, NA, FO 371/162879.   [193] Ibid.

told W. P. Cranston in September 1961 that the sheikhdom "had come to realise that she must use more of her wealth to establish herself in better light among her Arab neighbours": the government would have to "spend more in those countries."[194] Cranston was sympathetic to Kuwait's position, having written a month and a half earlier: "Indeed, it may well be that the promise of economic development may be part of the price which Kuwait will have to pay in order to secure her future independence and to remove the current feeling of resentment."[195] In fact, as early as June 1960, representatives of the Treasury, the Bank of England, and the Foreign Office agreed "in principle" that the British government "should support any move to invest part of Kuwait's surplus in Arab projects" because such investment would remove the "stigma of imperialism" associated with the sheikhdom's financial policies and silence the "criticism that the ruler had no interest in Arab development."[196] However, knowing that the British would worry about the ramifications for sterling of Kuwait's decision to play a role in Arab economic development, Omar assured Cranston that any funds for this purpose would come from Kuwait's current revenues, precluding any "large scale withdrawal" of overseas sterling investments.[197]

To facilitate Kuwaiti lending to Arab countries, Sheikh Abdullah, who since independence referred to himself as "emir," established the Kuwait Fund for Arab Economic Development (KFAED) in December 1961.[198] Initially capitalized at £50 million (and later £100 million), the KFAED provided loans that varied in both length and interest rates, depending on the nature of the proposal accepted. According to the fund's guidelines, applicants had to demonstrate their projects' technical soundness, economic feasibility, and high priority in their country's development program. Furthermore, no project could receive more than 50 percent

[194] Cranston to Walmsley, September 3, 1961, NA, FO 371/156865.
[195] Cranston to Mackay, July 16, 1961, NA, FO 371/156860.
[196] "Minutes of a Meeting Held in the Treasury on 5th May, 1960," NA, T 236/6314.
[197] Cranston to Walmsley, September 3, 1961, NA, FO 371/156865.
[198] Fakhri Shehab actually proposed a similar idea to British officials more than a year and a half earlier, telling Roger Stevens that the al-Sabah "might endanger their own position by locking up all their investments in the United Kingdom." He encouraged the British to persuade Abdullah to set aside £10 million for investment in the Arab world over a five-year period in commercial projects, the proposals for which would be vetted by "an authoritative body, whether international or set up by the state of Kuwait, and not giving money away." See Beaumont to Richmond, May 4, 1960, NA, T 236/6314. The most detailed study of the KFAED and its relationship to Arab economic development is Soliman Demir, *The Kuwait Fund and the Political Economy of Arab Regional Development* (New York: Praeger, 1976). Also see Ahmed A. Ahmed, "Kuwait Public Commercial Investments in Arab Countries," *Middle Eastern Studies*, 31, 2 (1995), 293–306.

of its financing from the KFAED, nor could any country receive more than 15 percent of the fund's resources at any one time.[199] By January 1964, the KFAED had disbursed £40.5 million in loans to the Arab world, including £6 million to Tunisia, £7 million to Sudan, £7.5 million to Jordan, £10 million to Algeria, and £10 million to the United Arab Republic.[200] None of the states contained in this list were oil producers and, therefore, they were most in need of loans for development. It is possible that the United Arab Republic and Algeria received the most money out of the group because they represented the Arab nationalist vanguard in the Middle East and North Africa at the time. But it is also possible that their projects simply demanded more money. Whether or not political considerations influenced the disbursement of KFAED funds depended on the case under consideration.[201]

Concerned about the possible economic repercussions for Britain of Kuwait's new and potentially widespread lending to Arab countries, British officials closely monitored the sheikhdom's outlays. What they saw assuaged any anxieties that they may have had. According to one Treasury observer, it seemed that two years of loans to Arab governments, whether under the auspices of the KFAED or directly from Kuwait's budget, had not yet affected Britain's balance of payments, nor were they likely to place "any great strain" on Britain's reserves. Of course, the disbursement of so much sterling increased Britain's export opportunities – although one could not be sure how or where the Arab countries that received Kuwaiti money would eventually spend it. Finally, given the sturdy management of Kuwait's balances up to that point, the running down of those balances would probably not be "great" or "unduly fast."[202]

Treasury officials still worried about losing influence over Kuwait's investment policy to competing parties inside and outside the sheikhdom. In May 1962, Robert Anderson – George Humphrey's successor as secretary of the treasury under Eisenhower – distressed members of the British Treasury when he and his investment firm, Interser, discussed with Sheikh Jabir the idea of forming a new investment company in Kuwait. Alistair Mackay described Anderson's proposal as a "matter of

---

[199] Minute by the Treasury, April 11, 1963, NA, T 317/323; "Kuwait Fund for Arab Economic Development: First Annual Report, 1962–1963" in NA, T 317/517.

[200] Sharp to Owen, January 10, 1964, NA, T 317/517.

[201] For example, the KFAED suspended its subsidy to Jordan during its civil war in 1970–1971, when the Jordanian army put down a Palestinian rebellion. See Demir, *The Kuwait Fund and the Political Economy of Arab Regional Development*, 21–22.

[202] "The Economy of Kuwait, 1950–1968," FCO Research Department, October 1969, NA, FCO 51/93.

great anxiety" for Britain, believing that if the US company were to hold sway over Kuwait's investment machinery, it would "cut the ground from under the feet of the Kuwait Investment Board in London."[203] The result might be that Anderson's firm would pull funds away from "established organizations" and precipitate a "rapid switch out of sterling."[204] Anderson assured Selwyn Lloyd, then the Chancellor of the Exchequer, that he would not make "any arrangement of any sort" without consulting Britain first and that he was "intent" that no withdrawal of existing sterling investments would occur.[205] Despite these assurances, Mackay believed that the sheikhdom's acceptance of Anderson's proposals was "bound to involve the risk of increasing American influence on Kuwait's investment policy to the detriment of [Britain's]."[206] Much to the relief of Treasury officials, nothing came of Anderson's scheme, at least not at first. Kuwaiti authorities thought that the proposed company would duplicate the functions of the indigenous and recently formed Kuwait Investment Company (KIC), and they feared that other Arabs would attack them for engaging in "speculation with Jewish bankers."[207] But, in the end, the scheme was revived and the Kuwait Capital Corporation (KCC) was established at the end of the year with an initial capitalization of $25 million, half of which would come from Kuwaiti sources – government and private – and the other half from Western interests. Since the group's funding was "relatively small," the Treasury's J. E. Lucas felt that the firm was "not likely to become very important."[208]

Although the creation of the KCC did not greatly perturb Lucas, he was nonetheless bothered by the rise in the number of organizations that handled the Kuwaiti government's investments. Along with the Kuwait Fund for Arab Economic Development and the Kuwait Capital Corporation, there was the Finance Committee of the Kuwait Finance

---

[203] Mackay to Milner-Barry, May 8, 1962, NA, T 317/121.

[204] "Brief for Mr. Anderson's Visit to the Chancellor," by Mackay, May 9, 1962, and the minutes of a meeting regarding "Kuwait: Investment," May 9, 1962, both in NA, T 317/121.

[205] "Note of Mr. Robert Anderson's Interview with the Chancellor of the Exchequer," by Mackay, May 15, 1962, NA, T 317/121.

[206] Mackay to Milner-Barry, July 16, 1962, NA, T 317/121.

[207] Milner-Barry to Rickett, June 22, 1962, NA, T 317/121; Richmond to Walmsley, June 30, 1962, NA, T 317/122.

[208] Lucas to Sharp, November 5, 1962, NA, T 317/322. Treasury officials also expressed concern about an IBRD mission to Kuwait, fearing that its survey of Kuwait's internal financial and economic administration would spill over into the investment of the sheikhdom's sterling balances. However, the investment of Kuwait's surplus sterling remained off the IBRD's agenda. See "Submission to the Lord Privy Seal from Milner-Barry," undated (most likely November 1960), and Mackay to Milner-Barry, February 15, 1961, NA, T 236/6315.

Department, which dealt with the investment proposals of visiting bankers and others. The Treasury figured that the committee had already invested £10 million, some of which went to Europe and Japan. Moreover, the Chase Manhattan Bank and the First National City Bank handled Kuwait's dollar income from Aminoil as well as that from the Japanese-owned Arabian Oil Company.[209] And while the aforementioned Kuwait Investment Company had not begun operations by early 1963, it had £15 million available for portfolio investment and was expected to draw future funds from both the government and the private sector. Finally, in 1966, the state would launch the Kuwait Foreign Trading Contracting and Investment Company (KFTCIC), a group that invested abroad exclusively and which received 80 percent of its funds, totaling £20 million, from the government.[210] Lucas commented: "We have never been too happy about this proliferation of investment organisations, the effect of which has inevitably been to reduce the importance of the Kuwait Investment Board." The British government may never have had any "direct influence" over the board's activities, but Lucas's concern about the KIB's diminished importance clearly derived from either the government's past ability to influence the board indirectly or the fact that the government and the board shared an understanding of what best served British economic interests.[211]

As Kuwait's Department of Finance took increasingly greater control over the state's investments from 1960 onward, Treasury officials tried to prevent the Kuwait Investment Board from becoming irrelevant, a process that began with efforts to install a Kuwaiti official on it. When board member Lord Kennet passed away, Roger Stevens at the Bank of England thought that British officials should take the opportunity to widen the KIB's scope and "bring it into a closer relationship" with Kuwait's Department of Finance.[212] But the board, especially its chairman, H. T. Kemp, rejected the idea of a Kuwaiti member. Kemp and his colleagues believed that, since the KIB was Sheikh Abdullah's "personal creation" and "responsible to him," it was up to him to decide on such a change, one that he had opposed in the past. They thought, moreover, that a Kuwaiti member would be "largely at sea in the atmosphere of the City" and would, therefore, try to "justify his existence" by criticizing the board to people in Kuwait behind their backs, eventually eroding

[209] Kuwait's total dollar holdings were around $150 million at the end of December 1962. See "Kuwait," (no signature) December 19, 1962, NA, T 317/322.
[210] "The Economy of Kuwait, 1950–1968," FCO Research Department, October 1969, NA, FCO 51/93.
[211] Lucas to Sharp, January 29, 1963, NA, FCO 51/93.
[212] Stevens to Rickett, July 28, 1960, NA, T 236/6314.

Abdullah's confidence in it.[213] J. E. Lucas, on the other hand, later wrote that the Treasury would "welcome changes" not only that included having Sheikh Jabir as chairman, but also whereby the board "would meet regularly in Kuwait."[214] His colleague, W. P. Cranston, argued that he "had no doubt" that to "leave things as they were" would ensure that the KIB would "gradually lose contact with what was going on in Kuwait."[215]

Because board member Lord Piercy was unwilling to have the KIB meet in Kuwait, and because H. T. Kemp was unable to travel there, the Treasury had to settle for the appointment to the Board of a Kuwaiti whose function was to improve communications with Sheikh Jabir and his staff.[216] Surprisingly, Jabir "showed no inclination" to change the organization of the board – at least as Lord Piercy understood his intentions – possibly because he wanted to keep its members at arm's length.[217] But a recommendation from the International Bank of Reconstruction and Development as well as the endorsement of the Foreign Office finally persuaded Amir Abdullah to nominate someone, and, in April 1962, he selected Khalifa Ghunaim, the Kuwaiti Ambassador to the United Kingdom, to serve on the KIB.[218] Both the Treasury and the Foreign Office welcomed the choice, and the Bank of England's C. E. Loombe regarded him as "suitably qualified and likely to be well disposed towards [Britain]."[219]

However, once Ghunaim was appointed to the board, Jabir felt that the ambassador's status "required" that he become chairman. Such a step went too far for Alistair Mackay, and he confessed a "certain uneasiness about the prospect of a Kuwaiti becoming not just a member of the KIB

---

[213] Record of conversation between Beaumont and Kemp, August 12, 1960, NA, T 236/6315.

[214] "Kuwait Investment Policy," Note for the record by J. E. Lucas, May 5, 1961, NA, T 236/6527.

[215] Mackay to Milner-Barry, May 17, 1961, NA, T 236/6527.

[216] Lucas to Sharp, January 25, 1963, NA, T 317/322.

[217] Mackay to Milner-Barry, May 17, 1961, NA, T 236/6527; No. 84 from the Foreign Office to Kuwait, January 19, 1962, and Cranston's record of conversation with Lord Piercy, January 31, 1962, both NA, T 317/120.

[218] The Foreign Office wrote, "We are much concerned at the criticism which may be directed at [the KIB's] exclusively British composition and at its consequent appearance of being isolated from Kuwait. Now that Kuwait has for some time been recognized as a fully independent State, she may be criticised, however unjustly, for allowing the greater part of her reserves to be administered by an exclusively British body, and it is not in the interest either of Kuwait or of Her Majesty's Government that grounds for such criticism should be given. If therefore the Kuwait Government were in favour of broadening the membership of the KIB by the appointment of a Kuwaiti, Her Majesty's Government would warmly welcome it." See No. 84 from the Foreign Office to Kuwait, January 19, 1962, NA, T 317/120.

[219] Lucas to Sharp, January 25, 1963, NA, T 317/322, Walmsley to Richmond, May 1, 1962, NA, T 317/121, and Mackay to Milner-Barry, April 18, 1962, NA, T 317/120.

but the chairman who would report to Sheikh Jabir." The "right sort of Kuwaiti," he said, might provide the advantage of "letting it be seen that the UK was not running the show," while the "wrong sort of Kuwaiti" could spell trouble.[220] Ghunaim was never appointed chairman, but the point was moot anyway. Kuwaiti authorities had already shoved the KIB to the periphery, eventually dissolving it several years later and replacing it with the Kuwait Investment Office (KIO), a bureau run by a Kuwaiti general manager who reported directly to the minister of finance and oil.[221]

The government's "high-powered," five-man Advisory Council became the most influential body regarding Kuwait's foreign investments. Established in 1963, the council, which was supposed to advise Kuwait's minister of finance on the state's "overall financial, budgetary and investment policies," emerged from discussions between Sheikh Jabir and Eugene Black – the former president of the IBRD – at the annual meeting of the International Monetary Fund in Washington in 1962. Apart from its chairman, Sheikh Jabir, the council's members represented five different countries, including Eugene Black himself and Lord Piercy of the KIB.[222] The council intended to meet two to three times a year in Kuwait and in other countries, receiving regular reports from the Kuwaiti government as well as from foreign experts who visited the state. The Treasury embraced the creation of the Advisory Council as a necessary means of coordinating Kuwait's financial and investment policies, and, for department officials, the participation of someone from the KIB was "a matter of great importance," even "essential." Alistair Mackay felt that Piercy's inclusion would provide a means of ensuring that Britain's "best advice and persuasion" could be "brought to bear on the Kuwaiti authorities in regard to sterling investment," and give British officials "the maximum warning of any development of thought in the central board away from sterling."[223]

Despite Lord Piercy's presence on the council, it had become clear that, since 1960 – and especially since Kuwait's independence – the Kuwait Investment Board's ability to exert influence over the state's

[220] Mackay to Milner-Barry, April 18, 1962, NA, T 317/120.
[221] "Kuwait: Background," Annex B, June 22, 1966, attached to Fogarty to Figgures, June 23, 1966, NA, T 317/844.
[222] The other members were Hermann Abs, president of the Deutsche Bank, Samuel Schweizer, chairman of the Swiss Bank Corporation, and Marcus Wallenberg, chairman of Asea, L. M. Ericsson, SAS, and Atlas Copco. See Richmond to the Earl of Home, June 19, 1963, NA, T 317/324 and Lucas to Sharp, January 29, 1963, NA, T 317/322.
[223] Mackay to Milner-Barry, April 18, 1962, NA, T 317/120; Lucas to Sharp, January 29, 1963, NA, T 317/322.

foreign investment policy had been much reduced. To protect Britain's sterling interests in Kuwait, Whitehall now had to rely upon an increasingly irrelevant KIB, a single voice on the Advisory Council, the British consular apparatus in Kuwait, Britain's historic ties with the al-Sabah, and finally, the ruling family's continued need for British military protection. But even this last factor seemed to become less important as Kuwait improved its links with the Arab world. The British government had been forced to accept diminished influence over Kuwait's investment policy and could only hope that sterling would remain stable enough to prevent the al-Sabah from wanting to make large transfers into other currencies. As a Cabinet paper revealed in 1957, "The best way of keeping the Ruler in sterling is to keep sterling strong."[224] The problem for Whitehall was that, throughout the 1960s, sterling showed signs of chronic weakness.

4.4   Britain's continuing balance-of-payments struggles, Whitehall's reconsideration of its military commitments in the Persian Gulf, and US efforts to maintain sterling and British forces east of Suez

Former Treasury official and noted economic historian Sir Alec Cairncross described the balance of payments as the "central problem" of the British economy in the 1960s.[225] Long-term capital investment outside the country, military spending, and foreign aid were among the chief culprits in the nation's trade account woes.[226] The deficit on the long-term capital account averaged £200 million a year from 1963 to 1966, and, ironically, large-scale foreign investment by oil companies – historically permitted in the postwar era owing to the future balance-of-payments benefits that such investment could produce – contributed significantly to this deficit, especially in 1964.[227] One member of the Foreign Office believed that government expenditure abroad "more than anything else"

---

[224] "Anglo-American Co-operation in the Middle East: Economic Development," OME (57) 14 (Revise), March 13, 1957, NA, CAB 134/2339.

[225] Sir Alec Cairncross, *Managing the British Economy in the 1960s: A Treasury Perspective* (London: Macmillan, 1996), 18.

[226] See Strange, *Sterling and British Policy*, ch. 4, for a detailed discussion of Britain's greater propensity to invest overseas compared with other industrialized countries.

[227] Cairncross and Eichengreen, *Sterling in Decline*, 19, 157. In 1964, the Kuwait Oil Company reached an agreement with the government of Kuwait to pay its income tax to the state on profits earned in the current year rather than the previous year as it had done previously. The upshot was that during a three-year transition period, from 1964 to 1966, the KOC would receive an extra £50 million in each of those years. See Lucas to Sharp, May 19, 1964, NA, T 317/683.

created Britain's current account problems in the 1960s, offering as evidence the rise of foreign aid grants from £50 million in 1955 to £115 million in 1964 and an increase in military spending from £155 million to £275 million during that same period.[228] Whitehall's efforts to maintain Britain's international political and military prestige in the 1950s and 1960s were subverting its efforts to maintain the country's international economic prestige. The fact that Britain's share of world trade in manufactures was falling, as it had been for years, did not help the nation's balance-of-payments prospects, nor did the fact that the British economy was growing at a slower rate than the economies of Western Europe and the United States.[229]

Throughout the 1960s, Britain seemed to go from one balance-of-payments crisis to another. In 1960, the country suffered a £171 million current account deficit due to a rise in demand for imports, a result of the previous year's economic boom (see Appendix 1). In an effort to restore equilibrium to Britain's trade account, the Bank of England raised interest rates from 4 to 7 percent in the first half of 1961 to deflate the economy – the "stop" part of the infamous "stop–go" economic cycle that characterized Conservative economic policy in the 1950s and 1960s. While the interest-rate hike produced the desired effect of returning the trade account to surplus, it did so by helping to trigger the recession of 1962–1963.[230] After thirteen years in the wilderness, the Labour Party regained power in 1964 under the stewardship of Harold Wilson, and, almost immediately, the new government had to contend with a record deficit in merchandise trade. It was induced by the "go" part of the "stop–go" cycle, which the Conservative government refused to brake in an election year.[231] After a brief recovery in the balance of payments in

[228] "The Balance of Payments," Foreign Office Minute by C. O'Neill, July 6, 1966, NA, FO 371/189661.

[229] Cairncross and Eichengreen, *Sterling in Decline*, 157. In the 1950s, the average growth rate of Britain's economy was 2.7 percent a year, while that of the United States was 3.2 percent and Western Europe's was 4.4 percent. See Eichengreen, *Globalizing Capital*, 125. Some scholars have attributed Britain's sluggish growth rate to the country's overreliance on trade with the empire instead of competing in the more dynamic markets of Western Europe, Japan, and the United States, a point that is a matter of debate. In *Sterling and British Policy*, Susan Strange writes, "British exporters were featherbedded both by discriminatory exchange controls in the sterling markets and by discriminatory capital controls in Britain. Both induced them to opt for their soft colonial markets," 70. In chapter 3 of *Britain and the Sterling Area*, Catherine Schenk rejects this assertion.

[230] Eichengreen, *Globalizing Capital*, 126–127. Sir Alec Cairncross offers a detailed discussion of the controversy over "stop–go" and Britain's lackluster growth rate in the 1960s in *Managing the British Economy in the 1960s*, 8–11. Cairncross and Eichengreen, *Sterling in Decline*, 157.

[231] Eichengreen, *Globalizing Capital*, 127.

the first quarter of 1965, Britain's current account once again slipped into the red, prompting a run on sterling that caused the country to lose £48 million during a single day in July.[232] Fears of devaluation, which persisted until sterling was, in fact, devalued in November 1967, regularly precipitated large, outward, short-term capital movements similar to that which occurred during the Suez episode a decade earlier. Thus, each crisis, including one in the summer of 1966, was exacerbated by a progressively deteriorating confidence in sterling.[233]

In this environment, Britain's access to Middle Eastern oil and the terms by which the nation procured it remained as important as ever to the British government. Two meetings between US and British officials in April and June 1963 illustrate the point. At the April 23–24 discussion in London on Anglo-American interests in the Gulf, British representatives stressed that the area remained of "vital" concern to the British government, which retained "its willingness and capability to preserve the British position there."[234] An important function of Britain's presence in the Gulf, they said, was "insuring the continued availability of oil to the UK and European economies on reasonable terms." Of all of its interests, though, "the continued availability of cheap sterling oil" was "pre-eminent" because "any disruption of this availability would seriously jeopardize the British balance-of-payments position."[235] At the June 10–14 meeting on international oil problems, the participants forecast that Middle East oil production would rise by 90 percent between 1961 and 1970, equaling the amount produced by the United States and representing about one-third of "Free World" production.[236] Among the conclusions reached was that Britain's balance of payments was "heavily dependent on the trading and investment of the British international oil companies," something that stood apart from Britain's "interest as a consumer in the security and continuity of supplies."[237] Sterling, having entered its weakest period since 1947–1951, continued to rely upon the uninterrupted flow of Middle Eastern oil to maintain stability.

The precarious state of the pound in the 1960s raised the level of anxiety among Kuwaiti officials about the potential for sterling devaluation,

---

[232] Cairncross, *Managing the British Economy in the 1960s*, 128–130.

[233] Tew, "Policies Aimed at Improving the Balance of Payments," 304. See Eichengreen, *Globalizing Capital*, 126, for a graph that plots the expected rate of sterling devaluation from 1961 to 1971.

[234] Airgram from the Embassy in the United Kingdom to the Department of State, May 31, 1963, *FRUS, 1961–1963, Vol. XVIII*, 559–561.

[235] Ibid.

[236] "Minute of UK–US Discussion on International Oil Problems," June 14, 1963, *FRUS, 1961–1963, Vol. XVIII*, 631–634.

[237] Ibid.

increasing the possibility that they would make large transfers out of the currency. Between 1962 and 1966, Kuwait repeatedly asked the British government for a guarantee that it would maintain the exchange value of its sterling reserves in the event of a devaluation. British representatives always responded by insisting that the government had no intention of devaluing, and that, even if it did, it could not give Kuwait an exchange guarantee without doing so for every member of the sterling area, which would defeat the purpose of a devaluation in the first place. But Whitehall did promise to give Kuwait 48-hours notice if a devaluation was in the offing, although such notice would almost certainly have to come on a Friday after the markets closed to prevent a run on the pound.[238] Therefore, during the balance-of-payments crisis of 1964, when the British and foreign press stirred a panic about devaluation in Kuwait, Sheikh Jabir wanted to raise with the Advisory Council the issue of increasing the dinar's gold cover from 50 to 80 percent. He also suggested that the Kuwait Investment Board should buy gold on the open market. One Bank of England official believed that although Britain could probably absorb the shock of a £25–50 million switch to gold, the "repercussions elsewhere" could be "extremely serious," possibly jeopardizing the "whole international payments system."[239] Fortunately for Britain, the Advisory Council recommended against Kuwait's using sterling to buy so much gold, both in 1965 and in 1966, "on the self-interested ground that to do so would lose both interest and the chance of capital appreciation."[240]

Despite the uncertainty surrounding the value of sterling, Kuwait never did make any large transfers out of the currency during the mid-1960s. For the most part, London remained the "principal depository of Kuwaiti funds" because no other country could offer "the combination of high rates with the security" that the government demanded, not even the United States.[241] Furthermore, according to an article by the financial editor of Britain's Daily Mail, Kuwaiti officials had some "unfortunate

---

[238] See, for example, Walmsley to Richmond, March 7, 1962, NA, T 317/844; "Note of a Discussion with Khalid Jaffar, Kuwaiti Ambassador in London," by C. E. Loombe, September 8, 1964, NA, T 317/683; "Note of the Governor's Conversation with the Kuwaiti Ambassador," by M. H. P., August 19, 1966, NA, T 318/127; and No. 697 from Crawford to the Foreign Office, October 21, 1966, NA, T 317/1003.

[239] "Note of a Discussion with Khalid Jaffar, Kuwaiti Ambassador in London," by C. E. Loombe, September 8, 1964, NA, T 317/683; Cromer to Rickett, March 9, 1965, NA, T 317/684; "Note for the Record" by J. E. Lucas, April 14, 1965.

[240] Fogarty to Lucas, February 4, 1966, NA, T 317/843.

[241] Jackson to Steward, January 7, 1966, NA, FO 371/185395; Fogarty to Lucas, NA, T 317/843; "The Economy of Kuwait, 1950–1968," FCO Research Department, October 1969, NA, FCO 51/93. C. E. Loombe of the Bank of England described Sheikh Jabir "and his colleagues" as "extremely interest conscious," Note by Loombe, May 8, 1965, NA, T 317/684.

Table 4.5 *Kuwait's reserves, 1962–1967 (in million pounds)*

Year	Government's foreign assets	Currency board's foreign assets	Gold	IMF	Dollar assets
1962		35	17.5		11.8
1963	270	39	17	4.5	16.6
1964	308	39	17	4.5	20.1
1965	288	44	18.5	4.5	12.7
1966	333	59	24	4.5	17.6
1967	301	66	48.7	4.5	13.0

Source: Strange, *Sterling and British Policy*, 111.

experiences" with Americans, and they also considered Wall Street less efficient than the City of London. Zurich was apparently "not worth the high commissions" that its financial sector charged.[242] Kuwait's Advisory Council exerted enough influence over the government to prevent it from making any sudden and large switches out of sterling, having convinced officials that such transactions would be detrimental to the state's interests by virtue of their "disruptive effects." But the council could not advise against, nor stop, the government from engaging in reasonable financial risk management by progressively moving its assets into forms of exchange other than sterling (see Table 4.5). One Treasury official wrote: "it would be surprising if some [sterling] holders did not decide to forgo the higher return on part of their funds, in order to spread their assets more widely."[243] Indeed, the Kuwaiti government constantly sought to diversify its currency cache, setting for itself the goal of reducing the proportion of its sterling holdings to an amount equal to that of the other currencies in its possession by buying foreign exchange with its surplus revenues.[244]

Another consequence of Britain's trade account problems for the Anglo-Kuwaiti relationship was Whitehall's decision to question the economic prudence of having so many forces deployed east of Suez.[245] As early as 1961, the British government began to assess whether its military presence in the Persian Gulf was worthwhile. Just as Harold Macmillan asked the Colonial Office's Colonial Policy Committee to undertake a

---

[242] "Why This Man Could Make the City TREMBLE," Patrick Sergeant, *The Daily Mail*, November 25, 1965, NA, T 317/685.

[243] Bell to Workman, November 18, 1966, NA, T 318/203.

[244] Lucas to Sharp, September 16, 1965, NA, T 317/685.

[245] For an analysis of the various measures used to stabilize Britain's balance of payments, see Tew, "Policies Aimed at Improving the Balance of Payments."

cost–benefit analysis of the empire in 1957, he ordered the Treasury to conduct a similar study regarding the Persian Gulf, requesting a balance sheet that contained the value of Britain's stake in Middle Eastern oil on one side and the cost of defending it on the other.[246] The resulting paper, prepared by officials at the Treasury and the Ministry of Fuel and Power – and in consultation with the Foreign Office and the Ministry of Defence – calculated the value of Middle Eastern oil, particularly Kuwait's, to Britain's balance of payments. It concluded that the £506 million worth of oil consumed annually in Britain and by British forces abroad would cost the country only £117 million in foreign exchange, representing a credit of nearly £400 million to its trade account. On the other side of the balance sheet, the government spent only £30–40 million a year on forces intended mainly to defend British interests in the Persian Gulf, although isolating the amount attributable to Kuwait alone in overall defense expenditure proved to be an impossible task.[247]

The exercise did not ultimately help the British government decide whether to attenuate its military commitment in the Persian Gulf. When Selwyn Lloyd submitted the paper to Harold Macmillan, he argued that "too many uncertainties and imponderabilia" existed to create a balance sheet "in any precise terms." Lloyd concluded that what Britain was in fact guarding against in Kuwait was "the danger that the British [oil] companies might have to face a substantially reduced share of production profits – perhaps of the order of £100 million."[248] Treasury Under-Secretary P. S. Milner-Barry provided a shrewd analysis of the study, going beyond its scope to take stock in the nature of Britain's position in Kuwait. He characterized the balance sheet exercise as "necessarily limited," even as a "factual analysis," and pointed out that the resulting paper did not attempt to deal with the most significant question implied by the project:

Is it worth while in present circumstances to continue incurring this very heavy bill for defence, including very large amounts of overseas expenditure, as an insurance against eventualities such as the possible exclusion of the British companies from

[246] For the Colonial Policy Committee's assessment of the financial worth of the empire to Britain, see Tony Hopkins, "Macmillan's Audit of Empire, 1957" in Clarke and Trebilcock, *Understanding Decline*, 234–259.

[247] The £30–40 million in defense expenditure included £13 million a year for Aden and the Gulf, "some part" of both the £10 million spent in East Africa and the £20 million in Cyprus and Libya. See "Kuwait and Middle East Oil," Minute by Lloyd, August 2, 1961, NA, PREM 11/3452.

[248] Lloyd to Macmillan, August 2, 1961, NA, T 236/6719. Alexander Frederick Douglas-Home, the secretary of state for foreign affairs, agreed with Lloyd's assessment. See Home to Macmillan, August 4, 1961, NA, T 236/6719.

the Middle East, or the lesser threat of a substantial reduction in the production profits being earned?[249]

Milner-Barry then considered the nature of the threat to British interests in Kuwait. "Internal subversion," he believed, constituted the greatest danger, not "direct military intervention," in which case, he wondered whether the British government intended to support a regime "with which a majority of its subjects were out of sympathy." And if a regime hostile to the West assumed power in Kuwait, he asked, would it not have to sell oil to the West anyway? The fact of the matter, Milner-Barry argued, was that Britain would have to expect that "an increasing share of the profits [of British oil companies] one way or another [would] go to the producing countries, and that the balance of payments [would] suffer accordingly." Therefore, he maintained, while Britain should not unilaterally repudiate its military agreement with Kuwait, "there would be little object" in allowing the agreement to persist when "it was in fact impossible to implement without making matters worse."[250]

In a letter written in 1962, Milner-Barry reiterated the point that he made one year earlier about the need for Britain to "face the fact" that Kuwait would inevitably "follow the example of all the oil producing countries in trying to extract better terms for herself" on the sale of its petroleum. He wrote, "I see no likelihood that a process of gradual erosion of our position and profits can be avoided."[251] Four years later, in 1966, Kuwait demanded a supplemental oil agreement from the Kuwait Oil Company that would give the state a greater share of the profits from its operations. During a deadlock in the negotiations, the Kuwaiti foreign minister and the minister of finance informed British officials that if the British government did not put pressure on British Petroleum "to make some concession" on the issue of profits, then they might make a significant switch out of sterling. With its balance of payments at risk on two different fronts, all that Britain could do was inform the Kuwaiti government that any sudden and large transfer out of sterling could harm the international payments system as a whole and could, thus, damage its own interests.[252] The ambassador, G. N. Jackson, was instructed to "maintain a firm front" in the face of Kuwait's threats, but "not to enter any argument" about the matter.[253] Few instances better demonstrate how much Britain's position in the Middle East had changed since the end of World War II. Whereas at one time Whitehall would have defended

[249] Milner-Barry to Rickett, July 31, 1961, NA, T 236/6719.   [250] Ibid.
[251] Milner-Barry to Peck, October 12, 1962, NA, T 317/122.
[252] Ryrie to Goldman, August 24, 1966, NA, T 312/1703.
[253] Goldman to Lavelle, August 24, 1966, NA, T 312/1703.

Britain's right to control access to Middle Eastern oil at prices that it deemed reasonable, now it could only appeal to Kuwait's self-interest to limit the damage that this small desert sheikhdom could do to the British economy. Britain had grown too economically weak and the countries of the South too politically strong for London to handle matters any other way.

Further balance-of-payments crises depicted in stark terms the harsh economic reality that Britain faced, with consequences for British overseas defense. Starting in 1965, the impact of defense spending on the balance of payments became a "constant theme" in the government's annual *Statements on the Defence Estimates*.[254] By the end of the year, the Treasury insisted that Whitehall maintain a £2,000 million ceiling on military spending, mandating that Britain cut its coat according to its cloth. The Defence White Paper of 1966 reflected the new directive: the government would not replace an aging and costly fleet of aircraft carriers, nor would it keep its forces in Aden once the South Arabian Federation became independent in 1968.[255] Based on the defense review of 1965, the British government also adjusted its military relationship with Kuwait, terminating its commitment to provide ground forces to defend the state and reducing its protective apparatus to air power alone. According to G. N. Jackson, Amir Sabah, Abdullah's successor, the prime minister, and the minister of defense "received the news calmly, saying it was their intention in the first instance, to rely on the Arab League to help them defend Kuwait."[256]

Policy-makers in the United States did not display similar equanimity in their discussions with British officials on the subject of Britain's decision to reduce commitments east of Suez, which included forces on and around British bases in Aden, the Persian Gulf, Singapore, and Malaysia. From the end of 1964 onward, Britain's persistent and worsening balance-of-payments problems, the Wilson government's intention to cut overseas defense expenditure as a result, and the future of Britain's role in global affairs, was a recurring topic of conversation among British and US officials at the highest levels.[257] On December 7, 1964,

---

[254] Tew, "Policies Aimed at Improving the Balance of Payments," 321.   [255] Ibid., 292.
[256] Jackson to Stewart, May 6, 1966, NA, FO 371/185396.
[257] The strategic-economic facet of Anglo-American relations during this period is well covered in Diane Kunz, "'Somewhat Mixed Up Together': Anglo-American Defence and Financial Policy during the 1960s" in Robert D. King and Robin Kilson (eds.), *The Statecraft of British Imperialism: Essays in Honour of Wm. Roger Louis* (London: Frank Cass 1999), 213–232. For the Middle East aspect, see Tore Tingvold Petersen, *The Decline of the Anglo-American Middle East, 1961–1969: A Willing Retreat* (Brighton: Sussex Academic Press, 2006), chs. 4 and 7, although I fundamentally disagree with his premise that "Wilson and the Labourites were intent, all along, on ending Britain's

Foreign Secretary Patrick Gordon Walker and Secretary of Defence Denis Healey met with their counterparts in Washington and set the tone for the rest of the decade. Healey informed Secretary of Defense Robert McNamara, Secretary of State Dean Rusk, and other US officials, that a recent gathering of British ministers, advisors, and service chiefs at Chequers – the prime minister's weekend retreat – focused on the future of British defense policy over the next ten years, "under the shadow of economic pressure."[258] The Chequers gathering pondered what role Britain expected to fill in the world, Healey reported, lamenting that no other European power contributed to both the defense of Europe and areas beyond the Continent – that Britain was "almost alone from Suez to Singapore." Rusk responded by urging Whitehall to "give full weight" to Britain's role as a world power. The United States wanted Britain to "play as large a role as possible," he said, adding that US officials would "look with the greatest concern at a diminution" of Britain's position because of the significant impact on what the United States could itself accomplish strategically. The interests of the free world as a whole, not just British interests, depended on the maintenance of Britain's international military commitments, the secretary argued.[259] In June, Chancellor of the Exchequer James Callaghan reassured McNamara that he believed that Britain should indeed "go on playing its role" but not under the weight of the country's current foreign exchange burden, which he insisted "must come down."[260]

It was becoming clear to US officials that Britain's position in the Middle East would "continue to erode," as Walt Rostow concluded in October 1965.[261] Rostow himself advocated that greater attention "be given to the provision of other capabilities 'over the horizon' to meet the continuing need for the West to be able to react quickly with small forces in local crises in the oil rich Persian Gulf and elsewhere in the region."[262] Writing several months earlier, the CIA had assessed that the sentiment at Whitehall was that reducing Britain's presence in the Gulf would benefit the pound more than dedicating military resources to protect the $300 million in sterling oil revenue that would "by and large still flow" to Britain.[263] Patrick Gordon Walker confirmed the CIA's judgment when

---

overseas commitments for reasons of ideology" and that "the poor shape of the British economy was just an added inducement to speed up the withdrawal process," 2.

[258] Memorandum of Conversation, *FRUS, 1964–1968, Vol. XII*, 475–479.

[259] Ibid.

[260] Memorandum of Conversation, June 30, 1965, *FRUS, 1964–1968, Vol. XII*, 493–496.

[261] Quoted in Little, *American Orientalism*, 139.   [262] Ibid.

[263] CIA Intelligence Memorandum, June 7, 1965, quoted in Petersen, *The Decline of the Anglo-American Middle East*, 113.

he said: "Why should we not, like other European countries, obtain oil from the Persian Gulf by paying for it instead of maintaining forces there?"[264]

The defense review that Whitehall would publish in February 1966 sparked another round of Anglo-American talks concerning Britain's role east of Suez. Harold Wilson met with Lyndon Johnson in the Oval Office in mid-December 1965 and discussed, among other topics, the broad outlines of the review without providing many details. Although the prime minister gave assurances that his government would maintain Britain's presence east of Suez – and continue its worldwide role – he said that there would have to be "readjustments in the British defense posture" in the Middle East and Southeast Asia. More specifically, he added, Aden "could not be regarded as a long-term base" and that, while Iran and Kuwait still needed protection, "generally it should be possible to lighten the British presence in the Gulf."[265] At the meeting, Wilson and Johnson agreed to have Michael Stewart, Patrick Gordon Walker's successor as foreign secretary, and Denis Healey present the key elements of the defense review to US officials in January 1966. Using stronger language than the prime minister, they confirmed in Washington that Britain "must withdraw" from its base at Aden, and would do so after 1968, but added that Britain would increase its forces in the Gulf to compensate for the South Arabian losses.[266] Given that the CIA had once described Aden as "one of Britain's most valuable military assets" and "a major British contribution to the world-wide Western Defense system," the definitive nature of Stewart and Healy's comments on Aden surely unsettled the Americans in the room.[267] Dean Rusk not only repeated what he had intoned at the December 1964 meeting regarding the importance of "Britain's retaining a world power role" but also added that "it would be

---

[264] Ibid.

[265] Memorandum Prepared by the Executive Secretary of the Department of State, "Visit of Prime Minister Wilson," undated, *FRUS, 1964–1968, Vol. XII*, 510–512.

[266] Memorandum of Conversation, January 27, 1966, *FRUS, 1964–1968, Vol. XII*, 516–528. At a February 4, 1966, meeting in Washington, Sir Roger Allen, the deputy under-secretary at the Foreign Office, and other British officials provided the details of the British plan for a "forces buildup in the Gulf," *FRUS, 1964–1968, Vol. XXI*, 162–165.

[267] Intelligence Memorandum, "The Security Situation in Aden," June 9, 1965, *FRUS, 1964–1968, Vol. XXI*, 143–145. The memorandum goes on to say: "Aden is a base for the protection of Persian Gulf oil; a garrison area for the defense of British interests in the Arabian Peninsula and in the Indian Ocean generally; and a major British contribution to the world-wide Western Defense system. As currently operated, it is the largest and busiest RAF station in the world and, after Singapore, the largest British base complex outside the UK itself. In terms of commercial strategy, Aden is the largest bunkering port in the world and the third largest port of any kind in the Commonwealth."

disastrous if the American people were to get the impression that the US is entirely alone."[268] Robert McNamara agreed with Rusk, saying that he "could not overemphasize" the secretary of state's point on the political dimension of the United States policing the world on its own.[269]

The Johnson Administration had previously sought to reinforce Britain's military position east of Suez with economic aid, offering and arranging both American and international financing to support sterling, as it did during the balance-of-payments crisis that struck Britain in the summer of 1965. In his meeting with British officials that June, Robert McNamara committed the United States to alleviating the foreign exchange component of Britain's "defense problem" by purchasing more from Britain as well as to reexamining "existing credit arrangements with a view to improving the terms." Such help, he stressed, was "conditional on there being no change in Britain's world-wide political commitments."[270] Under Secretary of State George Ball reiterated this point to Harold Wilson in London on September 9, 1965. Both he and the US Ambassador to Britain, David Bruce, explained that:

> it would be a great mistake if the United Kingdom failed to understand that the American effort to relieve Sterling was inextricably related to the commitment of the United Kingdom to maintain commitments around the world. All of the US Government activities in relation to Sterling or the economic problems of the United Kingdom were necessarily related to the commitment of the two Governments to engage together in a 5-year review of the United Kingdom's defense program.[271]

Ball and Bruce's stern attitude reflected the fact that the United States was preparing to contribute $400 million to a $900–1,000 million package of multilateral aid to support the pound that Britain would secure the next evening.[272]

When another balance-of-payments crisis undermined sterling in the summer of 1966, the tone in Washington changed regarding Britain's east of Suez deployments, at least outside the Pentagon. US Secretary of the Treasury Henry Fowler believed that the United States's first priority should be to "move the United Kingdom to save its long-term economic and financial position and thereby to prevent potentially disastrous consequences for the United States, our over-all foreign policy and the stability

---

[268] Memorandum of Conversation, January 27, 1966, *FRUS, 1964–1968, Vol. XXI*, 516–528.

[269] Ibid.

[270] Memorandum of Conversation, June 30, 1965, *FRUS, 1964–1968, Vol. XXI*, 493–496.

[271] Memorandum from Bundy to Johnson, September 10, 1965, *FRUS, 1964–1968, Vol. XXI*, 506–509.

[272] Barr to Johnson, September 10, 1965, *FRUS, 1964–1968, Vol. XXI*, 505–506.

of the Free World financial system."[273] He advised that the administration "leave it to the UK government to decide what it must do, short of devaluation, to save its national position." A "weak ally is of no use to us East of Suez, in Europe, in the international financial set-up, or anywhere else," he added, expressing what would eventually be the British argument in defense of its military retrenchment. Fowler consequently recommended against "leaning" on Wilson to "do something he would not otherwise do."[274] Similarly, Ball wanted the United States to "face the fact that it is basically unhealthy to encourage the United Kingdom to continue as America's poor relation, living beyond her means by periodic American bailouts."[275] In other words, the administration should "redefine the so-called 'special relationship' in terms consistent with the longer-range interests of both our nations." He concluded that US officials should resign themselves to the fact that, no matter how much pressure they applied, Britain would "inevitably cut down her overseas deployments." The United States would "have to pay an exorbitant price – both financial and political" to delay the process of British retrenchment when in all probability such outlays would "not materially affect Britain's inevitable withdrawal."[276]

By mid-1966, the Johnson Administration had accepted the likelihood that Britain would abdicate its east of Suez positions and started planning more seriously for the security of the Persian Gulf in Britain's absence. Building on the policies of the Eisenhower and Kennedy Administrations, Johnson and his advisors pursued a strategic framework for the Gulf that revolved around powerful regional actors – in this case, Saudi Arabia and Iran, eventually referred to as the "twin pillars." In preparation for the visit of Saudi Arabia's King Faisal to Washington in June 1966, Walt Rostow advised Johnson to ask the king how he planned to "fill the gap the British will leave in South Arabia and the Persian Gulf" and to encourage Faisal to get "excited about cooperating with his moderate neighbors."[277] In his June 21 meeting with Johnson, Faisal said that cooperating with other Middle Eastern states "to stem the tide of Communism" was "precisely his aim."[278] As for the Shah of Iran, the president wrote a letter to him on July 20, in which he declared: "At a time when the United States is heavily engaged in continued stability in the defense of freedom in Asia, we are no less interested in continued stability in the Persian Gulf area. We welcome your determination to help maintain

---

[273] Fowler to Johnson, July 18, 1966, *FRUS, 1964–1968, Vol. XXI*, 539–543.   [274] Ibid.
[275] Ball to Johnson, July 22, 1966, *FRUS, 1964–1968, Vol. XXI*, 545–555.   [276] Ibid.
[277] June 20, 1966, *FRUS, 1964–1968, Vol. XXI*, 520–521.
[278] Memorandum of Conversation, June 21, 1966, *FRUS, 1964–1968, Vol. XXI*, 527–530.

that stability."[279] The Johnson Administration provided arms packages to both regimes to promote their deterrent capabilities.[280] Referring to Iran, Rostow told Johnson that bolstering the Shah's military strength offered a cost-effective way of defending the Middle East, especially in light of Britain's intention to withdraw from Aden in 1968, its planned force reduction in the Persian Gulf, and the escalating war in Southeast Asia.[281] US officials nonetheless counted on Britain's presence in the region for the foreseeable future. In October 1967, amidst yet another British economic crisis, Under Secretary of State Nicholas Katzenbach wrote to the US Embassy in London: "US continues attach great importance to UK presence in Gulf. We support current British position and will encourage HMG to continue maintain military forces in Gulf equal to task for providing security for Shaikhdoms [sic]."[282] Earlier that year, the CIA assessed that it seemed "likely" that it would be "at least three to five years before the UK abandons its special military and political position in the Gulf," but the Agency ominously concluded: "increased trouble in the Gulf or economic problems at home might hasten British departure."[283]

---

[279] *FRUS, 1964–1968, Vol. XXII*, 287–288.   [280] Little, *American Orientalism*, 140–141.
[281] Ibid.   [282] October 2, 1967, *FRUS, 1964–1968, Vol. XXI*, 227.
[283] National Intelligence Estimate, May 18, 1967, *FRUS, 1964–1968, Vol. XXI*, 206–208.

Conclusion: the devaluation of 1967 and the end of empire

> Britain's severe economic problems have shaken the international monetary system and sealed a historic transformation of British foreign policy.
>
> Paper prepared in the Department of State, undated[1]

> We all hope the present period of international financial difficulties will be temporary. While some programs can be cut back now and started up again later without serious problems, the elimination of the UK military position in the Gulf would be an irreversible decision. The USG feels strongly that such an irrevocable act is warranted neither by present circumstances nor future prospects. Moreover, economies effected [*sic*] now could be penny-wise, pound-foolish if political changes in the Gulf were to bring about revisions in the terms by which the UK gets its oil.
>
> Lucius Battle, Assistant Secretary of State for Near Eastern and South Asian Affairs, US Department of State[2]

The continuing deterioration of Britain's balance-of-payments position in the mid to late 1960s culminated in a currency crisis that was sparked, in part, by a rise in the cost of obtaining Middle Eastern oil, which finally forced the Treasury to devalue sterling in November 1967. In a replay of what happened during the Suez crisis, another outbreak of war in the Middle East between Israel and the front-line Arab states, in June, prevented Britain from obtaining sterling oil through the Suez Canal. Adding to the problems caused by the waterway's disruption, the Arab oil-producing nations immediately cut off the flow of petroleum to countries that they deemed supporters of Israel, including the United States, Britain, and West Germany.[3] The upshot was that only 40 percent of the Middle Eastern oil destined for the West still traveled there once the conflict was underway, imposing a serious financial burden on Britain, which, at the time, fulfilled half of its petroleum-related energy

---

[1] *FRUS, 1964–1968, Vol. XII*, 618–624.

[2] Briefing Memorandum for Rusk, January 9, 1968, *FRUS, 1964–1968, Vol. XXI*, 256–258.

[3] "Text of Baghdad Oil Resolutions," NA, FCO 54/54.

requirements with oil from the Persian Gulf.[4] Worse still, the onset of
civil war in Nigeria meant that a relatively close, non-Arab source of oil
might be unavailable.[5] Despite the fact that Britain overcame the ensu-
ing supply shortage, thanks to the fortuitous combination of excess US
capacity, increased exports from Iran, Venezuela, and Indonesia, and the
eventual cooperation of moderate Arab states, including Kuwait, Saudi
Arabia, and Libya, Britain still had to pay 400 percent more in shipping
costs to acquire oil via the water route around the perimeter of Africa.[6]
As a result, the nation's trade account suffered by £90 million in 1967,
£45 million in 1968, and £40 million in 1969.[7]

The consequent decline in sterling confidence also hurt Britain's balance of payments by triggering a "heavy outflow" of private short-term
capital, transfers exacerbated by sterling-holding Arab countries.[8] During
the summer of 1967, the British government monitored "abnormal transactions in Middle East sterling movements" and noticed that between the
end of May and mid-September the sterling holdings of Arab states fell
by £236 million.[9] It appears that most of the transfers occurred in June,
with approximately £180 million "directly attributed to the effects of the
Middle East war," either because of "political hostility or pressure," fears
that Britain would block sterling, or the disbursement of grants to the
front-line Arab countries. The Bank of England believed that these movements cost Britain's reserves £80 million.[10] In the end, the Middle East
crisis, combined with dock strikes in Britain that autumn and the Wilson
government's commitment to a policy of economic reflation in the first
half of 1967, caused a drain of £500 million from the British reserves in

[4] Yergin, *The Prize*, 555; "The Closure of the Suez Canal: The Effect on Britain's Oil Operations," Memorandum by the Foreign and Commonwealth Office, June 12, 1969, NA, T 317/1362.
[5] Keir Thorpe, "The Forgotten Shortage: Britain's Handling of the 1967 Oil Embargo," *Contemporary British History*, 21, 2 (2007), 203–204. He describes the oil crisis as "an important milestone in the changing relationship between the UK and the Middle East," 217.
[6] Bamberg, *British Petroleum and Global Oil, 1950–1975*, 170. The cost of shipping Persian Gulf oil through the Suez Canal was 33 shillings a ton whereas it cost 134 shillings a ton to send the oil via the Cape route; see "The Closure of the Suez Canal and Oil," August 7, 1967, NA, T 317/1362.
[7] "The Closure of the Suez Canal: The Effect on Britain's Oil Operations," Memorandum by the Foreign and Commonwealth Office, June 12, 1969, NA, T 317/1362.
[8] "United Kingdom Balance of Payments in the Fourth Quarter and Year 1967," Central Statistical Office, March 13, 1968, NA, FCO 48/176.
[9] Morse to Rickett, July 24, 1967, NA, T 318/128. Kuwait exchanged £106 million, Libya £67 million, Iraq £28 million, Egypt £17 million, and other Arab countries £18 million. See Lavelle to Cheminant, September 21, 1967, NA, T 318/128.
[10] The other £100 million was thought to be held in sterling accounts in other countries, mainly Japan. See Lavelle to Cheminant, September 21, 1967.

the third quarter. Officials at Whitehall could no longer hold the line after a last-ditch effort of raising the discount rate (the interest rate charged to commercial banks) had no impact, leading them to devalue sterling on November 18, 1967 from $2.80 to $2.40.[11] Given how hard they and their predecessors had fought since 1949 to avoid such a drastic measure, the decision was both a major turning point and a humiliating moment, causing the resignation of James Callaghan as Chancellor of the Exchequer. It revealed an understanding and acceptance among British policy-makers of the profound weakness of the nation's international trade position as well as sterling itself. The decision certainly put to rest any notion that the currency could regain its former status in the global economy.

Even before the devaluation, Treasury and Bank of England officials had begun to question whether the benefits of maintaining sterling's position as an international trading and reserve currency – particularly in the form of invisible income – were worth the cost of its upkeep. In mid-1967, the Treasury's Invisible Earnings Committee proposed that the Treasury and the Bank undertake a study, in collaboration with City associations, to determine how much Britain's invisible income depended on sterling's international role.[12] Two years later, the Treasury's Group on the International Monetary System produced a report that concluded that the heavy burden – in the form of interest payments and economic policy constraints – placed on the British economy by preserving sterling as an international currency did not seem worth the estimated £70 million in City earnings. Furthermore, the report's authors asserted what has long since been demonstrated: that, while the emergence of the City of London was closely connected with the international use of sterling, its institutions would continue to prosper without the currency carrying on in that capacity. The City's dynamic and flexible investment houses adapted themselves quite well to the emerging Euro-dollar business in the late 1960s, and they would eventually adjust, with great success, to shifts in the British government's economic agenda and the ever-changing world of international finance.[13]

<hr/>

[11] "United Kingdom Balance of Payments in the Fourth Quarter and Year 1967," Central Statistical Office, March 13, 1968, NA, FCO 48/176 and Cairncross and Eichengreen, *Sterling in Decline*, 187–188.

[12] Copeman to Hubback, October 19, 1967, NA, T 312/2304.

[13] "Costs and Benefits of the International Role of Sterling and its Reduction," Group on the International Monetary System, IM (69) 31, September 9, 1969, NA, T 312/2305. For more on this subject, see Cain and Hopkins, *British Imperialism*, 640–644, and Schenk, "The New City and the State in the 1960s."

The City may have marched forward with great success in the years after devaluation, but the sterling area did not. It suffered a slow demise, beginning with a mass flight from sterling by OSA countries that wanted to minimize risk.[14] Seeking to prevent the kind of abrupt end to the system that would destabilize the British economy, Whitehall temporarily breathed life back into the currency group by negotiating the so-called "Basle Agreements" with area members.[15] The individual accords guaranteed the value of OSA sterling holdings against the dollar, and, in return, signatories promised to maintain a certain proportion of their foreign exchange reserves in pounds, a figure that varied by country. Providing the insurance that protected Britain against violations of the agreements was the Basle Facility, an arrangement by which the Bank for International Settlements and twelve industrialized countries consented to supply as much as $2 billion to Britain if sterling area holdings fell below a certain level. In this way, Britain could wind down the sterling area on its own terms, causing the least amount of disruption to the pound and the British economy.

The dollar could not avoid the fallout caused by the devaluation, despite contingency plans conceived to ensure that "the sterling problem" did not have an "unfavorable impact" on it.[16] Because countries around the world kept less sterling and more dollars in their reserves, the dollar was becoming increasingly exposed at a time when the United States could ill-afford the currency to be so vulnerable. With a growing number of US multinational corporations sending dollars to finance operations around the globe and with the US government emptying its treasury to maintain its worldwide military commitments – including the ongoing war in Southeast Asia – the United States, like Britain, also experienced severe balance-of-payments difficulties. The British devaluation made matters worse, prompting a "large decline" in gold reserves, creating a full-fledged gold crisis, and putting even greater pressure on the dollar.[17]

[14] Henry Fowler said that Britain was "losing large amounts of reserves not only because of widespread lack of confidence in sterling but also because several countries are diversifying their reserves" and, thus, "forcing Britain to recognize that the pound will not much longer be used as a reserve currency." "Summary Notes of the 587th Meeting of the National Security Council," June 5, 1968, *FRUS, 1964–1968, Vol. XII*, 624–627.

[15] Barber to Wilson, October 30, 1970, NA, PREM 15/329. The agreements were named for the city that housed the Bank for International Settlements (BIS), the coordinating body for the world's central banks through which Britain achieved the new sterling area framework.

[16] "Summary Notes of the 587th Meeting of the National Security Council," June 5, 1968, *FRUS, 1964–1968, Vol. XII*, 624–627.

[17] Undated Department of State Memorandum attached to a note from Walsh to Smith on June 1, 1968, and prepared for an NSC meeting scheduled for June 5, 1968, *FRUS, 1964–1968, Vol. XII*, 618–624.

Moreover, chronically large deficits in the US trade account rendered the dollar vulnerable to speculative attack, an experience that sterling constantly suffered throughout the postwar era. In a bid to reassure the markets, Lyndon Johnson held a news conference at the LBJ Ranch on New Year's Day, 1968, to announce the "firm and decisive step" that the US government had taken to reduce the country's balance-of-payments deficit by $3 billion.[18]

Before sterling's devaluation and subsequent retrenchment, US officials had relied on the pound to serve as a lightning rod to absorb market attacks that would otherwise strike the dollar. Along with the need to support British defense commitments east of Suez, sterling's crucial role as a decoy motivated the Johnson Administration to use US resources to support the currency. Indeed, on the cusp of the pound's devaluation, Walt Rostow wrote to the president: "I won't go into the pros and cons of letting the pound go. The main point is the risks for us are just too great to be worth the gamble."[19] With the dollar's first line of defense gone, and pressure continuing to mount from severe balance-of-payments problems, Johnson's successor, Richard Nixon, was forced to do what had been previously inconceivable and separate the link between the dollar and gold, thereby removing the linchpin of the Bretton Woods regime of fixed exchange rates.[20] By 1971, the dollar had simply become too weak to support the international monetary system, proving correct Henry Fowler's prediction two years earlier that "a large devaluation" of the pound "would put in jeopardy the entire structure of trade and payments."[21]

The strategic consequences of sterling's devaluation in 1967 were no less monumental. As previously discussed, Whitehall had announced in 1966 that Britain would leave Aden when Southwest Arabia gained independence in 1968, stirring anxiety in the Persian Gulf territories because of the importance of the British military base at Aden to regional defense. But when British authority in Southwest Arabia disintegrated at the end of 1967, Britain fled its longstanding base at Aden at gunpoint, making irrelevant plans for an orderly departure the following

[18] *Public Papers of the Presidents of the United States, Lyndon B. Johnson: Containing the Public Messages, Speeches, and Statements of the President, 1968–69 (in two books), Book I – January 1 to June 30, 1968* (Washington: United States Government Printing Office, 1970), 1.
[19] Rostow to Johnson, November 13, 1967. *FRUS, 1964–1968, Vol. VIII*, 437.
[20] For an account of the collapse of the Bretton Woods system, see Andrew Shonfield (ed.), *International Economic Relations of the Western World, 1959–1971, Part 1: Politics and Trade* (London: Oxford University Press, 1976), ch. 3. The pound itself was allowed to float in June 1972.
[21] Fowler to Johnson, August 6, 1965, *FRUS, 1964–1968, Vol. XII*, 503–505.

year. Even after Britain simultaneously devalued sterling and quit its disintegrating colony in Southwest Arabia, British representatives had assured the sheikhdoms that Britain would honor its treaty obligations with them. Only two months later, however, British officials conveyed to the Gulf rulers, with some measure of shame, what Labour Prime Minister Harold Wilson would declare to Parliament and the rest of the world on January 16, 1968: that the British government intended to withdraw all the nation's forces from east of Suez – including the Persian Gulf – by the end of 1971. The government would do so as part of the larger effort to reduce overseas expenditure and, thus, alleviate pressure on Britain's balance of payments.[22] Kuwait's foreign minister reported to British officials that the Gulf rulers were "severely shaken" and "quite bewildered" by Britain's decision, complaining that White-hall had "treated them badly."[23] The sheikhs worried about threats from states that had long had ambitions in the region, including Iran, Iraq, and Saudi Arabia, all of which relished the prospect of Britain's withdrawal. Members of the Treasury feared that the sheikhs would be so upset with Britain that they might diversify their sterling assets out of spite.[24]

Much like the Gulf rulers, the Johnson Administration did not take the news of Britain's decision well. British Foreign Minister George Brown revealed the Wilson government's policy in a meeting with US Secretary of State Dean Rusk in Washington on January 11, 1968. Upon hear-ing the news, Rusk said that he was "profoundly dismayed," describing Britain's decision as an "alarming development." When Rusk raised the point that Britain would save only £12 million yearly by leaving the Gulf – in exchange for potentially grave consequences – Brown said that "the decision was not based on the minor saving that might result, but that it was a logical outcome of the major decision to withdraw from the Far East." Brown later clarified that once Britain's Far East bases were gone, it "could only get hardware savings" by trimming its carrier force – by forgoing maintenance of its fleet "against theoretical possibili-ties." Resigned to the fact that his arguments would make no difference, Rusk remarked that he smelled "the acrid aroma of a fait-accompli."[25]

---

[22] Balfour-Paul, *The End of Empire in the Middle East*, 122–125. Saki Dockrill points out that the Wilson government had already made the decision to withdraw British forces from bases in Singapore and Malaysia in July 1967, and, thus, argues that the November devaluation merely hastened a process already underway. See *Britain's Retreat from East of Suez*, 211–212. Her point is well taken, but it was nonetheless chronic balance-of-payments problems in the 1960s that led to the decision to withdraw in the first place.

[23] No. 57 from Roberts to the Foreign Office, February 5, 1968, FCO 8/42.

[24] "Defence Cuts: The Danger of Diversification," Draft brief by W. S. Ryrie for the chancellor, January 10, 1968, T 312/1949.

[25] Memorandum of Conversation, *FRUS, 1964–1968, Vol. XII*, 603–608.

The entire conversation had the air of a divorce, with one side unilaterally ending the marriage and the other side trying to talk the former out of a decision that had already been made, long having signaled its intentions to the broken-hearted party. After receiving word from Rusk about the secretary's meeting with Brown, Lyndon Johnson expressed his own disappointment and concern in a letter to Harold Wilson: "I cannot conceal from you my deep dismay upon learning this profoundly discouraging news. If these steps are taken, they will be tantamount to British withdrawal from world affairs."[26] In a second letter, sent on January 15, Johnson wrote that "accelerated British withdrawal both from its Far Eastern bases and from the Persian Gulf would create most serious problems for the United States Government and for the security of the entire free world."[27] The next day, Washington *éminence grise* and US Ambassador at Large Averell Harriman spoke with the British Ambassador to the United States, Patrick Dean, about Wilson's policy and barked, "We cannot accept this decision as final. It must be reversed." Dean replied, "Well, it's been made," and added that "the US cannot be the only world power on the Free World side."[28]

There is no doubt that the timing of Britain's announcement provoked the highly charged responses from Johnson, Rusk, and other US officials. After all, the administration had known for a long time that Britain was reconsidering its military presence east of Suez. In January 1968, the central problem for Johnson and his advisors was the costly and escalating war in Southeast Asia. Britain's east of Suez policy represented a double blow for the United States by removing British forces from the theater where American troops were fighting as well as from a strategically vital region to which the United States could not afford – in treasure, personnel, or political capital – to send forces. Rusk had previously referred to Vietnam in the context of Britain's east of Suez deliberations in a memorandum that he sent to George Brown in April 1967, writing: "For the UK to announce that you will no longer carry this burden (even at a future date) at the very moment when we are deeply involved in Vietnam and when Thailand is under threat, would have the most serious effects here."[29] In addition to the worsening situation in Southeast Asia in early 1968, the Soviet Union and China proved increasingly influential in the newly established People's Democratic Republic of Yemen – the successor state to Britain's colony at Aden – and, thus, the Arabian Peninsula appeared to be under greater threat from communism than

---

[26] January 11, 1968, *FRUS, 1964–1968, Vol. XII*, 608–609.   [27] Ibid., 609–610.
[28] Quoted in Little, *American Orientalism*, 142.
[29] April 21, 1967, *FRUS, 1964–1968, Vol. XII*, 566–568.

ever. On January 9, 1968, Lucius Battle wrote: "a total withdrawal of British military forces in the next few years would seriously undermine the Western position in the Gulf." He added that there was "no politically feasible way for the US or other Western power to step in with an equally effective presence once the British are gone."[30] Because of prior assurances from the Foreign Office – even after the devaluation – that Britain had intended to maintain a military presence in the Gulf until the mid-1970s, US officials felt double-crossed by the British. At the very least, Britain would have to stay there until a local security arrangement was in place.[31] Under Secretary of State George Ball got it right when he asserted in 1965 that, if Britain "should make a big external move" in devaluing sterling, then it "would wreck more than the monetary system," adding: "Our foreign political and defense policies would be badly mangled."[32]

Another problem for the Johnson Administration was that Britain planned to announce its east of Suez decision *publicly*. In the April 1967 memorandum to George Brown from Dean Rusk, the secretary of state argued "against major reductions" in British forces east of Suez "in the near future" but argued "even more strongly against *any announcement now* of any intentions to withdraw from the area." By revealing its policy to the world, Rusk maintained, Britain risked: (1) setting in motion "strains and ambitions" that would create turmoil in Malaysia; (2) contradicting the administration's claim to the American public that US allies shared the burden of fighting communism in faraway places; (3) prompting administration critics in the US Senate to call for a reduction in the number of American forces in Europe; and (4) giving communists in North Vietnam and China an arsenal of propaganda regarding the Western position in Southeast Asia.[33] In a letter to Lyndon Johnson in July 1967, Harold Wilson addressed US requests to avoid announcing his government's east of Suez decisions – which, at the time, kept at least some forces in place until the mid-1970s: "The fact is that so much has appeared publicly in various parts of the world about our long-term intentions (and this was certainly not something that we either wished or accept responsibility for) that it is simply impossible for us to avoid giving some public indication of what they are." Otherwise, Wilson argued, Britain risked people believing that it was "planning a more rapid rundown than is in fact the case." He also explained that the government

[30] Battle to Rusk, January 9, 1968, *FRUS, 1964–1968, Vol. XXI,* 256–258.
[31] Battle to Rusk, November 20, 1967, *FRUS, 1964–1968, Vol. XXI,* 244–245.
[32] Ball to Fowler, July 28, 1965, *FRUS, 1964–1968, Vol. VIII,* 175–177.
[33] My emphasis. *FRUS, 1964–1968, Vol. XII,* 566–568.

"must in all fairness give our armed forces some idea of their long term size, shape and equipment when the process is completed in the middle 1970s, particularly as the careers of many are involved."[34]

On January 15, 1968, the day before Wilson delivered his speech to Parliament announcing the Labour government's decision to withdraw all British forces from east of Suez by 1971, he wrote a long letter to Johnson in an attempt to deepen the context of the decision and to combat the notion that it represented "a British withdrawal from world affairs":

> As I shall be explaining tomorrow, it is absolutely clear to us that our present political commitments are too great for the military capability of the forces that we can reasonably afford, if the economy is to be restored quickly and decisively; but without economic strength, we can have no real military credibility. If there is any lesson to be learned from the [illegible] way we have found ourselves obliged to lurch from one defence review to another in recent years, it is that we must now take certain major foreign policy decisions as the prerequisite of economies in our defence expenditure. Put simply, this only amounts to saying that we have come to terms with our role in the world. And we are confident that if we fully assert our economic strength, we can by realistic priorities, strengthen this country's real influence and power for peace in the world.

He concluded by describing the decisions that his government was making as "the most difficult and the heaviest" of any that he and his colleagues could remember in public life: "We are taking them because we are convinced that, in the longer term, only thus can Britain find the new place on the world stage that I firmly believe the British people ardently desire."[35]

One thing was certain: the United States did not want to take Britain's place in the Persian Gulf. As Under Secretary of State Eugene Rostow explained in a meeting of US oil company executives on Iranian oil, "the US does not have to fill every military vacuum left by a British or French withdrawal."[36] The Department of State repeated this sentiment in a telegram to the US Embassy in Aden instructing the ambassador to tell Southern Yemen's President, Qahtan al-Shaabi, that the United States had "no intention" of "replacing the British."[37] The ongoing war in Southeast Asia made such a move financially, logistically, and politically unfeasible. Referring to the last of the three hurdles, Lyndon Johnson wrote to Harold Wilson: "Americans will find great difficulty in supporting the idea that we must move in to secure areas which the United

---

[34] July, 13, 1967, *FRUS, 1964–1968, Vol. XII*, 575–578.   [35] Ibid., 611–614.

[36] Memorandum of Conversation, March 6, 1968, *FRUS, 1964–1968, Vol. XXXIV*, 401–404.

[37] February 3, 1968, *FRUS, 1964–1968, Vol. XXI*, 277–278.

5.1 British Prime Minister Harold Wilson and US President Lyndon Johnson in the Oval Office during the former's visit to the United States, February 1968.

Kingdom has abandoned."[38] That being the case, US officials wanted Britain to preserve as much of its "special role" as possible until British forces left in 1971 and believed that Whitehall should "maintain certain elements" of the British position beyond that time.[39] The Johnson Administration also hoped that Britain's "residual political and economic influence in the Middle East" would continue to redound to the West's benefit.[40] For its part, the British government intended to "leave an orderly political situation" in its wake and sought to enlist the US government's help as much as possible to achieve that goal, especially given the "profound and enduring" British economic interests in the region.[41]

Lacking the will to replace Britain in the Gulf, policy-makers in Washington fell back on the regional solution to the problem of security there. To start, Lucius Battle, among others, believed that the United States

[38] Message from Johnson to Wilson, January 15, 1968, *FRUS, 1964–1968, Vol. XII,* 609–611.
[39] "Visit of British Prime Minister Wilson," a background paper prepared by the Department of State, February 2, 1968, *FRUS, 1964–1968, Vol. XXI,* 274–275.
[40] Paper Prepared in the Department of State, undated, *FRUS, 1964–1968, Vol. XII,* 618–624.
[41] Circular Telegram from the Department of State to Certain Posts, February 12, 1968, *FRUS, 1964–1968, Vol. XXI,* 279.

should foster greater political and economic cooperation among the states to promote stabilization.[42] In addition, the Joint Chiefs of Staff recommended that the United States establish an arms policy for the lower Persian Gulf states and Kuwait and set up a Defense Attaché Office in the latter. While the United States should continue to regard Britain as the "primary arms supplier" for the area, the Joint Chiefs explained, it should nonetheless "be prepared to consider favorably – on a case-by-case basis – limited sales of arms to Kuwait and the lower Gulf States to meet legitimate defense needs" not met by Britain.[43] Department of State officials accepted the necessity of such an arms policy but cautioned against "an undue military buildup" in the area.[44] As for the sheikhdoms themselves, they sought a greater US role in the Gulf, hoping to substitute one "powerful protector" for another.[45] But much to their certain dismay, the key element of the US regional strategy was to have Iran and Saudi Arabia – local powers that the Emirates historically feared – police the area by proxy, a policy that had gained momentum in direct proportion to British decline since the Eisenhower Administration. Acknowledging the fact that the two states were fierce competitors for influence in the region, Walt Rostow wrote in January 1968: "Good relations between Saudi Arabia and Iran will be necessary to keep things under control when the British leave. The alternatives are instability with a strong chance of an increased Soviet presence. We don't want to have to replace the British, and we don't want the Russians there. So we must count on the Shah and Faisal."[46] Thus, the Johnson Administration laid the foundation for the US strategic approach to the Middle East for the next decade – although it was Richard Nixon whose name would be attached to the US strategy, the Nixon Doctrine, of using proxies to defend Western interests both in the Gulf and around the globe.[47]

Britain delivered on its promise to withdraw from the Gulf during Nixon's first term. That it did so without leaving chaos in its wake was a remarkable achievement given the array of forces militating against a

[42] Information Memorandum from Battle to Rusk, February 22, 1968, *FRUS, 1964–1968, Vol. XXI*, 281–283; "Visit of British Prime Minister Wilson," a background paper prepared by the Department of State, February 2, 1968, *FRUS, 1964–1968, Vol. XXI*, 274–275; "Paper Prepared in the Department of State," undated, *FRUS, 1964–1968, Vol. XII*, 618–624.
[43] Memorandum from the Joint Chiefs of Staff to McNamara, June 19, 1968, *FRUS, 1964–1968, Vol. XII*, 298–299.
[44] Information Memorandum from Battle to Rusk, February 22, 1968, *FRUS, 1964–1968, Vol. XII*, 281–283.
[45] Ibid.
[46] Action Memorandum from Rostow to Johnson, January 31, 1968, *FRUS, 1964–1968, Vol. XII*, 268–269.
[47] Little, *American Orientalism*, 143–145.

stable outcome, including: (1) Iran's advocacy of its historic claims to the island of Bahrain; (2) the return to power of British Conservatives who had denounced the Wilson government's Gulf policy and vowed to reverse it when elected; and (3) the uncertainty over the structure of the future political relationship between the protectorates. First, Britain was able to persuade Iran to acquiesce in its claims to Bahrain through the face-saving route of having the United Nations sanction the island's independence in 1970 – after a UN mission had determined that this represented the wishes of the majority of Bahrainis. Second, members of Edward Heath's Conservative government, elected in June 1970, discovered that they could not so easily reverse the process that Harold Wilson had set in motion three years earlier. Foreign Minister – and former Prime Minister – Alec Douglas-Home surveyed the government's options with a realist's gaze and persuaded Heath that the military links retained within a federation of the Trucial States, as well as the availability of British air and sea forces, would help keep the region stable. Third, through the tireless efforts of William Luce, the esteemed former political resident in the Persian Gulf whom the Conservative government called out of retirement, Britain resolved any lingering political and defense questions regarding the Gulf territories. Consequently, when Britain withdrew its forces from the region in December 1971, the Trucial States did as Whitehall had hoped and formed a political union, the United Arab Emirates. Britain then secured Treaties of Friendship with all three of the new political entities that had emerged from the original nine protectorates, including Bahrain and Qatar. The treaties provided for military consultation, air space and deployment rights for the British air force, and training facilities for British troops.[48] Compared with the disorder that it left behind when it ignominiously abandoned Southwestern Arabia, Britain could be pleased with the uneventful way that it departed from the Persian Gulf. Glen Balfour-Paul captures the moment perfectly: "It was not a heroic end but neither was it, as in Aden, a horrendous one."[49]

Decolonization happened much later in the Gulf than in the rest of the empire primarily owing to the economic importance of the region's oil to Britain, but forces external to Britain also supported its presence there. One was the sheikhdoms themselves. Because these semi-colonies did not resemble other parts of the formal empire in terms of size, population, or level of development – not to mention British intrusiveness – they had different goals and needs, particularly in the area of security. And the

---

[48] Balfour-Paul, *The End of Empire in the Middle East*, 126–136; Wm. Roger Louis, "The Withdrawal from the Gulf" in Louis, *Ends of British Imperialism*, 877–903.
[49] Balfour-Paul, *The End of Empire in the Middle East*, 135.

maintenance of their security depended entirely on outside assistance. Thus, whereas a nationalist-inspired "push" drove agents of imperialism from colonial Asia and Africa, a defense-led "pull" kept British troops in the Gulf to repel threats from Iran, Saudi Arabia, and others. A second buttress for Britain's presence in the area was the United States, which had looked to Britain to defend Western oil interests in the region throughout the postwar era, even as British influence waned elsewhere in the Middle East. Johnson Administration officials demonstrated just how important they considered the British role there in both words and deeds, the latter of which included arranging US and international support for sterling. The profound disappointment expressed by US officials on the Wilson government's decision to abandon the Gulf revealed the depth of US dependence on British forces to secure the region. And, as the quote from Lucius Battle that leads off this chapter demonstrates, at least one US policy-maker advocated for Britain's continuing position in the Gulf by employing the very same oil-related, financial argument that British officials themselves had once used to defend British policy in the Middle East. In 1967, however, conditions were such that Whitehall could no longer justify Britain's Gulf deployments, either economically or strategically.

By the mid to late 1960s, Britain's approach to securing access to Middle Eastern oil had changed, a shift that had begun in at least one part of Whitehall as early as 1962. As noted in chapter 4, Treasury Under-Secretary P. S. Milner-Barry acknowledged that Kuwait and other oil producers would continue to ask for – and receive – increasingly greater shares of the profits on the sale of their petroleum, causing the British balance of payments to suffer accordingly. He also understood that the British government was helpless to do anything to affect that trend because using military force to control the terms on which it procured oil from the region was no longer an option. The era of instigating coups and invading countries to protect petroleum interests in the Middle East ended with Suez, at which point the unfeasibility of these types of actions – at least for Britain – had become clear. As a result of its eroding political, economic, and military position, Britain could no longer impose its will in parts of the world where the superpowers, if not a consensus of like-minded nations, had veto authority over British policy. Moreover, Milner-Barry, and eventually Foreign Secretary Patrick Gordon Walker and other British officials, reached the conclusion that keeping British forces in the Gulf to protect against the *possibility* of some future event that denied Britain access to oil – or dramatically increased its price – was not worth the cost of keeping those forces there. Given that the scenarios in which the government would resort to military action were limited – as were the circumstances in which having troops on the ground provided some kind of tactical advantage – the British presence in the Gulf had become something like an insurance policy that had outlasted its usefulness.

Britain's decision to abandon the Gulf against US wishes – and the dismay that it provoked in Washington – continued a pattern of discord in the postwar Anglo-American "special relationship" that, at times, seemed much less than special. Just as with Britain's discrimination against dollar oil and Whitehall's responses to the twin nationalizations of the Iranian oil industry and the Suez Canal, US officials viewed Britain's Gulf policy as the narrow pursuit of British economic interests at the expense of the overall interests of the West. The Cold War always loomed large in US calculations. In 1950, Britain's oil-substitution policy irritated US officials because it hindered the spread of free-trade capitalism – to the ostensible detriment of the Western industrialized nations and their trading partners and redounding to the benefit of their communist enemies. Likewise, Washington chafed at British policies toward Iran in 1951, Egypt in 1956, and the Gulf in 1968, because US officials feared that the British approach would destabilize the Middle East in ways that promoted communist influence in the region. Officials in London argued that they pursued such policies to prevent Britain's further economic deterioration – or to save the nation from economic crisis – in part because they considered an economically debilitated Britain of no use to the United States as a strategic partner in fighting the Cold War. Although both governments liked to frame their policies as being driven by service to the greater Western good, national self-interest motivated policy-making in both London and Washington to be sure. That said, British and US officials genuinely believed that the fate of the West was tethered to the individual fates of their respective nations: in their minds, the national interest and the greater good were one and the same.

Unmet expectations exacerbated friction in the postwar Anglo-American relationship much in the same way that the bitterest disagreements can occur among friends. After suffering unprecedented physical and financial devastation during World War II, Britain expected the United States to be sympathetic to its need to resort to extreme measures, whether in economic or foreign policy, to shore up the British economy as a matter of survival. That the United States was dependent on Britain to help fight communism in faraway places merely reinforced this sentiment. On the other hand, US officials expected that Britain, the closest of allies, would consult with the United States on significant strategic and economic decisions that affected US interests. The provision of generous financial aid to Britain – ensuring that the British empire continued in receivership after the war, rather than being liquidated in a fire sale – also encouraged the belief in Washington that Britain should hew closely to US policy goals: "He who pays the piper calls the tune," as one British official remarked concerning the contingencies of the postwar American loan. Both sides grew frustrated when the actions of their counterparts did not conform to expectations that were oftentimes explicitly stated. Ultimately, the chief source of trouble in the Anglo-American relationship in the postwar era was the opposite trajectories of Britain and the United States as world powers. With the United States in ascendance and Britain in decline, US and British officials approached the world and each other from different angles and, consequently, with different interests. It was inevitable that those interests would collide and create conflict. Any discord, however, should be viewed in the larger context of fundamental Anglo-American agreement on broad postwar goals.

While Britain's withdrawal from the Persian Gulf – a decision made with only British interests in mind – may have signified the formal end to Britain's empire in the Middle East, the core of British influence in the region, the informal empire, unraveled long before then. Imagining a graphic representation of British decline, we can mark points on the trend line with key events: the oil nationalization crisis in Iran (1951); the Suez base agreement with Egypt (1954); Jordan's dismissal of the longtime British head of the Arab Legion (1956); the Suez crisis (1956); and the Iraqi revolution (1958). And just as with decolonization in Asia and Africa during the 1950s and 1960s, the origins of the informal empire's demise can be traced back to World War II. The conflict catalyzed the growth of nationalist movements previously stunted by British cooption or coercion and left Britain too diminished economically and politically to contain them any longer. When confronted with the manifestations of Iranian and Egyptian nationalisms in the respective takeovers of assets vital to the British economy – the Iranian oil industry and the Suez Canal – Britain's economic vulnerability proved critical in limiting Whitehall's options. Indeed, both cases demonstrated that Britain had ceded control over its own destiny to outside forces: not only to Iran and Egypt but also to the United States – on which Britain depended for both money and oil at a time when US officials began to determine the contours of Western policy in the Middle East. Britain's Suez debacle, which exposed the country's economic and political weakness – and further energized the spread of Arab nationalism in the region – represented the beginning of the end of Britain's informal influence there. In Iraq, Arab nationalism alchemized with the country's social upheaval and fervent animosity toward Britain and produced the bloody revolution that consumed the substance of what was left of Britain's informal empire in the Middle East. Any influence that remained in Jordan after July 1958 was negligible and waning – the stellar remnants from a supernova.

By undermining the structure of the country's informal empire in the Middle East, Britain's postwar economic weakness fed on itself by hindering the government's ability to dictate the terms on which the nation acquired oil from the region. It is worth repeating that, over the preceding pages, the economic consequences of Britain's dependence on foreign oil has not concerned the typical macroeconomic effects associated with the prohibitive cost of doing business in an industrial economy when oil prices rise, that is, higher transportation costs and the ripple effects that lead to a slower- or negatively growing economy. Rather, the focus here has been on the *financial* consequences of such dependence, namely the impact on Britain's balance of payments, and, hence, on its currency. The British empire's ability to procure petroleum cheaply and to pay for it in sterling – as facilitated by British-registered companies – contributed positively to Britain's balance of payments and strengthened the pound (as did the huge profits those companies generated). Its inability to do so had the opposite effect, producing higher inflation and interest rates and worsening the already harmful economic consequences of increasing oil prices. Owing to oil's being the largest item in Britain's balance of payments, the impact that it had on the nation's financial position in the postwar era was enormous. This was especially the case because the level of Britain's gold and foreign exchange reserves too often hovered just above the margin of peril – as a result of the nation's chronic inability to export more than it imported, forcing Britain to use its reserves to buy from abroad what it did not produce at home.

Britain's informal empire in the Middle East, of which the Anglo-Iranian Oil Company was both a beneficiary and an instrument, provided easy access to the kind of oil that would have the most salutary effect on the balance of payments: plentiful, cheap, and obtainable in sterling. As a result, British officials placed a premium on Middle Eastern oil after World War II. Anglo-Iranian's stake in Middle Eastern oil proved immensely advantageous for Britain. But as the first two chapters of this book demonstrate, the mutual interest of the British government and the firm in securing Middle Eastern oil did not necessarily translate into harmony between official British and AIOC policy. For the British government, the region's petroleum was first and foremost a national concern, critical to Britain's postwar economic recovery not only because it literally fueled reconstruction but also because it saved Britain dollars, giving sterling much-needed support. By strengthening the pound, or preventing it from weakening further, Middle Eastern oil also proved to be an important component in the bid by Labour and Conservative governments to maintain the currency's – and in turn Britain's – international prestige and influence. But, as noted above, preserving access to Middle Eastern oil during this period also meant averting balance-of-payments disasters, such as those associated with the Suez crisis and the Arab-Israeli War of 1967. A significant consequence, then, of Britain's waning influence in the Middle East was its diminishing ability to limit threats to the nation's economy associated with access to the region's oil. Considerable economic benefits accrued to Britain when its informal empire in the Middle East was robust. But, having grown dependent on the spoils of empire, Britain found itself in a precarious position when the system unraveled.

The same was true of the widespread use of sterling as a trading and reserve currency. As British Treasury officials noted, its premier status enabled Britain to do business around the world in its own currency. Furthermore, the economic influence that came with the pound's global reach also conferred political power upon Britain as a banker to a large part of the world. When sterling was strong, there seemed to be no downside to the currency's omnipresence. When it was weak, however – particularly after World War II – the disadvantages were significant. The pound's international exposure meant that it could be attacked from many different quarters, with large numbers of sterling-holders usually fleeing the currency at once, rendering Britain vulnerable to financial crisis. As has been demonstrated, sterling attacks did not occur only because users expected the currency to lose its value – that is, for purely economic reasons. They occurred for political reasons as well, as happened during the Suez crisis and the Arab-Israeli War of 1967. Ironically, then, sterling, once a primary source of Britain's international influence, had effectively become its Achilles heel.

This raises the issue of the Anglo-Kuwaiti relationship during the 1950s and 1960s. Beyond the fact that Kuwait was important to Britain as a major source of sterling oil, the sheikhdom had enormous sterling assets. In fact, once the independent petroleum companies broke the monopoly over Middle Eastern oil held by the major multinationals and ushered out the era of fifty–fifty contracts, the question of what Kuwait would do with its sterling revenues began to concern Whitehall more than the terms of British Petroleum's concession agreements with the sheikhdom. Sterling's decline and Arab nationalism's ascent after the Suez crisis stoked that anxiety, putting both economic and political pressure on Kuwait to diversify its assets out of sterling and concomitantly increasing pressure on Britain to prevent or limit such activity. Of course, the very fact of the pound's weakness and Arab nationalism's vigor undercut Britain's influence and rendered it less able to do so. Working in Britain's favor, though, were two forces that prevented Kuwait from making significant transfers out of sterling: first, any large move from sterling into gold, dollars, or other currencies would threaten the value of the assets that Kuwait continued to hold; and second, Kuwait depended on Britain for security. Indeed, the combination of Britain's strategic importance to Kuwait, the sheikhdom's economic importance to Britain, and Britain's post-Suez sense of restraint, ensured that Anglo-Kuwaiti relations remained stable during the period covered in this book.

Given the enormous liabilities that came from fighting two world wars – as well as an economy that consistently imported more than it exported – international sterling had become something like a business on the verge of bankruptcy in the wake of World War II. It was saved by an infusion of cash from the United States and a regulatory structure – the empire – that imposed restrictions on what its investors – the balance-holders – could do with their shares. Thus, the business of international sterling persisted after World War II, albeit hobbled, with Labour and Conservative governments determined to continue breathing life into it. Over time and across governments, prestige and influence provided the chief motivation for British officials, even more than the material benefits that sterling's international presence delivered – or was believed to deliver – to Britain. That said, the war's destruction of Britain's already declining industrial economy, and the continuing vitality of its service sector, provided added incentive for Conservatives to keep the business of international sterling going. They believed that the City's effectiveness depended on it. But even if British officials wanted to "sell off" the business of international sterling, how would they have done so without causing severe economic disruption at home? Harold Macmillan addressed this question to Anthony Eden after the Suez crisis in the context of the sterling area:

There is no way of avoiding the dangers to sterling which come from our being bankers to the sterling area. We have inherited an old family business which used to be very profitable and sound. The trouble is that the liabilities are four times the assets. In the old days, a business of this kind, like Coutt's or Cox's Bank, would have been sold to one of the big five [banking houses]. The trouble is I do not know who is to buy the sterling area banking system. I tried it out on [US Secretary of the Treasury George] Humphrey but he was not taking it. So we must either carry on the business with all its risks, or wind it up and pay 5 [shillings] to the [pound].[50]

[50] Macmillan to Eden, December 31, 1956, NA, PREM 11/1826.

The devaluation of 1967 forced Britain to wind down the business, with the Basle Facility serving as a de facto bankruptcy court that enabled Britain to liquidate its assets in an orderly fashion.

In the end, this book has been about the efforts of successive British governments to contend with Britain's decline as a world power after World War II. In their approach to foreign, colonial, and economic policy-making, the Attlee, Churchill, and Eden governments acknowledged Britain's limitations to some degree, while seeking unrepentantly to restore and maintain Britain's status as a world power – and they did so primarily by capitalizing on the advantages of empire. Both Labour and Conservative governments considered Middle Eastern oil and the widespread use of the pound sterling to be among the most important benefits that the empire provided to help preserve and promote Britain's international influence. But the forces unleashed by World War II – in the British economy, in the Middle East, and throughout the world – eventually limited Britain's ability to exploit the region's oil and sterling's global reach in the way that British officials had envisioned. As the postwar era evolved, when the Attlee, Churchill, and Eden governments tried to operate as though Britain and the world around it had not changed, they were confronted with their nation's diminishing ability to control events. British power failed to match its will, and, as a result, decline managed the British government more than the British government managed decline. Only under Macmillan and Wilson – primarily because of the lesson of Suez – did the reverse occur, as illustrated on a small scale by Britain's nuanced policy toward Kuwait and on a grand scale by the mostly orderly process of decolonization. If British action during the Suez crisis represented "the last gasp of declining power," as Macmillan told Dulles at the end of 1956, then the devaluation of 1967 signified the exhalation of that breath. It was then that, as a generation of British officials had feared, denial of oil from the Middle East helped finish off sterling as a prominent trading and reserve currency. The upshot was the end of empire itself.

Afterword

Historians tend to be cautious about viewing current events through the lens of the past or using historical analogies to analyze the present day. And rightly so: context matters, and, thus, no historical analogy can ever be perfect. Nonetheless, carefully deployed, such analogies can be enlightening. Indeed, the decline of the dollar, US dependence on foreign oil, and US efforts to preserve influence in the Middle East is so similar to parts of the British experience surveyed over the preceding pages that it begs for a short discussion. Ideally, some lessons can be drawn from that experience.

Much like sterling at its peak during the nineteenth century, the dollar has been the foremost trading and reserve currency in the global economy since World War II, owing to the dominant international position of US manufacturing and financial services. But, like Britain before it, the US share of manufacturing in the world economy has shrunk as competitors have captured an increasing share of the global market – particularly since the 1970s – and none more so than China during the first decade of the twenty-first century. Consequently, goods that the United States once produced domestically are now imported from other countries, in some cases where they are manufactured more cheaply in low-wage economies or in other cases where such goods have been made better. Because the United States has imported increasingly more than it has exported since 1975, it has had to borrow the savings of other countries to cover the trade gap, putting downward pressure on the dollar.[1] Record trade deficits, loss of confidence in a slowing US economy, and the subsequent implosion of the US financial sector in 2007–2008 has further added to that pressure. Unlike the adjustments that British officials made to sterling during the period covered by this book, however, in the post-Bretton Woods era of flexible exchange rates, currency devaluations

---

[1] "US Trade Deficit Sets Record, With China and Oil the Causes," *New York Times*, February 11, 2006.

happen automatically, as has more or less steadily happened to the dollar in the 2000s.

The decline of the dollar in nominal terms against a basket of major currencies – most notably the euro (the European Union's official currency since 1999) – was the subject of extensive discussion in 2007 and 2008.[2] Its free-fall started in the second half of 2001 and accelerated in 2007–2008, with the dollar losing 2.2 percent of its value against the euro on September 22, 2008, its biggest one-day drop since January 2001.[3] The preceding week was one of the worst for the US financial sector in decades, prompting historian Niall Ferguson to write an article in the *Washington Post* in which he assessed that "the days when the dollar was the sole international reserve currency" may be "coming to an end" – and put the dollar's woes in the context of sterling's post-World War II decline.[4] Similarly, almost a year earlier, *The Economist* wrote that "worrying parallels are seen between the dollar's recent fall and the decline of sterling as a reserve currency half a century ago."[5] And much like what happened to the pound, speculative selling of the dollar ensued, reaching nearly an all-time high in November 2007, according to a leading investment bank.[6] Indeed, the markets have demonstrated extreme skittishness about the dollar, so much so that mere mid-level Chinese officials caused the dollar to plummet by calling for China to diversify its reserves out of "weak" currencies such as the dollar and characterizing the dollar's status as a reserve currency as "shaky."[7] The fact that China has the world's largest cache of dollar reserves, comprising 60–70 percent of its roughly $1.9 trillion in total foreign exchange, certainly played a role in the overreaction by markets already on edge. In an effort to minimize risk, other countries with large dollar-denominated reserves have shown a "new willingness to dump the dollar in favor of the euro," as former British colonies did with their sterling balances in the 1960s.[8] To be worthy of reserve status, a currency must be a good store of value, a characteristic that the dollar exhibited over much of the latter half of the twentieth century. But the dollar's steep decline since 2001 relative to other major currencies has demonstrated that it may no longer be capable of playing such a role to the extent that it has previously. By the 2010s, it is possible that the dollar will no longer be the world's premier reserve

[2] For example, *The Economist* asks, "How long will the dollar remain the world's premier currency?", November 29, 2007.
[3] "Free Fall," *Economist.com*, March 16, 2008. From 2002 to 2007, the dollar lost 25 percent of its value against a basket of leading currencies, *The Economist*, November 29, 2007. *Washington Post*, September 23, 2008.
[4] "Rough Week, But America's Era Goes On," *Washington Post*, September 21, 2008.
[5] *The Economist*, November 29, 2007.   [6] Ibid.
[7] "Ready for a Rout?" *The Economist*, November 8, 2007.
[8] *New York Times*, January 2, 2007.

currency but rather will share that role with other leading currencies, such as the euro and the Chinese yuan, following the model of sterling during the interwar period.[9]

Just as British dependence on foreign oil hurt the pound during the post-World War II era, US dependence on foreign oil has helped accelerate the dollar's decline. According to official US government statistics, the United States imported 58 percent of the crude oil that it consumed in 2007, with Canada (18.2%), Mexico (11.4%), Saudi Arabia (11.0%), Venezuela (10.1%), and Nigeria (8.4%) representing the five biggest suppliers. Almost half of US crude oil imports came from the Western Hemisphere and 16 percent came from the Persian Gulf, including Saudi Arabia, Bahrain, Iraq, Kuwait, Qatar, and the United Arab Emirates.[10] Fortunately for the United States, the OPEC countries, led by Saudi Arabia, agreed to sell their oil exclusively for US dollars in 1974. As a result, the United States has the benefit of being able to trade dollar-denominated assets, purchased by oil producers, for crude, thus obviating the need to use foreign exchange for the biggest-ticket item in its trade account. In addition, pricing oil in dollars requires other oil importers to hold dollars for transaction purposes, thereby increasing demand for the currency and driving up its value. But US consumption of foreign oil still counts against the US balance of payments, which means that the dollar feels the downward pressure of the United States having to import a majority of the oil that it consumes. Furthermore, because OPEC prices its oil in dollars – an advantage when the dollar is strong – when the currency's value declines, more dollars are required to buy the same amount of oil. A vicious cycle occurs in which a rise in oil prices increases the US trade deficit and, consequently, puts downward pressure on the dollar. In 2005, the US trade deficit set a record due in part to "soaring energy prices that added tens of billions of dollars to the nation's bill for imported oil."[11] The price of oil reached record highs in inflation-adjusted dollars in 2008, and, in July, the trade deficit rose to a

[9] The dollar accounted for almost two-thirds of official international foreign-exchange reserves in 2008, according to the IMF; see "The Resilient Dollar," *The Economist*, October 2, 2008; "Losing Faith in the Greenback," *The Economist*, November 29, 2007; Barry Eichengreen and Marc Flandreau persuasively argue that the market has room for more than one dominant reserve currency at one time by demonstrating that the dollar surpassed sterling in central bank reserves as early as the mid-1920s – contrary to previous thinking – before falling behind sterling in the 1930s and then once again regaining its top status after World War II; see "The Rise and Fall of the Dollar, or When did the Dollar Replace Sterling as the Leading International Currency?" (National Bureau of Economic Research, Working Paper No. 14154, July 2008).

[10] Energy Information Administration, Official Energy Statistics from the US Government, http://tonto.eia.doe.gov/energy_in_brief/foreign_oil_dependence.

[11] "US Trade Deficit Sets Record, With China and Oil the Causes," *New York Times*, February 11, 2006.

sixteen-month high as a result.[12] In a likely demonstration of the connection between the value of the dollar and the price of oil, the deepening US financial crisis of 2008 caused the dollar's 2.2 percent plunge against the euro in September, while the price of oil per barrel had its biggest one-day rise in dollar terms, $16.37.[13]

The dollar's weakness has put the US economy in a vulnerable position with respect to the world's biggest oil producers. Those that peg their currencies to the dollar, such as the Gulf states, have shown an interest in severing that link. Kuwait did so in 2007, pegging the Kuwaiti dinar to a basket of currencies instead. The other Gulf states have considered following Kuwait's lead because the dollar's slide was exporting inflation to the region.[14] If countries such as the United Arab Emirates decided to separate their currencies from the dollar, demand for dollars would decline. A decision by oil producers to stop accepting dollars for their crude would decrease demand for the greenback even further as nations turned to the euro or other currencies to purchase one of the world's most heavily traded commodities. Iranian President Mahmoud Ahmadinejad has already threatened to refuse dollar payments for his country's oil, not only for economic reasons (he called the dollar a "worthless piece of paper") but certainly for political ones as well, given the longstanding hostility of the Iranian government to the United States.[15] Under the leadership of Hugo Chavez, another US *bête noire*, Venezuela could decide to go the same route. If enough producers choose to accept other currencies for their oil, they could spark a full-fledged financial crisis, as dollar-holders flee the currency in anticipation of even greater losses of value.[16] In this case, it would be worthwhile for US policy-makers to follow the example of the post-World War II generation of British officials who obsessed over the connection between imported oil and the value of their nation's currency.

[12] "Trade Deficit Rose to 16-Month High in July as Oil Prices Hit a Record," *New York Times*, September 12, 2008.
[13] "Currency's Dive Points to Further Pain," *Washington Post*, September 23, 2008.
[14] "Time to Break Free," *The Economist*, November 22, 2007.
[15] Ibid. "Losing Faith in the Greenback," *The Economist*, November 29, 2007.
[16] A community of conspiracy theorists, writing mostly on the internet, believes that the United States invaded Iraq because the country's ruler, Saddam Hussein, decided to sell Iraqi oil for euros, thus threatening to spark a mass movement in the international oil industry toward that currency and undermining the dollar's supremacy in the world economy. See, for example, William R. Clark, *Petrodollar Warfare: Oil, Iraq and the Future of the Dollar* (British Columbia: New Society, 2005), ch. 5. While the United States should take seriously the threat of oil being sold for other currencies because of the financial implications involved, we cannot properly assess whether this issue even factored into the Bush Administration's calculations in launching the Iraq War until all the US government documents related to the conflict become publicly available.

Like Britain after World War II, the United States has faced a nationalist trend in the Middle East in the 2000s that threatens its oil interests there – US oil interests being defined as the maintenance of petroleum flows to the West at stable prices. Whereas British officials once feared the spread of Pan-Arab nationalism through the Persian Gulf, US officials have been equally concerned about the broad appeal of Islamism – or Islamically oriented political movements – particularly as applied in the realm of law and government in Middle Eastern countries. The overthrow in 1979 of the Shah of Iran – one of the United States's closest allies – and the establishment of an Islamic theocracy in his government's place, was a severe blow to US influence in the Middle East. It was akin to the downfall of Iraq's Nuri al-Said for the British, not least because of the shock it generated among most US officials as well as the post-revolutionary hostility generated toward the *ancien régime*'s chief patron. An important difference between the two events, though, was that the Iraqi revolution occurred when British influence in the Middle East was plummeting, whereas the Iranian revolution merely reduced what continues to be, for now, robust US sway in the region.

Nonetheless, the Iranian revolution was a harbinger of what the United States would confront in the years to come, depicted in sharp relief with al-Qaeda's attack on the United States in 2001. And just as Britain invaded Egypt in 1956 to confront Nasser and Pan-Arab nationalism in an effort to preserve British influence in the Middle East, so did the United States invade Iraq to establish a Western-oriented democratic government in the heart of the Arab world in part to provide a countervailing force to Islamism. That is where the analogy between Suez and Iraq ends, however. The United States on the eve of the Iraq invasion much more resembled Britain before the First World War, a superpower with little competition – or in the case of the United States, no competition in terms of sheer military strength. But the United States could find itself exiting Iraq much like Britain finished World War II, diminished economically, with a currency driven down by the enormous debt that the United States has incurred from fighting the conflict – the cost of which will total roughly $1 trillion, not counting continuing payments for veterans' care, interest on the debt, and other expenses.[17] Future US administrations might want to follow the post-1958 Eisenhower model of recognizing that, like Arab nationalism of the 1950s, Islamism (1) comes

[17] The total cost could amount to $3 trillion, according to Joseph E. Stiglitz and Linda J. Bilmes, *The Three Trillion Dollar War: The True Cost of the Iraq Conflict* (New York: W. W. Norton, 2008).

in many different forms; (2) will not always run counter to US interests; and (3) in some cases, might be accommodated.[18]

While it would have been impossible for Britain to substitute oil with an energy alternative in the post-World War II era to eliminate or reduce the financial risk of dependence on foreign oil, the United States will have better options if it pursues the right policies. The steep fall in US demand for oil in the summer of 2008 – associated with the record-high cost of gasoline – demonstrated that the United States can significantly decrease its dependence on foreign oil even before turning to alternative energy sources. The US government can incentivize the continuation of such behavior when the price of oil falls – as it did steeply in the last quarter of 2008 and early 2009 as a result of the global economic downturn[19] – by increasing the federal gasoline tax. Pursuing such a policy would reduce the shock associated with a future spike in oil prices, which is assured when the global economy rebounds and a surge in demand overwhelms an oil supply limited by the current lack of investment as a result of low oil prices.[20] Economists have recommended increasing the gasoline tax ever since the oil shocks from the Arab-Israeli War of 1973 and the Iranian revolution in 1979 helped cripple the US economy during the 1970s.[21] A higher gasoline tax would prevent the United States from repeating the mistakes of the late 1980s and 1990s when a precipitous fall in the price of oil led the country to abandon – or, at the very least, not update – some of the conservation measures and practices developed during the Ford and Carter Administrations in response to record oil prices. Of course, the US government can also encourage the development of alternative energy sources, such as wind, solar, and safe nuclear power, through tax, subsidy, and investment policies.

The US government should also take care to manage the dollar's decline so that it does not lurch from crisis to crisis as the pound did during the post-World War II era. Fortunately for US policy-makers, while the dollar's slide from top-currency status may resemble that of sterling's half a century earlier, the dollar has had something in its favor that the pound did not: the US consumer. The global economy is too interconnected and too dependent on US consumption of foreign goods

---

[18] See Yaqub, *Containing Arab Nationalism*.

[19] After peaking at $147 per barrel in July 2008, the price plunged to roughly $34 per barrel in January 2009.

[20] "Well Prepared," *The Economist*, November 6, 2008; "Oil Closes Below $50, Lowest Price since May 2005," *New York Times*, November 21, 2008; "Down it Goes," *The Economist*, December 2, 2008.

[21] James Akins, the future US Ambassador to Saudi Arabia, recommended such a course to the Nixon Administration in 1971. See Robert D. Kaplan, *The Arabists: The Romance of an American Elite* (New York: Free Press, 1993), 173.

to allow the currency of the world's biggest economy to collapse. Once the United States emerges from the deep recession that began in 2008, however, it will have to find a way to consume more responsibly because record government and household debt has, among other things, put unrelenting downward pressure on the dollar in the twenty-first century, potentially leading to much higher inflation and interest rates in the future. Since the 1970s, the country has been able to support a habit of living beyond its means by borrowing cheaply in its own currency – a luxury that no other country enjoys to the degree that the United States does – from countries whose own economies have depended on exporting to the United States. Foreign lenders will not continue to sustain US debt-driven consumption forever, though, and certainly not if the dollar's value continues to decline. Therefore, the US government will have to cooperate with its foreign counterparts to ensure a soft landing for the currency. After all, at some point central banks may seek to cut the losses on their dollar reserves and try to get out in front of a wave of selling by other central banks – which would also fear such losses – and thereby instigate further dollar-dumping, a panic, and ultimately a currency crisis.[22] Global cooperation in the face of the worst financial crisis since the 1930s offers reason for optimism that such an outcome may not occur.

In the end, the crisis of 2008 may diminish New York's place at the center of international finance the way that World War I undercut London's position after 1918. Wall Street almost single-handedly precipitated the global credit crunch by peddling risky mortgage-backed securities (and their derivatives) that became worthless when the US housing market crashed. In other words, searching for ever-greater profits, legendary and too loosely regulated Wall Street investment banks such as Lehman Brothers, Bear Stearns, and others, took excessive risks and imploded as a result, tarnishing Wall Street's reputation in the process. It is now possible to see a future where New York becomes one of several important hubs in a multi-polar system of international finance, as London was during the interwar period.[23] Indeed, the multi-polar character of the interwar period is likely where the world is headed, with the United States, the European Union, and China competing for markets, resources, and political power.[24] The main question to be answered is how the United States gets there. It may be useful to look to the British experience for some answers.

[22] "Losing Faith in the Greenback," *The Economist*, November 29, 2007.
[23] "America and the New Financial World," *Wall Street Journal*, October 6, 2008.
[24] On this subject, see Parag Khanna, *The Second World: Empires and Influence in the New Global Order* (New York: Random House, 2008).

Appendices

Appendix 1 *United Kingdom balance of payments: current account, 1946–1967 (in million pounds)*

	1946	1947	1948	1949	1950	1951	1952	1953	1954	1955	1956	1957	1958	1959	1960	1961	1962	1963	1964	1965	1966	1967
1 Trade in goods	-101	-358	-152	-137	-54	-692	-272	-244	-210	-315	50	-29	34	-116	-404	-144	-104	-123	-551	-263	-111	-601
2 Trade in services	-274	-197	-64	-43	-4	32	123	123	115	42	26	121	119	118	39	51	50	4	-34	-66	44	157
3 Balance (1 + 2)	-375	-555	-216	-180	-58	-660	-149	-121	-95	-273	76	92	153	2	-365	-93	-54	-119	-585	-329	-67	-444
4 Compensation of employees	-20	-19	-20	-20	-21	-21	-22	-25	-27	-27	-30	-32	-34	-37	-35	-35	-37	-38	-33	-34	-39	-39
5 Investment income	88	159	252	234	426	365	265	238	261	175	237	257	303	269	235	259	346	416	420	467	413	411
6 Total income (4 + 5)	68	140	232	214	405	344	243	213	234	148	207	225	269	232	200	224	309	378	387	433	374	372
7 Current transfers	166	123	96	29	39	29	169	143	55	43	2	-5	4	-	-6	-9	-14	-37	-62	-66	-89	-117
8 Current balance (3 + 6 + 7)	-141	-292	112	63	386	-287	263	235	194	-82	285	312	426	234	-171	122	241	222	-260	38	218	-189

Source: Paul Dickman (ed.), *National Statistics: Economic Trends Annual Supplement, 2000 Edition*, No. 26 (London: The Stationery Office, 2000), 98.

Appendix 2 *United Kingdom oil account transactions: visible and invisible trade, 1946–1958 (in million pounds)*[a]

		1946	1947	1948	1949	1950	1951	1952	1953	1954	1955	1956	1957	1958
Visible trade	1 Imports	62.4	97.7	128.5	122.8	149.8	199.2	185.5	200.9	222.9	246.7	258.5	307.9	316
	2 Exports	33.1	43.9	62.3	63.8	48.8	72.1	113.8	140.3	145.7	146.1	187.2	184.2	187.2
	3 Balance (2−1)	−29.3	−53.8	−66.2	−59.0	−101.0	−127.1	−71.7	−60.6	−77.2	−100.6	−71.3	−123.7	−128.8
Invisible trade	4 Debits[b]	166.9	202.8	278.4	329.3	378.5	559.1	707.5	754.2	813.9	1,030.5	1,262.3	1,371.7	1,360.5
	5 Credits	169.2	263.9	420.2	464.2	633.6	748.3	858.2	916.7	1,003.7	1,155.6	1,404.0	1,549.0	1,595.0
	6 Balance (5−4)	2.3	61.1	141.8	134.9	255.1	189.2	150.7	162.5	189.8	125.1	141.7	177.3	234.5
	7 Dollar cost	111.5	148.9	155.0	157.8	143.6	269.7	257.2	236.8	178.1	167.7	140.5	199.7	–

Source: Bank of England, March 1959, NA, POWE 33/1845.
Notes: [a] I was unable to find figures for years after 1958. [b] Government debits represent oil for British forces abroad.

Appendix 3 *United Kingdom reserves and sterling exchange rate, 1945–1967*

Year	Reserves ($ millions)[a]	Exchange rate ($ per £)
1945	2,476	4.00
1946	2,696	4.00
1947	2,079	4.00
1948	1,856	4.00
1949	1,688	3.70
1950	3,300	2.80
1951	2,335	2.80
1952	1,846	2.80
1953	2,518	2.80
1954	2,762	2.80
1955	2,120	2.80
1956	2,133	2.80
1957	2,273	2.80
1958	3,069	2.80
1959	2,736	2.80
1960	3,231	2.80
1961	3,318	2.80
1962	2,806	2.80
1963	949	2.80
1964	827	2.80
1965	1,073	2.80
1966	1,107	2.80
1967	1,123	2.40

Source: Dickman, *Economic Trends Annual Supplement*, 229.
Note: [a]Year-end totals.

Select bibliography

ARCHIVES

BANK OF ENGLAND ARCHIVE, LONDON

G1   Governor's files

Economic Intelligence Department
EID3   Balance of Payments Estimates

Exchange Control Department
EC4   Defence (Finance) Regulations: Files
EC5   Exchange Control Act: Files

Overseas Department
OV 23   Iraq
OV 44   Sterling and Sterling Area Policy

BP ARCHIVE, UNIVERSITY OF WARWICK, COVENTRY

NATIONAL ARCHIVES OF THE UNITED KINGDOM, KEW
Cabinet Office
CAB 128   Minutes
CAB 134   Miscellaneous Committees: Minutes and Papers

Foreign and Commonwealth Office
FCO 48   Commonwealth Office: Aid Department and Commonwealth
          Financial Policy Department
FCO 51   Foreign and Commonwealth Office and Predecessors: Research
          Department
FCO 54   Foreign Office: Oil Department

Foreign Office
FO 371   Political Departments: General Correspondence
FO 800   Private Offices: Various Ministers' and Officials' Papers

Ministry of Fuel and Power
POWE 17   Mines Department and Successor: Coal Division: Emergency Services, Correspondence and Papers
POWE 33   Petroleum Division

Prime Minister's Office
PREM 8   Correspondence and Papers, 1945–1951
PREM 11   Correspondence and papers, 1951–1964

Treasury Office
T 172   Chancellor of the Exchequer's Office: Miscellaneous Papers
T 229   Central Economic Planning Staff, and Treasury, Central Economic Planning Section
T 234   Home and Overseas Planning Staff Division
T 236   Overseas Finance Division
T 312   Overseas Finance and Co-ordination Division and Finance (International Monetary) Division
T 317   Finance: Overseas Development Divisions
T 318   Finance (Statistics) Division and Finance (Balance of Payments) Division

NATIONAL ARCHIVES AND RECORDS ADMINISTRATION, WASHINGTON, DC

Decimal Files

Record Group 59. Records of the Department of State

Records of the Petroleum Division

PUBLISHED GOVERNMENT DOCUMENTS

Dickman, Paul (ed.). *National Statistics: Economic Trends Annual Supplement, 2000 Edition*, No. 26 (London: The Stationery Office, 2000).
Glover, Stephen and Edward Parker. "Invisible Earnings: The UK's Hidden Strength: HM Treasury Occasional Paper 7." London: HM Treasury, 1996.
Gorst, Anthony and Lewis Johnman (eds.). *The Suez Crisis*. London: Routledge, 1997.
HM Treasury. *United Kingdom Balance of Payments, 1946–1957* (London: Her Majesty's Stationery Office, 1959).
Johnson, Lyndon B. *Public Papers of the Presidents of the United States, Lyndon B. Johnson: Containing the Public Messages, Speeches, and Statements of the President, 1968–69 (in two books), Book I – January 1 to June 30, 1968.* Washington: United States Government Printing Office, 1970.

Parliamentary Debates (*Hansard*), Fifth Series, Vol. 51, House of Commons, Official Report, Second Session of the Forty-First Parliament, Session 1956–7 Comprising period from 26th November to 7th December, 1956.

US Department of State. *Papers Related to the Foreign Relations of the United States, 1919, Vol. II.* Washington: United States Government Printing Office, 1934.

Foreign Relations of the United States, Diplomatic Papers, 1944, Vol. III: The British Commonwealth and Europe. Washington: United States Government Printing Office, 1965.

Foreign Relations of the United States, Diplomatic Papers, 1944, Vol. V: The Near East, South Asia, Africa, and the Far East. Washington: United States Government Printing Office, 1965.

Foreign Relations of the United States, Diplomatic Papers, 1945, Vol. VI: The British Commonwealth; the Far East. Washington: United States Government Printing Office, 1969.

Foreign Relations of the United States, 1947, Vol. III: The British Commonwealth; Europe. Washington: United States Government Printing Office, 1972.

Foreign Relations of the United States, 1947, Vol. V: The Near East and Africa. Washington: United States Government Printing Office, 1972.

Foreign Relations of the United States, 1948, Vol. III: Western Europe. Washington: United States Government Printing Office, 1974.

Foreign Relations of the United States, 1949, Vol. IV: Western Europe. Washington: United States Government Printing Office, 1975.

Foreign Relations of the United States, 1949, Vol. VI: The Near East, South Asia, and Africa. Washington: United States Government Printing Office, 1977.

Foreign Relations of the United States, 1950, Vol. III: Western Europe. Washington: United States Government Printing Office, 1977.

Foreign Relations of the United States, 1950, Vol. V: The Near East, South Asia, and Africa. Washington: United States Government Printing Office, 1978.

Foreign Relations of the United States, 1951, Vol. V: The Near East and Africa. Washington: United States Government Printing Office, 1982.

Foreign Relations of the United States, 1952–1954, Vol. VI: Western Europe and Canada (in two parts). Washington: United States Government Printing Office, 1986.

Foreign Relations of the United States, 1952–1954, Vol. IX: The Near and Middle East (in two parts). Washington: United States Government Printing Office, 1986.

Foreign Relations of the United States, 1952–1954, Vol. X: Iran, 1951–1954. Washington: United States Government Printing Office, 1989.

Foreign Relations of the United States, 1955–1957, Vol. XII: Near East Region; Iran; Iraq. Washington: United States Government Printing Office, 1992.

Foreign Relations of the United States, 1955–1957, Vol. XIV: Arab-Israeli Dispute, 1955. Washington: United States Government Printing Office, 1989.

Foreign Relations of the United States, 1955–1957, Vol. XV: Arab-Israeli Dispute, January 1–July 26, 1956. Washington: United States Government Printing Office, 1989.

Foreign Relations of the United States, 1955–1957, Vol. XVI: Suez Crisis, July 26–December 31, 1956. Washington: United States Government Printing Office, 1990.

Foreign Relations of the United States, 1955–1957, Vol. XXVII: Western Europe and Canada. Washington: United States Government Printing Office, 1992.

Foreign Relations of the United States, 1958–1960, Vol. XII: Near East Region; Iraq; Iran; Arabian Peninsula. Washington: United States Government Printing Office, 1993.

Foreign Relations of the United States, 1961–1963, Vol. XVII: Near East, 1961–1962. Washington: United States Government Printing Office, 1995.

Foreign Relations of the United States, 1961–1963, Vol. XVIII: Near East, 1962–1963. Washington: United States Government Printing Office, 1995.

Foreign Relations of the United States, 1964–1968, Vol. VIII: International Monetary and Trade Policy. Washington: United States Government Printing Office, 1998.

Foreign Relations of the United States, 1964–1968, Vol. XII: Western Europe. Washington: United States Government Printing Office, 2001.

Foreign Relations of the United States, 1964–1968, Vol. XXI: Near East Region; Arab Peninsula. Washington: United States Government Printing Office, 2000.

Foreign Relations of the United States, 1964–1968, Vol. XXII: Iran, Washington: United States Government Printing Office, 1999.

US Office of Naval Petroleum and Oil Shale Reserves. *Twentieth Century Petroleum Statistics,* 37th edition. Dallas: DeGolyer and MacNaughton, 1981.

NEWSPAPERS AND MAGAZINES

The Economist

Financial Times

The (London) *Times*

New York Times

Wall Street Journal

Washington Post

MEMOIRS AND SECONDARY SOURCES

Abadi, Jacob. *Britain's Withdrawal from the Middle East: The Economic and Strategic Imperatives.* Princeton: The Kingston Press, 1982.

Abrahamian, Ervand. *Iran between Two Revolutions.* Princeton University Press, 1982.

Acheson, Dean. *Present at the Creation: My Years in the State Department.* New York: W. W. Norton and Company, 1969.

Ahmed A. Ahmed. "Kuwait Public Commercial Investments in Arab Countries," *Middle Eastern Studies*, 31, 2 (1995), 293–306.

Al-Sabah, Y. S. F. *The Oil Economy of Kuwait*. London: Kegan Paul International, 1980.

Anderson, Irvine. *Aramco, the United States, and Saudi Arabia: A Study of the Dynamics of Foreign Oil Policy, 1933–1950*. Princeton University Press, 1981.

Ashton, Nigel John. *Eisenhower, Macmillan and the Problem of Nasser: Anglo-American Relations and Arab Nationalism, 1955–59*. New York: St. Martin's Press, 1996.

Assiri, Abdul-Reda. *Kuwait's Foreign Policy: City-State in World Politics*. Boulder: Westview Press, 1990.

Balfour-Paul, Glen. *The End of Empire in the Middle East: Britain's Relinquishment of Power in Her Last Three Arab Dependencies*. Cambridge University Press, 1991.

"Britain's Informal Empire in the Middle East" in Judith Brown and Wm. Roger Louis (eds.), *The Oxford History of the British Empire, Volume IV: The Twentieth Century*. Oxford University Press, 1999, 490–514.

Bamberg, J. H. *British Petroleum and Global Oil, 1950–1975*. Cambridge University Press, 2000.

The History of the British Petroleum Company, Volume II: The Anglo-Iranian Years, 1928–1954. Cambridge University Press, 1994.

Baran, Paul. *The Political Economy of Growth*. New York: Monthly Review Press, 1957.

Bartlett, C. J. *"The Special Relationship": A Political History of Anglo-American Relations since 1945*. London: Longman, 1992.

Batatu, Hanna. *The Old Social Classes and the Revolutionary Movements of Iraq: A Study of Iraq's Old Landed and Commercial Classes and of its Communists, Ba'thists, and Free Officers*. Princeton University Press, 1989.

Bell, Philip W. *The Sterling Area in the Postwar World: Internal Mechanism and Cohesion, 1946–1952*. Oxford: Clarendon Press, 1956.

Beloff, Max. *The Future of British Foreign Policy*. London: Secker and Warburg, 1969.

Bialer, Uri. *Oil and the Arab-Israeli Conflict, 1948–1963*. New York: St. Martin's Press, 1999.

Bill, James A. *The Eagle and the Lion: The Tragedy of American–Iranian Relations*. New Haven: Yale University Press, 1988.

Blyth, Robert J. "Britain versus India in the Persian Gulf: The Struggle for Political Control, *c.*1928–48," *The Journal of Imperial and Commonwealth History*, 28, 1 (2000), 90–111.

Bostock, Frances and Geoffrey Jones (eds.). *Planning and Power in Iran: Ebtehaj and Economic Development under the Shah*. London: Frank Cass, 1989.

Bowie, Robert R., "Eisenhower, Dulles, and the Suez Crisis" in Wm. Roger Louis and Roger Owen (eds.), *Suez 1956: The Crisis and its Consequences*. Oxford: Clarendon Press, 1989, 189–214.

Brown, Judith. "India" in Judith M. Brown and Wm. Roger Louis (eds.), *The Oxford History of the British Empire, Volume IV: The Twentieth Century*. Oxford University Press, 1999, 421–446.

Burnham, Peter. *Remaking the Postwar World Economy: Robot and British Policy in the 1950s*. New York: Palgrave Macmillan, 2003.

Cain, P. J. and A. G. Hopkins. *British Imperialism, 1688–2000*, second edition. London: Longman, 2002.

Cairncross, Sir Alec. "The Bank of England and the British Economy" in Richard Roberts and David Kynaston (eds.), *The Bank of England: Money, Power and Influence, 1694–1994*. Oxford: Clarendon Press, 1995, 56–82.

The British Economy since 1945: Economic Policy and Performance, 1945–1990. Oxford: Blackwell, 1992.

"A British Perspective on Bretton Woods" in Orin Kirshner (ed.), *The Bretton Woods–GATT System: Retrospect and Prospect after Fifty Years*. New York: M. E. Sharpe, 1996, 70–81.

Managing the British Economy in the 1960s: A Treasury Perspective. London: Macmillan, 1996.

Years of Recovery: British Economic Policy, 1945–1951. London: Methuen, 1985.

Cairncross, Sir Alec and Barry Eichengreen, *Sterling in Decline: The Devaluations of 1931, 1949 and 1967*. Oxford: Basil Blackwell, 1983.

Cassis, Youssef. "Financial Elites Revisited" in Ranald Michie and Philip Williamson (eds.), *The British Government and the City of London in the Twentieth Century*. Cambridge University Press, 2004, 76–95.

Chapman, Richard A. *The Treasury in Public Policy-Making*. London: Routledge, 1997.

Childs, David. *Britain since 1945: A Political History*, third edition. London: Routledge, 1997.

Clark, William R. *Petrodollar Warfare: Oil, Iraq and the Future of the Dollar*. British Columbia: New Society, 2005.

Cohen, Michael J. "The Strategic Role of the Middle East after the War" in Michael J. Cohen and Martin Kolinsky (eds.), *Demise of the British Empire in the Middle East: Britain's Responses to Nationalist Movements, 1943–1955*. London: Frank Cass, 1998, 23–37.

Conan, A. R. *The Sterling Area*. London: Macmillan, 1952.

Cooper, Richard N. *The International Monetary System*. Cambridge: MIT Press, 1987.

Cottam, Richard. *Nationalism in Iran*. University of Pittsburgh Press, 1964.

Cottrell, P. L. "The Bank of England in its International Setting, 1918–1972" in Richard Roberts and David Kynaston (eds.), *The Bank of England: Money, Power and Influence, 1694–1994*. Oxford: Clarendon Press, 1995, 83–139.

Crafts, N. F. R. and N. W. C. Woodward (eds.). *The British Economy since 1945*. Oxford: Clarendon Press, 1991.

Crystal, Jill. *Oil and Politics in the Gulf: Rulers and Merchants in Kuwait and Qatar*. Cambridge University Press, 1990.

Darwin, John. *Britain and Decolonization: The Retreat from Empire in the Post-War World*. New York: St. Martin's Press, 1988.

Britain, Egypt, and the Middle East. New York: St. Martin's Press, 1981.

The End of the British Empire: The Historical Debate. Oxford: Basil Blackwell, 1991.

De Macedo, Jorge Braga, Barry Eichengreen, and Jaime Reis (eds.). *Currency Convertibility: The Gold Standard and Beyond.* London: Routledge, 1996.

Dell, Edmund. *The Chancellors: A History of the Chancellors of the Exchequer, 1945–1990.* London: HarperCollins, 1996.

Demir, Soliman. *The Kuwait Fund and the Political Economy of Arab Regional Development.* New York: Praeger, 1976.

Dessouki, Ali E. Hillal. "Nasser and the Struggle for Independence" in Wm. Roger Louis and Roger Owen (eds.), *Suez 1956: The Crisis and its Consequences.* Oxford: Clarendon Press, 1989, 31–41.

Divine, Robert A. *Eisenhower and the Cold War.* New York: Oxford University Press, 1981.

Dobson, Alan P. *The Politics of the Anglo-American Economic Special Relationship, 1940–1987.* New York: St. Martin's Press, 1988.

Dockrill, Saki. *Britain's Retreat from East of Suez: The Choice between Europe and the World?* New York: Palgrave Macmillan, 2002.

Dow, J. C. R. *The Management of the British Economy, 1945–60.* Cambridge University Press, 1964.

Drummond, Ian M. *The Floating Pound and the Sterling Area, 1931–1939.* Cambridge University Press, 1981.

Imperial Economic Policy, 1917–1939: Studies in Expansion and Protection. London: George Allen and Unwin, 1974.

Dutton, David. *Anthony Eden: A Life and Reputation.* London: Arnold, 1997.

Eden, Anthony. *Full Circle: The Memoirs of Anthony Eden.* Cambridge, UK: The Riverside Press, 1960.

Eichengreen, Barry. *Globalizing Capital: A History of the International Monetary System.* Princeton University Press, 1996.

El Mallakh. *Kuwait: Trade and Investment.* Boulder: Westview Press, 1979.

Elm, Mostafa. *Oil, Power, and Principle: Iran's Oil Nationalization and its Aftermath.* Syracuse University Press, 1992.

Elwell-Sutton, L. P. *Persian Oil: A Study in Power Politics.* Westport: Greenwood Press, 1975.

Farmanfarmaian, Manucher and Roxane Farmanfarmaian. *Memoirs of a Persian Prince.* New York: Random House, 1997.

Farnie, D. A. *East and West of Suez: The Suez Canal in History: 1854–1956.* Oxford: Clarendon Press, 1969.

Farouk-Sluglett, Marion and Peter Sluglett. *Iraq since 1958: From Revolution to Dictatorship.* London: I. B. Tauris, 1990.

Ferrier, R. W. *The History of the British Petroleum Company, Volume I: The Developing Years, 1901–1932.* Cambridge University Press, 1982.

Fforde, John. *The Bank of England and Public Policy, 1941–1958.* Cambridge University Press, 1992.

Frank, André Gunder. *Capitalism and Underdevelopment in South America.* New York: Monthly Review Press, 1967.

Gardner, Richard N. *Sterling–Dollar Diplomacy: The Origins and the Prospects of our International Economic Order*, new expanded edition. New York: McGraw-Hill, 1969.

"Sterling–Dollar Diplomacy in Current Perspective" in Wm. Roger Louis and Hedley Bull (eds.), *The Special Relationship: Anglo-American Relations since 1945*. Oxford: Clarendon Press, 1986, 185–200.

Gavin, Francis J. "The Gold Battles within the Cold War: American Monetary Policy and the Defense of Europe, 1960–1963," *Diplomatic History*, 26, 1 (2002), 61–94.

Gold, Dollars, and Power: The Politics of International Monetary Relations, 1958–1971. Chapel Hill: University of North Carolina Press, 2004.

"Politics, Power, and US Policy in Iran, 1950–1953," *Journal of Cold War Studies*, 1, 1 (1999), 56–90.

Green, E. H. H. "The Conservatives and the City" in Ranald Michie and Philip Williamson (eds.), *The British Government and the City of London in the Twentieth Century*. Cambridge University Press, 2004, 153–173.

Greenstein, Fred I. *The Hidden-Hand Presidency: Eisenhower as Leader*. New York: Basic Books, 1982.

Hack, Karl. *Defence and Decolonisation in Southeast Asia: Britain, Malaya and Singapore, 1941–1968*. Richmond: Curzon Press, 2001.

Hathaway, Robert M. *Great Britain and the United States: Special Relations since World War II*. Boston: Twayne, 1990.

Heikal, Mohammed. *Cutting the Lion's Tail: Suez through Egyptian Eyes*. London: André Deutsch, 1986.

Heiss, Mary Ann. *Empire and Nationhood: The United States, Great Britain, and Iranian Oil, 1950–1954*. New York: Columbia University Press, 1997.

Hinds, Allister. *Britain's Sterling Colonial Policy and Decolonization, 1939–1958*. Westport: Greenwood Press, 2001.

Hobsbawm, Eric. *Industry and Empire: An Economic History of Britain since 1750*. London: Weidenfeld and Nicolson, 1968.

Hobson, J. A. *Imperialism: A Study*. Ann Arbor: University of Michigan Press, 1965.

Hollowell, Jonathan (ed.). *Twentieth-Century Anglo-American Relations*. Houndmills: Palgrave, 2001.

Holtfrerich, Carl-Ludwig (ed.). *Interactions in the World Economy: Perspectives from International Economic History*. New York: New York University Press, 1989.

Hopkins, Tony. "Macmillan's Audit of Empire, 1957" in Peter Clarke and Clive Trebilcock (eds.), *Understanding Decline: Perceptions and Realities of British Economic Performance*. Cambridge University Press, 1997, 234–260.

Hopwood, Derek (ed.). *The Arabian Peninsula: Society and Politics*. London: George Allen and Unwin, 1972.

Horne, Alistair. *Macmillan, 1894–1956: Volume I of the Official Biography*. London: Macmillan, 1988.

Howarth, Stephen. *A Century in Oil: The "Shell" Transport and Trading Company, 1897–1997*. London: Weidenfeld and Nicholson, 1997.

Hyam, Ronald. *Britain's Declining Empire: The Road to Decolonisation, 1918–1968*. Cambridge University Press, 2006.

Ingram, Edward. *Britain's Persian Connection, 1798–1828: Prelude to the Great Game in Asia*. Oxford: Clarendon Press, 1992.

Johnman, Lewis. "Defending the Pound: The Economics of the Suez Crisis, 1956" in Anthony Gorst, Lewis Johnman, and W. Scott Lucas (eds.), *Postwar Britain, 1945–64: Themes and Perspectives.* London: Pinter, 1989, 166–188.

Jones, Geoffrey. *Banking and Empire in Iran: The History of the British Bank of the Middle East*, 2 volumes. Cambridge University Press, 1986 and 1987.

Joyce, Miriam. *Kuwait, 1945–1996: An Anglo-American Perspective.* London: Frank Cass, 1998.

"Preserving the Sheikhdom: London, Washington, Iraq and Kuwait, 1958–1961," *Middle Eastern Studies*, 31, 2 (1995), 281–292.

Kaplan, Robert D. *The Arabists: The Romance of an American Elite.* New York: Free Press, 1993.

Katz, Samuel I. "Sterling Instability and the Postwar Sterling System," *Review of Economics and Statistics*, 31, 1 (1954), 81–87.

"Sterling's Recurring Postwar Payments Crises," *The Journal of Political Economy*, 68, 3 (1955), 216–226.

Keddie, Nikki R. *Roots of Revolution: An Interpretive History of Modern Iran.* New Haven: Yale University Press, 1981.

Kegley, Charles W. Jr. and Pat McGowan. *The Political Economy of Foreign Policy Behavior.* Beverly Hills: Sage, 1981.

Kelly, J. B. *Arabia, the Gulf and the West.* New York: Basic Books, 1980.

Kenen, Peter B. *British Monetary Policy and the Balance of Payments, 1951–1957.* Cambridge, MA: Harvard University Press, 1967.

Khanna, Parag. *The Second World: Empires and Influence in the New Global Order.* New York: Random House, 2008.

Khouja, M. W. and P. G. Sadler. *The Economy of Kuwait: Development and Role in International Finance.* London: Macmillan, 1979.

Kindleberger, Charles. *The World in Depression, 1929–1939*, revised and enlarged edition. Berkeley: University of California Press, 1986.

Kingston, Paul W. T. *Britain and the Politics of Modernization in the Modern Middle East, 1945–1958.* New York: Cambridge University Press, 1996.

Kirshner, Orin (ed.). *The Bretton Woods–GATT System: Retrospect and Prospect after Fifty Years.* New York: M. E. Sharpe, 1996.

Krozewski, Gerold. "Finance and Empire: The Dilemma Facing Great Britain in the 1950s," *International History Review*, 18, 1 (1996), 48–69.

Money and the End of Empire: British International Economic Policy and the Colonies, 1947–1958. Houndmills: Palgrave, 2001.

"Sterling, the 'Minor Territories,' and the End of Formal Empire, 1939–1958," *Economic History Review*, 46, 2 (1993), 239–265.

Kunz, Diane B. *The Economic Diplomacy of the Suez Crisis.* Chapel Hill: University of North Carolina Press, 1991.

"'Somewhat Mixed Up Together': Anglo-American Defence and Financial Policy during the 1960s" in Robert D. King and Robin Kilson (eds.), *The Statecraft of British Imperialism: Essays in Honour of Wm. Roger Louis.* London: Frank Cass, 1999, 213–232.

Kyle, Keith. *Suez.* London: Weidenfeld and Nicolson, 1991.

Kynaston, David. *The City of London, Volume IV: A Club No More, 1945–2000.* London: Chatto and Windus, 2001.

Landes, David. *Bankers and Pashas: International Finance and Economic Imperialism in Egypt*. Cambridge, MA: Harvard University Press, 1958.

The Wealth and Poverty of Nations: Why Some are so Rich and Some so Poor. New York: W.W. Norton, 1998.

Little, Douglas. *American Orientalism: The United States and the Middle East since 1945*. Chapel Hill: University of North Carolina Press, 2002.

Lloyd, Selwyn. *Suez 1956: A Personal Account*. London: Jonathan Cape, 1978.

Longrigg, Stephen Hemsley. *Oil in the Middle East: Its Discovery and Development*, third edition. London: Oxford University Press, 1968.

Longstreth, Frank. "The City, Industry, and the State" in Colin Crouch (ed.), *State and Economy in Contemporary Capitalism*. London: Croom Helm, 1979, 157–190.

Louis, Wm. Roger. "American Anti-Colonialism and the Dissolution of the British Empire" in Wm. Roger Louis and Hedley Bull (eds.), *The Special Relationship: Anglo-American Relations since 1945*. Oxford: Clarendon Press, 1986, 261–284.

The British Empire in the Middle East, 1945–1951: Arab Nationalism, the United States, and Postwar Imperialism. Oxford: Clarendon Press, 1984.

"The British and the Origins of the Iraqi Revolution" in Robert Fernea and Wm. Roger Louis (eds.), *The Iraqi Revolution of 1958: The Old Social Classes Revisited*. London: I. B. Tauris, 1991, 31–61.

"The Dissolution of the British Empire" in Judith M. Brown and Wm. Roger Louis (eds.), *The Oxford History of the British Empire, Volume IV: The Twentieth Century*. Oxford University Press, 1999, 329–356.

"Dulles, Suez, and the British" in Richard H. Immerman (ed.), *John Foster Dulles and the Diplomacy of the Cold War*. Princeton University Press, 1990, 133–158.

"The End of the Palestine Mandate" in Wm. Roger Louis (ed.), *Ends of British Imperialism: The Scramble for Empire, Suez and Decolonization*. London: I. B. Tauris, 2006, 419–447.

Imperialism at Bay: The United States and the Decolonization of the British Empire, 1941–1945. New York: Oxford University Press, 1978.

Imperialism: The Robinson and Gallagher Controversy. New York: New Viewpoints, 1976.

"Musaddiq and the Dilemmas of British Imperialism" in James Bill and Wm. Roger Louis (eds.), *Musaddiq, Iranian Nationalism, and Oil*. Austin: University of Texas Press, 1988, 228–260.

"Public Enemy Number One: Britain and the United Nations in the Aftermath of Suez" in Wm. Roger Louis (ed.), *Ends of British Imperialism: The Scramble for Empire, Suez and Decolonization*. London: I. B. Tauris, 2006, 689–724.

"The Withdrawal from the Gulf" in Wm. Roger Louis (ed.), *Ends of British Imperialism: The Scramble for Empire, Suez and Decolonization*. London: I. B. Tauris, 2006, 877–903.

Louis, Wm. Roger and Ronald Robinson. "The Imperialism of Decolonization" in Wm. Roger Louis (ed.), *Ends of British Imperialism: The Scramble for Empire, Suez and Decolonization*. London: I. B. Tauris, 2006, 451–502.

Lytle, Mark Hamilton. *The Origins of the Iranian–American Alliance, 1941–1953*. New York: Holmes and Meier, 1987.

Macmillan, Harold. *Riding the Storm, 1956–1959*. London: Harper and Row, 1971.

McGhee, George. *Envoy to the Middle World: Adventures in Diplomacy*. New York: Harper and Row, 1983.

Mansergh, Nicholas. *The Commonwealth Experience*, second edition. London: Macmillan, 1982.

Marlowe, John. *Anglo-Egyptian Relations, 1800–1956*. London: Frank Cass, 1965.

Marsh, Steve. "Anglo-American Crude Diplomacy: Multinational Oil and the Iranian Oil Crisis, 1951–53." *Contemporary British History*, 21, 1 (2007), 25–53.

  Anglo-American Relations and Cold War Oil: Crisis in Iran. New York: Palgrave Macmillan, 2003.

Menderhausen, Horst. "Dollar Shortage and Oil Surplus in 1949–1950," *Essays in International Finance*, No. 11, 1950.

Michie, Ranald. "The City of London and the British Government: The Changing Relationship" in Ranald Michie and Philip Williamson (eds.), *The British Government and the City of London in the Twentieth Century*. Cambridge University Press, 2004, 31–55.

Miller, J. D. B. *Britain and the Old Dominions*. Baltimore: The Johns Hopkins University Press, 1966.

  Survey of Commonwealth Affairs: Problems of Expansion and Attrition, 1953–1969. London: Oxford University Press, 1974.

Monroe, Elizabeth. *Britain's Moment in the Middle East, 1914–1971*. London: Chatto and Windus, 1981.

Newton, Scott. "Britain, the Sterling Area and European Integration, 1945–50," *The Journal of Imperial and Commonwealth History*, 13, 3 (1985), 163–182.

Oren, Michael B. *Six Days of War: June 1967 and the Making of the Modern Middle East*. Oxford University Press, 2002.

Ovendale, Ritchie. *Anglo-American Relations in the Twentieth Century*. New York: St. Martin's Press, 1998.

  Britain, the United States and the Transfer of Power in the Middle East, 1945–1962. London: Leicester University Press, 1996.

Owen, Nicholas. "Britain and Decolonization: The Labour Governments and the Middle East" in Michael J. Cohen and Martin Kolinsky (eds.), *Demise of the British Empire in the Middle East: Britain's Responses to Nationalist Movements, 1943–1955*. London: Frank Cass, 1998, 3–22.

Painter, David S. *Oil and the American Century: The Political Economy of US Foreign Oil Policy, 1941–1954*. Baltimore: The Johns Hopkins University Press, 1986.

Peden, G. C. "The Treasury and the City" in Ranald Michie and Philip Williamson (eds.), *The British Government and the City of London in the Twentieth Century*. Cambridge University Press, 2004, 117–134.

Perkins, Bradford. "Unequal Partners: The Truman Administration and Great Britain" in Roger Louis and Hedley Bull (eds.), *The "Special Relationship": Anglo-American Relations since 1945*. Oxford: Clarendon Press, 1986, 43–64.

Petersen, Tore Tingvold. "Anglo-American Rivalry in the Middle East: The Struggle for the Buraimi Oasis, 1952–1957," *The International History Review*, 14, 1 (1992), 71–91.

"Crossing the Rubicon? Britain's Withdrawal from the Middle East, 1964–1968: A Bibliographical Review," *The International History Review*, 22, 2 (2000), 318–340.

The Decline of the Anglo-American Middle East, 1961–1969: A Willing Retreat. Brighton: Sussex Academic Press, 2006.

The Middle East between the Great Powers: Anglo-American Conflict and Cooperation, 1952–1957. Houndmills: Macmillan, 2000.

Phillips, Kevin. *Bad Money: Reckless Finance, Failed Politics, and the Global Crisis of American Capitalism.* New York: Penguin, 2008.

Platt, D. C. M. *Finance, Trade, and Politics in British Foreign Policy, 1815–1914.* Oxford: Clarendon Press, 1968.

Pressnell, L. S. *External Economic Policy since the War, Volume I: The Post-War Financial Settlement.* London: Her Majesty's Stationery Office, 1986.

Pridham, B. R. (ed.). *The Arab Gulf and the Arab World.* London: Croom Helm, 1988.

Roseveare, Henry. *The Treasury: The Evolution of a British Institution.* New York: Columbia University Press, 1969.

Rostow, W. W. *The Stages of Economic Growth: A Non-Communist Manifesto*, third edition. Cambridge University Press, 1990.

Rotter, Andrew J. *The Path to Vietnam: Origins of the American Commitment to Southeast Asia.* Ithaca: Cornell University Press, 1987.

Said, Edward W. *Orientalism.* New York: Vintage Books, 1978.

Sampson, Anthony. *The Seven Sisters: The Great Oil Companies and the World They Shaped.* New York: The Viking Press, 1975.

Sanders, David. *Losing an Empire, Finding a Role: An Introduction to British Foreign Policy since 1945.* New York: St. Martin's Press, 1989.

Schenk, Catherine R. *Britain and the Sterling Area: From Devaluation to Convertibility in the 1950s.* London: Routledge, 1994.

"Closing the Hong Kong Gap: The Hong Kong Free Dollar Market in the 1950s," *The Economic History Review*, 47, 2 (1994), 335–353.

"Exchange Controls and Multinational Enterprise: The Sterling–Dollar Oil Controversy in the 1950s," *Business History*, 38, 4 (1996), 21–41.

"Finance and Empire: Confusions and Complexities: A Note," *The International History Review*, 18, 4 (1996), 868–872.

"The New City and the State in the 1960s" in Ranald Michie and Philip Williamson (eds.), *The British Government and the City of London in the Twentieth Century.* Cambridge University Press, 2004, 322–339.

"The Origins of a Central Bank in Malaya and the Transition to Independence, 1954–1959," *Journal of Imperial and Commonwealth History*, 21, 2 (1993), 409–431.

Scott, M. F. G. "The Balance of Payments Crises" in G. D. N. Worswick and P. H. Ady (eds.), *The British Economy in the Nineteen-Fifties.* Oxford: Clarendon Press, 1962, 205–230.

A Study of United Kingdom Imports. Cambridge University Press, 1963.

Shonfield, Andrew. *British Economic Policy since the War*. London: Penguin, 1958.
(ed.). *International Economic Relations of the Western World, 1959–1971, Part 1: Politics and Trade*. London: Oxford University Press, 1976.
Shwadran, Benjamin. *The Middle East, Oil, and the Great Powers*, third edition. New York: Wiley, 1974.
Silverfarb, Daniel. *Britain's Informal Empire in the Middle East: A Case Study of Iraq, 1929–1941*. New York: Oxford University Press, 1986.
Skidelsky, Robert. *John Maynard Keynes, Volume III: Fighting for Britain, 1937–1946*. London: Macmillan, 2000.
Smith, Charles D. *Palestine and the Arab-Israeli Conflict*, second edition. New York: St. Martin's Press, 1992.
Smith, Michael, Steve Smith, and Brian White (eds.), *British Foreign Policy: Tradition, Change, and Transformation*. London: Unwin Hyman, 1988.
Smith, Simon. *Kuwait, 1950–1965: Britain, the al-Sabah, and Oil*. Oxford University Press, 1999.
Stephens, Robert. *Nasser: A Political Biography*. New York: Simon and Schuster, 1971.
Stiglitz, Joseph E. and Linda J. Bilmes. *The Three Trillion Dollar War: The True Cost of the Iraq Conflict*. New York: W. W. Norton, 2008.
Stoff, Michael. *Oil, War, and American Security: The Search for a National Policy on Foreign Oil, 1941–1947*. New Haven: Yale University Press, 1980.
Strange, Susan. *Sterling and British Policy: A Political Study of an International Currency in Decline*. London: Oxford University Press, 1971.
Supple, Barry. "Fear of Failing: Economic History and the Decline of Britain" in Peter Clarke and Clive Trebilcock (eds.), *Understanding Decline: Perceptions and Realities of British Economic Performance*. Cambridge University Press, 1997, 9–29.
Takeyh, Ray. *The Origins of the Eisenhower Doctrine: The US, Britain, and Nasser's Egypt, 1953–1957*. New York: St. Martin's Press, 2000.
Tew, J. H. B. "Policies Aimed at Improving the Balance of Payments" in F. T. Blackaby (ed.), *British Economic Policy, 1960–74*. Cambridge University Press, 1978, 304–358.
Thorpe, Keir. "The Forgotten Shortage: Britain's Handling of the 1967 Oil Embargo," *Contemporary British History*, 21, 2 (2007), 201–222.
Tibi, Bassam. *Arab Nationalism: A Critical Enquiry*, second edition, edited and translated by Marion Farouk Sluglett and Peter Sluglett. New York: St. Martin's Press, 1990.
Tomlinson, B. R. "Imperialism and After: The Economy of the Empire on the Periphery" in Judith M. Brown and Wm. Roger Louis (eds.), *The Oxford History of the British Empire, Volume IV: The Twentieth Century*. Oxford University Press, 1999, 357–378.
The Political Economy of the Raj, 1914–1947: The Economics of Decolonization in India. London: Macmillan, 1979.
Tomlinson, Jim. "Labour Party and the City, 1945–1970" in Ranald Michie and Philip Williamson (eds.), *The British Government and the City of London in the Twentieth Century*. Cambridge University Press, 2004, 174–192.

Van Dormael, Armand. *Bretton Woods: Birth of a Monetary System.* New York: Holmes and Meier, 1978.

Wallerstein, Immanuel. *The Capitalist World Economy.* Cambridge University Press, 1979.

Watt, D. Cameron. *Succeeding John Bull: America in Britain's Place, 1900–1975.* Cambridge University Press, 1984.

Williamson, Philip. "The City of London and Government in Modern Britain: Debates and Politics" in Ranald Michie and Philip Williamson (eds.), *The British Government and the City of London in the Twentieth Century.* Cambridge University Press, 2004, 5–30.

Wilson, Harold. *The Labour Government, 1964–1970: A Personal Record.* London: Weidenfeld and Nicolson, 1971.

Wilson, Keith M. (ed.). *Imperialism and Nationalism in the Middle East: The Anglo-Egyptian Experience, 1882–1982.* London: Mansell, 1983.

Wilson, Rodney. "Economic Aspects of Arab Nationalism" in Michael J. Cohen and Martin Kolinsky (eds.), *Demise of the British Empire in the Middle East: Britain's Responses to Nationalist Movements, 1943–1955.* London: Frank Cass, 1998, 64–78.

Winks, Robin W. (ed.). *The Oxford History of the British Empire, Volume V: Historiography.* Oxford University Press, 1999.

Yapp, M. E. *The Near East since the First World War.* London: Longman, 1991.

Yaqub, Salim. *Containing Arab Nationalism: The Eisenhower Doctrine and the Middle East.* Chapel Hill: University of North Carolina Press, 2004.

Yergin, Daniel. *The Prize: The Epic Quest for Oil, Money, and Power.* New York: Simon and Schuster, 1991.

Zahlan, Rosemarie Said. *The Making of the Modern Gulf States: Kuwait, Bahrain, Qatar, The United Arab Emirates and Oman.* London: Unwin Hyman, 1989.

Zupnik, Elliot. *Britain's Postwar Dollar Problem.* New York: Columbia University Press, 1957.

Index

DATE DUE